Ethics Introduced

READINGS IN MORAL PHILOSOPHY

Bassim Hamadeh, CEO and Publisher
Angela Schultz, Senior Field Acquisitions Editor
Michelle Piehl, Project Editor
Abbey Hastings, Associate Production Editor
Miguel Macias, Senior Graphic Designer
Stephanie Kohl, Licensing Associate
Don Kesner, Interior Designer
Natalie Piccotti, Director of Marketing
Kassie Graves, Vice President of Editorial
Jamie Giganti, Director of Academic Publishing

Ethics Introduced

READINGS IN MORAL PHILOSOPHY

Dennis Arjo, Dawn Gale, and Omar Conrad

Johnson County Community College

Contents

Part 4: Applied Ethics: Thinking Through Contemporary Controversies

PART 1

Meta-ethics

ARE THERE MORAL TRUTHS?

Meta-ethics

INTRODUCTION TO META-ETHICS

Meta-ethics is a major concern of ethical inquiry. Meta-ethics asks the question, How is it possible for a moral claim to be true or false? To see the import of this question, compare the following claims:

1. World War I began in 1914.
2. The first atomic bomb exploded in 1950.
3. F = ma.
4. KE = mv^2.
5. Adultery is morally wrong.
6. Giving 10 percent of your disposable income away to charity is an evil thing to do.

Claims 1 and 2 are historical claims. Claim 1 happens to be true. World War I began in 1914, so when someone claims "World War I began in 1914," they claim something true. Claim 1 lines up with the facts of history. Claim 2 happens to be false. The first atomic bomb actually exploded on July 16, 1945, in Alamogordo, New Mexico. So, when someone claims that "the first atomic bomb exploded in 1950," they have claimed something false. Claim 2 doesn't line up with the facts of history.

Claims 3 and 4 are scientific claims. Claim 3 is the equation for force where *F* stands for force, *m* for mass, and *a* for acceleration. Claim 3 is true. Claim 4 attempts to give the equation for Kinetic Energy, where *KE* stands for Kinetic Energy, *m* for mass, and *v* for velocity. Claim 4 is false, however, because the actual equation for KE is ½ mv^2. (Claim 4 is false because it doubles this amount!)

Claims 5 and 6 are moral claims—claims about how we should and should not live our lives. Most of us would probably say that Claim 5 is true. Adultery seems morally wrong. And most of us would probably say that Claim 6 is false. It doesn't seem evil to give away some of your disposable income to charity. It seems instead like a good thing to do.

The meta-ethical question is, How can claims like 5 and 6 be either true or false? Notice that claims 5 and 6 are not reporting historical events in the world. So, it doesn't seem like there is anything in the world that we could point to and say, "Claim 5 is true because it corresponds to reality." Moral claims about what we should and should not do, do not seem analogous to historical facts about what has and has not been. Further notice that Claims 5 and 6 do not seem analogous to scientific descriptions of patterns that we see throughout nature. So, how is it possible for the claim "adultery is morally wrong" to be true? Or, if you think Claim 5 is false, how is that possible?

There are at least four possible approaches to answering the fundamental meta-ethical question: moral nihilism, moral subjectivism, moral relativism, and moral objectivism.

Moral nihilists claim that moral reasoning is impossible. Moral claims such as "murder is wrong" have no meaning according to the moral nihilists. Moral nihilists believe that moral claims cannot be true or false. It is hard to imagine a more skeptical view regarding moral theory than this. If the moral nihilists are right, then there seems little reason to study ethics. We will read Friedrich Nietzsche's *On the Uses and Disadvantages of History for Life* as our selection on moral nihilism.

Moral subjectivists believe that moral claims only apply to the person making the claim. Morality is merely a matter of personal opinion, taste, or creed according to the moral subjectivist. Each of us would thus have our own private morality. Moral subjectivism is not as skeptical as moral nihilism regarding the possibility of moral truth. But it is close. Moral relativists believe that moral claims are the product of culture. Each culture has its own creed of praiseworthy, permissible, and wrong actions or values. Moral relativism holds that moral claims, such as "One should give to charity," are meaningful and can be true or false in the sense that a culture accepts them as true or false. Moral relativism is not as skeptical as moral subjectivism and is far less skeptical than moral nihilism. And it has significant utility. I can pass judgement on other people's actions, give moral counsel, et cetera as long as we both share the same culture. We will read Ruth Benedict as an example of a moral relativist. If the moral relativists are right, then there seems to be a basic problem—and perhaps an unsolvable problem—for how one culture can pass judgment on another culture. This problem is analogous to a problem with moral subjectivism. If the moral subjectivists are right, then there seems to be no way for us to judge someone other than oneself.

In contrast to the nihilists, subjectivists, and relativists, the moral objectivists believe that moral claims are true or false independent of what any one of us happens to think about them. A moral objectivist might say it is true that murder is wrong regardless of whether Charles Manson or Nazi Germany agree or not. Moral objectivism is the most optimistic position one can take in meta-ethics. If the moral objectivist is right, then objective moral judgements can be made on individuals and even entire cultures. But of course, there is a problem with moral objectivism too. Where would the objectivity of morality come from? We will read Michael Smith defend moral objectivism.

READING 1.1

On the Uses and Disadvantages
of History for Life

Friedrich Nietzsche

∾

Foreword

"Incidentally, I despise everything which merely instructs me without increasing or immediately enlivening my activity." These are Goethe's words. With them, as with a heartfelt expression of *ceterum censeo,* our consideration of the worth and the worthlessness of history may begin. For this work is to set down why, in the spirit of Goethe's saying, we must seriously despise instruction without vitality, knowledge which enervates activity, and history as an expensive surplus of knowledge and a luxury, because we lack what is still most essential to us and because what is superfluous is hostile to what is essential. To be sure, we need history. But we need it in a manner different from the way in which the spoilt idler in the garden of knowledge uses it, no matter how elegantly he may look down on our coarse and graceless needs and distresses. That is, we need it for life and action, not for a comfortable turning away from life and action or merely for glossing over the egotistical life and the cowardly bad act. We wish to use history only insofar as it serves living. But there is a degree of doing history and a valuing of it through which life atrophies and degenerates. To bring this phenomenon to light as a remarkable symptom of our time is every bit as necessary as it may be painful. ...

Observe the herd which is grazing beside you. It does not know what yesterday or today is. It springs around, eats, rests, digests, jumps up again, and so from morning to night and from day to day, with its likes and dislikes closely tied to the peg of the moment, and thus neither melancholy nor weary.

Friedrich Nietzsche, Selection from *On the Use and Abuse of History for Life*, trans. Ian Johnston. Copyright © 2010 by Richer Resources Publications. Reprinted with permission.

To witness this is hard for man, because he boasts to himself that his human race is better than the beast and yet looks with jealousy at its happiness. For he wishes only to live like the beast, neither weary nor amid pains, and he wants it in vain, because he does not will it as the animal does. One day the man demands of the beast: "Why do you not talk to me about your happiness and only gaze at me?" The beast wants to answer, too, and say: "That comes about because I always immediately forget what I wanted to say." But by then the beast has already forgotten this reply and remains silent, so that the man wonders on once more.

But he also wonders about himself, that he is not able to learn to forget and that he always hangs onto past things. No matter how far or how fast he runs, this chain runs with him. It is something amazing: the moment, in one sudden motion there, in one sudden motion gone, before nothing, afterwards nothing, nevertheless comes back again as a ghost and disturbs the tranquillity of each later moment. A leaf is continuously released from the roll of time, falls out, flutters away–and suddenly flutters back again into the man's lap. For the man says, "I remember," and envies the beast, which immediately forgets and sees each moment really perish, sink back in cloud and night, and vanish forever. Thus the animal lives unhistorically, for it gets up in the present like a number without any odd fraction left over; it does not know how to play a part, hides nothing, and appears in each moment exactly and entirely what it is.

Thus a beast can be nothing other than honest. By contrast, the human being resists the large and ever increasing burden of the past, which pushes him down or bows him over. It makes his way difficult, like an invisible and dark burden which he can for appearances' sake even deny, and which he is only too happy to deny in his interactions with his peers, in order to awaken their envy. Thus, it moves him, as if he remembered a lost paradise, to see the grazing herd or, something more closely familiar, the child, which does not yet have a past to deny and plays in blissful blindness between the fences of the past and the future. Nonetheless this game must be upset for the child. He will be summoned all too soon out of his forgetfulness. For he learns to understand the expression "It was," that password with which struggle, suffering, and weariness come over human beings, so as to remind him what his existence basically is–a never completed past tense. If death finally brings the longed for forgetting, it nevertheless thereby destroys present existence and thus impresses its seal on the knowledge that existence is only an uninterrupted living in the past, something which exists for the purpose of self-denial, self-destruction, and self-contradiction.

If happiness or if, in some sense or other, a reaching out for new happiness is what holds the living onto life and pushes them forward into life, then perhaps no philosopher has more justification than the cynic. For the happiness of the beast, like that of the complete cynic, is the living proof of the rightness of cynicism. The smallest happiness, if only it is uninterrupted and creates happiness, is incomparably more happiness than the greatest which comes only as an episode, as it were, like a mood, as a fantastic interruption between nothing but boredom, cupidity, and deprivation. However, with the smallest and with the greatest good fortune, happiness becomes happiness in the same way: through forgetting or, to express the matter in a more scholarly fashion, through the capacity, for as long as the happiness lasts, to sense things unhistorically. The person who cannot set himself down on the crest of the moment, forgetting everything from the past, who is not capable of standing on a single point, like a goddess of victory, without dizziness or fear, will never know what happiness is. Even worse, he will never do anything to make other people happy. Imagine the most extreme example, a person who did not possess the power of forgetting at all, who would be condemned to see everywhere a coming into being. Such a person no longer believes in his own being, no longer believes in himself, sees everything in moving points flowing out of each other, and loses himself in this stream of becoming. He will, like the true pupil of Heraclitus, finally hardly dare any more to lift his finger. Forgetting belongs to all action, just as both light and darkness belong in the life of all organic things. A person who wanted to feel utterly and only historically would be like someone who was forced to abstain from sleep, or like the beast that is to continue its life only from rumination to constantly repeated rumination. For this reason, it is possible to live almost without remembering, indeed, to live happily, as the beast demonstrates; however, it is generally completely impossible to live without forgetting. Or, to explain myself more clearly concerning my thesis: *There is a degree of insomnia, of rumination, of the historical sense, through which living comes to harm and finally is destroyed, whether it is a person or a people or a culture.*

In order to determine this degree of history and, through that, the borderline at which the past must be forgotten if it is not to become the gravedigger of the present, we have to know precisely how great the plastic force of a person, a people, or a culture is. I mean that force of growing in a different way out of oneself, of reshaping and incorporating the past and the foreign, of healing wounds, compensating for what has been lost, rebuilding shattered forms out of one's self. There are people who possess so little of this force that they bleed to death incurably from a single experience, a single pain, often even from a single tender injustice, as from a really small bloody scratch. On the other hand, there are people whom the wildest and most horrific accidents in life and even actions of their own wickedness injure so little that right in the middle of these experiences or shortly after they bring the issue to a reasonable state of well being with a sort of quiet conscience.

The stronger the roots which the inner nature of a person has, the more he will appropriate or forcibly take from the past. And if we imagine the most powerful and immense nature, then we would recognize there that for it there would be no frontier at all beyond which the historical sense would be able to work as an injurious overseer. Everything in the past, in its own and in the most alien, this nature would draw upon, take it into itself, and, as it were, transform into blood. What such a nature does not subjugate it knows how to forget. It is there no more. The horizon is closed completely, and nothing can recall that there still are men, passions, instruction, and purposes beyond it. This is a general principle: each living being can become healthy, strong, and fertile only within a horizon. If he is incapable of drawing a horizon around himself and too egotistical to enclose his own view within an alien one, then he wastes away there, pale or weary, to an early death. Cheerfulness, good conscience, joyful action, trust in what is to come–all that depends, with the individual as with a people, on the following facts: that there is a line which divides the observable brightness from the unilluminated darkness, that we know how to forget at the right time just as well as we remember at the right time, that we feel with powerful instinct the time when we must perceive historically and when unhistorically. This is the specific principle which the reader is invited to consider: *that for the health of a single individual, a people, and a culture the unhistorical and the historical are* equally essential.

At this point everyone brings up the comment that a person's historical knowledge and feeling can be very limited, his horizon hemmed in like that of an inhabitant of an Alpine valley; in every judgment he might set down an injustice and in every experience a mistake, which he was the first to make, and nevertheless in spite of all injustice and every mistake he stands there in invincible health and vigour and fills every eye with joy, while close beside him the far more just and scholarly person grows ill and collapses, because the lines of his horizon are always being shifted about restlessly, because he cannot wriggle himself out of the much softer nets of his justices and truths to strong willing and desiring. By contrast, we saw the beast, which is completely unhistorical and which lives almost in the middle of a sort of horizon of points, and yet exists with a certain happiness, at least without weariness and pretence. Thus, we will have to assess the capacity of being able to feel to a certain degree unhistorically as more important and more basic, to the extent that in it lies the foundation above which something right, healthy, and great, something truly human, can generally first grow. The unhistorical is like an enveloping atmosphere in which life generates itself alone, only to disappear again with the destruction of this atmosphere.

The truth is that, in the process by which the human being, in thinking, reflecting, comparing, separating, and combining, first limits that unhistorical

sense, the process in which inside that surrounding misty cloud a bright gleam-
ing beam of light arises, only then, through the power of using the past for living
and making history out of what has happened, does a person first become a
person. But in an excess of history the human being stops once again; without
that cover of the unhistorical he would never have started or dared to start.
Where do the actions come from which men are capable of doing without previously having gone into that misty patch of the unhistorical? Or to set pictures
to one side and to grasp an example for illustration: we picture a man whom a
violent passion, for a woman or for a great idea, shakes up and draws forward.
How his world is changed for him! Looking backwards, he feels blind; listening
to the side he hears the strangeness like a dull sound empty of meaning. What
he is generally aware of he has never yet perceived as so true, so perceptibly
close, coloured, resounding, illuminated, as if he is comprehending with all the
senses simultaneously. All his estimates of worth are altered and devalued. He
is unable any longer to value so much, because he can hardly feel it any more.
He asks himself whether he has been the fool of strange words and strange
opinions for long. He is surprised that his memory turns tirelessly in a circle
but is nevertheless too weak and tired to make a single leap out of this circle.
It is the most unjust condition of the world, narrow, thankless with respect to
the past, blind to what has passed, deaf to warnings, a small living vortex in
a dead sea of night and forgetting: nevertheless this condition—unhistorical,
thoroughly anti-historical—is the birthing womb not only of an unjust deed
but much more of every just deed. And no artist would achieve his picture,
no field marshal his victory, and no people its freedom, without previously
having desired and striven for them in that sort of unhistorical condition. As
the active person, according to what Goethe said, is always without conscience,
so he is also always without knowledge. He forgets most things in order to do
one thing; he is unjust towards what lies behind him and knows only one right,
the right of what is to come into being now. So every active person loves his
deed infinitely more than it deserves to be loved, and the best deeds happen
in such a excess of love that they would certainly have to be unworthy of this
love, even if their worth were otherwise incalculably great.

Should a person be in a position to catch in many examples the scent of
this unhistorical atmosphere, in which every great historical event arose, and
to breathe it in, then such a person might perhaps be able, as a knowledgeable
being, to elevate himself up to a superhistorical standpoint, in the way Niebuhr
once described a possible result of historical research: "In one thing at least," he
says, "is history, clearly and thoroughly grasped, useful, the fact that one knows,
as even the greatest and highest spirits of our human race do not know, how
their eyes have acquired by chance the way in which they see and the way in
which they forcefully demand that everyone see, forcefully because the intensity

of their awareness is particularly great. Someone who has not, through many examples, precisely determined, known, and grasped this point is overthrown by the appearance of a mighty spirit who in a given shape presents the highest form of passionate dedication."

We could call such a standpoint superhistorical, because a person who assumes such a stance could feel no more temptation to continue living and to participate in history. For he would have recognized the single condition of every event, that blindness and injustice in the soul of the man of action. He himself would have been cured from now on of taking history excessively seriously. But in the process he would have learned, for every person and for every experience, among the Greeks or Turks, from a moment of the first or the nineteenth century, to answer for himself the question how and why they conducted their lives. Anyone who asks his acquaintances whether they would like to live through the last ten or twenty years again will easily perceive which of them has been previously educated for that superhistorical point of view. For they will probably all answer "No!", but they will substantiate that "No!" differently, some of them perhaps with the confident hope "But the next twenty years will be better." Those are the ones of whom David Hume mockingly says:

'And from the dregs of life hope to receive
What the first sprightly running could not give.'

We will call these the historical people. The glance into the past pushes them into the future, fires their spirit to take up life for a longer time yet, kindles the hope that justice may still come and that happiness may sit behind the mountain towards which they are walking. These historical people believe that the meaning of existence will come increasingly to light in the course of its process. Therefore they look backwards only to understand the present by considering previous process and to learn to desire the future more keenly. In spite of all their history, they do not understand at all how unhistorically they think and act and also how their concern with history stands, not in service to pure knowledge, but to living.

But that question whose first answer we have heard can be answered again in a different way, that is, once more with a "No!" but with a "No!" that has a different grounding. The denial comes from the superhistorical person, who does not see healing in the process and for whom the world is much more complete and at its end in every moment. What could ten new years teach that the past ten years has not been able to teach!

Now, whether the meaning of the theory is happiness, resignation, virtue, or repentance, on that issue the superhistorical people have not been united. But contrary to all the historical ways of considering the past, they do come to

In Defense of Relativism

selection from *Anthropology and the Abnormal*
by Ruth Benedict

Modern social anthropology has become more and more a study of the varieties and common elements of cultural environment and the consequences of these in human behavior. For such a study of diverse social orders primitive peoples fortunately provide a laboratory not yet entirely vitiated by the spread of a standardized worldwide civilization. Dyaks and Hopis, Fijians and Yakuts are significant for psychological and sociological study because only among these simpler peoples has there been sufficient isolation to give opportunity for the development of localized social forms. In the higher cultures the standardization of custom and belief over a couple of continents has given a false sense of the inevitability of the particular forms that have gained currency, and we need to turn to a wider survey in order to check the conclusions we hastily base upon this near-universality of familiar customs. Most of the simpler cultures did not gain the wide currency of the one which, out of our experience, we identify with human nature, but this was for various historical reasons, and certainly not for any that gives us as its carriers a monopoly of social good or of social sanity. Modern civilization, from this point of view, becomes not a necessary pinnacle of human achievement but one entry in a long series of possible adjustments.

These adjustments, whether they are in mannerisms like the ways of showing anger, or joy, or grief in any society, or in major human drives like those of sex, prove to be far more variable than experience in any one culture would suggest. In certain fields, such as that of religion or of formal marriage arrangements, these wide limits of variability are well known and can be fairly described. In others it is not yet possible to give a generalized account, but that does not

Ruth Benedict, "Anthropology and the Abnormal: In Defense of Relativism," *The Journal of General Psychology*, vol. 10, no. 1, pp. 59-62, 64-65, 71-74, 76-77. Copyright © 1934 by Taylor & Francis Group. Reprinted with permission.

absolve us of the task of indicating the significance of the work that has been done and of the problems that have arisen.

One of these problems relates to the customary modern normal-abnormal categories and our conclusions regarding them. In how far are such categories culturally determined, or in how far can we with assurance regard them as absolute? In how far can we regard inability to function socially as diagnostic of abnormality, or in how far is it necessary to regard this as a function of the culture?

As a matter of fact, one of the most striking facts that emerge from a study of widely varying cultures is the ease with which our abnormals function in other cultures. It does not matter what kind of "abnormality" we choose for illustration, those which indicate extreme instability, or those which are more in the nature of character traits like sadism or delusions of grandeur or of persecution, there are well-described cultures in which these abnormals function at ease and with honor, and apparently without danger or difficulty to the society.

The most notorious of these is trance and catalepsy. Even a very mild mystic is aberrant in our culture. But most peoples have regarded even extreme psychic manifestations not only as normal and desirable, but even as characteristic of highly valued and gifted individuals. This was true even in our own cultural background in that period when Catholicism made the ecstatic experience the mark of sainthood. It is hard for us, born and brought up in a culture that makes no use of the experience, to realize how important a rôle it may play and how many individuals are capable of it, once it has been given an honorable place in any society.

Some of the Indian tribes of California accorded prestige principally to those who passed through certain trance experiences. Not all of these tribes believed that it was exclusively women who were so blessed, but among the Shasta (10) this was the convention. Their shamans were women, and they were accorded the greatest prestige in the community. They were chosen because of their constitutional liability to trance and allied manifestations. One day the woman who was so destined, while she was about her usual work, would fall suddenly to the ground. She had heard a voice speaking to her in tones of the greatest intensity. Turning, she had seen a man with drawn bow and arrow. He commanded her to sing on pain of being shot through the heart by his arrow, but under the stress of the experience she fell senseless. Her family gathered. She was lying rigid, hardly breathing. They knew that for some time she had had dreams of a special character which indicated a shamanistic calling, dreams of escaping grizzly bears, falling off cliffs or trees, or of being surrounded by swarms of yellow jackets. The community knew therefore what to expect. After a few hours the woman began to moan gently and to roll about upon the ground, trembling violently. She was supposed to be repeating the song which she had been told to sing and which during the trance had been taught her by the spirit. As she revived her moaning became more and more clearly the spirit's song until at last she called out the name of the spirit itself, and immediately blood oozed from her mouth.

When the woman had come to herself after the first encounter with her spirit she danced that night her first initiatory shamanistic dance, holding herself by a rope that was swung from the ceiling. For three nights she danced, and on the third night she had to receive in her body her power from her spirit. She was dancing, and as she felt the approach of the moment she called out, "He will shoot me, he will shoot me." Her friends stood close, for when she reeled in a kind of cataleptic seizure, they had to seize her before she fell or she would die. From this time on she had in her body a visible materialization of her spirit's power, an icicle-like object which in her dances thereafter she would exhibit, producing it from one part of her body and returning it to another part. From this time on she continued to validate her supernatural power by further cataleptic demonstrations, and she was called upon in great emergencies of life and death, for curing and for divination and for counsel. She became in other words by this procedure a woman of great power and importance.[1]

It is clear that, so far from regarding cataleptic seizures as blots upon the family escutcheon and as evidences of dreaded disease, cultural approval had seized upon them and made of them the pathway to authority over one's fellows. They were the outstanding characteristic of the most respected social type, the type which functioned with most honor and reward in the community. It was precisely the cataleptic individuals who in this culture were singled out for authority and leadership. ...

It is clear that culture may value and make socially available even highly unstable human types. If it chooses to treat their peculiarities as the most valued variants of human behavior, the individuals in question will rise to the occasion and perform their social rôles without reference to our usual ideas of the types who can make social adjustments and those who cannot.

Cataleptic and trance phenomena are, of course, only one illustration of the fact that those whom we regard as abnormals may function adequately in other cultures. Many of our culturally discarded traits are selected for elaboration in different societies. Homosexuality is an excellent example, for in this case our attention is not constantly diverted, as in the consideration of trance, to the interruption of routine activity which it implies. Homosexuality poses the

---

1 In all cultures behavior which is socially rewarded attracts persons who are attracted by the possibility of leadership, and such individuals may simulate the required behavior. This is as true when society rewards prodigality as when it rewards catalepsy. For the present argument the amount of shamming is not considered though it is of obvious importance. It is a matter which cultures standardize quite as much as they standardize the type of rewarded behavior.

problem very simply. A tendency toward this trait in our culture exposes an individual to all the conflicts to which all aberrants are always exposed, and we tend to identify the consequences of this conflict with homosexuality. But these consequences are obviously local and cultural. Homosexuals in many societies are not incompetent, but they may be such if the culture asks adjustments of them that would strain any man's vitality. Wherever homosexuality has been given an honorable place in any society, those to whom it is congenial have filled adequately the honorable roles society assigns to them. Plato's *Republic* is, of course, the most convincing statement of such a reading of homosexuality. It is presented as one of the major means to the good life, and it was generally so regarded in Greece at that time.

The cultural attitude toward homosexuals has not always been on such a high ethical plane, but it has been very varied. Among many American Indian tribes there exists the institution of the berdache (12, 15), as the French called them. These men-women were men who at puberty or thereafter took the dress and the occupations of women. Sometimes they married other men and lived with them. Sometimes they were men with no inversion, persons of weak sexual endowment who chose this rôle to avoid the jeers of the women. The berdaches were never regarded as of first-rate supernatural power, as similar men-women were in Siberia, but rather as leaders in women's occupations, good healers in certain diseases, or, among certain tribes, as the genial organizers of social affairs. In any case, they were socially placed. They were not left exposed to the conflicts that visit the deviant who is excluded from participation in the recognized patterns of his society. ...

Behavior honored upon the Northwest Coast is one which is recognized as abnormal in our civilization, and yet it is sufficiently close to the attitudes of our own culture to be intelligible to us and to have a definite vocabulary with which we may discuss it. The megalomaniac paranoid trend is a definite danger in our society. It is encouraged by some of our major preoccupations, and it confronts us with a choice of two possible attitudes. One is to brand it as abnormal and reprehensible, and is the attitude we have chosen in our civilization. The other is to make it an essential attribute of ideal man, and this is the solution in the culture of the Northwest Coast.

These illustrations, which it has been possible to indicate only in the briefest manner, force upon us the fact that normality is culturally defined. An adult shaped to the drives and standards of either of these cultures, if he were transported into our civilization, would fall into our categories of abnormality. He would be faced with the psychic dilemmas of the socially unavailable. In his own culture, however, he is the pillar of society, the end result of socially inculcated mores, and the problem of personal instability in his case simply does not arise.

No one civilization can possibly utilize in its mores the whole potential range of human behavior. Just as there are great numbers of possible phonetic articulations, and the possibility of language depends on a selection and standardization of a few of these in order that speech communication may be possible at all, so the possibility of organized behavior of every sort, from the fashions of local dress and houses to the dicta of a people's ethics and religion, depends upon a similar selection among the possible behavior traits. In the field of recognized economic obligations or sex tabus this selection is as non-rational and subconscious a process as it is in the field of phonetics. It is a process which goes on in the group for long periods of time and is historically conditioned by innumerable accidents of isolation or of contact of peoples. In any comprehensive study of psychology, the selection that different cultures have made in the course of history within the great circumference of potential behavior is of great significance.

Every society,[2] beginning with some slight inclination in one direction or another, carries its preference farther and farther, integrating itself more and more completely upon its chosen basis, and discarding those types of behavior that are uncongenial. Most of those organizations of personality that seem to us most incontrovertibly abnormal have been used by different civilizations in the very foundations of their institutional life. Conversely the most valued traits of our normal individuals have been looked on in differently organized cultures as aberrant. Normality, in short, within a very wide range, is culturally defined. It is primarily a term for the socially elaborated segment of human behavior in any culture; and abnormality, a term for the segment that that particular civilization does not use. The very eyes with which we see the problem are conditioned by the long traditional habits of our own society.

It is a point that has been made more often in relation to ethics than in relation to psychiatry. We do not any longer make the mistake of deriving the morality of our own locality and decade directly from the inevitable constitution of human nature. We do not elevate it to the dignity of a first principle. We recognize that morality differs in every society, and is a convenient term for socially approved habits. Mankind has always preferred to say, "It is a morally good," rather than "It is habitual," and the fact of this preference is matter enough for a critical science of ethics. But historically the two phrases are synonymous.

The concept of the normal is properly a variant of the concept of the good. It is that which society has approved. A normal action is one which falls well within the limits of expected behavior for a particular society. Its variability among different peoples is essentially a function of the variability of the

---

2   This phrasing of the process is deliberately animistic. It is used with no reference to a group mind or a superorganic, but in the same sense in which it is customary to say, "Every art has its own canons."

behavior patterns that different societies have created for themselves, and can never be wholly divorced from a consideration of culturally institutionalized types of behavior.

Each culture is a more or less elaborate working-out of the potentialities of the segment it has chosen. In so far as a civilization is well integrated and consistent within itself, it will tend to carry farther and farther, according to its nature, its initial impulse toward a particular type of action, and from the point of view of any other culture those elaborations will include more and more extreme and aberrant traits.

Each of these traits, in proportion as it reinforces the chosen behavior patterns of that culture, is for that culture normal. Those individuals to whom it is congenial either congenitally, or as the result of childhood sets, are accorded prestige in that culture, and are not visited with the social contempt or disapproval which their traits would call down upon them in a society that was differently organized. On the other hand, those individuals whose characteristics are not congenial to the selected type of human behavior in that community are the deviants, no matter how valued their personality traits may be in a contrasted civilization. …

I have spoken of individuals as having sets toward certain types of behavior, and of these sets as running sometimes counter to the types of behavior which are institutionalized in the culture to which they belong. From all that we know of contrasting cultures it seems clear that differences of temperament occur in every society. The matter has never been made the subject of investigation, but from the available material it would appear that these temperament types are very likely of universal recurrence. That is, there is an ascertainable range of human behavior that is found wherever a sufficiently large series of individuals is observed. But the proportion in which behavior types stand to one another in different societies is not universal. The vast majority of the individuals in any group are shaped to the fashion of that culture. In other words, most individuals are plastic to the moulding force of the society into which they are born. In a society that values trance, as in India, they will have supernormal experience. In a society that institutionalizes homosexuality, they will be homosexual. In a society that sets the gathering of possessions as the chief human objective, they will amass property. The deviants, whatever the type of behavior the culture has institutionalized, will remain few in number, and there seems no more difficulty in moulding the vast malleable majority to the "normality" of what we consider an aberrant trait, such as delusions of reference, than to the normality of such accepted behavior patterns as acquisitiveness. The small proportion of the number of the deviants in any culture is not a function of the sure instinct with which that society has built itself upon the fundamental sanities, but of

Indeed, something like this view of moral practice seems to explain our preoccupation with moral argument. What seems to give moral argument its point and poignancy is the idea that, since we are all in the same boat, a careful mustering and assessment of the reasons for and against our moral opinions is the best way to discover what the moral facts really are. If the participants are open-minded and thinking correctly then, we seem to think, such an argument should result in a *convergence* in moral opinion—a convergence upon the truth. Individual reflection may serve the same purpose, but only when it simulates a real moral argument; for only then can we be certain that we are giving each side of the argument due consideration.

We may summarize this first feature of moral practice in the following terms: we seem to think moral questions have correct answers, that the correct answers are made correct by objective moral facts, that moral facts are determined by circumstances, and that, by moralizing, we can discover what these objective moral facts determined by the circumstances are. The term 'objective' here simply signifies the possibility of a convergence in moral views of the kind just mentioned.

A second and rather different feature of moral practice concerns the practical implications of moral judgement, the way in which moral questions gain in their significance for us because of the special influence our moral opinions are supposed to have upon our actions. The idea is that when, say, we come to think that we did the wrong thing in refusing to give to famine relief, we come to think that we failed to do something for which there was a good reason. And this has motivational implications. For now imagine the situation if we refuse to give to famine relif when next the opportunity arises. Our refusal will occasion serious puzzlement, for we will have refused to do what we are known to think we have a good reason to do. Perhaps we will be able to explain ourselves. Perhaps we thought there was a better reason to do something else, or perhaps we were weak-willed. But, the point remains, an explanation of some sort will need to be forthcoming. An explanation will need to be forthcoming because, we seem to think, other things being equal, to have a moral opinion simply *is* to find yourself with a corresponding motivation to act.

These two distinctive features of moral practice—the *objectivity* and the *practicality* of moral judgement–are widely thought to have both metaphysical and psychological implications. However, and unfortunately, these implications are the exact opposite of each other. In order to see why this is thought to be so, we need to pause for a moment to reflect more generally on the nature of human psychology.

According to the standard picture of human psychology—a picture we owe to David Hume, the famous Scottish philosopher of the eighteenth century—there are two main kinds of psychological state. On the one hand there are beliefs, states that purport to represent the way the world is. Since our beliefs purport to represent the world, they are subject to rational criticism: specifically, they are assessable in terms of truth and falsehood according to whether or not they succeed in representing the world to be the way it really is.

On the other hand, however, there are also desires, states that represent how the world is to be. Desires are unlike beliefs in that they do not even purport to represent the way the world is. They are therefore not assessable in terms of truth and falsehood. Indeed, according to the standard picture, our desires are at bottom not subject to any sort of rational criticism at all. The fact that we have a certain desire is, with a proviso to be mentioned presently, simply a fact about ourselves to be acknowledged. It may be unfortunate that we have certain combinations of desires—perhaps our desires cannot all be satisfied together—but, *in themselves*, our desires are all on a par, rationally neutral.

This is important, for it suggests that though we may make discoveries about the world, and though these discoveries may rightly affect our beliefs, such discoveries should, again with one proviso to be mentioned presently, have no rational impact upon our desires. They may of course, have some *non*-rational impact. Seeing a spider I may be overcome with a morbid fear and desire never to be near one. However, this is not a change in my desires mandated by reason. It is a *non*-rational change in my desires.

Now for the proviso. Suppose, contrary to the example I just gave, that I acquire the desire never to be near a spider because I come to believe, falsely, that spiders give off an unpleasant odour. Then we would certainly ordinarily say that I have an 'irrational desire'. However, the reason we would say this clearly doesn't go against the spirit of what has been said so far. For my desire never to be near a spider is *based on* a further desire and belief: my desire not to smell that unpleasant odour and my belief that that odour is given off by spiders. Since I can be rationally criticized for having the belief, as it is false, I can be rationally criticized for having the desire it helps to produce.

The proviso is thus fairly minor: desires are subject to rational criticism, but only insofar as they are based on beliefs that are subject to rational criticism. Desires that are not related in some such way to beliefs that can be rationally criticized are not subject to rational criticism at all. We will return to this point presently.

According to the standard picture, then, there are two kinds of psychological state–beliefs and desires–utterly distinct and different from each other. The standard picture of human psychology is important because it provides us with a model for understanding human action. Human action is, according to this picture, produced by a combination of the two. Crudely, our beliefs tell us how the world is, and thus how it has to be changed, so as to make it the way our desires tell us it is to be. An action is thus the product of these two forces:

a desire representing the way the world is to be and a belief telling us how the world has to be changed so as to make it that way.

Let's now return to consider the two features of moral judgment we discussed earlier. Consider first the objectivity of such judgement: the idea that moral questions have correct answers, that the correct answers are made correct by objective moral facts, that moral facts are determined by circumstances, and that, by moralizing, we can discover what these objective moral facts are. The metaphysical and psychological implications of this may now be summarized as follows. Metaphysically, the implication is that, amongst the various facts there are in the world, there aren't just facts about (say) the consequences of our actions on the well-being of our families and friends, there are also distinctively *moral* facts: facts about the rightness and wrongness of our actions having these consequences. And, psychologically, the implication is thus that when we make a moral judgement we thereby express our *beliefs* about the way these moral facts are. In forming moral opinions we acquire beliefs, representations of the way the world is morally.

Given the standard picture of human psychology, there is a further psychological implication. For whether or not people who have a certain moral belief desire to act accordingly must now be seen as a further and entirely separate question. They may happen to have a corresponding desire, they may not. However, either way, they canot be rationally criticized. Having or failing to have a corresponding desire is simply a further fact about a person's psychology.

But now consider the second feature, the practicality of moral judgment. We saw earlier that to have a moral opinion simply *is*, contrary to what has just been said, to find ourselves with a corresponding motivation to act. If we think it right to give to famine relief then, other things being equal, we must be motivated to give to famine relief. The practicality of moral judgement thus seems to have a psychological and a metaphysical implication of its own. Psychologically, since making a moral judgement requires our having a certain desire, and no recognition of a fact about the world could rationally compel us to have one desire rather than another, our judgement must really simply *be* an expression of that desire. And this psychological implication has a metaphysical counterpart. For it seems to follow that, contrary to initial appearance, when we judge it right to give to famine relief we *are not* responding to any moral fact—the rightness of giving to famine relief. Indeed, moral facts are an idle postulate. In judging it right to give to famine relief we are really simply expressing our desire that people give to famine relief. It is as if we were yelling 'Hooray for giving to famine relief!'—no mention of a moral fact there, in fact, no factual claim at all.

We are now in a position to see why philosophers have been worried about the whole business of moral appraisal. The problem is that the *objectivity* and the *practicality* of moral judgement pull in quite opposite directions from each other. The objectivity of moral judgement suggests that there are moral facts, determined by circumstances, and that our moral judgements express our beliefs about what these facts are. This enables us to make good sense of moral argument, and the like, but it leaves it entirely mysterious how or why having a moral view is supposed to have special links with what we are motivated to do. And the practicality of moral judgement suggests just the opposite, that our moral judgements express our desires. While this enables us to make good sense of the link between having a moral view and being motivated, it leaves it entirely mysterious what a moral argument is supposed to be an argument about.

The idea of a moral judgement thus looks like it may well be incoherent, for what is required to make sense of such a judgement is a queer sort of fact about the universe: a fact whose recognition necessarily impacts upon our desires. But the standard picture tells us that there are no such facts. Nothing could be everything a moral judgement purports to be—or so it may now seem.

At long last we are in a position to see what this essay is about. For *moral realism* is simply the metaphysical (or ontological) view that there exist moral facts. The psychological counterpart to realism is called 'cognitivism', the view that moral judgements express our beliefs about what these moral facts are, and that we can come to discover what these facts are by engaging in moral argument and reflection.

Moral realism thus contrasts with two alternative metaphysical views about morality: *irrealism* (sometimes called 'anti-realism') and *moral nihilism*. According to the irrealists, there are no moral facts, but neither are moral facts required to make sense of moral practice. We can happily acknowledge that our moral judgements simply express our desires about how people behave. This, the psychological counterpart to irrealism, is called 'non-cognitivism'. (There are different versions of irrealism: e.g. emotivism, prescriptivism, and projectivism. For a fuller discussion of these theories see Article 36, INTUITIONISM, Article 38, SUBJECTIVISM, and Article 40, UNIVERSAL PRESCRIPTIVISM.)

By contrast, according to the moral nihilists, the irrealists are right that there are no moral facts, but wrong about what is required to make sense of moral practice. The nihilist thinks that without moral facts moral practice is all a sham, much like religious practice without belief in God.

I have taken some time before introducing the ideas of moral realism, irrealism, and nihilism because, as it seems to me, each has much to be said both in its favour and against it. In what follows I will explain in more detail some of the substantive views people have taken in this whole debate. However, I want to emphasize at the outset that nearly every substantive position is fraught with difficulty and controversy. The long introduction will hopefully have given some hint of why this is so. The very idea of moral practice may well be in deep trouble, much as the moral nihilist suggests.

Remember that, according to the irrealist, when we judge it right to give to famine relief we are expressing our desire that people give to famine relief; it is as if we were yelling 'Hooray for giving to famine relief!' Irrealism is certainly an option to be considered. But it seems to me that it is ultimately an unattractive option.

To be sure, irrealists have a perfect explanation of the practicality of moral judgement. But it seems utterly implausible to suppose, as they therefore must, that moral judgements aren't truth-assessable at all. They must say this because they model a moral judgement on a yell of approval or disapproval. But when I yell 'Hooray for giving to famine relief!', though my yell may be sincere or insincere, it can hardly be true or false. My yell reveals something about myself–that I have a certain desire–not about the world.

The problem here isn't just that we *say* that moral judgements can be true or false, though we certainly do do that. The problem is rather that the whole business of moral argument and moral reflection only makes sense on the assumption that moral judgements *are* truth-assessable. When we agonize over our moral opinions, we seem to be agonizing over whether our reasons for our beliefs are good enough reasons for believing what we believe to be true. And no irrealist surrogate seems up to the task of explaining this appearance away. For example, it seems utterly hopeless to suppose that we are agonizing over whether we *really* have the desires we have. Surely *this* question isn't so hard to answer!

Indeed, in this context, it is worthwhile asking what the irrealists' view of moral argument is supposed to be. They presumably imagine that what we are trying to do, when we engage in moral argument, is to get our opponent to have the same desires as we have. But, at bottom, they must also say that we are trying to do this *not* because the opponent rationally should have these desires–remember that, subject to the proviso mentioned, desires aren't supposed to be subject to rational criticism at all—but rather just because these are the desires *we* want him to have. But in that case moral argument begins to look massively self-obsessed, an imposition of *our* wants on others.

Irrealism isn't an attractive option. The irrealist's account of moral judgement as the expression of a desire simply fails to make sense of moral reflection. And the irrealist's account of moral argument makes moral persuasion look like it is itself immoral! What about the alternative, moral realism?

It might be thought that, since the moral realist admits the existence of moral facts, he has therefore no problem explaining the objectivity of moral judgement and the related phenomena of moral reflection and moral argument. It might be thought that the realist's only problem is that, if he is to eschew the existence of 'queer' moral properties whose recognition connects necessarily with the will, then he cannot explain the practicality of moral judgement. But matters are in fact much more complicated.

Certainly the moral realist needs to face up to the fact that the practicality of moral judgement is problematic, from his point of view. But his problem is more than that. His problem is that, *because* he has no explanation of the practicality of moral judgement, he has no plausible story about what *kind* of fact a moral fact is. And if he has no plausible story about the kind of fact a moral fact is, then, despite initial appearance, he has no plausible story about what moral reflection and moral argument are all about.

In order to see this, remember what we said at the outset when we first introduced the idea of the practicality of moral judgement. We said then that the practicality of moral judgement is a consequence of the fact that judgements about right and wrong are judgements about what we have reason to do and reason not to do. This is the subject matter of moral reflection and moral argument, *our reasons for action*. But the moral realist who admits an array of moral facts about which we may be motivationally neutral must reject such a conception of rightness and wrongness. After all, we could hardly remain motivationally neutral about what we think we have reason to do! The challenge such a realist faces is thus to provide us with some alternative account of what *kind* of fact a moral fact is; an alternative account of what moral reflection and moral argument are *about*.

Some moral realists do face up to this challenge. They have claimed, for example, that moral facts are facts that play a certain *explanatory role* in the social world: right acts are those that tend towards social stability, whereas wrong acts are those that tend towards social unrest. An Aristotelian version of this might be: right acts are those in accord with the 'proper function' of human beings—a quasi-biological notion—wrong acts are those that are not in accord with this proper function. Moral reflection and moral argument are thus, they suggest, arguments about which features of actions feed this tendency towards unrest and stability. Or, in the Aristotelian version, they are arguments about which acts are in accord with the proper function of humans (and thus, ultimately, about what the proper function of a human being is). The word 'tendency' is not idle here, for such realists are quick to emphasize that other factors may mitigate the tendency towards stability and unrest, or may stop humans actually having their proper function.

Let's focus for a moment on the suggestion that a moral fact can be characterized in terms of a tendency towards social stability or unrest. This suggestion cannot be dismissed out of hand, for reflection of an armchair-sociological kind does suggest that the acts we are disposed to think of as right—those that provide for a more equitable satisfaction of different people's interests, say—do tend towards social stabilty, and that the acts we are disposed to think of as wrong—those that provide for a less equitable satisfaction of different people's interests, say—do tend towards social unrest. It is thus best to assume that we have here two *competing* conceptions of a moral fact. Which conception seems the more plausible?

On the one hand, we have the idea of a moral fact as a fact about what we have reason to do or not to do. On the other, we have the idea of a moral fact in terms of what tends towards social stability and unrest. If the question is 'Which conception allows us to make the best sense of moral argument?' then the answer must surely be the former. For, to the extent that moral argument does focus on what tends towards social stability, it does so because social stability is deemed morally important, an outcome we have reason to produce.

Indeed, it seems to me that even this kind of moral realist's focus on *explanation* pushes us back in the direction of the idea of a moral fact as a fact about what we have reason to do. For, again, to the extent that we think of right acts as acts that tend towards social stability, we think that they have this tendency *because* they represent the reasonable thing for people to do. It is the tendency people have to do what is reasonable that is doing the explanatory work, But that, too, simply returns us to the original conception of a moral fact in terms of what we have reason to do. (We might say similar things about the idea that we can characterize a moral fact in terms of the proper function of human beings; for insofar as we understand the idea of the 'proper function' of human beings, we think that their proper function is to be reasonable and rational.)

In the end, then, we might object that this kind of moral realist fails to provide us with a real *alternative* to our original conception of a moral fact. The real question, then, is whether the moral realist is forced to reject the idea that rightness and wrongness have to do with what we have reason to do and reason not to do. In the remainder of this essay I want to explore this question.

The devil of the piece is what I have been calling the 'standard picture' of human psychology. For the standard picture gives us a model of what it is to have a reason in terms of a desire/belief pair. If the moral realist is to make headway in combining the objectivity and the practicality of moral judgement without appealing to 'queer' moral facts, he must challenge this standard picture.

The trouble is, however, that the standard picture looks substantially correct as an account of human motivation. After all, it is uncontroversial that the psychological states that motivate actions must be dispositions of some sort, dispositions to produce acts of the relevant kind. And it is also uncontroversial that actions are motivated by psychological states that have content: either they are produced by states that represent the way the world is (beliefs) or by states that represent the way the world is to be (desires), or, as the standard picture has it, they are produced by a pairing of the two (a desire and a belief).

But now reflect for a moment. A disposition to produce acts of some relevant kind, if it has content, must have, as its content, a representation of the way the world is to be, and so it must be a desire. For how else could the psychological state in question *target* the state of affairs to be produced? (And how could it produce what is to be produced without having targeted it?) Moreover, if this state is to produce the targeted state of affairs, it must also be paired with a representation of how the world is, and so it must be paired with a belief. For only so will the relevant *change* in the world be produced so as to bring about the targeted state of affairs.

It therefore seems that the standard picture is right in insisting that desires are required in order to motivate actions. The place to challenge the standard picture, then, is not in its account of what motivates action, but rather in its tacit conflation of *reasons* with *motives*. Seeing why this is a conflation also enables us to see why we may legitimately talk about our *beliefs* about the reasons we have, and why having such beliefs makes it rational to have corresponding desires.

Imagine that you are giving the baby a bath. As you do, it begins to scream uncontrollably. Nothing you do seems to help. As you watch it scream, you are overcome with a desire to drown the baby in the bathwater. Certainly you may now be *motivated* to drown the baby. (You may even actually drown it.) But does the mere fact that you have this desire, and are thus motivated, mean that you have a *reason* to drown the baby?

One commonsensical answer is that, since the desire is not *worth* satisfying, it does not provide you with such a reason; that, in this case, you are motivated to do something you have *no* reason to do. However, the standard picture seems utterly unable to accept this answer. After all, your desire to drown the baby need be based on no false belief. As such, it is entirely beyond rational criticism—or so that standard picture tells us.

The problem, here, is that the standard picture gives no special privilege to what we would want if we were 'cool, calm and collected' (to use a flippant phrase). Yet we seem ordinarily to think that not being cool, calm and collected may lead to all sorts of irrational emotional outbursts. Having those desires that we would have if we were cool, calm and collected thus seems to be an independent rational ideal. When cool, calm and collected, you would wish for the baby not to be drowned, no matter how much it screams, and no matter how overcome you may be, in your uncool, uncalm and uncollected state, with a desire to drown it. This is why you have no reason to drown the baby.

Perhaps we have already said enough to reconcile the objectivity of moral judgement with its practicality. Judgements of right and wrong are judgements about what we have reason to do and reason not to do. But what sort of fact is a fact about what we have reason to do? The preceding discussion suggests an answer. It suggests that facts about what we have reason to do are not facts about what we *do* desire, as the standard picture would have it, but are rather facts about what we *would* desire if we were in certain idealized conditions of reflection: if, say, we were well-informed, cool, calm and collected. According to this account, then, I have a reason to give to famine relief in my particular circumstances just in case, if I were in such idealized conditions of reflection, I would desire that, even when in my particular circumstances, I give to famine relief. And this sort of fact may certainly be the object of a belief.

Moreover, this account of what it is to have a reason makes it plain why the standard picture of human psychology is wrong to insist that beliefs and desires are altogether distinct; why, on the contrary, having certain beliefs, beliefs about what we have reason to do, does make it rational for us to have certain desires, desires to do what we believe we have reason to do.

In order to see this, suppose I believe that I would desire to give to famine relief if I were cool, calm and collected–i.e. more colloquially, I believe I have a reason to give to famine relief—but, being uncool, uncalm and uncollected, I don't desire to give to famine relief. Am I rationally criticizable for not having the desire? I surely am. After all, from my own point of view my beliefs and desires form a more coherent, and thus a rationally preferable, package if I do in fact desire to do what I believe I would desire to do if I were cool, calm and collected. This is because, since it is an independent rational ideal to have the desires I would have if I were cool, calm and collected, so, from my own point of view, if I believe that I would have a certain desire under such conditions and yet fail to have it, then my beliefs and desires fail to meet this ideal. To believe that I would desire to give to famine relief if I were cool, calm and collected, and yet to fail to desire to give to famine relief, is thus to manifest a commonly recognizable species of rational failure.

If this is right, then it follows that, contrary to the standard picture of human psychology, there is in fact no problem at all in supposing that I may have genuine *beliefs* about what I have reason to do, where having those beliefs makes it rational for me to have the corresponding *desires*. And if there is no problem at all in supposing that this may be so, then there is no problem in reconciling the practicality of moral judgement with the claim that moral judgements express our beliefs about the reasons we have.

However, this doesn't yet suffice to solve the problem facing the moral realist. For moral judgements aren't *just* judgements abut the reasons we have. They are judgements about the reasons we have *where those reasons are supposed to be determined entirely by our circumstances.* As I put it earlier, people in the same circumstances face the same moral choice: if they did the same action then either they both acted rightly (they both did what they had reason to do) or they both acted wrongly (they both did what they had reason not to do). Does the account of what it is to have a reason just given entail that this is so?

Suppose our circumstances are identical, and let's ask whether it is right for each of us to give to famine relief: that is, whether we each have a reason to do so, According to the account on offer it is right that I give to famine relief just in case I have a reason to give to famine relief, and I have such a reason just in case, if I were in idealized conditions of reflection—well-informed, cool, calm and collected—I would desire to give to famine relief. And the same is true of you. If our circumstances are the same then, supposedly, we should both have such a reason or both lack such a reason. But do we?

The question is whether, if we were well-informed, cool, calm and collected, we would tend to *converge* in the desires we have. Would we converge or would there always be the possibility of some non-rationally-explicable difference in our desires *even under such conditions?* The standard picture of human psychology now returns to centre-stage. For it tells us that there is *always* the possibility of some non-rationally-explicable difference in our desires even under such idealized conditions of reflection. This is the residue of the standard picture's conception of desire as a psychological state that is beyond rational criticism.

If this is right then the moral realist's attempt to combine the objectivity and the practicality of moral judgement must be deemed a failure. We are forced to accept that there is a *fundamental relativity* in the reasons we have. What we have reason to do is relative to what we would desire under certain idealized conditions of reflection, and this may differ from person to person. It is not wholly determined by our circumstances, as moral facts are supposed to be.

Many philosophers accept the standard picture's pronouncement on this point. But accepting there is such a fundamental relativity in our reasons seems altogether premature to me. It puts the cart before the horse. For surely moral practice is itself the forum in which we will *discover* whether there is a fundamental relativity in our reasons.

After all, in moral practice we attempt to change people's moral beliefs by engaging them in rational argument: i.e. by getting their beliefs to approximate those they would have under more idealized conditions of reflection. And sometimes we succeed. When we succeed, other things being equal, we succeed in changing their desires. But if we accept that there is a fundamental relativity in our reasons then we can say, in advance, that this procedure will never result in a massive *convergence* in moral beliefs; for we know in advance that there will never be a convergence in the desires we have under such idealized conditions of reflection. Or rather, and more accurately, if there is a fundamental relativity in our reasons then it follows that any convergence we find in our moral beliefs, and thus in our desires, must be entirely contingent. It could in no way be explained by, or suggestive of, the fact that the desires that emerge have some *privileged* rational status.

My question is: 'Why accept this?' Why not think, instead, that if such a convergence emerged in moral practice then that would itself suggest that these particular moral beliefs, and the corresponding desires, *do* enjoy a privileged rational status? After all, something like such a convergence in mathematical practice lies behind our conviction that mathematical claims enjoy a privileged rational status. So why not think that a like convergence in moral practice would show that moral judgements enjoy the same privileged rational status? At this point, the standard picture's insistence that there is a fundamental relativity in our reasons begins to sound all too much like a hollow dogma.

The kind of moral realism described here endorses a conception of moral facts that is a far cry from the picture presented at the outset: moral facts as queer facts about the universe whose recognition necessarily impacts upon our desires. Instead, the realist has eschewed queer facts about the universe in favour of a more 'subjectivist' conception of moral facts. This emerged in the realist's analysis of what it is to have a reason. (For a fuller discussion of subjectivist theories see Article 38, SUBJECTIVISM.) The realist's point, however, is that such a conception of moral facts may make them subjective only in the innocuous sense that they are facts about what we would *want* under certain idealized conditions of reflection, where wants are, admittedly, a kind of psychological state enjoyed by subjects. But moral facts remain objective insofar as they are facts about what *we,* not just *you* or *I,* would want under such conditions. The existence of a moral fact—say, the rightness of giving to famine relief in certain circumstances—requires that, under idealized conditions of reflection, rational creatures would *converge* upon a desire to give to famine relief in such circumstances.

Of course, it must be agreed on all sides that moral argument has not yet produced the sort of convergence in our desires that would make the idea of a moral fact–a fact about the reasons we have entirely determined by our circumstances–look plausible. But neither has moral argument had much of a history in times in which we have been able to engage in free reflection unhampered by a false biology (the Aristotelian tradition) or a false belief in God (the Judeo-Christian tradition). It remains to be seen whether sustained moral argument can elicit the requisite convergence in our moral beliefs, and corresponding desires, to make the idea of a moral fact look plausible. The kind of moral realism described here holds out the hope that it will. Only time will tell.

Further Reading

Ayer, A.J.: 'Critique of ethics and theology', in his *Language, Truth and Logic* (London: 1936); (London: Gollancz, 1970).

Harman, G.: *The Nature of Morality* (Oxford: Oxford University Press, 1977).

Honderich, T., ed.: *Morality and Objectivity* (London: Routledge and Kegan Paul, 1985), especially the papers by Blackburn and Williams.

Hume, D.: *A Treatise of Human Nature* (1738): ed. L. A. Selby-Bigge (Oxford: Clarendon Press, 1978), especially Book II, Part III, Section III.

Mackie, J.: *Ethics: Inventing Right and Wrong* (Harmondsworth: Penguin, 1977), especially ch. 1.

Nagel, T.: *The View From Nowhere* (Oxford: Oxford University Press, 1986), especially ch. 8.

Sayre-McCord, G., ed.: *Essays on Moral Realism* (Ithaca, NY: Cornell University Press, 1988). This is the best book to read on the topic of moral realism, if you can only manage one, as it collects together papers by many of the leading figures: e.g. Ayer, Blackburn, Harman, Mackie, McDowell, Wiggins, Williams and others. Sayre-McCord's introduction is also well worth reading.

Smith, M., Lewis, D. and Johnston, M.: Symposium on 'Dispositional theories of value', *Proceedings of the Aristotelian Society,* Supplementary Volume (1989).

Williams, B.: 'Internal and external reasons', in his *Moral Luck* (Cambridge: Cambridge University Press, 1981).

——: *Ethics and the Limits of Philosophy* (Cambridge, Mass.: Harvard University Press, 1985), especially the first four chapters.

Nietzsche, *On the Uses of and Disadvantages of History for Life*

1. According to Nietzsche, how does memory separate humans from other animals? How does this cause humans to be dishonest?
2. Why does Nietzsche say forgetfulness is necessary for happiness? How does this support his claim that cynicism is the only warranted philosophical position?
3. What is the difference between the historical and superhistorical people? Why is Nietzsche happy to concede to the latter their wisdom? What does he hope for instead of wisdom?
4. Why does Nietzsche think the active person is without both conscience and knowledge?

Benedict, *Anthropology of the Abnormal*

1. Is modern civilization a pinnacle of human achievement? Why or why not?
2. What striking feature does Benedict note about "abnormal"? What is her primary example?
3. What does Benedict think it would be a mistake to do regarding human nature?
4. What is Benedict's conclusion regarding "normality" or morality? What is her evidence?

Michael Smith, *Realism*

1. What is implied by our desire to get the answers to moral questions right? What should argument about what is morally right accomplish?
2. What is the first feature of moral practice? What is the second feature of moral practice? What is the problem with these two features of moral practice?
3. Who do we owe the standard picture of human psychology to? What two kinds of psychological states are there according to the standard picture? Which type is capable of being true or false? Which type is not capable of being true or false? Why have some philosophers been worried about moral appraisal?
4. What does Smith think the standard picture of human psychology wrongly conflates? What is the problem with the standard picture of human psychology? How does the "baby bath" example illustrate this problem?

5. What question does Smith raise about convergence? What would the standard picture of human psychology tell us about convergence? Why is this a problem for the moral realist? What does Smith believe about the "forum" of moral practice? Why does he believe this? Why does Smith accuse the standard picture of being a "hollow dogma"?

SUGGESTIONS FOR FURTHER READING OR VIEWING

Blackburn, Simon. *Ethics: A Very Short Introduction.* Oxford: Oxford University Press, 2009.

PART 2

The Good Life

WHAT SHOULD WE VALUE THE MOST?

Imagine going on a first date and being asked by your date, What do you value most in the world? What would you say? What answer would you hope to hear from your date when you ask them the same question? Are there answers that would mean no second date?

Here are some possible answers your date might give to the question, What do you value most in the world?

- Family: I would give my life for my children. I respect and honor my parents by the way I live my life. I would give my life for my siblings. I would do anything to protect them.
- Country: If I have to die, let it be for my country. And if I have any regrets, let it be that I have only one life to give to my country.
- God: I love God with all my heart, all my soul, and all my strength.
- Honor: When I give my word, I keep it. My reputation as an honorable person means more to me than anything else.
- Beauty: I want to experience as much beauty in my life as possible.
- Happiness: I want to be happy. At the end of my life, I want to be happy with the life I lived.

The last answer, happiness, is a quite popular one and it is endorsed by utilitarians such as Jeremy Bentham and John Stuart Mill. Many of us value happiness more than we value anything else: we want to be happy and we want our children to grow up to be happy. As you might suspect, however, philosophers disagree about what happiness is, and many reject the idea that happiness is the most important thing. Nietzsche, over a hundred years ago, joked, "Man does not strive after happiness, only the Englishman does."*

*Friedrich Nietzsche. *Twilight of the Idols*. In *The Portable Nietzsche*, translated by Walter Kaufmann. Penguin Books, 1977. See Maxims and Arrows" No. 12, p. 468.

The joke is funny in part because Bentham and Mill were Englishmen. In the same aphorism, Nietzsche adds that "If we have our *why* of life, we will put up with any *how*." His point is that while some people may value happiness more than anything else, many of us don't. What the rest of us want is a *why*. We want a purpose to our lives. We want our lives to mean something. And if we have a *why*, if we have a purpose, then we will endure any *how*, no matter how hard that *how* is, no matter how much sacrifice and suffering that *how* requires.

The next few selections will consider what we should value the most. Our readings will range from the view, endorsed by Epicurus, that pleasure and freedom from pain is the most important thing, to the Buddhist view that a wrong-headed pursuit of pleasure leads to suffering. In between are Aristotle and Confucius, who present distinctive and influential pictures of human well-being or flourishing.

Hedonism

INTRODUCTION TO HEDONISM

Hedonism is a philosophical theory that emphasizes the pursuit of pleasure above all other activities and enterprises. There are two main types of hedonism: psychological hedonism and what might be described as "ethical" or "evaluative" hedonism. Psychological hedonism holds that the pursuit of pleasure and avoidance of pain are the sole motivators of human action. According to this view, people ultimately only act in order to gain pleasure or avoid pain; nothing else is capable of driving human action. Psychological hedonism is a descriptive theory that isn't making any sort of value judgment about what has worth nor is it prescribing anything about what we ought to pursue. Rather, it simply describes human psychology. On the other hand, hedonism in the ethical or evaluative sense offers a theory of value and as such is normative in nature. As a value theory, hedonism does not offer an account of what actions are right or wrong, but it does provide an account of what sorts of things have value and are worth pursuing. In this sense, hedonism is the view that pleasure and the absence of pain are the sole objects of inherent (or intrinsic) value. This means that pleasure and the absence of pain are the only things that are desirable as ends in themselves and that all other objects of desire are worthy only so far as they produce pleasure or eliminate pain.

In its modern form, hedonism was introduced and popularized by Jeremy Bentham's *An Introduction to the Principles of Morals and Legislation* in the nineteenth century and is often associated with classical utilitarianism. Both Jeremy Bentham and John Stuart Mill define happiness in terms of pleasure and the absence of pain and are often classified as hedonistic utilitarians, although there is some debate about classifying Mill in this fashion. However, philosophical discussion of hedonism and criticism of the view date back to ancient philosophy and the works of Plato and Aristotle. Perhaps the most famous defense of hedonism can be found in the work of Epicurus, roughly

300 years before the Common Era, in his *Letter to Menoeceus*. One of the main critiques of hedonism stems from the contemporary political philosopher Robert Nozick's Experience Machine. This thought experiment presents a hypothetical situation where the audience has the chance to be attached to a machine that simulates a reality with nothing but pleasure for the remainder of their lives. Nozick appeals to the audience's reluctance to sign up for this opportunity as evidence that pleasure and the absence of pain are not the sole objects of inherent value.

Epicurus's *Letter to Menoeceus* begins by introducing some of his basic teachings about the gods, death, and moral theory. He argues that while the gods do in fact exist, their nature is distinct from what most people believe and they are not really involved in the affairs of humans. Epicurus's discussion of death emphasizes his materialistic metaphysics and denial of an afterlife by characterizing death as "the end of all consciousness." From this conclusion, Epicurus defends the notion that there is no reason to spend our lives in fear of death. Rather, Epicurus holds that we ought to focus on living a happy life. In his discussion of moral theory, Epicurus introduces hedonism, acknowledging that while the pursuit of pleasure is natural, there is time when it is vain and there are some pleasures that are necessary and others that are not. Epicurus differentiates between types of pleasures and emphasizes prudence as the chief virtue in living a life of pleasure.

READING 2.1

Letter to Menoeceus

Epicurus

Greeting

Let no one be slow to seek wisdom when he is young nor weary in the search thereof when he is grown old. For no age is too early or too late for the health of the soul. And to say that the season for studying philosophy has not yet come, or that it is past and gone, is like saying that the season for happiness is not yet or that it is now no more. Therefore, both old and young ought to seek wisdom, the former in order that, as age comes over him, he may be young in good things because of the grace of what has been, and the latter in order that, while he is young, he may at the same time be old, because he has no fear of the things which are to come. So we must exercise ourselves in the things which bring happiness, since, if that be present, we have everything, and, if that be absent, all our actions are directed toward attaining it.

Those things which without ceasing I have declared to you, those do, and exercise yourself in those, holding them to be the elements of right life. First believe that God is a living being immortal and happy, according to the notion of a god indicated by the common sense of humankind; and so of him [...] agree [...] with whatever may uphold both his happyness and his immortality. For truly there are gods, and knowledge of them is evident; but they are not such as the multitude believe, seeing that people do not steadfastly maintain the notions they form respecting them. Not the person who denies the gods worshipped by the multitude, but he who affirms of the gods what the multitude believes about them is truly impious. For the utterances of the multitude about the gods are not true preconceptions but false assumptions; hence it is

Epicurus, "Letter to Menoeceus," trans. Robert Drew Hicks.

that the greatest evils happen to the wicked and the greatest blessings happen to the good from the hand of the gods, seeing that they are always favorable to their own good qualities and take pleasure in people like to themselves, but reject as alien whatever is not of their kind.

Accustom yourself to believe that death is nothing to us, for good and evil imply awareness, and death is the privation of all awareness; therefore a right understanding that death is nothing to us makes the mortality of life enjoyable, not by adding to life an unlimited time, but by taking away the yearning after immortality. For life has no terror; for those who thoroughly apprehend that there are no terrors for them in ceasing to live. Foolish, therefore, is the person who says that he fears death, not because it will pain when it comes, but because it pains in the prospect.

Whatever causes no annoyance when it is present, causes only a groundless pain in the expectation. Death, therefore, the most awful of evils, is nothing to us, seeing that, when we are, death is not come, and, when death is come, we are not. It is nothing, then, either to the living or to the dead, for with the living it is not and the dead exist no longer. But in the world, at one time people shun death as the greatest of all evils, and at another time choose it as a respite from the evils in life. The wise person does not deprecate life nor does he fear the cessation of life. The thought of life is no offense to him, nor is the cessation of life regarded as an evil. And even as people choose of food not merely and simply the larger portion, but the more pleasant, so the wise seek to enjoy the time which is most pleasant and not merely that which is longest. And he who admonishes the young to live well and the old to make a good end speaks foolishly, not merely because of the desirability of life, but because the same exercise at once teaches to live well and to die well. Much worse is he who says that it were good not to be born, but when once one is born to pass with all speed through the gates of Hades. For if he truly believes this, why does he not depart from life? It were easy for him to do so, if once he were firmly convinced. If he speaks only in mockery, his words are foolishness, for those who hear believe him not.

We must remember that the future is neither wholly ours nor wholly not ours, so that neither must we count upon it as quite certain to come nor despair of it as quite certain not to come.

We must also reflect that of desires some are natural, others are groundless; and that of the natural some are necessary as well as natural, and some natural only. And of the necessary desires some are necessary if we are to be happy, some if the body is to be rid of uneasiness, some if we are even to live. He who has a clear and certain understanding of these things will direct every preference and aversion toward securing health of body and tranquillity of mind, seeing that this is the sum and end of a happy life. For the end of all our actions is to be free from pain and fear, and, when once we have attained all this, the tempest of the soul is laid; seeing that the living creature has no need to go in search of something that is lacking, nor to look anything else by which the good of the soul and of the body will be fulfilled. When we are pained [...], then, and then only, do we feel the need of pleasure. For this reason we call pleasure the alpha and omega of a happy life. Pleasure is our first and kindred good. It is the starting-point of every choice and of every aversion, and to it we come back, inasmuch as we make feeling the rule by which to judge of every good thing. And since pleasure is our first and native good, for that reason we do not choose every pleasure whatever, but often pass over many pleasures when a greater annoyance ensues from them. And often we consider pains superior to pleasures when submission to the pains for a long time brings us as a consequence a greater pleasure. While therefore all pleasure because it is naturally akin to us is good, not all pleasure is worthy of choice, just as all pain is an evil and yet not all pain is to be shunned. It is, however, by measuring one against another, and by looking at the conveniences and inconveniences, teat all these matters must be judged. Sometimes we treat the good as an evil, and the evil, on the contrary, as a good. Again, we regard, independence of outward things as a great good, not so as in all cases to use little, but so as to be contented with little if we have not much, being honestly persuaded that they have the sweetest enjoyment of luxury who stand least in need of it, and that whatever is natural is easily procured and only the vain and worthless hard to win. Plain fare gives as much pleasure as a costly diet, when one the pain of want has been removed, while bread an water confer the highest possible pleasure when they are brought to hungry lips. To habituate one's [self] therefore, to simple and inexpensive diet supplies [all] that is needful for health, and enables a person to meet the necessary requirements of life without shrinking and it places us in a better condition when we approach at intervals a costly fare and renders us fearless of fortune.

When we say, then, that pleasure is the end and aim, we do not mean the pleasures of the prodigal or the pleasures of sensuality, as we are understood to do by some through ignorance, prejudice, or willful misrepresentation. By pleasure we mean the absence of pain in the body and of trouble in the soul. It is not an unbroken succession of drinking-bouts and of merrymaking, not sexual love, not the enjoyment of the fish and other delicacies of a luxurious table, which produce a pleasant life; it is sober reasoning, searching out the grounds of every choice and avoidance, and banishing those beliefs through which the greatest disturbances take possession of the soul. Of all this the [end] is prudence. For this reason prudence is a more precious thing even than the other virtues, for [...] a life of pleasure which is not also a life of prudence, honor, and justice; nor lead a life of prudence, honor, and justice, which is not also a life of pleasure. For the virtues have grown into one with a pleasant life, and a pleasant life is inseparable from them.

Who, then, is superior in your judgment to such a person? He holds a holy belief concerning the gods, and is altogether free from the fear of death. He has diligently considered the end fixed by nature, and understands how easily the limit of good things can be reached and attained, and how either the duration or the intensity of evils is but slight. Destiny which some introduce as sovereign over all things, he laughs to scorn, affirming rather that some things happen of necessity, others by chance, others through our own agency. For he sees that necessity destroys responsibility and that chance or fortune is inconstant; whereas our own actions are free, and it is to them that praise and blame naturally attach. It were better, indeed, to accept the legends of the gods than to bow beneath destiny which the natural philosophers have imposed. The one holds out some faint hope that we may escape if we honor the gods, while the necessity of the naturalists is deaf to all entreaties. Nor does he hold chance to be a god, as the world in general does, for in the acts of a god there is no disorder; nor to be a cause, though an uncertain one, for he believes that no good or evil is dispensed by chance to people so as to make life happy, though it supplies the starting-point of great good and great evil. He believes that the misfortune of the wise is better than the prosperity of the fool. It is better, in short, that what is well judged in action should not owe its successful issue to the aid of chance.

Exercise yourself in these and kindred precepts day and night, both by yourself and with him who is like to you; then never, either in waking or in dream, will you be disturbed, but will live as a god among people. For people lose all appearance of mortality by living in the midst of immortal blessings.

ॐ

STUDY GUIDE QUESTIONS FOR READINGS

Epicurus, *Letter to Menoeceus*

1. Why is the study of philosophy important for both the young and the old man according to Epicurus?
2. Offer a brief characterization of Epicurus's views about the gods and death and how these views connect to his defense of hedonism.
3. Explain Epicurus's classifications of desire as natural or vain and of some desires as necessary and others merely natural.
4. How does Epicurus reconcile his view that pleasure is the greatest good with the fact that some pleasures should be chosen while others should not?
5. What is the source of true pleasure according to Epicurus? What is the role of prudence and how are these notions connected? Explain.

SUGGESTIONS FOR FURTHER READING OR VIEWING

Epicurus. *The Essential Epicurus*. Translated by Eugene O'Connor. London: The Big Nest, 2014.

Konstan, David. "Epicurus." In *The Stanford Encyclopedia of Philosophy, edited by Edward N. Zalta. Stanford University,* Fall 2016 edition. https://plato.stanford.edu/archives/fall2016/entries/epicurus/.

Moore, Andrew. "Hedonism." In *The Stanford Encyclopedia of Philosophy, edited by Edward N. Zalta. Stanford University,* Winter 2103 Edition. https://plato.stanford.edu/archives/win2013/entries/hedonism/.

Nozick, Robert. *Anarchy, State, and Utopia.* New York, NY: Basic Books, 1974.

Aristotle

INTRODUCTION TO ARISTOTLE

Aristotle is one of the towering figures in moral philosophy, and nearly two and a half millennia after his death he remains one of the most relevant and widely discussed ethicists in the Western tradition. Aristotle is today associated with what is known as **virtue ethics**, an approach to moral thinking that begins with considerations of what kinds of people we ought to be, and continues with questions about what we ought and ought not to do based on the identification of morally desirable traits or qualities of character—the virtues.

Our selections are from Aristotle's major work in moral philosophy, *Nichomachean Ethics*, named after his son Nichomas, which is where he presents his theory of **virtue**. Aristotle argues first that a virtue is a quality of a thing that makes it more perfect, or "excellent." In a famous passage often called "the function argument," Aristotle elaborates on this by suggesting virtues enable a thing to perform its function. In other words, a virtue enables a thing to do well at what things of that kind are supposed to do in the way that sharpness helps a knife cut well, which is the function of a knife. Humans don't exactly have a function in the way a knife does, but Aristotle argues that we do have a nature, and this defines for us what it is we're supposed to be. Humans are, he argues, "rational animals." So basically, it is our job, so to speak, to become successful rational animals, and a virtue is any trait that helps us do this.

The second key part of Aristotle's theory of virtue is the Doctrine of the Mean, which tells us that each virtue is a mean, or midpoint, between two extremes. Each virtue is tied to a feeling, and so the idea behind the Doctrine of the Mean is the idea that having a tendency to have too much or too little of the feeling in question is bad—these extremes are **vices**, not virtues. The virtue comes when we have the right amount, neither too much nor too little.

Courage, for example, lies between a tendency to have too much fear—cowardice—and too little fear, which leads us to be rash. A courageous person is able to be rational in facing danger.

Aristotle also considers the question of how we acquire virtues. He does not suppose we are simply born with them or that they are impossible to acquire. A bit more hopeful, he supposes that we can come to have them by regularly behaving in certain ways and not in others. This is where his theory adds a concern with actions. Aristotle's account focuses on what he calls habituation, which you can think of as practice in the sense of practicing a musical instrument or a sport. Because we will not fall into the right habits automatically—in fact Aristotle suggests we begin life being prone to vice—we need teachers to steer us toward what is good until we are able to identify it ourselves. This means we need a moral education—a proper upbringing that helps to instill virtuous traits through habituation.

Aristotle's Nicomachean Ethics, Book 1

Robert C. Bartlett and Susan D. Collins

Chapter One

1094a Every art and every inquiry, and similarly every action as well as choice, is held to aim at some good.[1] Hence people have nobly[2] declared that the good is that at which all things aim. But there appears to be a certain difference among the ends: some ends are activities, others are certain works apart from the activities themselves, and in those cases in which there are certain ends apart from the
5 actions, the works are naturally better than the activities.[3]

Now, since there are many actions, arts, and sciences,[4] the ends too are many: of medicine, the end is health; of shipbuilding, a ship; of generalship, victory; of household management, wealth. And in all things of this sort that

---

1 Aristotle introduces several central terms here: *technē*, a technical art or craft, such as shoemaking, and the knowledge that goes together with it; *praxis*, action, which issues from the parts of the soul characterized by longing and desiring; and *proairesis*, choice, closely tied to action. See the glossary for these and other key terms. The verb Aristotle uses here for "is held to" (*dokein*) is related to the noun translated as "opinion" (*doxa*); it may mean simply that something "seems" to be the case or that it is "held" to be so by opinion.

2 *Kalōs*: the adverb related to a central term, *to kalon*, which has a range of meanings for which English requires at least three: "noble," "beautiful," and "fine." It denotes (physical) beauty but also and above all, in the *Ethics*, what is admirable in a moral sense. It will be translated most frequently as "the noble" ("noble," "nobly," "in a noble manner") and, in the rare cases in which it refers unambiguously to physical beauty, as "beautiful." In the present instance, Aristotle may say that the declaration in question is a "noble" one because it expresses a noble sentiment—that all things aim at the good—but not necessarily a true one: the conclusion drawn does not in fact follow from the premises given in the first sentence.

3 Another set of key terms is introduced here: *telē* (singular, *telos*), the "end" or goal of a thing; see also *teleios*, n. 37 below. *Energeiai* (singular, *energeia*), "activity," means the state of being engaged in an act or the carrying out of a deed (*ergon*); it is thus related to the next term, *erga* (singular, *ergon*). *Ergon* cannot be captured by one English word; it may be translated as "work," "product," "task" or—especially when used in contrast to "speech" (*logos*)—"deed."

4 Or, "knowledge" in the strict sense (*epistēmē*, here in the plural). We use "science" or "scientific knowledge" to distinguish *epistēmē* from the other term Aristotle uses for knowledge, *gnosis*.

fall under some one capacity[5]—for just as bridle making and such other arts 10
as concern equestrian gear fall under horsemanship, while this art and every
action related to warfare fall under generalship, so in the same manner, some
arts fall under one capacity, others under another—in *all* of them, the ends of
the architectonic ones are more choice-worthy than all those that fall under 15
them, for these latter are pursued for the sake of the former. And it makes no
difference at all whether the ends of the actions are the activities themselves
or something else apart from these, as in the sciences mentioned.

Chapter Two

If, therefore, there is some end of our actions that we wish for on account of
itself, the rest being things we wish for on account of this end, and if we do not
choose all things on account of something else—for in this way the process will 20
go on infinitely such that the longing[6] involved is empty and pointless—clearly
this would be the good, that is, the best.[7] And with a view to our life, then, is
not the knowledge of this good of great weight, and would we not, like archers
in possession of a target, better hit on what is needed? If this is so, then one 25
must try to grasp, in outline at least, whatever it is and to which of the sciences
or capacities it belongs.

But it might be held to belong to the most authoritative and most architectonic one,[8] and such appears to be the political art.[9] For it ordains what sciences
there must be in cities and what kinds each person in turn must learn and up 1094b
to what point. We also see that even the most honored capacities—for example,
generalship, household management, rhetoric—fall under the political art.
Because it makes use of the remaining sciences and, further, because it legislates 5
what one ought to do and what to abstain from, its end would encompass those
of the others, with the result that this would be the human good. For even if
this is the same thing for an individual and a city, to secure and preserve the
good of the city appears to be something greater and more complete: the good
of the individual by himself is certainly desirable enough, but that of a nation
and of cities is nobler and more divine.

The inquiry, then, aims at these things, since it is a sort of political inquiry. ...

---

5 Or, "power" (*dunamis*), here and throughout.
6 This is the first instance of the term *orexis*, which we translate as "longing" and which refers in general to the appetency of the soul, of which *epithumia*, "desire," is a species. The term is related to the verb *oregein*, which we translate as "to long for."
7 *To ariston*: the superlative of *to agathon*, "the good." Although some translators render this term as the "highest" or "chief " good, we consistently translate it as "the best" to capture the sense that it is indeed a peak but may also be simply the best of the goods available to human beings.
8 "One" might refer to "science" (*epistēmē*), "art" (*technē*), or "capacity" (*dunamis*).
9 Aristotle here uses substantively the feminine singular adjective *politikē* (the political), without therefore specifying the noun it is meant to modify, as can be easily done

Chapter Seven

15 Let us go back again to the good being sought, whatever it might be. For it appears to be one thing in one action or art, another in another: it is a different thing in medicine and in generalship, and so on with the rest. What, then, is the good in each of these? Or is it that for the sake of which everything else is
20 done? In medicine, this is health; in generalship, victory; in house building, a house; and in another, it would be something else. But in *every* action and choice, it is the end involved, since it is for the sake of this that all people do everything else. As a result, if there is some end of *all* actions, this would be the good related to action; and if there are several, then it would be these. So as the argument proceeds, it arrives at the same point. But one ought to try to
25 make this clearer still.

Since the ends appear to be several, and some of these we choose on account of something else—for example, wealth, an aulos,[10] and the instrumental things generally—it is clear that not all ends are complete,[11] but what is the best appears to be something complete. As a result, if there is some one thing that is complete in itself, this would be what is being sought, and if there are several, then
30 the most complete of these. We say that what is sought out for itself is more complete than what is sought out on account of something else, and that what is never chosen on account of something else is more complete than those things chosen both for themselves and on account of this [further end]. The simply complete thing, then, is that which is always chosen for itself and never on account of something else.

1097b   Happiness above all seems to be of this character, for we always choose it on account of itself and never on account of something else. Yet honor, pleasure, intellect, and every virtue we choose on their own account—for even if nothing resulted from them, we would choose each of them—but we choose
5 them also for the sake of happiness, because we suppose that, through them, we will be happy. But nobody chooses happiness for the sake of these things, or, more generally, on account of anything else.

The same thing appears to result also on the basis of self-sufficiency, for the complete good is held to be self-sufficient. We do not mean by *self-sufficient* what suffices for someone by himself, living a solitary life, but what is sufficient also with respect to parents, offspring, a wife, and, in general, one's friends and 10 fellow citizens, since by nature a human being is political. But it is necessary to grasp a certain limit to these; for if one extends these to include the parents [of

---

10 A double-reed instrument not unlike the modern oboe; the noun here is plural in the Greek.
11 Or, "perfect" (*teleios*); the adjective is related to the noun *telos* and suggests that which reached or fulfilled the end or goal appropriate to a given thing (see also n. 3 above).

parents],[12] and descendants, and the friends of friends, it will go on infinitely. But this must be examined further later on. As for the self-sufficient, we posit 15 it as that which by itself makes life choiceworthy[13] and in need of nothing, and such is what we suppose happiness to be.

Further, happiness is the most choiceworthy of all things because it is not just one among them—and it is clear that, were it included as one among many things, it would be more choiceworthy with the least addition of the good things; for the good that is added to it results in a superabundance of goods, and the greater number of goods is always more choiceworthy. So 20 happiness appears to be something complete and self-sufficient, it being an end of our actions.

But perhaps saying that "happiness is best" is something manifestly agreed on, whereas what it is still needs to be said more distinctly. Now, perhaps this would come to pass if the work[14] of the human being should be grasped. For 25 just as in the case of an aulos player, sculptor, and every expert, and in general with those who have a certain work and action, the relevant good and the doing of something well seem to reside in the work, so too the same might be held to be the case with a human being, if in fact there is a certain work that is a human being's. Are there, then, certain works and actions of a carpenter and shoemaker, but none of a human being: would he, by contrast, be naturally 30 "without a work"[15]? Or just as there appears to be a certain work of the eye, hand, and foot, and in fact of each of the parts in general, so also might one posit a certain work of a human being apart from all these?

So whatever, then, would this work be? For living appears to be something common even to plants, but what is peculiar [to human beings] is being 1098a sought. One must set aside, then, the life characterized by nutrition as well as growth. A certain life characterized by sense perception would be next, but it too appears to be common to a horse and cow and in fact to every animal. So there remains a certain active life of that which possesses reason; and what possesses reason includes what is obedient to reason, on the one hand, and what possesses it and thinks, on the other. But since this [life of reason in 5 the second sense] also is spoken of in a twofold way, one must posit the life [of that which possesses reason] in accord with an activity, for this seems to be its more authoritative meaning.[16] And if the work of a human being is an

---

12 This additional phrase, not present in the MSS, seems necessary in order to make the text consistent with 1097b9–10; it is suggested by Rassow and accepted by both Burnet and Gauthier and Jolif.

13 Some MSS add at this point the words "and sufficient" (*arkion*) (or, "sufficient and choiceworthy").

14 *To ergon*: see n. 3 as well as the glossary.

15 *Argon*: literally, without an *ergon*, a work, task, or function, and so by extension idle.

16 The subject of the sentence is unclear, and we supply the immediately preceding referent, the life in accord with the part of the soul that possesses reason and thinks; of this part, there is both an activity and a characteristic (*hexis*); and, as Aristotle will argue in 1.8, happiness consists in the activity or use

activity of soul in accord with reason, or not without reason, and we assert that the work of a given person is the same in kind as that of a serious[17] person, just as it would be in the case of a cithara[18] player and a serious cithara player,
10 and this would be so in all cases simply when the superiority in accord with the virtue is added to the work; for it belongs to a cithara player to play the cithara, but to a serious one to do so well. But if this is so[19]—and we posit the work of a human being as a certain life, and this is an activity of soul and actions accompanied by reason, the work of a serious man being to do these
15 things well and nobly, and each thing is brought to completion well in accord with the virtue proper to it—if this is so, then the human good becomes an activity of soul in accord with virtue, and if there are several virtues, then in accord with the best and most complete one.

But, in addition, in a complete life. For one swallow does not make a spring, nor does one day. And in this way, one day or a short time does not make someone blessed and happy either.
20 Let the good have been sketched in this way, then, for perhaps one ought to outline it first and then fill it in later. It might seem to belong to everyone to advance and fully articulate things whose sketch is in a noble condition, and time is a good discoverer of or contributor to such things: from this
25 have arisen the advances in the arts too, for it belongs to everyone to add what is lacking.

But one must remember the points mentioned previously as well, to the effect that one must not seek out precision in all matters alike but rather in each thing in turn as accords with the subject matter in question and insofar as is appropriate to the inquiry. For both carpenter and geometer
30 seek out the right angle but in different ways: the former seeks it insofar as it is useful to his work; the latter seeks out what it is or what sort of a thing it is, for he is one who contemplates[20] the truth. One ought to act in the same manner also in other cases, so that things extraneous to the works involved not multiply. And one should not demand the cause in all things 1098b

rather than the mere possession of a characteristic. Burnet recommends dropping the immediately preceding phrase, which distinguishes the two parts of the soul; he argues that the phrase "interrupts the argument and destroys the grammar." On his reading, the referent would be simply the active life of that which possesses reason.

17 The first appearance of the term *spoudaios*. The "serious" (*spoudaios*) human being is characterized by the correct devotion to and exercise of moral virtue, although Aristotle extends the term to anything that does its own "work" well, including horses and eyes: see 2.6.

18 A plucked instrument with a tortoiseshell soundboard.

19 Bywater brackets everything within the dashes on the grounds that it is both awkward and a repetition of points already raised. The grammar here is difficult; Burnet, who accepts the text, confesses that he "hardly [likes] to put a limit to the capacity of Aristotle for long and complicated protases even when they involve repetitions and grammatical awkwardnesses."

20 Or, is an "observer," "spectator" (*theatēs*); the term is related to the words translated as "contemplation" and "contemplative" (*theōretikē, theōretikos*).

alike either; rather, it is enough in some cases to have nobly pointed out the "that"—such is the case in what concerns the principles—and the "that" is the first thing and a principle. Some principles are observed[21] by means of induction,[22] some by perception, some by a certain habituation, and others in other ways. One ought to try to go in search of each in turn in the manner 5 natural to them and to be serious about their being nobly defined. For they are of great weight in what follows from them: the beginning[23] seems to be more than half of the whole, and many of the points being sought seem to become manifest on account of it.

∾

---

21 Again, "contemplated," "beheld," or "seen" (*theōrein*).

22 A technical term of Aristotelian logic (*epagōgē*); see also 6.3.

23 *Archē*: "principle" or "beginning point" (see n. 20).

Aristotle's Nicomachean Ethics, Book 2

Robert C. Bartlett and Susan D. Collins

$\backsim$

Chapter One

Virtue, then, is twofold, intellectual and moral. Both the coming-into-being and
increase of intellectual virtue result mostly from teaching—hence it requires
experience and time—whereas moral virtue is the result of habit, and so it is
that moral virtue got its name [*ēthikē*] by a slight alteration of the term *habit*
[*ethos*]. It is also clear, as a result, that none of the moral virtues are present in
us by nature, since nothing that exists by nature is habituated to be other than
it is. For example, a stone, because it is borne downward by nature, could not be
habituated to be borne upward, not even if someone habituates it by throwing it
upward ten thousand times. Fire too could not be borne downward, nor could
anything else that is naturally one way be habituated to be another. Neither
by nature, therefore, nor contrary to nature are the virtues present; they are
instead present in us who are of such a nature as to receive them, and who are
completed[1] through habit.

Further, in the case of those things present in us by nature, we are first
provided with the capacities associated with them, then later on display the
activities, something that is in fact clear in the case of sense perceptions. For
it is not as a result of seeing many times or hearing many times that we came
to have those sense perceptions; rather, it is, conversely, because we have them
that we use them, and not because we use them that we have them. But the
virtues we come to have by engaging in the activities first, as is the case with
the arts as well. For as regards those things we must learn how to do, we
learn by doing them—for example, by building houses, people become house

1103a15

20

25

30

---

1 Or, "who are perfected." The same participle (*teleioumenois*) may also be taken to be in the middle
rather than the passive voice: "and who complete or perfect themselves through habit."

builders, and by playing the cithara, they become cithara players. So too, then, 1103b
by doing just things we become just; moderate things, moderate; and courageous
things, courageous. What happens in the cities too bears witness to this, for by
habituating citizens, lawgivers make them good, and this is the wish of every
lawgiver; all who do not do this well are in error, and it is in this respect that 5
a good regime² differs from a base regime.

Further, as a result of and on account of the same things, every virtue both
comes into being and is destroyed,³ as is similarly the case also with an art.
For it is as a result of playing the cithara that both good and bad cithara players
arise, and analogously with house builders and all the rest: as a result of build- 10
ing houses well, people will be good house builders; but as a result of doing so
badly, they will be bad ones. If this were not the case, there would be no need
of a teacher, but everyone would come into being already good or bad. So
too in the case of the virtues: by doing things in our interactions with human 15
beings, some of us become just, others unjust; and by doing things in terrifying
circumstances and by being habituated to feel fear or confidence, some of us
become courageous, others cowards. The case is similar as regards desires and
bouts of anger. For some people become moderate and gentle, others licentious
and irascible, the former as a result of conducting themselves in the one way, the 20
latter as a result of doing so in the other. And so, in a word, the characteristics
come into being as a result of the activities akin to them. Hence we must make
our activities be of a certain quality, for the characteristics correspond to the
differences among the activities. It makes no small difference, then, whether
one is habituated in this or that way straight from childhood but a very great 25
difference—or rather the whole difference.

Chapter Two

Now, since the present subject is taken up, not for the sake of contemplation,
as are others—for we are conducting an examination, not so that we may know
what virtue is, but so that we may become good, since otherwise there would
be no benefit from it—it is necessary to examine matters pertaining to actions,
that is, how one ought to perform them. For these actions have authoritative 30
control over what sorts of characteristics come into being, just as we have said.
Now, "acting in accord with correct reason"⁴ is commonly granted, and let it

---

2 The first appearance of this important political term (*politeia*), which refers to the authoritative
ruling element in a political community. Aristotle's sixfold classification of regimes is found in 8.10.

3 Or, perhaps, "ruined," "corrupted" (*phtheirein*).

4 This famous phrase (*orthos logos*), which translators have often rendered as "right reason," is as
ambiguous as its components: what is "correct" (*orthos*) may or may not be true, and a *logos* may be a
rational argument or merely a "speech," rational or not.

be posited for now—what pertains to it will be spoken of later, both what "correct reason" is and how it relates to the virtues.[5]

1104a　But let it be agreed to in advance that every argument concerned with what ought to be done[6] is bound to be stated in outline only and not precisely—just as we said at the beginning as well, that the demands made of given arguments should accord with the subject matter in question. Matters of action and those
5　pertaining to what is advantageous have nothing stationary about them, just as matters of health do not either. And since such is the character of the general argument, still less precise is the argument concerned with particulars, for it does not fall under an art or any set of precepts. Instead, those who act ought themselves always to examine what pertains to the opportune moment [when
10　it presents itself], as is the case with both medicine and piloting. Although such is the character of the present argument, one must nonetheless attempt to be of assistance.

　　This, then, is the first thing that must be contemplated. Such things [as the virtues] are naturally destroyed through deficiency and excess, just as we see in the case of strength and health (for one ought to make use of manifest things as
15　witnesses on behalf of what is immanifest): excessive as well as deficient gymnastic exercises destroy strength, and, similarly, both drink and food destroy health as they increase or decrease in quantity, whereas the proportionate amounts create, increase, and preserve health. So it is too with moderation,
20　courage, and the other virtues: he who avoids and fears all things and endures nothing becomes a coward, and he who generally fears nothing but advances toward all things becomes reckless. Similarly, he who enjoys every pleasure and abstains from none becomes licentious; but he who avoids every pleasure, as the boorish do, is a sort of "insensible" person.[7] Moderation and courage are
25　indeed destroyed by excess and deficiency, but they are preserved by the mean.[8]

　　But not only do the coming-into-being and increase [of the virtues], as well as their destruction, occur as a result of the same things and through the same things, but the activities [associated with the virtues] too will be found in the same things [as are responsible for their coming-into-being and increase]. For this is the case also with other, more manifest things—for example, in the case 30 of strength: it comes into being as a result of taking much nourishment and enduring many exertions, and he who is strong would especially be able to do just these things. So too in the case of the virtues, for as a result of abstaining

---

5　Literally, "to the other virtues."

6　The reading of the principal MSS accepted by Burnet, but Bywater, following Bekker and Susemihl, emends the text to read in translation: "concerned with actions."

7　That is, someone lacking in sense perception (*anaisthetos*); Aristotle will note later (1107b8) that there really is no name for such persons, since they "do not come into being very much" (see also 1108b21, 1109a4, 1114a10, and 1119a7).

8　The first appearance of this famous term (*hē mesotēs*) in Aristotle's account of the moral phenomena.

from pleasures, we become moderate; and by so becoming, we are especially able 35
to abstain from them. Similar is the case of courage as well: by being habituated 1104b
to disdain frightening things and to endure them, we become courageous, and
by so becoming, we will be especially able to endure frightening things.

Chapter Three

The pleasure or pain that accompanies someone's deeds ought to be taken as 5
a sign of his characteristics: he who abstains from bodily pleasures and enjoys
this very abstention is moderate, but he who is vexed in doing so is licentious;
he who endures terrifying things and enjoys doing so, or at any rate is not
pained by it, is courageous, but he who is pained thereby is a coward. For moral
virtue is concerned with pleasures and pains: it is on account of the pleasure
involved that we do base things, and it is on account of the pain that we abstain 10
from noble ones. Thus one must be brought up in a certain way straight from
childhood, as Plato asserts, so as to enjoy as well as to be pained by what one
ought, for this is correct education.

Further, if the virtues are concerned with actions and passions, and pleasure
and pain accompany every passion and every action, then on this account too 15
virtue would be concerned with pleasures and pains. Punishments are indicative
of this as well, since they arise through these [pains]: they are a sort of curative
treatment, and curative treatments naturally take place through contraries.

Further, as we said just recently too, every characteristic of soul shows its
nature in relation to and in its concern for the sorts of things by which it nat- 20
urally becomes worse or better: it is through pleasures and pains that people
become base, by pursuing and avoiding these, either the pleasures and pains
that one ought not to pursue or avoid, or when one ought not, or as one ought
not, or in as many other such conditions as are defined by reason.⁹ Thus people
even define the virtues as certain dispassionate and calm states, though such
a definition is not good; for they say simply this much but not "as one ought," 25
"as one ought not," "when," and any other things posited in addition. Virtue,
therefore, has been posited as being such as to produce the best [actions] in
relation to pleasures and pains, and vice as being the contrary.

But that [virtue and vice] are concerned with the same things might become
manifest to us also from these considerations: there being three objects of 30
choice and three of avoidance—the noble, the advantageous, and the pleasant
together with their three contraries, the shameful, the harmful, and the painful—in all these the good person is apt to be correct, the bad person to err,
but especially as regards pleasure. For pleasure is common to the animals and

---

9 Or, "the argument" (*ho logos*). The phrase may well refer to "[correct] reason"; see also n. 4 above.

35   attendant upon all things done through choice, since both what is noble and
1105a   what is advantageous appear pleasant.

Further, pleasure has been a part of the upbringing of us all from infancy; it
is difficult to remove this experience, since our life has been so ingrained with
it. We also take pleasure and pain as the rule of our actions, some of us to a
5   greater degree, some to a lesser. It is on account of this, then, that one's entire
concern necessarily pertains to pleasure and pain, for taking delight and feeling pain make no small contribution to our actions' being well or badly done.

Further, it is more difficult to battle against pleasure than against spiritedness,
as Heraclitus[10] asserts, and art and virtue always arise in connection with that
10   which is more difficult: the doing of something well is better when it is more
difficult. As a result, and on account of this, the whole matter of concern in
both virtue and the political art is bound up with pleasures and pains. For he
who deals with these well will be good, but he who does so badly will be bad.

Let it be said, then, that virtue concerns pleasures and pains; that it both
15   increases as a result of those actions from which it comes into being and is
destroyed when these are performed in a different manner; and that it becomes
active in just those activities as a result of which it also came into being.

Chapter Four

But someone might be perplexed as to what we mean when we say that to
become just, people must do just things or, to become moderate, do moder-
20   ate things. For if they do just and moderate things, they already *are* just and
moderate, just as if they do what concerns letters and music, they are by that
fact skilled [or artful] in letters and in music. Or is this not so even in the case
of the arts? For it is possible to do something skillful in letters by chance or on
the instructions of another. A person will actually be skilled in letters, then,
25   when he both does something skillful and does it in a skillful way, and this
is what accords with the art of letters that resides within the person himself.

Further, what pertains in the arts is not at all similar to what pertains in
the virtues. For the excellence in whatever comes into being through the arts
resides in the artifacts themselves. It is enough, then, for these artifacts to be
in a certain state. But whatever deeds arise in accord with the virtues are not
done justly or moderately if they are merely in a certain state, but only if he   30
who does those deeds is in a certain state as well: first, if he acts knowingly;
second, if he acts by choosing and by choosing the actions in question for their

---

10   Heraclitus of Ephesus lived in the late sixth century and is numbered among the most famous of
the pre-Socratic philosophers. It is uncertain what remark Aristotle here refers to, and the fragment
most frequently cited by commentators ("with *thumos* it is difficult to do battle / for whatever it craves is
purchased at the price of soul") appears to use *thumos* (translated in the text above by "spiritedness," its
usual meaning in later Attic Greek) as an equivalent of, rather than in contrast to, craving or desire (see
Gauthier and Jolif). Aristotle cites this line also in the *Politics* (1315a30–31) and *Eudemian Ethics* (1223b23).

own sake; and, third, if he acts while being in a steady and unwavering state. But these criteria are irrelevant when it comes to possessing the arts—except 1105b for the knowledge itself involved. But when it comes to the virtues, knowledge has no, or little, force, whereas the other two criteria amount to not a small part of but rather the whole affair—criteria[11] that are in fact met as a result of our doing just and moderate things many times. Matters of action are said to 5 be just and moderate, then, when they are comparable in kind to what the just or moderate person would do. And yet he who performs these actions is not by that fact alone just and moderate, but only if he also acts as those who are just and moderate act.

It is well said, then, that as a result of doing just things, the just person comes 10 into being and as a result of doing moderate things, the moderate person; without performing these actions, nobody would become good. Yet most people [or the many] do not do them; and, seeking refuge in argument, they suppose that they are philosophizing and that they will in this way be serious, thereby 15 doing something similar to the sick who listen attentively to their physicians but do nothing prescribed. Just as these latter, then, will not have a body in good condition by caring for it in this way, so too the former will not have a soul in good condition by philosophizing in this way.

Chapter Five

After this, what virtue is must be examined. Now, since there are three things that are present in the soul—passions, capacities, and characteristics—virtue 20 would be one of these. I mean by *passions* the following: desire, anger, fear, confidence, envy, joy, friendly affection,[12] hatred, yearning, emulation, pity— in general, those things that pleasure or pain accompany. And *capacities* are those things in reference to which we are said to be able to undergo these passions—for example, those in reference to which we are able to feel anger, 25 pain, or pity. But *characteristics* are those things in reference to which we are in a good or bad state in relation to the passions; for example, if we feel anger intensely or weakly, we are in a bad condition, but if in a measured[13] way, we are in a good condition, and similarly with the other passions as well. Neither the 30 virtues nor the vices, then, are passions, because we are not said to be serious

---

11 The reading of the MSS (*haper*). Perhaps better is Bywater's slight emendation of the text (*eiper*), adopted also by Burnet and Gauthier and Jolif, which might be rendered as follows: "the whole affair, if in fact [the virtues] are gained as a result of doing just and moderate things many times."

12 Or, "friendship." Although Aristotle uses exactly the same word (*philia*) for both the moral virtue taken up in 4.6 and the association of two friends discussed in books 8–9, he argues that the former does not really have a name, "though it seems most like friendship," and that the latter is finally something other than moral virtue.

13 Or, in a manner characteristic of the middle (*mesos*), a term related to Aristotle's doctrine of moral virtue as a "mean" (*mesotēs*) or "middle" (*to meson*). See also n. 15 below.

or base in reference to the passions but in reference to the virtues and vices, and because we are neither praised nor blamed in reference to the passions simply (for neither he who is afraid nor he who is angry is praised, nor is he

1106a who is simply angry blamed, but only he who is such in a certain way). Rather, it is in reference to the virtues and vices that we are praised or blamed. Further, we are angry and afraid in the absence of choice, but the virtues are certain choices or not without choice. In addition to these considerations, in the case

5 of the passions we are said to be moved; but in that of the virtues and vices, we are not said to be moved but rather to have a certain disposition.

On account of these considerations as well, the virtues and vices are not capacities either. For we are not said to be either good or bad by dint of possessing the capacity simply to undergo the passions, nor are we praised or blamed. Further, we are possessed of capacities by nature, but we do not by

10 nature become good or bad. But we spoke about this before.

If, then, the virtues are neither passions nor capacities, it remains that they are characteristics. What virtue is with respect to its genus, then, has been said.

Chapter Six

Yet one ought to say not only this—that virtue is a characteristic—but also what

15 sort of characteristic it is. So it must be stated that every virtue both brings that of which it is the virtue into a good condition and causes the work belonging to that thing to be done well. For example, the virtue of the eye makes both the eye and its work excellent,[14] for by means of the virtue of the eye, we see well. Similarly,

20 the virtue of a horse makes the horse both excellent and good when it comes to running, and carrying its rider, and standing its ground before enemies. If indeed this is so in all cases, then the virtue of a human being too would be that characteristic as a result of which a human being becomes good and as a result of which he causes his own work to be done well. And how this will be, we have already stated.

25 But virtue will be further manifest also as follows—if we contemplate what sort of thing its nature is. In everything continuous and divisible, it is possible to grasp the more, the less, and the equal, and these either in reference to the thing itself or in relation to us. The equal is also a certain middle term[15] between excess and deficiency. I mean by "a middle term of the thing" that which stands 30 at an equal remove from each of the extremes, which is in fact one and the same thing for all; though in relation to us, it is that which neither takes too much nor is deficient. But this is not one thing, nor is it the same for all. For example, if ten is much but two is few, six is a middle term for those who take it

---

14 Or, "serious" (*spoudaios*), here and in the next sentence.

15 *To meson* (the middle term, the middle—though not necessarily the literal center of something) as distinguished from *hē mesotēs*, which will always be rendered as "the mean." The two are etymologically close.

in reference to the thing itself. For it both exceeds and is exceeded by an equal amount, and this is the middle term according to the arithmetic proportion. But 35 one ought not to grasp in this way the middle term relative to us, for if eating 1106b ten pounds is a lot but two pounds too little, the trainer will not prescribe six pounds, since perhaps even this is a lot or a little for him who will take it: for Milo,[16] it would be too little; for someone just starting gymnastic training, it would be too much. It is similar in the case of running and in that of wrestling.

Thus every knower of the excess and the deficiency avoids them, but seeks 5 out the middle term and chooses this—yet not a middle belonging to the thing in question but rather the one relative to us. Indeed, every science in this way brings its work to a good conclusion, by looking to the middle term and guiding the works toward this. Hence people are accustomed to saying that 10 there is nothing to take away from or add to works that are in a good state, on the grounds that the good state is destroyed by excess and deficiency but the mean preserves it; and the good craftsmen, as we say, perform their work by looking to this. Virtue is more precise and better than every art, as is nature as 15 well. If all this is so, then virtue would be skillful in aiming at the middle term.

But I mean moral virtue, for it is concerned with passions and actions, and it is in these that excess, deficiency, and the middle term reside. For example, it is possible to be afraid, to be confident, to desire, to be angry, to feel pity, and, in general, to feel pleasure and pain to a greater or lesser degree than one 20 ought, and in both cases this is not good. But to feel them when one ought and at the things one ought, in relation to those people whom one ought, for the sake of what and as one ought—all these constitute the middle as well as what is best, which is in fact what belongs to virtue. Similarly, in the case of actions too, there is an excess, a deficiency, and the middle term. Virtue is 25 concerned with passions and actions, in which the excess is in error and the deficiency is blamed;[17] but the middle term is praised and guides one correctly, and both [praise and correct guidance] belong to virtue. Virtue, therefore, is a certain mean, since it, at any rate, is skillful in aiming at the middle term.

Further, while it is possible to be in error in many ways (for what is bad is unlimited [or indeterminate], as the Pythagoreans used to conjecture, what is 30 good, limited [or determinate]), there is only one way to guide someone correctly. And thus the former is easy, the latter hard: it is easy to miss the target, hard to hit it. On account of these considerations, then, to vice belongs the excess and the deficiency, to virtue the mean.

---

16   A famous wrestler of the late sixth century, hailing from Croton. He is said to have won six victories in the Olympic Games and six in the Pythian.

17   The reading of the MSS defended by Gauthier and Jolif. Bywater, followed by Burnet and others, deletes the verb translated as "is blamed."

35   For [people] are good[18] in one way, but in all kinds of ways bad

    Virtue, therefore, is a characteristic marked by choice, residing in the mean
1107a relative to us, a characteristic defined by reason and as the prudent person
would define it.[19] Virtue is also a mean with respect to two vices, the one vice
related to excess, the other to deficiency; and further, it is a mean because some
vices fall short of and others exceed what should be the case in both passions
5 and actions, whereas virtue discovers and chooses the middle term. Thus, with
respect to its being and the definition that states what it is, virtue is a mean; but
with respect to what is best and the doing of something well, it is an extreme.
    But not every action or every passion admits of the mean, for some have
10 names that are immediately associated with baseness—for example, spitefulness,
shamelessness, envy, and, when it comes to actions, adultery, theft , and murder.
For all these things, and those like them, are spoken of as being themselves
base, rather than just their excesses or deficiencies. It is never possible, then, to
15 be correct as regards them, but one is always in error; and it is not possible to
do what concerns such things well or not well—by committing adultery with
the woman one ought and when and as one ought. Rather, doing any of these
things whatever is simply in error. Similar to this, then, is thinking it right that,
as regards committing injustice, being a coward, and acting licentiously, there is
20 a mean, an excess, and a deficiency: in this way there will be a mean of an excess
and of a deficiency, an excess of an excess, and a deficiency of a deficiency! And
just as there is no excess and deficiency of moderation and courage, on account
of the middle term's being somehow an extreme, so too there would not be a
25 mean or an excess and a deficiency of those [base acts mentioned above]; rather,
however they are done, they are in error. For in general there is neither a mean
of an excess and of deficiency nor an excess and deficiency of a mean.

Chapter Seven

One must not only state this [definition] in general terms but also make it harmo-
30 nize with the particulars involved. For in the case of arguments concerning actions,
the general arguments are of wider application,[20] whereas those pertaining to a
part are truer: actions concern particulars, and it is with these that the arguments
ought to accord. One must grasp these particulars from the [following] outline.

---

18 Not the usual word translated as "good" (*agathos*) but the more poetic *esthlos*. The author of the
verse is unknown.

19 An alternative reading suggested by Alexander of Aphrodisias, among others, and adopted by
Bywater, would give the following translation: "residing in the mean relative to us, a mean defined by
that argument by which the prudent person would define it."

20 ²⁰˙ Or, "are common to more things" (*koinoteroi*). Some translators and commentators follow an
alternative reading (*kenōteroi*) that might be rendered as follows: "the general arguments are emptier."

Concerning fear and confidence, then, courage is a mean. Among those characterized by an excess, he who is excessive in fearlessness is nameless (in 1107b fact, many of these characteristics are nameless), and he who is excessive in feeling confident is reckless; he who is excessive in being afraid and deficient in feeling confident is a coward. Concerning pleasures and pains—not all of them, and to a lesser degree as regards pains—the mean is moderation, the 5 excess, licentiousness. But those who are deficient when it comes to pleasures do not arise very much, and thus people of this sort too have not attained a name; let them be "the insensible."

Concerning the giving and taking of money, the mean is liberality, the excess and deficiency, prodigality and stinginess[21] respectively. But they are excessive 10 and deficient in contrary respects: the prodigal person is excessive in spending but deficient in taking, whereas the stingy is excessive in taking but deficient in spending. Now, at present we are speaking in outline and summarily, being satisfied with just that, but later what pertains to them will be defined more 15 precisely. Concerning money, there are also other dispositions: the mean is magnificence (for the magnificent person differs from the liberal, the former being concerned with great things, the latter with small); the excess is vulgarity and crassness; the deficiency, parsimony. These differ from matters related to 20 liberality, but how they differ will be stated later.

Concerning honor and dishonor, the mean is greatness of soul; the excess, what is said to be a certain vanity; the deficiency, smallness of soul. And just as we were saying that liberality bears a relation to magnificence, though it differs by being concerned with small things, so also there is a certain [other] virtue 25 that bears a relation to greatness of soul, the latter being concerned with great honor, the former with small. For it is possible to long for honor as one ought and more or less than one ought; the person who is excessive in his longings in this regard is said to be ambitious,[22] the deficient unambitious, while the one in the middle is nameless. And the dispositions are in fact nameless, except 30 the ambition of the ambitious person. This is why people at the extremes lay claim to the middle ground, and we sometimes call the person in the middle "ambitious," sometimes "unambitious"; and sometimes we praise the ambi- 1108a tious person, sometimes the unambitious one. What the cause is, on account of which we do this, will be stated subsequently. For now, let us speak about what remains in the manner that has guided us thus far.

In what concerns anger too there is an excess, a deficiency, and a mean; and 5 although these are pretty much nameless, let us call the mean gentleness, since we speak of the person in the middle as gentle. Of those at the extremes, let he

---

21 Literally, "illiberality" (*aneleutheria*).
22 Literally, "a lover of honor" (*philotimos*).

who is excessive be irascible, the vice irascibility, and let he who is deficient be a sort of "unirascible" person, the deficiency "unirascibility."

10   There are also three other means, and though they bear a certain similarity to one another, they also differ from one another. For all are concerned with our sharing in speeches and actions, but they differ because one of them is concerned with the truth in such speeches and actions, the others with what is pleasant in them. Of these latter, one is found in times of play, the other in all 15 that relates to life [as a whole]. One must speak about these too, then, so that we may see better that in all things, the mean is praiseworthy and the extremes are neither praiseworthy nor correct but instead blameworthy. Now, the majority of these are nameless, and yet one must try, as in the case of the others as well, to fashion a name for them for the sake of clarity and ease of following along.

Concerning the truth, then, let the person in the middle be said to be some-20 body truthful and the mean, truthfulness; the pretense that exaggerates is boastfulness, and he who possesses it, a boaster, whereas that which understates is irony and he who possesses it, an ironist. As for what is pleasant in times of play, he who is in the middle is witty and the disposition, wittiness; the excess 25 is buffoonery and he who possesses it, a buffoon, while he who is deficient is a sort of boor, and the characteristic, boorishness. As for the remaining part of what is pleasant, which is found in life [as a whole], he who is pleasant as he ought to be is friendly and the relevant mean, friendliness.[23] But he who is 30 friendly in excess is obsequious, if he is such for no reason, but if he is excessively friendly for his own advantage, he is a flatterer; he who is deficient and is in all things unpleasant is a sort of quarrelsome and surly person.

There are also means in the passions and concerning the passions. For a sense of shame is not a virtue, but he who is bashful[24] is praised: in these things too there is one person said to be in the middle, another who is in excess, 35 like the shy person who feels shame in everything. He who is deficient in this or is generally ashamed of nothing is shameless, whereas he who is in the 1108b middle is bashful. Indignation[25] is a mean between envy and spitefulness, and these concern pleasure and pain at the fortunes that befall one's neighbors: the indignant person is pained at those who fare well undeservedly; the envious 5 person exceeds him because he is pained at anyone's faring well; the spiteful is so deficient in feeling pain [at the misfortune of others] that he even delights in it. But about these types, there will be an opportunity to speak elsewhere.

---

23   Or simply, "friendship" (*philia*). Books 8 and 9 examine *philia*, understood there not as a moral virtue but as a kind of community or association that the virtues help make possible.

24   The word translated as "bashful" (*aidēmōn*) shares the same root as the word translated as "a sense of shame" (*aidōs*), which can also refer to the "awe" or "reverence" due to the gods and the divine things, for example.

25   Literally, "nemesis," also the name of a Greek goddess, the divine personification of righteous indignation or revenge (see Hesiod, *Works and Days* 200, *Theogony* 223 and contexts).

As for justice, since it is not spoken of in a simple way, after we have gone through each [of the meanings of *justice*], we will say how they are means, and similarly also with the rational virtues.[26]   10

Chapter Eight

There are, then, three dispositions, two of them vices—one relating to an excess, the other to a deficiency—and one of them a virtue, namely, the mean. All are in some way opposed to all: the extremes are contrary both to the middle disposition and to each other, while the middle disposition is contrary to the extremes. For just as the equal is greater when compared to what is lesser and 15 lesser when compared to what is greater, so the middle characteristics are excessive when compared to the deficient characteristics but deficient when compared to the excessive, in both passions and actions. For the courageous person appears reckless when compared to the coward, but when compared to 20 the reckless, a coward. And similarly, the moderate person appears licentious when compared to the "insensible" one, but when compared to the licentious, "insensible"; the liberal person, when compared to the stingy, appears prodigal, but when compared to the prodigal, stingy. Hence each of those at the extremes pushes the person in the middle over to the other extreme: the coward calls the courageous man reckless, the reckless calls him a coward, and analogously in 25 the case of the others. And although these are opposed to one another in this way, the greatest contrariety lies with the extremes in relation to each other rather than in relation to the middle term; for these extremes stand at a greater remove from each other than they do from the middle term, just as the great stands at a greater remove from the small and the small from the great than either stands from the equal.   30

Further, there appears to be a certain similarity of some extremes to the middle term, as recklessness has some similarity to courage and prodigality to liberality, but the extremes have the greatest dissimilarity to one another. (Things at the greatest remove from one another are defined as contraries, with the result that the more they are removed from one another, the more they are 35 contraries of one another.)

In some cases, it is the deficiency that is more opposed to a given middle 1109a term, in some cases it is the excess. For example, it is not recklessness, which is an excess, but rather cowardice, which is a deficiency, that is more opposed to courage. Then again, it is not "insensibility," which is a deficiency, but rather licentiousness, an excess, that is more opposed to moderation. This 5 occurs through two causes, one being the result of the thing itself: by dint of the one extreme's being closer and more similar to the middle, we set not this

---

26 The phrase "rational virtues" (*logikai aretai*) appears nowhere else in the *Nicomachean Ethics*.

extreme but rather its contrary in greater opposition [to the middle term]. For example, since recklessness seems more similar and closer to courage, but cowardice less similar, we posit cowardice as being in greater opposition
10 [to the middle term than is recklessness]: things at a greater remove from the middle term seem to be more contrary to it. This, then, is one cause, which results from the thing itself.

The other cause results from us ourselves. For those things to which we
15 somehow more naturally incline appear to a greater degree contrary to the middle term. For example, we ourselves are naturally more inclined toward pleasures; hence we have a greater propensity toward licentiousness than orderliness. We say, then, that those things toward which our tendency is greater are to a greater degree contraries [of the mean]; and on this account licentiousness, which is an excess, is more contrary to moderation [than is "insensibility"].

Chapter Nine

20 That moral virtue is a mean, then, and how it is such; that it is a mean between two vices, the one relating to excess, the other to deficiency; and that it is such on account of its being skilled in aiming at the middle term in matters of passion and action, have been stated adequately. Hence it is in fact a task to be serious,
25 for in each case it is a task to grasp what resides in the middle. For example, to grasp the middle of a circle belongs not to everyone but to a knower. And so too, to become angry belongs to everyone and is an easy thing, as is also giving and spending money; but to whom [one ought to do so], how much, when, for the sake of what, and how—these no longer belong to everyone nor
30 are easy. Thus in fact acting well is rare, praiseworthy, and noble. Hence he who aims at the middle term must first depart from what is more contrary to it, just as Calypso too advises:

From this smoke and swell, keep the ship[27]

For of the extremes, the one is more in error, the other less. Now, since it is
35 difficult to hit on the middle with extreme precision, we must, in accord with "the second sailing,"[28] as they say, grasp the least of the bad things, and this 1109b
will occur most of all in the way we are speaking of.

---

27 In the text of Homer's *Odyssey* as it has come down to us, these words are spoken by Odysseus to his men, as the result of Circe's advice (*Odyssey* 12.219). According to Burnet, "[s]ome inferior MSS. have *Kirkē* [Circe, rather than Calypso] which is more nearly right."
28 A proverbial expression roughly equivalent to "the next best thing." Socrates, for example, uses the expression of his turn away from the natural philosophy of his predecessors and to his characteristic examination of "the speeches": see Plato, *Phaedo* 99c9–d1 and context.

But one must examine what we ourselves readily incline toward, for some of us naturally incline to some things, others to other things. This [object of our inclination] will be recognizable from the pleasure and the pain that occur in our case. And we must drag ourselves away from it toward its con- 5 trary; for by leading ourselves far from error, we will arrive at the middle term, which is in fact what those who straighten warped lumber do. But in everything one must be especially on guard against the pleasant and pleasure, for we do not judge it impartially. What the town elders felt toward Helen, then, is what we too ought to feel toward pleasure; and in all cases we ought 10 to utter their remark, for by thus dismissing pleasure, we will err less.[29] By doing these things, then—to speak in summary fashion—we will be most able to hit on the middle term.

But perhaps this is hard, and especially so in particular cases; for it is not easy to define how, with whom, at what sorts of things, and for how long a 15 time one ought to be angry: sometimes we praise those who are deficient and assert that they are gentle, sometimes those who are harsh, calling them manly. But he who deviates a little from what is well done is not blamed, whether he does so in the direction of what is more [than the mean] or in that of what is 20 less than it. But he who deviates more than that *is* blamed, for he does not go unnoticed. Yet at what point and to what extent he is blameworthy is not easy to define by means of argument, for neither is anything else that is subject to perception; such things reside in the particulars involved, the relevant decision too residing in the perception [of the particulars].

This much, then, is clear: the middle characteristic in all cases is praisewor- thy, but one ought to incline sometimes toward the excess, sometimes toward 25 the deficiency, for in this way we will most easily hit on the middle term and what is well done.

---

29 See *Iliad* 3.154–160:

And when they saw Helen moving along the city walls
Softly they uttered winged words to one another:
"No indignation [*nemesis*: see n. 25] at the Trojans and well-greaved Achaeans, Who for the sake of this woman have long suffered pains.
Terribly does she resemble, in our eyes, immortal goddesses.
But, even such as she is, let her go home in the ships
And not remain, for us and our children, a calamity hereafter."

Aristotle, Nichomachean Ethics, Book I

1. What is the Good according to Aristotle? What characteristics must the Good have on his account?
2. What is the human function according to Aristotle? How does this account relate his understanding of the Good?

Aristotle, Nichomachean Ethics, Book II

1. Using an example such as generosity, explain the Doctrine of the Mean.
2. According to Aristotle, what kinds of things don't have a mean? Is this a problem for his theory?
3. What are the differences between the intellectual and the moral virtues and how they are acquired?
4. How does Aristotle argue that human nature is to be a rational animal?
5. Why does Aristotle suggest that we may initially be more attracted to vice than virtue?

SUGGESTIONS FOR FURTHER READING OR VIEWING

Kraut, Richard. "Aristotle's Ethics." In *The Stanford Encyclopedia of Philosophy*, edited by Edward N. Zalta. Stanford University, Winter 2103 Edition. https://plato.stanford.edu/entries/aristotle-ethics/.

MacIntyre, Alasdair. *After Virtue: A Study in Moral Theory.* 4th ed. Indiana: University of Notre Dame Press, 2007.

Brodie, Sarah. *Ethics with Aristotle.* New York: Oxford University Press, 1991.

Confucianism

INTRODUCTION TO CONFUCIANISM

Confucianism arose in China during the later days of the Zhou Dynasty (1046–256 BCE), a time of growing turmoil and political upheaval throughout the Chinese world. Confucius (551–479 BCE)—*Kongfuzi* in Chinese—responded to increasing conflict, political corruption, and moral decline by developing a picture of moral self-cultivation focused on our abilities to live well in the communities and relationships which define us as human. Emphasizing the need to preserve and enrich the customs and traditions of early Zhou culture, Confucius presents a distinct understanding of morality that has influenced cultures in East Asia for some 2500 years. As the most important Chinese thinker, Confucius has arguably influenced the values and beliefs of more human beings than any other single person. Importantly, however, Confucius himself saw his work and teaching as growing out of a living tradition, and that his ideas and teachings themselves were developed and extended by numerous thinkers after him. In this section we will consider some of the teachings of Confucius, as recorded by his students after his death, as well some thoughts recorded by two of his most important successors, Mencius—*Mengzi* in Chinese—and Xunzi.

While the *Analects of Confucius* can be bewildering on a first read, it helps to see the various sayings as elaborating on a handful of key ideas, which are frequently illustrated in short exchanges between Confucius ("the master") and his students. One such idea is that of the *junzi*, or in the translation included here, the "gentleman." This is a person of unusual moral accomplishment—as other translators render it, the *junzi* is a "morally exemplary person" who has reached a high level of sophistication in their moral development. The junzi is the kind of person each of us should aspire to be, which raises the question of what it is to be such a person—what does a *junzi* look like? Here, a couple of additional key ideas are important. Above all a *junzi* is *ren*—translated here as "benevolent" or "benevolence" but in other translations as "humane," "human hearted," "humanity," "authoritative," or "consummate." The key components of *ren* are concern for the well-being of others and a skillful ability to translate that concern into effective action.

A final question is how we become *ren*, and so progress toward becoming a *junzi*. Here, two ideas are essential. One is the very distinctive Confucian emphasis on *xiao*, or filial piety. This is a pattern of deference to and respect for our elders, starting with our parents. As one of Confucius' most celebrated students *Youzi*, or Master You, puts it, *xiao* is the "root of *ren*," the basis of our ability to develop into a *junzi*. This focus again reflects Confucianism's focus on the centrality of relationships in human lives, with an added stress on family relationships.

The second key component of Confucian moral development is *li*, translated here as "rites"; other translates often go with "rituals" or "ritual propriety." *Li* has to do with the shared expectations that tell us how to behave in various social activities and situations—think of how we are expected to dress and speak, and address people at weddings, funerals, job interviews, graduations, fancy dinners, and so on. The Confucian belief is that mastering the *li* of a vibrant and morally sound culture refines our sensibilities and allows us to become the kinds of people who perform well in our various relationships.

All of these key Confucian ideas are found and developed in the texts by Mencius and Xunzi, where a few additional themes emerge as well. Menicus offers thoughts about those parts of our psychology that matter to our moral development. Here he develops a compelling image of the *xin*, or heart. In the Chinese imagination, the heart is the seat of both our feelings and our thoughts (hence a common translation of late has been "heart-mind"). Arguing by way of his arresting image of a child about to fall into a well, Mencius presents us with the four "sprouts," or innate feelings that develop and "grow" as we develop into a *junzi*. Each sprout is paired with a virtue that it can become when all goes well in our upbringing and education.

Based on this image of the heart-mind as naturally inclined toward moral development, Mencius famously declares human nature to be good. This claim is flatly contradicted by Mencius' near contemporary Xunzi, who bluntly declares human nature to be evil or bad. Using his own stock of well-chosen examples and metaphors, Xunzi portrays our innate psychological endowment as something that drives us toward base appetites and conflict with others. For Xunzi, human nature is something to be overcome and changed, not nurtured. For all his criticisms of Mencius, however, Xunzi agrees with Mencius that moral development is possible, as a proper upbringing and Confucian education will enable us to overcome our initial tendencies. This need for moral training, Xunzi, insists, shows morality to be a result of "conscious effort," or something that needs to be learned.

In considering these challenging texts, look for both similarities and differences with more familiar works in moral philosophy. Many see points of contact with the ethical approach of Aristotle in particular and marked contrasts with the more rule-based moral theories of Kant and Mill.

Analects of Confucius

∽

Book I

1. The Master said, 'Is it not a pleasure, having learned something, to try it out at due intervals? Is it not a joy to have friends come from afar? Is it not gentlemanly not to take offence when others [fail] to appreciate your abilities?'

2. Yu Tzu[1] said, 'It is rare for a man whose character is such that he is good as a son and obedient as a young man to have the inclination to transgress against his superiors; it is unheard of for one who has no such inclination to be inclined to start a rebellion. The gentleman devotes his efforts to the roots, for once the roots are established, the Way will grow therefrom. Being good as a son and obedient as a young man is, perhaps, the root of a man's character.' [*i*][2]

3. The Master said, 'It is rare, indeed, for a man with cunning words and an ingratiating face to be benevolent.'

4. Tseng Tzu said, 'Every day I examine myself on three counts. In what I have undertaken on another's behalf, have I failed to do my best? In my dealings with my friends have I failed to be trustworthy in what I say? Have I passed on to others anything that I have not tried out myself?'

5. The Master said, 'In guiding a state of a thousand chariots, approach your duties with reverence and be trustworthy in what you say; avoid excesses in expenditure and love your fellow men; employ the labour of the common people only in the right seasons.'

6. The Master said, 'A young man should be a good son at home and an obedient young man abroad, sparing of speech but trustworthy in what he says, and should love the multitude at large but

---

1   For names of persons and places see Glossary.
2   Numbers in square brackets refer to Textual Notes on p. 234.

16. The Master said, 'Ssu, only with a man like you can one discuss the *Odes*. Tell such a man something and he can see its relevance to what he has not been told.'

The Master said, 'It is not the failure of others to appreciate your abilities that should trouble you, but rather your failure to appreciate theirs.'

BOOK II

1. The Master said, 'The rule of virtue can be compared to the Pole Star which commands the homage of the multitude of stars without leaving its place.'

2. The Master said, 'The *Odes* are three hundred in number. They can be summed up in one phrase, Swerving not from the right path.'[3]

3. The Master said, 'Guide them by edicts, keep them in line with punishments, and the common people will stay out of trouble but will have no sense of shame. Guide them by virtue, keep them in line with the rites, and they will, besides having a sense of shame, reform themselves.'

4. The Master said, 'At fifteen I set my heart on learning; at thirty I took my stand; at forty I came to be free from doubts; at fifty I understood the Decree of Heaven; at sixty my ear was atuned;[4] at seventy I followed my heart's desire without overstepping the line.'

5. Meng Yi Tzu asked about being filial. The Master answered, 'Never fail to comply.'

Fan Ch'ih was driving. The Master told him about the interview, saying, 'Meng-sun asked me about being filial. I answered, "Never fail to comply." '

Fan Ch'ih asked, 'What does that mean?'

The Master said, 'When your parents are alive, comply with the rites in serving them; when they die, comply with the rites in burying them; comply with the rites in sacrificing to them.'

6. Meng Wu Po asked about being filial. The Master said, 'Give your father and mother no other cause for anxiety than illness.'

7. Tzu-yu asked about being filial. The Master said, 'Nowadays for a man to be filial means no more than that he is able to provide his parents with food. Even hounds and horses are, in some way, provided with food. If a man shows no reverence, where is the difference?'

8. Tzu-hsia asked about being filial. The Master said, 'What is difficult to manage is the expression on one's face. As for the young taking on the burden

---

3   This line is from Ode 297 where it describes a team of horses going straight ahead without swerving to left or right.

4   The expression *erh shun* is very obscure and the translation is tentative.

when there is work to be done or letting the old enjoy the wine and the food when these are available, that hardly deserves to be called filial.'

9. The Master asked, 'I can speak to Hui all day without his disagreeing with me in any way. Thus he would seem to be stupid. However, when I take a closer look at what he does in private after he has withdrawn from my presence, I discover that it does, in fact, throw light on what I said. Hui is not stupid after all.'

10. The Master said, 'Look at the means a man employs, observe the path he takes and examine where he feels at home.[5] In what way is a man's true character hidden from view? In what way is a man's true character hidden from view?'

11. The Master said, 'A man is worthy of being a teacher who gets to know what is new by keeping fresh in his mind what he is already familiar with.'

12. The Master said, 'The gentleman is no vessel.'[6]

13. Tzu-kung asked about the gentleman. The Master said, 'He puts his words into action before allowing his words to follow his action.'

14. The Master said, 'The gentleman enters into associations but not cliques; the small man enters into cliques but not associations.'

15. The Master said, 'If one learns from others but does not think, one will be bewildered. If, on the other hand, one thinks but does not learn from others, one will be in peril.'

16. The Master said, 'To attack a task from the wrong end can do nothing but harm.'

17. The Master said, 'Yu, shall I tell you what it is to know. To say you know when you know, and to say you do not when you do not, that is knowledge.'

18. Tzu-chang was studying with an eye to an official career. The Master said, 'Use your ears widely but leave out what is doubtful; repeat the rest with caution and you will make few mistakes. Use your eyes widely and leave out what is hazardous; put the rest into practice with caution and you will have few regrets. When in your speech you make few mistakes and in your action you have few regrets, an official career will follow as a matter of course.'

19. Duke Ai asked, 'What must I do before the common people will look up to me?'

Confucius answered, 'Raise the straight and set them over the crooked[7] and the common people will look up to you. Raise the crooked and set them over the straight and the common people will not look up to you.'

20. Chi K'ang Tzu asked, 'How can one inculcate in the common people the virtue of reverence, of doing their best and of enthusiasm?'

---

5   cf. 'The benevolent man feels at home in benevolence.' (IV. 2)

6   i.e., he is no specialist, as every vessel is designed for a specific purpose only.

7   cf. XII. 22.

The Master said, 'Rule over them with dignity and they will be reverent; treat them with kindness and they will do their best; raise the good and instruct those who are backward and they will be imbued with enthusiasm.'

21. Someone said to Confucius, 'Why do you not take part in government?'

The Master said, 'The *Book of History* says, "Oh! Simply by being a good son and friendly to his brothers a man can exert an influence upon government."[8] In so doing a man is, in fact, taking part in government. How can there be any question of his having actively to "take part in government"?'

22. The Master said, 'I do not see how a man can be acceptable who is untrustworthy in word? When a pin is missing in the yoke-bar of a large cart or in the collar-bar of a small cart, how can the cart be expected to go?'

23. Tzu-chang asked, 'Can ten generations hence be known?'

The Master said, 'The Yin built on the rites of the Hsia. What was added and what was omitted can be known. The Chou built on the rites of the Yin. What was added and what was omitted can be known. Should there be a successor to the Chou, even a hundred generations hence can be known.'

24. The Master said, 'To offer sacrifice to the spirit of an ancestor not one's own is obsequious.

'Faced with what is right, to leave it undone shows a lack of courage.' …

BOOK IV

1. The Master said, 'Of neighbourhoods benevolence is the most beautiful. How can the man be considered wise who, when he has the choice, does not settle in benevolence?'

2. The Master said, 'One who is not benevolent cannot remain long in straitened circumstances, nor can he remain long in easy circumstances.

'The benevolent man is attracted to benevolence because he feels at home in it. The wise man is attracted to benevolence because he finds it to his advantage.'

3. The Master said, 'It is only the benevolent man who is capable of liking or disliking other men.'

4. The Master said, 'If a man sets his heart on benevolence, he will be free from evil.'

5. The Master said, 'Wealth and high station are what men desire but unless I got them in the right way I would not remain in them. Poverty and low station

---

8 This is from a lost chapter of the *Shu ching* but has been incorporated in a modified form into the spurious *Chün shih* chapter. See *Shu ching chu shu*, 18.10a.

are what men dislike, but even if I did not get them in the right way I would not try to escape from them.[9]

'If the gentleman forsakes benevolence, in what way can he make a name for himself? The gentleman never deserts benevolence, not even for as long as it takes to eat a meal. If he hurries and stumbles one may be sure that it is in benevolence that he does so.'

6. The Master said, 'I have never met a man who finds benevolence attractive or a man who finds unbenevolence[10] repulsive. A man who finds benevolence attractive cannot be surpassed. A man who finds unbenevolence repulsive can, perhaps, be counted as benevolent, for he would not allow what is not benevolent to contaminate his person.

'Is there a man who, for the space of a single day, is able to devote all his strength to benevolence? I have not come across such a man whose strength proves insufficient for the task. There must be such cases of insufficient strength, only I have not come across them.'[11]

7. The Master said, 'In his errors a man is true to type. Observe the errors and you will know the man.' [i]

8. The Master said, 'He has not lived in vain who dies the day he is told about the Way.'

9. The Master said, 'There is no point in seeking the views of a Gentleman[12] who, though he sets his heart on the Way, is ashamed of poor food and poor clothes.'

10. The Master said, 'In his dealings with the world the gentleman is not invariably for or against anything. He is on the side of what is moral.'

11. The Master said, 'While the gentleman cherishes benign rule, the small man cherishes his native land. While the gentleman cherishes a respect for the law, the small man cherishes generous treatment.'[13]

12. The Master said, 'If one is guided by profit in one's actions, one will incur much ill will.'

13. The Master said, 'If a man is able to govern a state by observing the rites and showing deference, what difficulties will he have in public life? [4] If he is unable to govern a state by observing the rites and showing deference, what good are the rites to him?'

---

9 This sentence is most likely to be corrupt. The negative is probably an interpolation and the sentence should read: 'Poverty and low station are what men dislike, but if I got them in the right way I would not try to escape from them.'

10 The word 'unbenevolence' has been coined because the original word has a positive meaning lacking in 'non-benevolence'.

11 Cf. VI. 12.

12 For the use of 'Gentleman' and 'gentleman' in the present translation see n. 3 on p. 12.

13 The distinction here between 'the gentleman' and 'the small man' is not, as is often the case, drawn between the ruler and the ruled but within the class of the ruled.

14. The Master said, 'Do not worry because you have no official position. Worry about your qualifications. Do not worry because no one appreciates your abilities. Seek to be worthy of appreciation.'

15. The Master said, 'Ts'an! There is one single thread binding my way together.'

Tseng Tzu assented.

After the Master had gone out, the disciples asked, 'What did he mean?'

Tseng Tzu said, 'The way of the Master consists in doing one's best and in using oneself as a measure to gauge others. That is all.'

16. The Master said, 'The gentleman understands what is moral. The small man understands what is profitable.'

17. The Master said, 'When you meet someone better than yourself, turn your thoughts to becoming his equal. When you meet someone not as good as you are, look within and examine your own self.'

18. The Master said, 'In serving your father and mother you ought to dissuade them from doing wrong in the gentlest way. If you see your advice being ignored, you should not become disobedient but remain reverent. You should not complain even if in so doing you wear yourself out.'

19. The Master said, 'While your parents are alive, you should not go too far afield in your travels. If you do, your whereabouts should always be known.'

20. The Master said, 'If, for three years, a man makes no changes to his father's ways, he can be said to be a good son.'[14]

21. The Master said, 'A man should not be ignorant of the age of his father and mother. It is a matter, on the one hand, for rejoicing and, on the other, for anxiety.'

22. The Master said, 'In antiquity men were loath to speak. This was because they counted it shameful if their person failed to keep up with their words.'

23. The Master said, 'It is rare for a man to miss the mark through holding on to essentials.'

24. The Master said, 'The gentleman desires to be halting in speech but quick in action.'

25. The Master said, 'Virtue never stands alone. It is bound to have neighbours.'

26. Tzu-yu said, 'To be importunate with one's lord will mean humiliation. To be importunate with one's friends will mean estrangement.'

---

14   This saying also forms part of I. 11.

READING 2.5

Mencius

❧

6. Mencius said, 'No man is devoid of a heart sensitive to the suffering of others. Such a sensitive heart was possessed by the Former Kings and this manifested itself in compassionate government. With such a sensitive heart behind compassionate government, it was as easy to rule the Empire as rolling it on your palm.

'My reason for saying that no man is devoid of a heart sensitive to the suffering of others is this. Suppose a man were, all of a sudden, to see a young child on the verge of falling into a well. He would certainly be moved to compassion, not because he wanted to get in the good graces of the parents, nor because he wished to win the praise of his fellow villagers or friends, nor yet because he disliked the cry of the child. From this it can be seen that whoever is devoid of the heart of compassion is not human, whoever is devoid of the heart of shame is not human, whoever is devoid of the heart of courtesy and modesty is not human, and whoever is devoid of the heart of right and wrong is not human. The heart of compassion is the germ of benevolence; the heart of shame, of dutifulness; the heart of courtesy and modesty, of observance of the rites; the heart of right and wrong, of wisdom. Man has these four germs just as he has four limbs. For a man possessing these four germs to deny his own potentialities is for him to cripple himself; for him to deny the potentialities of his prince is for him to cripple his prince. If a man is able to develop all these four germs that he possesses, it will be like a fire starting up or a spring coming through. When these are fully developed, he can tend the whole realm within the Four Seas, but if he fails to develop them, he will not be able even to serve his parents.'

7. Mencius said, 'Is the maker of arrows really more unfeeling than the maker of armour? The maker of arrows is afraid lest he should fail to harm people, whereas the maker of armour is afraid lest they should be harmed. The case

is similar with the sorcerer-doctor and the coffin-maker. For this reason one cannot be too careful in the choice of one's calling.

'Confucius said, "The best neighbourhood is where benevolence is to be found. Not to live in such a neighbourhood when one has the choice cannot by any means be considered wise."[1] Benevolence is the high honour bestowed by Heaven and the peaceful abode of man. Not to be benevolent when nothing stands in the way is to show a lack of wisdom. A man neither benevolent nor wise, devoid of courtesy and dutifulness, is a slave. A slave ashamed of serving is like a maker of bows ashamed of making bows, or a maker of arrows ashamed of making arrows. If one is ashamed, there is no better remedy than to practise benevolence. Benevolence is like archery: an archer makes sure his stance is correct before letting fly the arrow, and if he fails to hit the mark, he does not hold it against his victor. He simply seeks the cause within himself.'

8. Mencius said, 'Whenever anyone told him that he had made a mistake, Tzu-lu was delighted. Whenever he heard a fine saying, Yü bowed low before the speaker. The Great Shun was even greater. He was ever ready to fall into line with others, giving up his own ways for theirs, and glad to take from others that by which he could do good. From the time he was a farmer, a potter and a fisherman to the time he became Emperor, there was nothing he did that he did not take from others. To take from others that by which one can do good is to help them do good. Hence there is nothing more important to a gentleman than helping others do good.'

❧

·

---

1 *The best neighbourhood . . . be considered wise':* Cf. *the Analects of* Confucius, IV. 1.

Xunzi

 ∽

MAN'S NATURE IS EVIL (Section 23)

Man's nature is evil; goodness is the result of conscious activity. The nature of man is such that he is born with a fondness for profit. If he indulges this fondness, it will lead him into wrangling and strife, and all sense of courtesy and humility will disappear. He is born with feelings of envy and hate, and if he indulges these, they will lead him into violence and crime, and all sense of loyalty and good faith will disappear. Man is born with the desires of the eyes and ears, with a fondness for beautiful sights and sounds. If he indulges these, they will lead him into license and wantonness, and all ritual principles and correct forms will be lost. Hence, any man who follows his nature and indulges his emotions will inevitably become involved in wrangling and strife, will violate the forms[1] and rules of society, and will end as a criminal. Therefore, man must first be transformed by the instructions of a teacher and guided by ritual principles, and only then will he be able to observe the dictates of courtesy and humility, obey the forms and rules of society, and achieve order. It is obvious from this, then, that man's nature is evil, and that his goodness is the result of conscious activity.

A warped piece of wood must wait until it has been laid against the straightening board, steamed, and forced into shape before it can become straight; a piece of blunt metal must wait until it has been whetted on a grindstone before it can become sharp. Similarly, since man's nature is evil, it must wait for the instructions of a teacher before it can become upright, and for the guidance of ritual principles before it can become orderly. If men have no teachers to instruct them, they will be inclined towards evil and not upright; and if they

---

1 Reading *wen* instead of *fen*.

have no ritual principles to guide them, they will be perverse and violent and lack order. In ancient times the sage kings realized that man's nature is evil, and that therefore he inclines toward evil and violence and is not upright or orderly. Accordingly they created ritual principles and laid down certain regulations in order to reform man's emotional nature and make it upright, in order to train and transform it and guide it in the proper channels. In this way they caused all men to become orderly and to conform to the Way. Hence, today any man who takes to heart the instructions of his teacher, applies himself to his studies, and abides by ritual principles may become a gentleman, but anyone who gives free rein to his emotional nature, is content to indulge his passions, and disregards ritual principles becomes a petty man. It is obvious from this, therefore, that man's nature is evil, and that his goodness is the result of conscious activity.

Mencius states that man is capable of learning because his nature is good, but I say that this is wrong. It indicates that he has not really understood man's nature nor distinguished properly between the basic nature and conscious activity. The nature is that which is given by Heaven; you cannot learn it, you cannot acquire it by effort. Ritual principles, on the other hand, are created by sages; you can learn to apply them, you can work to bring them to completion. That part of man which cannot be learned or acquired by effort is called the nature; that part of him which can be acquired by learning and brought to completion by effort is called conscious activity. This is the difference between nature and conscious activity.

It is a part of man's nature that his eyes can see and his ears can hear. But the faculty of clear sight can never exist separately from the eye, nor can the faculty of keen hearing exist separately from the ear. It is obvious, then, that you cannot acquire clear sight and keen hearing by study. Mencius states that man's nature is good, and that all evil arises because he loses his original nature. Such a view, I believe, is erroneous. It is the way with man's nature that as soon as he is born he begins to depart from his original naïveté and simplicity, and therefore he must inevitably lose what Mencius regards as his original nature.[2] It is obvious from this, then, that the nature of man is evil.

Those who maintain that the nature is good praise and approve whatever has not departed from the original simplicity and naïveté of the child. That is, they consider that beauty belongs to the original simplicity and naïveté and goodness to the original mind in the same way that clear sight is inseparable from the eye and keen hearing from the ear. Hence, they maintain that [the nature possesses goodness] in the same way that the eye possesses clear vision

---

2   Mencius, it will be recalled, stated: "The great man is he who does not lose his child's-heart" (*Mencius*, IVB, 12). If I understand Xunzi correctly, he is arguing that this "child's-heart," i.e., the simplicity and naïveté of the baby, will inevitably be lost by all men simply in the process of growing up, and therefore it cannot be regarded as the source of goodness.

or the ear keenness of hearing. Now it is the nature of man that when he is hungry he will desire satisfaction, when he is cold he will desire warmth, and when he is weary he will desire rest. This is his emotional nature. And yet a man, although he is hungry, will not dare to be the first to eat if he is in the presence of his elders, because he knows that he should yield to them, and although he is weary, he will not dare to demand rest because he knows that he should relieve others of the burden of labor. For a son to yield to his father or a younger brother to yield to his elder brother, for a son to relieve his father of work or a younger brother to relieve his elder brother—acts such as these are all contrary to man's nature and run counter to his emotions. And yet they represent the way of filial piety and the proper forms enjoined by ritual principles. Hence, if men follow their emotional nature, there will be no courtesy or humility; courtesy and humility in fact run counter to man's emotional nature. From this it is obvious, then, that man's nature is evil, and that his goodness is the result of conscious activity.

Someone may ask: if man's nature is evil, then where do ritual principles come from? I would reply: all ritual principles are produced by the conscious activity of the sages; essentially they are not products of man's nature. A potter molds clay and makes a vessel, but the vessel is the product of the conscious activity of the potter, not essentially a product of his human nature. A carpenter carves a piece of wood and makes a utensil, but the utensil is the product of the conscious activity of the carpenter, not essentially a product of his human nature. The sage gathers together his thoughts and ideas, experiments with various forms of conscious activity, and so produces ritual principles and sets forth laws and regulations. Hence, these ritual principles and laws are the products of the conscious activity of the sage, not essentially products of his human nature.

Phenomena such as the eye's fondness for beautiful forms, the ear's fondness for beautiful sounds, the mouth's fondness for delicious flavors, the mind's fondness for profit, or the body's fondness for pleasure and ease—these are all products of the emotional nature of man. They are instinctive and spontaneous; man does not have to do anything to produce them. But that which does not come into being instinctively but must wait for some activity to bring it into being is called the product of conscious activity. These are the products of the nature and of conscious activity respectively, and the proof that they are not the same. Therefore, the sage transforms his nature and initiates conscious activity; from this conscious activity he produces ritual principles, and when they have been produced he sets up rules and regulations. Hence, ritual principles and rules are produced by the sage. In respect to human nature the sage is the same as all other men and does not surpass[3] them; it is only in his conscious activity that he differs from and surpasses other men.

It is man's emotional nature to love profit and desire gain. Suppose now that a man has some wealth to be divided.[4] If he indulges his emotional nature, loving profit and desiring gain, then he will quarrel and wrangle even with his own brothers over the division. But if he has been transformed by the proper forms of ritual principle, then he will be capable of yielding even to a complete stranger. Hence, to indulge the emotional nature leads to the quarreling of brothers, but to be transformed by ritual principles makes a man capable of yielding to strangers.

Every man who desires to do good does so precisely because his nature is evil. A man whose accomplishments are meager longs for greatness; an ugly man longs for beauty; a man in cramped quarters longs for spaciousness; a poor man longs for wealth; a humble man longs for eminence. Whatever a man lacks in himself he will seek outside. But if a man is already rich, he will not long for wealth, and if he is already eminent, he will not long for greater power. What a man already possesses in himself he will not bother to look for outside. From this we can see that men desire to do good precisely because their nature is evil. Ritual principles are certainly not a part of man's original nature. Therefore, he forces himself to study and to seek to possess them. An understanding of ritual principles is not a part of man's original nature, and therefore he ponders and plans and thereby seeks to understand them. Hence, man in the state in which he is born neither possesses nor understands ritual principles. If he does not possess ritual principles, his behavior will be chaotic, and if he does not understand them, he will be wild and irresponsible. In fact, therefore, man in the state in which he is born possesses this tendency towards chaos and irresponsibility. From this it is obvious, then, that man's nature is evil, and that his goodness is the result of conscious activity.

Mencius states that man's nature is good, but I say that this view is wrong. All men in the world, past and present, agree in defining goodness as that which is upright, reasonable, and orderly, and evil as that which is prejudiced, irresponsible, and chaotic. This is the distinction between good and evil. Now suppose that man's nature was in fact intrinsically upright, reasonable, and orderly—then what need would there be for sage kings and ritual principles? The existence of sage kings and ritual principles could certainly add nothing to the situation. But because man's nature is in fact evil, this is not so. Therefore, in ancient times the sages, realizing that man's nature is evil, that it is prejudiced and not upright, irresponsible and lacking in order, for this reason established

3   Reading *guo* instead of *yi*.
4   Omitting the words *dixiung*, which do not seem to belong here.

the authority of the ruler to control it, elucidated ritual principles to transform it, set up laws and standards to correct it, and meted out strict punishments to restrain it. As a result, all the world achieved order and conformed to goodness. Such is the orderly government of the sage kings and the transforming power of ritual principles. Now let someone try doing away with the authority of the ruler, ignoring the transforming power of ritual principles, rejecting the order that comes from laws and standards, and dispensing with the restrictive power of punishments, and then watch and see how the people of the world treat each other. He will find that the powerful impose upon the weak and rob them, the many terrorize the few and extort from them, and in no time the whole world will be given up to chaos and mutual destruction. It is obvious from this, then, that man's nature is evil, and that his goodness is the result of conscious activity.

Those who are good at discussing antiquity must demonstrate the validity of what they say in terms of modern times; those who are good at discussing Heaven must show proofs from the human world. In discussions of all kinds, men value what is in accord with the facts and what can be proved to be valid. Hence if a man sits on his mat propounding some theory, he should be able to stand right up and put it into practice, and show that it can be extended over a wide area with equal validity. Now Mencius states that man's nature is good, but this is neither in accord with the facts, nor can it be proved to be valid. One may sit down and propound such a theory, but he cannot stand up and put it into practice, nor can he extend it over a wide area with any success at all. How, then, could it be anything but erroneous?

If the nature of man were good, we could dispense with sage kings and forget about ritual principles. But if it is evil, then we must go along with the sage kings and honor ritual principles. The straightening board is made because of the warped wood; the plumb line is employed because things are crooked; rulers are set up and ritual principles elucidated because the nature of man is evil. From this it is obvious, then, that man's nature is evil, and that his goodness is the result of conscious activity. A straight piece of wood does not have to wait for the straightening board to become straight; it is straight by nature. But a warped piece of wood must wait until it has been laid against the straightening board, steamed, and forced into shape before it can become straight, because by nature it is warped. Similarly, since man's nature is evil, he must wait for the ordering power of the sage kings and the transforming power of ritual principles; only then can he achieve order and conform to goodness. From this it is obvious, then, that man's nature is evil, and that his goodness is the result of conscious activity.

Someone may ask whether ritual principles and concerted conscious activity are not themselves a part of man's nature, so that for that reason the sage is capable of producing them. But I would answer that this is not so. A potter may mold clay and produce an earthen pot, but surely molding pots out of clay is not a part of the potter's human nature. A carpenter may carve wood and produce a utensil, but surely carving utensils out of wood is not a part of the carpenter's human nature. The sage stands in the same relation to ritual principles as the potter to the things he molds and produces. How, then, could ritual principles and concerted conscious activity be a part of man's basic human nature?

As far as human nature goes, the sages Yao and Shun possessed the same nature as the tyrant Jie or Robber Zhi, and the gentleman possesses the same nature as the petty man. Would you still maintain, then, that ritual principles and concerted conscious activity are a part of man's nature? If you do so, then what reason is there to pay any particular honor to Yao, Shun,[5] or the gentleman? The reason people honor Yao, Shun, and the gentleman is that they are able to transform their nature, apply themselves to conscious activity, and produce ritual principles. The sage, then, must stand in the same relation to ritual principles as the potter to the things he molds and produces. Looking at it this way, how could ritual principles and concerted conscious activity be a part of man's nature? The reason people despise Jie, Robber Zhi, or the petty man is that they give free rein to their nature, follow their emotions, and are content to indulge their passions, so that their conduct is marked by greed and contentiousness. Therefore, it is clear that man's nature is evil, and that his goodness is the result of conscious activity.

Heaven did not bestow any particular favor upon Zengzi, Min Ziqian, or Xiaoyi that it withheld from other men.[6] And yet these three men among all others proved most capable of carrying out their duties as sons and winning fame for their filial piety. Why? Because of their thorough attention to ritual principles. Heaven has not bestowed any particular favor upon the inhabitants of Qi and Lu which it has withheld from the people of Qin. And yet when it comes to observing the duties of father and son and the separation of roles between husband and wife, the inhabitants of Qin cannot match the filial reverence and respect for proper form which marks the people of Qi and Lu.[7] Why? Because the people of Qin give free rein to their emotional nature, are content to indulge their passions, and are careless of ritual principles. It is certainly not due to any difference in human nature between the two groups.

The man in the street can become a Yu.[8] What does this mean? What made the sage emperor Yu a Yu, I would reply, was the fact that he practiced

---

5   Reading *Shun* instead of *Yu* here and in the following sentence to conform to the sentence above.

6   Min Ziqian and Zengzi were disciples of Confucius famed for their filial conduct. Xiaoyi is identified by commentators as the heir apparent of Gaozong—i.e., King Wuding—of the Yin dynasty.

7   Reading *gong* instead of *ju*, *wen* instead of *fu*, and adding the words *Qinren* at the beginning of the sentence. Qi and Lu were of course the main centers of Confucian learning.

8   This was apparently an old saying. Cf. *Mencius* VIB, 2: "Jia of Cao asked, 'It is said that all men may become Yaos or Shuns. Is this so?' Mencius replied, 'It is.'"

benevolence and righteousness and abided by the proper rules and standards. If this is so, then benevolence, righteousness, and proper standards must be based upon principles which can be known and practiced. Any man in the street has the essential faculties needed to understand benevolence, righteousness, and proper standards, and the potential ability to put them into practice. Therefore it is clear that he can become a Yu.

Would you maintain that benevolence, righteousness, and proper standards are not based upon any principles that can be known and practiced? If so, then even a Yu could not have understood or practiced them. Or would you maintain that the man in the street does not have the essential faculties needed to understand them or the potential ability to put them into practice? If so, then you are saying that the man in the street in his family life cannot understand the duties required of a father or a son and in public life cannot comprehend the correct relationship between ruler and subject. But in fact this is not true. Any man in the street *can* understand the duties required of a father or a son and *can* comprehend the correct relationship between ruler and subject. Therefore, it is obvious that the essential faculties needed to understand such ethical principles and the potential ability to put them into practice must be a part of his make-up. Now if he takes these faculties and abilities and applies them to the principles of benevolence and righteousness, which we have already shown to be knowable and practicable,[9] then it is obvious that he can become a Yu. If the man in the street applies himself to training and study, concentrates his mind and will, and considers and examines things carefully, continuing his efforts over a long period of time and accumulating good acts without stop, then he can achieve a godlike understanding and form a triad with Heaven and earth. The sage is a man who has arrived where he has through the accumulation of good acts.

∽

---

9   Following the rearrangement of the text suggested by Tao Hongqing and Kanaya.

STUDY QUESTIONS FOR READINGS

Confucius, *The Analects*

1. Why does Youzi say filial piety is the root benevolence?
2. In 2.3, how does Confucius suggest a ruler best governs? How can the rites lead people to reform themselves?
3. Looking at 2.4, what is the course of Confucius's own moral development? What is he able to do by the time he is seventy years old? What might he mean by this?
4. In Book 4, what are the different ways in which Confucius characterizes the benevolent person? Putting them together, what would such a person be like?

Mencius

1. How does Mencius think we would respond to seeing a child about to fall into a well? What does he think this tell us about our nature?
2. What are the four "sprouts"? What does each of them "grow" into?
3. What point is Mencius making in Book 4A.8 in the passage about Ox Mountain? What does this tell us about human nature and how people actually are?

Xunzi

1. In what sense does Xunzi think human nature is evil? What enables us to be good?
2. Why does Xunzi think Mencius doesn't understand human nature? How does Xunzi distinguish human nature and "conscious effort"?
3. Compare Mencius's metaphors for the process of moral development to Xunzi's. What do these different images tell about how each envisions the process of moral education?

SUGGESTIONS FOR FURTHER READING OR VIEWING

Ivanhoe, Philip J., and Bryan W. Van Norden. *Readings in Chinese Philosophy*. 2nd ed. Indianapolis, IN: Hackett, 2005.

Lau, D. C. "Theories of Human Nature in Mencius and Xunzi." *Bulletin of the School of Oriental and African Studies* 15 (1953): 541–65. Reprinted in Kline, T. C., III, and Philip J. Ivanhoe, eds. *Virtue, Nature, and Moral Agency in the Xunzi*. Cambridge, MA: Hackett, 2000.

Littlejohn, Ronnie. *Confucianism: An Introduction*. London: I. B. Tauris, 2010.

Rosemont, Henry, Jr. "State and Society in the Hsun Tzu: A Philosophical Commentary." *Monumenta Serica* 29 (1970): 38–78. Reprinted in Kline, T. C., III, and Philip J. Ivanhoe, eds. *Virtue, Nature, and Moral Agency in the Xunzi*. Cambridge, MA: Hackett, 2000.

Buddhism

INTRODUCTION TO BUDDHISM

Buddhism begins with the life of a historical person, Siddhartha Gautama (sixth century BCE), who became recognized by his followers as "the Buddha," or the Enlightened One. Buddhist tradition holds that Siddartha was born in what is now Nepal to a privileged life, but in young adulthood he began feeling a deep dissatisfaction with his life. Startled, the story goes, by encounters with old age, sickness, and death, the future Buddha saw in the figure of a "renouncer"—one who has dropped out of society to seek liberation from life's seemingly constant suffering—a way to contend with his growing unhappiness. These encounters with suffering and the hope of relief became known as the Four Signs.

The traditional accounts of the Buddha's life would show it to be a familiar one within its cultural setting. The dominant religious practices of his time and place focused on liberation from suffering. Different sects within a religious tradition based on the Vedas—sacred texts that are at the core of what we now call Hinduism—had developed various aesthetic practices designed to free devotees from suffering (lasting versions of these include the various schools and techniques of yoga). As Siddhartha set out on his own quest for liberation, he turned first to these familiar practices. However, the tradition holds, he found they failed to end his suffering. Ultimately, he settled on a different path—a "middle way" between aestheticism and the materialistic life of his youth.

As a tradition, Buddhism is marked today by a great deal of diversity as different and competing schools emerged soon after the death of Siddhartha Gautama. At their core, however, all of the three main branches of Buddhism continue to share these basic convictions that make up the core of the Buddha's teachings, or *Dhamma* (Sanskrit: *Dharma*). Moreover, the basic elements of Buddhist ethics also derive from these basic teachings, and so we will focus on these here.

The Buddha's teachings begin with the Four Noble Truths. The first of these is that the world is marked by *dukkha* (Sanskrit: *dukhka*), a Pali word most typically translated as "suffering." While much of what we think of as suffering would be included in the common understanding of *dukkha*, the Buddha's claim is not that we invariably live in abject misery. Rather, the idea is that even at its best and most pleasurable, life is marked by a sense of things not being complete or fully satisfying. Like a wheel not turning on its axel properly—a commonly used image for *dukkha*—even the best of lives is colored by doubts, disappointments, and feelings of dissatisfaction.

The second Noble Truth is that there is a single, underlying cause of the suffering that marks life, namely cravings and attachment to goods that ultimately prove to be unattainable. We will say more about this shortly.

Being able to identify the ultimate cause of suffering is in the Buddhist moral imagination a good thing, as it enables us to see that there is a way to relieve the suffering that marks our lives. This is the third Noble Truth. Just as identifying the underlying cause of the symptoms of an illness is the first step to treating them, figuring out what is causing our unhappiness is key to overcoming the struggles of life.

The last of the Noble Truths identifies the "cure," so to speak, for suffering. This is the Noble Eightfold Path that defines, at its most basic, Buddhist belief and practice. As we will see, this is where we find the ethical core of Buddhism.

To grasp this ethical core, we need to return the second Noble Truth. It was said above that this is cravings or attachment. While this may suggest we make ourselves miserable when we pine for unattainable wealth or beauty or what have you—which is certainly true—there is a deeper point. The unhealthy cravings identified by Buddhism turn on a misunderstanding of our true nature as humans, a kind of ignorance that feeds and is fed by some of our worst psychological tendencies. As a cure for suffering, Buddhism works on two levels—it encourages a more productive understanding of our selves while working to transform our psychology. In the Buddhist picture, we must work to overcome the Three Poisons of ignorance, anger, and envy. Only through such a transformation can we reach *nibbana*—more commonly known by the Sanskrit word *nirvana*. This is a frequently misunderstood word that literally means "extinction" and refers to the elimination or cessation of the destructive patterns of thoughts and desires that cause us to suffer.

What then are the misunderstandings that drive the cravings that cause suffering? We can start with the idea of Interdependent Arising (Pali: *paṭiccasamuppāda*; Sanskrit: *Pratītyasamutpāda*), which is the claim that all things are interrelated and connected. The point here is a conceptual one—on the Buddhist picture, it is a mistake to suppose any thing stands on its own, enjoying an identity independent of other things. An image the Buddha uses is a tree, making the point that to consider a tree without noticing its reliance on the soil in which it grows, the sun and water that sustains it, the life it in turn nourishes, is to fundamentally misunderstand it. As wheels are necessarily tied to axels and roof beams to roofs, so all things are tied together in a network of connections with other things.

A second element of the Buddhist picture is Impermanence, the recognition that this interconnected world of interwoven elements is dynamic—things come and go constantly in this world, and so the network defined by Interdependent Arising is one of constant flux. In such a world, nothing lasts or stays the same, as a change in one brings about a change in all.

Putting Interdependent Arising and Impermanence together and applying it to ourselves leads to the idea of *Annata* (Sanskrit: *Anatman*), or No Self, perhaps the most challenging of all Buddhist ideas The logic, however, is compelling: if all things are interconnected and impermanent, then this is true of ourselves, which is to say we have no core, unchanging identity—no soul, no Self, no "I." Rather, we are simply an aggregation of various physical and psychological processes known in Buddhism as the Five Aggregates or *Khandhas* (Sanskrit: *Skandhas*).

The problem is that we have a deeply embedded tendency to see ourselves as independent and permanent beings. Such misconceptions encourage selfish wants and feelings, and these lead to actions that not only harm others, and so perpetuate suffering, but which also encourage more selfishness. This, of course, just leads to more destructive acts, and so the pattern continues. The root of such cycles of damaging feelings and actions, according to Buddhism, is a destructive focus on ourselves that is evidence of a profound lack of wisdom. This leads to a final Buddhist concept that is important to its ethical commitments, namely *kamma*, which is more well known in its Sanskrit version as *karma*.

In Buddhism, karma is tied deeply to the idea of Interdependent Arising: if everything is interconnected, it is impossible to escape the consequences of our actions as measured by their contributions to the suffering of the world. Actions, then, can be judged according to their merit. Do they contribute to the alleviation of suffering or do they compound it? Either way, the effects touch us as we cannot but live in the world we help create for better or worse. The teaching of karma also entails that at each moment we are working through the consequences of our past actions—we continuously confront situations that are in part of our own making, or that are "conditioned" by past actions. The idea is not that if I steal I will be stolen from. It is more that if I steal I am contributing to world in which theft is a reality, and this will be a world of greater suffering, not less. As a consequence of Interdependent Arising, I too will have to contend with the difficulties of living in such a world.

has slipped from its position, report it to me." "Yes, sire", the man replied. And after many hundreds and thousands of years the man saw that the sacred Wheel-Treasure had slipped from its position. Seeing this, he reported the fact to the King. Then King Daḷhanemi sent for his eldest son, the crown prince, and said: "My son, the sacred Wheel-Treasure has slipped from its position. And I have heard say that when this happens to a wheel-turning monarch, he has not much longer to live. I have had my fill [60] of human pleasures, now is the time to seek heavenly pleasures. You, my son, take over control of this ocean-bounded land. I will shave off my hair and beard, don yellow robes, and go forth from the household life into homelessness." And, having installed his eldest son in due form as king, King Daḷhanemi shaved off his hair and beard, donned yellow robes, and went forth from the household life into homelessness. And, seven days after the royal sage had gone forth, the sacred Wheel-Treasure vanished.

4. 'Then a certain man came to the anointed Khattiya King and said: "Sire, you should know that the sacred Wheel-Treasure has disappeared." At this the King was grieved and felt sad. He went to the royal sage and told him the news. And the royal sage said to him: "My son, you should not grieve or feel sad at the disappearance of the Wheel-Treasure. The Wheel-Treasure is not an heirloom from your fathers. But now, my son, you must turn yourself into an Ariyan wheel-turner. [786] And then it may come about that, if you perform the duties of an Ariyan wheel-turning monarch, on the fast-day of the fifteenth,[787] when you have washed your head and gone up to the verandah on top of your palace for the fast-day, the sacred Wheel-Treasure will appear to you, thousand-spoked, complete with felloe, hub and all appurtenances."

[61] 5. '"But what, sire, is the duty of an Ariyan wheel-turning monarch?" "It is this, my son: Yourself depending on the Dhamma, honouring it, revering it, cherishing it, doing homage to it and venerating it, having the Dhamma as your badge and banner, acknowledging the Dhamma as your master, you should establish guard, ward and protection according to Dhamma for your own household, your troops, your nobles and vassals, for Brahmins and householders, town and country folk, ascetics and Brahmins, for beasts and birds.[788] Let no crime[789] prevail in your kingdom, and to those who are in need, give property. And whatever ascetics and Brahmins in your kingdom have renounced the life of sensual infatuation and are devoted to forbearance and gentleness, each one taming himself, each one calming himself and each one striving for the end of craving, from time to time you should go to them and consult them as to what is wholesome and what is unwholesome, that is blameworthy and what is blameless, what is to be followed and what is not to be followed, and what action will in the long run lead to harm and sorrow, and what to welfare and happiness. Having listened to them, you should avoid evil and do what is good.[790] That, my son, is the duty of an Ariyan wheel-turning monarch.'

"'Yes, sire", said the King, and he performed the duties of an Ariyan wheel-turning monarch. And as he did so, on the fast-day of the fifteenth, when he had washed his head and gone up to the verandah on top of his palace for the fast-day, the sacred Wheel-Treasure appeared to him, thousand-spoked, complete with felloe, hub and all appurtenances. Then the King thought: "I have heard that when a duly anointed [62] Khattiya king sees such a wheel on the fast-day of the fifteenth, he will become a wheel-turning monarch. May I become such a monarch!"[791]

6. 'Then, rising from his seat, covering one shoulder with his robe, the King took a gold vessel in his left hand, sprinkled the Wheel with his right hand, and said: "May the noble Wheel-Treasure turn, may the noble Wheel-Treasure conquer!" The Wheel turned to the east, and the King followed it with his fourfold army. And in whatever country the Wheel stopped, the King took up residence with his fourfold army. And those who opposed him in the eastern region came and said: "Come, Your Majesty, welcome! We are yours, Your Majesty. Rule us, Your Majesty." And the King said: "Do not take life. Do not take what is not given. Do not commit sexual misconduct. Do not tell lies. Do not drink strong drink. Be moderate in eating."[792] And those who had opposed him in the eastern region became his subjects.

7. 'Then the Wheel turned south, west, and north ... (as verse 6). Then the Wheel-Treasure, having conquered the lands from sea to sea, returned to the royal capital and stopped before the King's palace as he was trying a case, as if to adorn the royal palace.

8. 'And a second wheel-turning monarch did likewise, and a third, a fourth, a fifth, a sixth, and a seventh king also ... told a man to see if the Wheel had slipped from its position (as verse 3). [64] And seven days after the royal sage had gone forth the Wheel disappeared.

9. 'Then a man came to the King and said: "Sire, you should know that the sacred Wheel-Treasure has disappeared." At this the King was grieved and felt sad. But he did not go to the royal sage and ask him about the duties of a wheel-turning monarch. Instead, he ruled the people according to his own ideas, and, being so ruled, the people did not prosper so well as they had done under the previous kings who had performed the duties of a wheel-turning monarch. Then the ministers, counsellors, treasury officials, guards and doorkeepers, and the chanters of mantras came to the King and said: [65] "Sire, as long as you rule the people according to your own ideas, and differently from the way they were ruled before under previous wheel-turning monarchs, the people do not prosper so well. Sire, there are ministers ... in your realm, including ourselves, who have preserved the knowledge of how a wheel-turning monarch should rule. Ask us, Your Majesty, and we will tell you!"

10. 'Then the King ordered all the ministers and others to come together, and he consulted them. And they explained to him the duties of a wheel-turning monarch. And, having listened to them, the King established guard and protection, but he did not give property to the needy, and as a result poverty became rife. With the spread of poverty, a man took what was not given, thus committing what was called theft. They arrested him, and brought him before the King, saying: "Your Majesty, this man took what was not given, which we call theft." The King said to him: "Is it true that you took what was not given—which is called theft?" "It is, Your Majesty." "Why?" "Your Majesty, I have nothing to live on." [66] Then the King gave the man some property, saying: "With this, my good man, you can keep yourself, support your mother and father, keep a wife and children, carry on a business and make gifts to ascetics and Brahmins, which will promote your spiritual welfare and lead to a happy rebirth with pleasant result in the heavenly sphere." "Very good, Your Majesty", replied the man.

11. 'And exactly the same thing happened with another man.

12. 'Then people heard that the King was giving away property to those who took what was not given, and they thought: "Suppose we were to do likewise!" And then another man took what was not given, and they brought him before the King. [67] The King asked him why he had done this, and he replied: "Your Majesty, I have nothing to live on." Then the King thought: "If I give property to everybody who takes what is not given, this theft will increase more and more. I had better make an end of him, finish him off once for all, and cut his head off." So he commanded his men: "Bind this man's arms tightly behind him with a strong rope, shave his head closely, and lead him to the rough sound of a drum through the streets and squares and out through the southern gate, and there finish by inflicting the capital penalty and cutting off his head!" And they did so.

13. 'Hearing about this, people thought: "Now let us get sharp swords made for us, and then we can take from anybody what is not given [which is called theft], [68] we will make an end of them, finish them off once for all and cut off their heads." So, having procured some sharp swords, they launched murderous assaults on villages, towns and cities, and went in for highway-robbery, killing their victims by cutting off their heads.

14. 'Thus, from the not giving of property to the needy, poverty became rife, from the growth of poverty, the taking of what was not given increased, from the increase of theft, the use of weapons increased, from the increased use of weapons, the taking of life increased—and from the increase in the taking of life, people's life-span decreased, their beauty decreased, and as a result of this decrease of life-span and beauty, the children of those whose life-span had been eighty thousand years lived for only forty thousand.

'And a man of the generation that lived for forty thousand years took what was not given. He was brought before the King, who asked him: "Is it true that you took what was not given—what is called theft?" "No, Your Majesty", he replied, thus telling a deliberate lie.

15. 'Thus, from the not giving of property to the needy,... the taking of life increased, and from the taking of life, lying increased, [69] from the increase in lying, people's life-span decreased, their beauty decreased, and as a result, the children of those whose life-span had been forty thousand years lived for only twenty thousand.

'And a man of the generation that lived for twenty thousand years took what was not given. Another man denounced him to the King, saying: "Sire, such-and-such a man has taken what was not given", thus speaking evil of another.[793]

16. 'Thus, from the not giving of property to the needy,... the speaking evil of others increased, and in consequence, people's life-span decreased, their beauty decreased, and as a result, the children of those whose life-span had been twenty thousand years lived only for ten thousand.

'And of the generation that lived for ten thousand years, some were beautiful, and some were ugly. And those who were ugly, being envious of those who were beautiful, committed adultery with others' wives.

17. 'Thus, from the not giving of property to the needy,... sexual misconduct increased, and in consequence people's life-span decreased, their beauty decreased, and as a result, the children of those whose life-span had been ten thousand years lived for only five thousand.

'And among the generation whose life-span was five thousand years, two things increased: harsh speech and idle chatter, in consequence of which people's life-span decreased, their beauty decreased, and as a result, the children of those whose life-span had been five thousand years [70] lived, some for two-and-a-half thousand years, and some for only two thousand.

'And among the generation whose life-span was two-and-a-half thousand years, covetousness and hatred increased, and in consequence people's life-span decreased, their beauty decreased, and as a result, the children of those whose life-span had been two-and-a-half thousand years lived for only a thousand.

'Among the generation whose life-span was a thousand years, false opinions[794] increased... and as a result, the children of those whose life-span had been a thousand years lived for only five hundred.

'And among the generation whose life-span was five hundred years, three things increased: incest, excessive greed and deviant practices[795]... and as a result, the children of those whose life-span had been five hundred years lived, some for two hundred and fifty years, some for only two hundred.

'And among those whose life-span was two hundred and fifty years, these things increased: lack of respect for mother and father, for ascetics and Brahmins, and for the head of the clan.

18. 'Thus, from the not giving of property to the needy,... [71] lack of respect for mother and father, for ascetics and Brahmins, and for the head of the clan increased, and in consequence people's life-span and beauty decreased, and the children of those whose life-span had been two-and-a-half centuries lived for only a hundred years.

19. 'Monks, a time will come when the children of these people will have a life-span of ten years. And with them, girls will be marriageable at five years old. And with them, these flavours will disappear: ghee, butter, sesame-oil, molasses and salt. Among them, kudrūsa-grain[796] will be the chief food, just as rice and curry are today. And with them, the ten courses of moral conduct will completely disappear, and the ten courses of evil will prevail exceedingly: for those of a ten-year lifespan there will be no word for "moral"[797] so how can there be anyone who acts in a moral way? Those people who have [72] no respect for mother or father, for ascetics and Brahmins, for the head of the clan, will be the ones who enjoy honour and prestige. Just as it is now the people who show respect for mother and father, for ascetics and Brahmins, for the head of the clan, who are praised and honoured, so it will be with those who do the opposite.

20. 'Among those of a ten-year life-span no account will be taken of mother or aunt, of mother's sister-in-law, of teacher's wife or of one's father's wives and so on—all will be promiscuous in the world like goats and sheep, fowl and pigs, dogs and jackals. Among them, fierce enmity will prevail one for another, fierce hatred, fierce anger and thoughts of killing, mother against child and child against mother, father against child and child against father, brother against brother, brother against sister, just as the hunter feels hatred for the beast he stalks... [73]

21. 'And for those of a ten-year life-span, there will come to be a "sword-interval"[798] of seven days, during which they will mistake one another for wild beasts. Sharp swords will appear in their hands and, thinking: "There is a wild beast!" they will take each other's lives with those swords. But there will be some beings who will think: "Let us not kill or be killed by anyone! Let us make for some grassy thickets or jungle-recesses or clumps of trees, for rivers hard to ford or inaccessible mountains, and live on roots and fruits of the forest." And this they will do for seven days. Then, at the end of the seven days, they will emerge from their hiding-places and rejoice together of one accord, saying: "Good beings, I see that you are alive!" And then the thought will occur to those beings: "It is only because we became addicted to evil ways that we suffered this loss of our kindred, so let us now do good! What good things can we do? Let

us abstain from the taking of life—that will be a good practice." And so they will abstain from the taking of life, and, having undertaken this good thing, will practise it. And through having undertaken such wholesome things, they will increase in life-span and beauty. [74] And the children of those whose life-span was ten years will live for twenty years.

22. 'Then it will occur to those beings: "It is through having taken to wholesome practices that we have increased in life-span and beauty, so let us perform still more wholesome practices. Let us refrain from taking what is not given, from sexual misconduct, from lying speech, from slander, from harsh speech, from idle chatter, from covetousness, from ill-will, from wrong views; let us abstain from three things: incest, excessive greed, and deviant practices; let us respect our mothers and fathers, ascetics and Brahmins, and the head of the clan, and let us persevere in these wholesome actions."

'And so they will do these things, and on account of this they will increase in life-span and in beauty. The children of those whose life-span is twenty years will live to be forty, their children will live to be eighty, their children to be a hundred and sixty, their children to be three hundred and twenty, their children to be six hundred and forty; the children of those whose life-span is six hundred and forty years will live for two thousand years, their children for four thousand, their children for eight thousand, and their children for twenty thousand. The children of those whose life-span is twenty thousand years will [75] live to be forty thousand, and their children will attain to eighty thousand years.

23. 'Among the people with an eighty thousand-year lifespan, girls will become marriageable at five hundred. And such people will know only three kinds of disease: greed, fasting, and old age.[800] And in the time of those people this continent of Jambudipa will be powerful and prosperous, and villages, towns and cities will be but a cock's flight one from the next.[801] This Jambudipa, like Avīci,[802] will be as thick with people as the jungle is thick with reeds and rushes. At that time the Vārānasi[803] of today will be a royal city called Ketumatī, powerful and prosperous, crowded with people and well-supplied. In Jambudipa there will be eighty-four thousand cities headed by Ketumati as the royal capital.

24. 'And in the time of the people with an eighty thousand-year life-span, there will arise in the capital city of Ketumati a king called Sankha, a wheel-turning monarch, a righteous monarch of the law, conqueror of the four quarters... (as verse 2).

25. 'And in that time of the people with an eighty thousand-year life-span, [76] there will arise in the world a Blessed Lord, an Arahant fully-enlightened Buddha named Metteyya,[803] endowed with wisdom and conduct, a Well-Farer, Knower of the worlds, incomparable Trainer of men to be tamed, Teacher of gods and humans, enlightened and blessed, just as I am now. He will thoroughly know by his own super-knowledge, and proclaim, this universe with its devas

and maras and Brahmas, its ascetics and Brahmins, and this generation with its princes and people, just as I do now. He will teach the Dhamma, lovely in its beginning, lovely in its middle, lovely in its ending, in the spirit and in the letter, and proclaim, just as I do now, the holy life in its fullness and purity. He will be attended by a company of thousands of monks, just as I am attended by a company of hundreds.

26. 'Then King Sankha will re-erect the palace once built by King Mahā-Panāda[804] and, having lived in it, will give it up and present it to the ascetics and Brahmins, the beggars, the wayfarers, the destitute. Then, shaving off hair and beard, he will don yellow robes and go forth from the household life into homelessness under the supreme Buddha Metteyya. Having gone forth, he will remain alone, in seclusion, ardent, eager and resolute, and before long he will have attained in this very life, by his own super-knowledge and resolution, [77] that unequalled goal of the holy life, for the sake of which young men of good family go forth from the household life into homelessness, and will abide therein.

27. 'Monks, be islands unto yourselves, be a refuge unto yourselves with no other refuge. Let the Dhamma be your island, let the Dhamma be your refuge with no other refuge. And how does a monk dwell as an island unto himself...? Here, a monk abides contemplating body as body, ardent, clearly aware and mindful, having put aside hankering and fretting for the world, he abides contemplating feelings as feelings, ... he abides contemplating mind as mind, ... he abides contemplating mind-objects as mind-objects, ardent, clearly aware and mindful, having put aside hankering and fretting for the world.

28. 'Keep to your own preserves, monks, to your ancestral haunts. If you do so, your life-span will increase, your beauty will increase, your happiness will increase, your wealth will increase, your power will increase.

'And what is length of life for a monk? Here, a monk develops the road to power which is concentration of intention accompanied by effort of will, the road to power which is concentration of energy..., the road to power which is concentration of consciousness..., the road to power which is concentration of investigation accompanied by effort of will. [805] By frequently practising these four roads to power he can, if he wishes, live for a full century,[806] or the remaining part of a century. That is what I call length of life for a monk.

'And what is beauty for a monk? Here, a monk practises right conduct, is restrained according to the discipline, [78] is perfect in behaviour and habits, sees danger in the slightest fault, and trains in the rules of training he has undertaken. That is beauty for a monk.

'And what is happiness for a monk? Here, a monk, detached from sense-desires ... enters the first jhāna, ... (as Sutta 22, verse 21), the second, third, fourth jhāna, ... purified by equanimity and mindfulness. That is happiness for a monk.

'And what is wealth for a monk? Here, a monk, with his heart filled with loving-kindness, dwells suffusing one quarter, the second, the third, the fourth. Thus he dwells suffusing the whole world, upwards, downwards, across—everywhere, always with a mind filled with loving-kindness, abundant, unbounded, without hate or ill-will. Then, with his heart filled with compassion,... with his heart filled with sympathetic joy, ... with his heart filled with equanimity,... he dwells suffusing the whole world, upwards, downwards, across, everywhere, always with a mind filled with equanimity, abundant, unbounded, without hate or ill-will.[807] That is wealth for a monk.

'And what is power for a monk? Here, a monk, by the destruction of the corruptions., enters into and abides in that corruptionless liberation of heart and liberation by wisdom which he has attained, in this very life, by his own super-knowledge and realisation. That is power for a monk.

'Monks, I do not consider any power[808] so hard to conquer as the power of Māra. [79] It is just by this building-up of wholesome states that this merit increases.'[809]

Thus the Lord spoke, and the monks were delighted and rejoiced at his words.

Notes

781 We seem to be back in the 'fairy-tale' world of some previous Suttas, but with a difference. RD, in another brilliant introduction in which he develops his theory of Normalism (the belief, in contrast to Animism, in a certain rule, order, or law), fails to analyse the structure of this fable (which is what, rather than a fairy-tale, it really is). The narrative part is framed by certain important remarks by the Buddha which, announced at the beginning, are repeated in elaborated form at the end (n.809).

782 Cf. DN 16.2.26 and n.395 there.

783 Cf. DN 22.1.

784 Gocare: lit. 'pastures'.

785 Pettike visaye: 'the range of your fathers'.

786 Cakkavatti-vatte vattāhi. RD points out the play on 'turning into a Wheel-Turner': vatta meaning both 'turning' and 'duty'.

787 Cf. DN 17.1.8.

788 A truly Buddhist touch! Asoka, who made some effort to live up to the ideal of a wheel-turning monarch, established animal hospitals.

789 Adhamma-kāro: 'non-Dhamma-doing'.

790 The word rendered 'good' is the same, kusala, as rendered just previously by 'wholesome. The literal 'skilful' is also sometimes to be preferred. A case where variation in translation is desirable—but it should be indicated.

791 All as in DN 17.

792 But see n.472. Warder (as n.801) has 'rule (collect taxes) in moderation'.

793 Even though the charge was justified! But the denunciation was malicious.

794 Micchā-diṭṭhi: see n.708.

795 Micchā-dhamma. DA says 'men with men, women with women'.

796 Said by RD to be 'a kind of rye'. The dictionaries are less specific.

797 Kusala (see n.790). The real meaning is 'skilful' in regard to knowing the karmic consequences of one's actions—in other words not having micchā-diṭṭhi (see n.708).

798 RD's note is barely intelligible, or at least unhelpful: 'Satthantarakappa. Sattha is sword; antarakappa is a period included in another period. Here the first period, the one included, is seven days. See Ledi Sadaw in the Buddhist Review, January 1916'—a journal not all readers will have to hand. On Antarakappa, Childers (as often) is more helpful than PED: 'Each Asankheyyakappa ["incalculable aeon"] contains twenty Antarakappas, an Antarakappa being the interval that elapses while the age of man increases from ten years to an asaṅkheyya, and then decreases again to ten years.' Clearly this immense period—which, in regard to the human life-span, is not canonical—is not meant here, but the reference to 'ten years' is relevant. DA distinguishes three kinds of Antarakappa: Dubbhikkhantarakappa, Rogantarakappa, and Satthantarakappa,caused by greed, delusion and hatred respectively. RD ignores all this.

Cf. EB under Antarakalpa, where a parallel to this commentarial passage is cited from the 11th-century Sanskrit-Tibetan dictionary called Mahāvyutpatti. The article concludes: 'Yet, the context in which the term satthantara-kappa occurs in the Dīgha Nikāya (III, 73) seems to suggest that the word could also be used in a very general sense to mean a period which is not of the same duration as an antarakappa.' The context in fact suggests that this period of one week marks a turning-point which is the beginning of an Antarakappa in the sense mentioned by Childers.

799 There will be, it seems, no real disease at all: death will result only from excessive or inadequate nourishment or the inevitable onset of old age. Accidents also seem to be excluded.

800 This seems to be the meaning of a doubtful expression.

801 In the commentaries and later literature Avici denotes the lowest of the hells (or 'purgatories', as RD and other translators have it, to indicate that no such hell is eternal). This, and a parallel passage at AN 3.56, is the only passage in the first four Nikāyas where it is mentioned, and 'hell' does not seem to be its meaning (RD renders it 'the Waveless Deep'), though its exact sense is doubtful. Warder, in his paraphrase of this Sutta (Indian Buddhism, 168) says parenthetically: '"like purgatory", the Buddha remarks ambiguously, thinking probably of his preference for seclusion.' The Buddhist hells grow steadily worse in the popular imagination, but most of their horrors find little support in the Suttas (though see MN 129, 130). Cf. n.244 and Introduction, p. 40.

802 Benares.

803 The next Buddha, perhaps better known by the Sanskrit name Maitreya.

804 This had been drowned in the Ganges.

805 Cf. DN 16.3.3. and 18.22.

806 See n.400.

807 As DN 13.76, 78.

808 The word bala 'power' is repeated from just before.

809 As RD fails to mention (though it is surely significant), the conclusion (verses 27–28) repeats the Buddha's words in verse 1, the reference there to Mara being expanded after the first sentence of verse 28, Māra and his power being again alluded to before the last sentence of verse 1 is repeated. The fable shows the large-scale effect of keeping morality, and indicates how monks are to use this lesson.

STUDY QUESTIONS FOR READINGS

Cakkavatti Sihadana Sutta

1. What do you think is meant by a "wheel-turning" monarch? How does the seventh king fail to perform the duties of a wheel-turning monarch? What kind of moral failing does the text suggests leads to the decline of the community?
2. What key Buddhist ideas are represented by the chain reaction of moral collapse that begins with such a seemingly small error by the ruler?
3. How does the text illustrate Buddhist ethics as found in the Five Precepts and Ten Virtues? How are moral lapses tied to the loss of beauty, health, social institutions, and our very humanity?
4. How is the moral decline finally brought to an end? What does the story as a whole suggest about the connection between living well and living ethically?

SUGGESTIONS FOR FURTHER READING OR VIEWING

The Dhammapada, available at http://www.accesstoinsight.org/tipitaka/kn/dhp/dhp.intro. budd.html. This is an early Buddhist text that focuses on its moral teachings.

Harvey, Paul. *An Introduction to Buddhist Ethics*. Cambridge: Cambridge University Press, 2000.

Hershock, Peter D. *Reinventing the Wheel: A Buddhist Response to the Information Age*. Albany: State University of New York Press, 1999.

Keown, Damien. *Buddhism: A Very Short Introduction*. Oxford: Oxford University Press. 2013. Ethics textbook.

PART 3

Normative Ethics

HOW DO WE KNOW WHAT TO DO?

S uppose you convince someone that you always try to do the right thing,
only to be asked: how do you decide what the right thing to do is?
Here are some possible answers you might give:

- I always try to do what is best for myself. I look out for number one. I
always try to make myself happy. The only person any of us truly have
moral obligations to is ourselves.

- I try to please God in everything that I do. I believe God created me and
everything else for the purpose of his glory. When I obey God, I please
him and thus glorify him.

- I try to make everyone happy, myself included, by every choice I make.
All others deserve happiness as much as I do, so I try to maximize
happiness for everyone.

- I try to follow what some call the bronze rule: I do unto others before they do
unto me. Because everyone in this world is out to get you, it's best to strike
first and get them before they get you. It's a kill or be killed world we're living in.

- I try to follow the silver rule: I do unto others as they do unto me. If
others are kind to me, I am kind back. If others hurt me, I hurt them back.

- I try to follow the golden rule: I do unto others as I would like them to do
unto me. I don't hurt others because I would not want them to hurt me.

While all of these might help you decide what to do, philosophers point to assumptions lurking in the backgrounds of each. For example, the second answer above
assumes both the existence of God and that we can know God's will. The third
answer above instead assumes that happiness matters most, that everyone's
happiness matters. The final three answers point to the idea that our actions should
take into account the actions and intentions of others. A great deal of normative
ethics is devoted to uncovering and examining these kinds of assumptions. The
next set of readings will consider some prominent theories in normative ethics.

Egoism

INTRODUCTION TO EGOISM

Egoism is a philosophical theory that emphasizes the self above all other entities and considerations. There are two main types of egoism: psychological egoism and ethical egoism. These two views are sometimes conflated; however, they are distinct and it is possible to hold one without automatically believing the other.

Psychological egoism holds that self-interest is the sole motivator of human action. In other words, according to this view, people ultimately only act in order to benefit themselves; nothing else is capable of driving human action. If it appears that someone is acting altruistically or for another, that is only because doing so ultimately is of benefit to the self. If it appears that someone is acting in a fashion that does not benefit the self, psychological egoism holds they are only doing so because of some perceived benefit to the self. Psychological egoism is a descriptive theory that isn't making any sort of value judgment about what has worth nor is it prescribing anything about what we ought to pursue. Rather, it simply describes human psychology and what motivates human action. On the other hand, ethical egoism offers a theory of value and as such is normative in nature.

Ethical egoism offers an account of what sorts of things have value and are worth pursuing (things that benefit oneself) and also offers an account of right and wrong. According to this view, actions are right insofar as they are in one's own long-term self-interest and wrong insofar as they detract from one's own long-term self-interest. It is important to note that this view of ethics is consequentialist. However, according to ethical egoism the only end results that are significant to moral consideration is the effect on the agent's own long-term self-interest.

Philosophical discussion and criticisms of egoism in its various forms date back to ancient philosophy and the works of Plato. While there is no necessary link between psychological egoism and ethical egoism as noted above, some proponents of egoism try to argue for ethical egoism on the grounds of psychological egoism, a move that faces much criticism. Another significant criticism of ethical egoism comes from G. E. Moore, who argued that such a view is self-contradictory, sparking a series of related criticisms and responses in the philosophical literature on this topic. Some advocates of egoism argue that the most plausible form of egoism is rational egoism, the philosophical view that it is both necessary and sufficient for an action to be rational that it maximizes one's self interest.

Plato's *Republic*, Book 2, draws the reader into a discussion between Socrates, Glaucon, and Adeimantus regarding the nature of justice. In this discussion, Glaucon proposes that to do injustice is by its nature good but to be victim of injustice is by its nature evil because injustice benefits the perpetrator but harms the recipient. He argues that because of this people compromise and agree to uphold certain principles of justice involuntarily only because they lack the power to behave unjustly without the potential for becoming a victim of injustice. Glaucon introduces the Myth of Gyges to reinforce his point, ultimately portraying an egoistic view of humanity.

The Republic

Plato

Book II
Socrates–Glaucon

WITH these words I was thinking that I had made an end of the discussion; but the end, in truth, proved to be only a beginning. For Glaucon, who is always the most pugnacious of men, was dissatisfied at Thrasymachus' retirement; he wanted to have the battle out. So he said to me: Socrates, do you wish really to persuade us, or only to seem to have persuaded us, that to be just is always better than to be unjust?

I should wish really to persuade you, I replied, if I could.

Then you certainly have not succeeded. Let me ask you now:—How would you arrange goods—are there not some which we welcome for their own sakes, and independently of their consequences, as, for example, harmless pleasures and enjoyments, which delight us at the time, although nothing follows from them?

I agree in thinking that there is such a class, I replied.

Is there not also a second class of goods, such as knowledge, sight, health, which are desirable not only in themselves, but also for their results?

Certainly, I said.

And would you not recognize a third class, such as gymnastic, and the care of the sick, and the physician's art; also the various ways of money-making—these do us good but we regard them as disagreeable; and no one would choose them for their own sakes, but only for the sake of some reward or result which flows from them?

There is, I said, this third class also. But why do you ask?

Because I want to know in which of the three classes you would place justice?

Plato, Selection from "Book II," *The Republic*, trans. Benjamin Jowett.

In the highest class, I replied,—among those goods which he who would be happy desires both for their own sake and for the sake of their results.

Then the many are of another mind; they think that justice is to be reckoned in the troublesome class, among goods which are to be pursued for the sake of rewards and of reputation, but in themselves are disagreeable and rather to be avoided.

I know, I said, that this is their manner of thinking, and that this was the thesis which Thrasymachus was maintaining just now, when he censured justice and praised injustice. But I am too stupid to be convinced by him.

I wish, he said, that you would hear me as well as him, and then I shall see whether you and I agree. For Thrasymachus seems to me, like a snake, to have been charmed by your voice sooner than he ought to have been; but to my mind the nature of justice and injustice have not yet been made clear. Setting aside their rewards and results, I want to know what they are in themselves, and how they inwardly work in the soul. If you, please, then, I will revive the argument of Thrasymachus. And first I will speak of the nature and origin of justice according to the common view of them. Secondly, I will show that all men who practise justice do so against their will, of necessity, but not as a good. And thirdly, I will argue that there is reason in this view, for the life of the unjust is after all better far than the life of the just—if what they say is true, Socrates, since I myself am not of their opinion. But still I acknowledge that I am perplexed when I hear the voices of Thrasymachus and myriads of others dinning in my ears; and, on the other hand, I have never yet heard the superiority of justice to injustice maintained by any one in a satisfactory way. I want to hear justice praised in respect of itself; then I shall be satisfied, and you are the person from whom I think that I am most likely to hear this; and therefore I will praise the unjust life to the utmost of my power, and my manner of speaking will indicate the manner in which I desire to hear you too praising justice and censuring injustice. Will you say whether you approve of my proposal?

Indeed I do; nor can I imagine any theme about which a man of sense would oftener wish to converse.

I am delighted, he replied, to hear you say so, and shall begin by speaking, as I proposed, of the nature and origin of justice.

Glaucon

They say that to do injustice is, by nature, good; to suffer injustice, evil; but that the evil is greater than the good. And so when men have both done and suffered injustice and have had experience of both, not being able to avoid the one and obtain the other, they think that they had better agree among themselves to have neither; hence there arise laws and mutual covenants; and that which is ordained by law is termed by them lawful and just. This they affirm to be the origin and nature of justice;—it is a mean or compromise, between the best of all, which is to do injustice and not be punished, and the worst of all, which is to suffer injustice without the power of retaliation; and justice, being at a middle point between the two, is tolerated not as a good, but as the lesser evil, and honoured by reason of the inability of men to do injustice. For no man who is worthy to be called a man would ever submit to such an agreement if he were able to resist; he would be mad if he did. Such is the received account, Socrates, of the nature and origin of justice.

Now that those who practise justice do so involuntarily and because they have not the power to be unjust will best appear if we imagine something of this kind: having given both to the just and the unjust power to do what they will, let us watch and see whither desire will lead them; then we shall discover in the very act the just and unjust man to be proceeding along the same road, following their interest, which all natures deem to be their good, and are only diverted into the path of justice by the force of law. The liberty which we are supposing may be most completely given to them in the form of such a power as is said to have been possessed by Gyges the ancestor of Croesus the Lydian. According to the tradition, Gyges was a shepherd in the service of the king of Lydia; there was a great storm, and an earthquake made an opening in the earth at the place where he was feeding his flock. Amazed at the sight, he descended into the opening, where, among other marvels, he beheld a hollow brazen horse, having doors, at which he stooping and looking in saw a dead body of stature, as appeared to him, more than human, and having nothing on but a gold ring; this he took from the finger of the dead and reascended. Now the shepherds met together, according to custom, that they might send their monthly report about the flocks to the king; into their assembly he came having the ring on his finger, and as he was sitting among them he chanced to turn the collet of the ring inside his hand, when instantly he became invisible to the rest of the company and they began to speak of him as if he were no longer present. He was astonished at this, and again touching the ring he turned the collet outwards and reappeared; he made several trials of the ring, and always with the same result-when he turned the collet inwards he became invisible, when outwards he reappeared. Whereupon he contrived to be chosen one of the messengers who were sent to the court; where as soon as he arrived he seduced the queen, and with her help conspired against the king and slew him, and took the kingdom. Suppose now that there were two such magic rings, and the just put on one of them and the unjust the other; no man can be imagined to be of such an iron nature that he would stand fast in justice. No man would keep his hands off what was not his own when he could safely take what he liked out of the market, or go into houses and lie with any one at his pleasure, or kill or release from prison whom he would, and in all respects be like a God among men. Then the actions of the just would be as the actions of the unjust; they would both come at last to the same point. And this we may truly affirm to be a great proof that a man is just, not willingly or because he thinks that justice is any good to him individually, but of necessity, for wherever any one thinks that he can safely be unjust, there he is unjust. For all men believe in their hearts that injustice is far more profitable to the individual than justice, and he who argues as I have been supposing, will say that they are right. If you could imagine any one obtaining this power of becoming invisible, and never doing any wrong or touching what was another's, he would be thought by the lookers-on to be a most wretched idiot, although they would praise him to one another's faces, and keep up appearances with one another from a fear that they too might suffer injustice. Enough of this.

Now, if we are to form a real judgment of the life of the just and unjust, we must isolate them; there is no other way; and how is the isolation to be effected? I answer: Let the unjust man be entirely unjust, and the just man entirely just; nothing is to be taken away from either of them, and both are to be perfectly furnished for the work of their respective lives. First, let the unjust be like other distinguished masters of craft; like the skilful pilot or physician, who knows intuitively his own powers and keeps within their limits, and who, if he fails at any point, is able to recover himself. So let the unjust make his unjust attempts in the right way, and lie hidden if he means to be great in his injustice (he who is found out is nobody): for the highest reach of injustice is: to be deemed just when you are not. Therefore I say that in the perfectly unjust man we must assume the most perfect injustice; there is to be no deduction, but we must allow him, while doing the most unjust acts, to have acquired the greatest reputation for justice. If he have taken a false step he must be able to recover himself; he must be one who can speak with effect, if any of his deeds come to light, and who can force his way where force is required his courage and strength, and command of money and friends. And at his side let us place the just man in his nobleness and simplicity, wishing, as Aeschylus says, to be and not to seem good. There must be no seeming, for if he seem to be just he will be honoured and rewarded, and then we shall not know whether he is just for the sake of justice or for the sake of honours and rewards; therefore, let him be clothed in justice only, and have no other covering; and he must be imagined in a state of life the opposite of the former. Let him be the best of men, and let him be thought the worst; then he will have been put to the proof; and we shall see whether he will be affected by the fear of infamy and its consequences. And let him continue thus to the hour of death; being just and seeming to be unjust. When both have reached the uttermost extreme, the one of justice and the other of injustice, let judgment be given which of them is the happier of the two.

STUDY GUIDE QUESTIONS FOR READINGS

Plato, *Republic*

1. Why does Glaucon believe injustice is by nature good and justice is by nature bad? Do you find this account compelling? Why or why not?
2. Why does Glaucon believe people are only just involuntarily? Do you agree with his conclusion? Why or why not?
3. Summarize the Myth of Gyges. What type of egoism is suggested by this story and how does Glaucon use this story to support his claims about justice and injustice?
4. How do Socrates and Adeimantus respond to Glaucon? Whose perspective do you find most compelling?
5. If the Myth of Gyges offers an accurate account of human nature, what, if any, ethical implications follow from this account? Explain your answers.

SUGGESTIONS FOR FURTHER READING OR VIEWING

Moseley, Alexander. "Egoism." In *The Internet Encyclopedia of Philosophy*, 2017. www.iep.utm.edu/egoism/.

Shaver, Robert. "Egoism." In *The Stanford Encyclopedia of Philosophy*, edited by Edward N. Zalta. Stanford University, Spring 2015 edition. https://plato.stanford.edu/entries/egoism/.

Divine Command Theory

INTRODUCTION TO DIVINE COMMAND THEORY

D ivine command theory holds that God determines what is morally forbidden and what we are morally obligated to do by decree. Judaism, Christianity, and Islam all have traditions of moral theology and philosophy that can be described as versions of divine command theory. These monotheistic faiths have many things in common, all tracing their roots back to Abraham. Hence, they are sometimes called the Abrahamic faiths. All stress the importance of God's laws or commandments and our duties to defer to God's will.

Divine command theory is an important theory in normative ethics. It is ancient, influential, and has many followers today. Judaism is 3000 or more years old, Christianity 2000 years old, and Islam 1400 years old. Two other major ethical theories we will study, natural law and Kantianism, echo many of the moral teachings of divine command theory. Today there are approximately 2.2 billion Christians, 1.6 billion Muslims, and 14.2 million Jews. Taken together, that is over half the world's population of 7.1 billion people. No other ethical theory can boast these kinds of numbers.

Divine command theorists hold that morality is objective. Adultery, for example, is objectively wrong, and would be wrong even if a vast majority of people came to believe it is permissible. According to divine command theory, the source of this objectivity is God—adultery is wrong because God has forbidden it. Divine command theorists hold that what we should value most is God.

The sacred text selections that follow will focus on some of the famous commandments of each of the three Abrahamic faiths. Included are excerpts from the sacred text of Judaism, the *Torah*; the sacred text of Christianity, the

Bible, specifically the New Testament; and the sacred text of Islam, the *Qur'an* (sometimes rendered as *The Koran*). Look for similarities and differences among the three selections.

Robert Mortimer's *Christian Ethics* elaborates on the details of a Christian version of divine command theory. That said, most of what he says applies to Judaism and Islam as well. The main exception is his discussion of the second function of revelation, which involves the death and resurrection of Jesus Christ, which Judaism and Islam importantly reject. Mortimer stresses God's perfection and our duties to obey the will of the being to whom we owe our lives in arguing for the moral authority of God's commandments.

Plato's *Euthyphro* is often read as a critique of divine command theory by way of something known as the Euthyphro Dilemma. We won't read responses to Plato's *Euthyphro* or the Euthyphro Dilemma that theologians and philosophers of religion have offered but be aware such responses exist; some are listed in the suggested readings.

The Ten Commandments

selection from the Torah

∾

Deuteronomy Chapter 5:7–22

6 I am the LORD thy God, who brought thee out of the land of Egypt, out of the house of bondage. Thou shalt have no other gods before Me. **7** Thou shalt not make unto thee a graven image, even any manner of likeness, of any thing that is in heaven above, or that is in the earth beneath, or that is in the water under the earth. **8** Thou shalt not bow down unto them, nor serve them; for I the LORD thy God am a jealous God, visiting the iniquity of the fathers upon the children, and upon the third and upon the fourth generation of them that hate Me, **9** and showing mercy unto the thousandth generation of them that love Me and keep My commandments. {**S**} **10** Thou shalt not take the name of the LORD thy God in vain; for the LORD will not hold him guiltless that taketh His name in vain. {**S**} **11** Observe the sabbath day, to keep it holy, as the LORD thy God commanded thee. **12** Six days shalt thou labour, and do all thy work; **13** but the seventh day is a sabbath unto the LORD thy God, in it thou shalt not do any manner of work, thou, nor thy son, nor thy daughter, nor thy man-servant, nor thy maid-servant, nor thine ox, nor thine ass, nor any of thy cattle, nor thy stranger that is within thy gates; that thy man-servant and thy maid-servant may rest as well as thou. **14** And thou shalt remember that thou was a servant in the land of Egypt, and the LORD thy God brought thee out thence by a mighty hand and by an outstretched arm; therefore the LORD thy God commanded thee to keep the sabbath day. {**S**} **15** Honour thy father and thy mother, as the LORD thy God commanded thee; that thy days may be long, and that it may go well with thee, upon the land which the LORD thy God giveth thee. {**S**} **16** Thou shalt not murder. {**S**} Neither shalt thou commit adultery. {**S**} Neither shalt thou steal. {**S**} Neither shalt thou bear false witness against thy neighbour. {**S**} **17** Neither shalt thou covet thy neighbour's wife; {**S**} neither shalt thou desire thy neighbour's house, his field, or his man-servant,

Selection from "Deuteronomy," New Jewish Publication Society of America Tanakh.

or his maid-servant, his ox, or his ass, or any thing that is thy neighbour's. {S} **18** These words the LORD spoke unto all your assembly in the mount out of the midst of the fire, of the cloud, and of the thick darkness, with a great voice, and it went on no more. And He wrote them upon two tables of stone, and gave them unto me. **19** And it came to pass, when ye heard the voice out of the midst of the darkness, while the mountain did burn with fire, that ye came near unto me, even all the heads of your tribes, and your elders; **20** and ye said: 'Behold, the LORD our God hath shown us His glory and His greatness, and we have heard His voice out of the midst of the fire; we have seen this day that God doth speak with man, and he liveth. **21** Now therefore why should we die? for this great fire will consume us; if we hear the voice of the LORD our God any more, then we shall die. **22** For who is there of all flesh, that hath heard the voice of the living God speaking out of the midst of the fire, as we have, and lived?

Deuteronomy Chapter 6:4–5

4 Hear, O Israel: the LORD our God, the LORD is one. **5** And thou shalt love the LORD thy God with all thy heart, and with all thy soul, and with all thy might.

Leviticus 19:33–34

{S} **33** And if a stranger sojourn with thee in your land, ye shall not do him wrong. **34** The stranger that sojourneth with you shall be unto you as the home-born among you, and thou shalt love him as thyself; for ye were strangers in the land of Egypt: I am the LORD your God.

Leviticus 25:35–37

35 And if thy brother be waxen poor, and his means fail with thee; then thou shalt uphold him: as a stranger and a settler shall he live with thee. **36** Take thou no interest of him or increase; but fear thy God; that thy brother may live with thee. **37** Thou shalt not give him thy money upon interest, nor give him thy victuals for increase.

Leviticus 26:14–18

14 But if ye will not hearken unto Me, and will not do all these commandments; **15** and if ye shall reject My statutes, and if your soul abhor Mine ordinances, so that ye will not do all My commandments, but break My covenant; **16** I also will do this unto you: I will appoint terror over you, even consumption and fever, that shall make the eyes to fail, and the soul to languish; and ye shall sow your seed in vain, for your enemies shall eat it. **17** And I will set My face against you, and ye shall be smitten before your enemies; they that hate you shall rule over you; and ye shall flee when none pursueth you. **18** And if ye will not yet for these things hearken unto Me, then I will chastise you seven times more for your sins.

Christian Moral Teachings

selection from the Bible

∽

Matthew 5:21–39

21 "You have heard that it was said to the people long ago, 'You shall not murder,[a] and anyone who murders will be subject to judgment.' 22 But I tell you that anyone who is angry with a brother or sister[b][c] will be subject to judgment. Again, anyone who says to a brother or sister, 'Raca,'[d] is answerable to the court. And anyone who says, 'You fool!' will be in danger of the fire of hell.

23 "Therefore, if you are offering your gift at the altar and there remember that your brother or sister has something against you, 24 leave your gift there in front of the altar. First go and be reconciled to them; then come and offer your gift.

25 "Settle matters quickly with your adversary who is taking you to court. Do it while you are still together on the way, or your adversary may hand you over to the judge, and the judge may hand you over to the officer, and you may be thrown into prison. 26 Truly I tell you, you will not get out until you have paid the last penny.

27 "You have heard that it was said, 'You shall not commit adultery.'[e] 28 But I tell you that anyone who looks at a woman lustfully has already committed adultery with her in his heart. 29 If your right eye causes you to stumble, gouge it out and throw it away. It is better for you to lose one part of your body than for your whole body to be thrown into hell. 30 And if your right hand causes you to stumble, cut it off and throw it away. It is better for you to lose one part of your body than for your whole body to go into hell.

31 "It has been said, 'Anyone who divorces his wife must give her a certificate of divorce.'[f]

[32] But I tell you that anyone who divorces his wife, except for sexual immorality, makes her the victim of adultery, and anyone who marries a divorced woman commits adultery.

[33] "Again, you have heard that it was said to the people long ago, 'Do not break your oath, but fulfill to the Lord the vows you have made.' [34] But I tell you, do not swear an oath at all: either by heaven, for it is God's throne; [35] or by the earth, for it is his footstool; or by Jerusalem, for it is the city of the Great King. [36] And do not swear by your head, for you cannot make even one hair white or black. [37] All you need to say is simply 'Yes' or 'No'; anything beyond this comes from the evil one.[g]

[38] "You have heard that it was said, 'Eye for eye, and tooth for tooth.'[h] [39] But I tell you, do not resist an evil person. If anyone slaps you on the right cheek, turn to them the other cheek also.

Matthew 19:16–24

[16] Just then a man came up to Jesus and asked, "Teacher, what good thing must I do to get eternal life?"

[17] "Why do you ask me about what is good?" Jesus replied. "There is only One who is good. If you want to enter life, keep the commandments."

[18] "Which ones?" he inquired.

Jesus replied, "'You shall not murder, you shall not commit adultery, you shall not steal, you shall not give false testimony, [19] honor your father and mother,'[a] and 'love your neighbor as yourself.'[b]"

[20] "All these I have kept," the young man said. "What do I still lack?"

[21] Jesus answered, "If you want to be perfect, go, sell your possessions and give to the poor, and you will have treasure in heaven. Then come, follow me."

[22] When the young man heard this, he went away sad, because he had great wealth.

[23] Then Jesus said to his disciples, "Truly I tell you, it is hard for someone who is rich to enter the kingdom of heaven. [24] Again I tell you, it is easier for a camel to go through the eye of a needle than for someone who is rich to enter the kingdom of God."

Matthew 22:37–40

[37] Jesus replied: "'Love the Lord your God with all your heart and with all your soul and with all your mind.'[a] [38] This is the first and greatest commandment. [39] And the second is like it: 'Love your neighbor as yourself.'[b] [40] All the Law and the Prophets hang on these two commandments."

Acts 10:34–35

[34] Then Peter began to speak: "I now realize how true it is that God does not show favoritism [35] but accepts from every nation the one who fears him and does what is right.

Galatians 3:26–29

[26] So in Christ Jesus you are all children of God through faith, [27] for all of you who were baptized into Christ have clothed yourselves with Christ. [28] There is neither Jew nor Gentile, neither slave nor free, nor is there male and female, for you are all one in Christ Jesus. [29] If you belong to Christ, then you are Abraham's seed, and heirs according to the promise.

Islamic Moral Teachings

selection from the Qur'an

∾

The Cow (2):275–276

Those who swallow usury will not rise, except as someone driven mad by Satan's touch. That is because they say, "Commerce is like usury." But God has permitted commerce, and has forbidden usury. Whoever, on receiving advice from his Lord, refrains, may keep his past earnings, and his case rests with God. But whoever resumes—these are the dwellers of the Fire, wherein they will abide forever. God condemns usury, and He blesses charities. God does not love any sinful ingrate.

Women (4):10 & 36

10. Those who consume the wealth of orphans illicitly consume only fire into their bellies; and they will roast in a Blaze.

36. Worship God, and ascribe no partners to Him, and be good to the parents, and the relatives, and the orphans, and the poor, and the neighbor next door, and the distant neighbor, and the close associate, and the traveler, and your servants. God does not love the arrogant showoff.

The Table Spread (5):32 & 90

32. Because of that We ordained for the Children of Israel: that whoever kills a person—unless it is for murder or corruption on earth—it is as if he killed the whole of mankind; and whoever saves it, it is as if he saved the whole of mankind. Our messengers came to them with clarifications, but even after that, many of them continue to commit excesses in the land.

90. O you who believe! Intoxicants, gambling, idolatry, and divination are abominations of Satan's doing. Avoid them, so that you may prosper.

Selections from *The Holy Qur'an*, trans. Maulana Muhammad Ali.

The Spoils (8):15–16

15. O you who believe! When you meet those who disbelieve on the march, never turn your backs on them.

16. Anyone who turns his back on them on that Day, except while maneuvering for battle, or to join another group, has incurred wrath from God, and his abode is Hell—what a miserable destination!

The Light (24):23

23. Those who slander honorable, innocent, believing women are cursed in this life and in the Hereafter. They will have a terrible punishment.

The Cow (2):256

256. There shall be no compulsion in religion; the right way has become distinct from the wrong way. Whoever renounces evil and believes in God has grasped the most trustworthy handle; which does not break. God is Hearing and Knowing.

The Bee (16):82

82. But if they turn away, your only duty is clear communication.

The Overwhelming (88):21, 22

21. So remind. You are only a reminder.

22. You have no control over them.

The Family of Imran (3):31

31. Say, "If you love God, then follow me, and God will love you, and will forgive you your sins." God is Forgiving and Merciful.

The Table Spread (5):9

9. God has promised those who believe and work righteousness: they will have forgiveness and a great reward.

The Cow (2):62

62. Those who believe, and those who are Jewish, and the Christians, and the Sabeans—any who believe in God and the Last Day, and act righteously—will have their reward with their Lord; they have nothing to fear, nor will they grieve.

∽

Christian Ethics

Robert Mortimer

∾

CHAPTER I

The Bible And Ethics

THE Christian religion is essentially a revelation of the nature of God. It tells men that God has done certain things. And from the nature of these actions we can infer what God is like. In the second place the Christian religion tells men what is the will of God for them, how they must live if they would please God. This second message is clearly dependent on the first. The kind of conduct which will please God depends on the kind of person God is. This is what is meant by saying that belief influences conduct. The once popular view that it does not matter what a man believes so long as he acts decently is nonsense. Because what he considers decent depends on what he believes. If you are a Nazi you will behave as a Nazi, if you are a Communist you will behave as a Communist, and if you are a Christian you will behave as a Christian. At least, in general. For a man does not always do what he knows he ought to do, and he does not always recognize clearly the implications for conduct of his belief. But in general our conduct, or at least our notions of what constitutes right conduct, are shaped by our beliefs. The man who knows about God—has a right faith—knows or may learn what conduct is pleasing to God and therefore right.

The Christian religion has a clear revelation of the nature of God, and by means of it instructs and enlightens the consciences of men. The first foundation is the doctrine of God the Creator. God made us and all the world. Because of that he has an absolute claim on our obedience. We do not exist in our own right, but only as His creatures, who ought therefore to do and be what He desires. We do not possess anything in the world, absolutely, not even our own bodies; we hold things in trust for God, who created them, and are bound, therefore, to use them only as He intends that they should be used. This is the doctrine contained in the first chapters of Genesis. God created man and placed him in the Garden of Eden with all the animals and the fruits of the earth at his disposal, subject to God's own law. "Of the fruit of the tree of the knowledge of good and evil thou shall not eat." Man's ownership and use of the material world is not absolute, but subject to the law of God.

From the doctrine of God as the Creator and source of all that is, it follows that a thing is not right simply because we think it is, still less because it seems to be expedient, It is right because God commands it. This means that there is a real distinction between right and wrong which is independent of what we happen to think. It is rooted in the nature and will of God. When a man's conscience tells him that a thing is right, which is in fact what God wills, his conscience is true and its judgement correct; when a man's conscience tells him a thing is right which is, in fact, contrary to God's will, his conscience is false and telling him a lie. It is a lamentably common experience for a man's conscience to play him false, so that in all good faith he does what is wrong, thinking it to be right. "Yea the time cometh that whosoever killeth you will think that he doeth God service." But this does not mean that whatever you think is right is right. It means that even conscience can be wrong: that the light which is in you can be darkness.

It is impossible to lay too great a stress on this fundamental principle, that there is a real and objective difference between right and wrong which is rooted in the will of God. It is the acceptance of this principle which distinguishes Christian ethics from Utilitarianism and Relativism. Utilitarianism distinguishes between right and wrong solely by reference to pleasure or expediency. That is right which tends to make me happy. The rightness of an action is to be judged by whether its consequences will bring more pleasure than pain, either to me or to society. By that, and that alone. When a man judges by reference to his own pleasure only, he is called a hedonist. Such a man is essentially selfish; for even though he may perform actions which give pleasure to others, his reason for doing so is that he himself derives pleasure from giving pleasure. That is why he thinks the action right. Utilitarians, properly so called, are those who think that right conduct consists not in pursuing their own pleasure but in promoting "the greatest happiness of the greatest number." In either case the decisive objection is that there is no means of distinguishing between one pleasure and another, except by its intensity. It is as right, perhaps more right, to indulge a passion for another man's wife than to listen to a classical concert.

Moreover any action may be justified by its end: if, on balance, it causes more happiness than pain, it is right. Thus it would be right to murder an irritating mother-in-law and so restore peace and harmony to a whole family.

It is a curious irony that in the public mind Christian ethics have become identified with hedonistic utilitarianism. "Christian" conduct has come to mean kindness. And by kindness is meant giving people what they want. Thus it is unkind and "unchristian" to insist that married people should live together if they do not want to. It is unkind and "unchristian" to insist that a man should keep his word, when it has become irksome to do so. He would be so much happier if he broke his word, and we ought to promote happiness. The cause of this ironical situation lies in the partial truth contained in Utilitarianism. God does indeed desire men's happiness, and it is a duty to promote happiness and not to cause pain. But the human happiness which God desires is the happiness of maturity, of having reached our human goal of perfection. And for this many lower and transient pleasures have to be sacrificed, the good giving way to the better. The rightness of conduct has to be judged not in reference to the present only or to the immediate future—though these are relevant—but in reference also to the total good of the whole man, a good which extends beyond this life and is only fully realized in the society of heaven. Every man's true happiness lies in acquiring a full and developed personality, harmonious and controlled, and in taking his place in a community of such persons. Many of the things which we call happiness are, when persisted in, fatal obstacles to the growth of such a personality: many of the things which we call tragedies are its unavoidable birth-pangs. The distinction between right and wrong is the distinction between those things which foster and those which fatally hinder man's growth to perfect manhood, his attainment of his eternal destiny to be fully himself. What these things are which advance a man towards the true end of his nature, are determined, and immutably determined, by God the author of that nature. He has laid down the path of growth. Man cannot alter it. He can only fail to perceive it.

Relativism holds that there is no ultimate and objective distinction between right and wrong. It is all a matter of taste and opinion. Different people have different ideas. They are all equally right or equally wrong. Because there is not any real distinction. It is all a matter of how people feel about things. And that depends chiefly on how they were brought up. There are as many different codes as there are different societies and cultures. But these codes are only convenient patterns of behaviour. They do not correspond to anything in the nature of things, but either they are only devices on the part of those in power to keep their subjects docile, or else they are general, if unconscious, agreements between the individual members of a society for the sake of a quiet life. The logical conclusion from such a view is that superior and intelligent persons who see through this pretence are above the so-called moral law, and are free to do what they like. Their behaviour is not to be limited by any moral considerations but only by their power to get what they want. Might is right. The conclusion for less powerful and superior persons is that it is never any good arguing with people about right and wrong. People have different ideas. Live and let live. It is as stupid to be angry with a person who sees no wrong in being cruel to a child as it is to be angry with a person who likes eating snails. In the end this comes to a position of complete scepticism. Nobody *knows* anything about anything. They merely have ideas and opinions, likes and dislikes. It is improbable that anyone holds this view in its fulness, for we all have a strong bias towards believing and asserting that our own opinions are actually true and those of other people false. But it is this kind of relativism which underlies the modern tolerance of divergent codes of behaviour.

As against Utilitarianism and Relativism alike, Christianity holds strongly to the objective distinction between right and wrong. It appeals to the common-sense conviction that "I ought" does not mean the same thing as "I want" or "it would pay me." It appeals to the universal innate consent to the proposition that we must do good and avoid evil, and to the conviction that, in general and in outline, what is good and what is evil is the same for all men at all times, being determined by the intrinsic nature of man.

There is such a thing as human nature, which is the same in all men. It exists, like everything else, in order to become fully itself, to achieve its end. What that end is can be perceived, at any rate to a great extent, by the use of reason alone, unaided by any special divine revelation. For example, everybody has some idea of what is meant by a good man or a noble man. Everybody has some idea of what makes a society "advanced" or developed and what makes it primitive or decadent. Or again, that mind should control matter, the reason order the emotions, is clearly demanded by the very structure of our nature, in which there is a hierarchy of spirit, mind and body. To make the body obey the reason is in harmony with nature, to allow the body to dominate the mind is to violate nature. Temperance, self-control, has always been recognized as a virtue. Indeed there has always been a general recognition of what the virtues are: justice, courage, temperance, consideration for others. The man who has these is well on the way to realizing his true nature, to becoming a man. The coward, the thief, the libertine, the ruthless oppressor is stunting and maiming himself. He becomes less and less a man, as he becomes more and more the slave of some dominant impulse and obsession. He is unbalanced and only partially developed.

All this means that there is a pattern of general behaviour, a code of things to do and not to do, which derives necessarily from nature itself, from the simple fact that man is man. It is what is called natural law. The knowledge of it is not peculiar to Christians: it is common to man. It may make things plainer, to give an illustration or two.

It is clear that man's power of memory, by means of which he can use the experience of the past as a guide for the present and can in some measure forecast the future and so provide for coming needs out of present super-fluity—it is clear that this power of memory indicates the duty of thrift and prudence and condemns prodigality as unnatural. Man is meant to acquire control of his environment by such use of reason and to live free of the bondage of chance and desperate need. Wilful neglect to make provision for the future is to violate the law of nature and to incur the risk of the penalties which such violations incur.

Again, nature makes it abundantly clear that the survival and education of human offspring require a long and close union of the two parents. Kittens and puppies may survive birth from promiscuous unions, being adequately cared for by the mother alone, and quickly reaching an age of self-sufficiency. Not so human babies, whose slow development to maturity involves them in a long helpless dependence on their parents, and creates for the parents a long period of shared responsibility for the lives they have brought into the world. Hence the institution of marriage, found at all levels of human culture, and the general recognition of the virtue of chastity and of fidelity to the marriage bond.

Again, it is clear that the isolated individual man, the fictional solitary inhabitant of a desert island, cannot, or does not easily attain to, the full devel-opment of his personality and power. It is by sharing the fruits of their diverse labour, by each contributing that for which he has a special aptitude, that men accumulate wealth, and by wealth get leisure. It is by mutual intercourse and the exchange of thought that men acquire and distribute wisdom, and are able to practise and appreciate the arts. It is by living together that men develop their spiritual and mental powers and become persons. In other words, as Aristotle said, Man is by nature a political animal. He is not meant to live alone but in society. From this follows the universal recognition of the virtue of justice. Without justice there can be no stable society. Justice demands that all respect each other's rights, so that all may live together in peaceable enjoyment of that which is their own. The particular determinations of justice, the decision as to what are each man's rights has always been difficult, and subject to constant variation; but the general principle that rights are to be respected has been universally admitted and finds expression in such universal prohibitions as "thou shalt not kill" and "thou shalt not steal."

The fact that there is (in this way) a pattern of behaviour by which alone man can attain to his full stature, that this pattern is laid down by the consti-tution of his nature as created by God, and that it can, at least in part and in general, be perceived by the light of unaided reason, that it can indeed be so easily perceived that in many cases it appears to be self-evident and axiomatic, so that ignorance of it is impossible to all but infants and imbeciles—for who can be ignorant that adultery is wrong or truthfulness right. All this must not be allowed to involve us in the error of supposing that this pattern of behaviour or natural law is a ready-made code, which every man has only to look within himself to read. The application of this law to the changing circumstances of evolving societies leaves room for every sort of error. And our knowledge of it is still crude and capable of endless refinement, as we penetrate more deeply into the mystery which surrounds human nature and sharpen our moral sensitiveness.

It is certain that human perception of the content and implications of natural law has developed with the emergence of man from his primitive condition—the history of the institution of marriage is but one, if the clearest, illustration of this. It is equally certain that it has also regressed; that from time to time different human societies have lost, or failed to reach, a grasp of certain of the most elementary of its contents. Anthropologists have little difficulty in showing that there is scarcely one of the generally accepted moral axioms which has not somewhere at some time been denied. Cannibalism, thievery, even prostitution have in some societies not merely been practised, but extolled as moral duties. And in our own day we have been amazed at the Nazi moral code, which inculcated cruelty and lies as patriotic virtues.

Some have used these facts as an argument in favour of relativism and against the very existence of a natural law of divinely constituted human behaviour. But the facts will not bear this argument, any more than ignorance of the solar system proves that the earth does not go round the sun. Existence of law and knowledge of that law are not the same thing. The law may well exist, and yet men be in ignorance of it. Knowledge of the law of nature in its more delicate implications and determinations demands refinement of moral sensitiveness and a quality of prophetic insight. Even in its elementary content, in such precepts as the ten commandments, passion, self-interest, long-standing custom can blind men to truths which to others seem self-evident. The elementary right to individual freedom has often been denied to slaves in the name of the law of nature itself. There is no limit to the perversity of the human reason when clouded and Weakened by unredeemed sin. It is the fact of universal human selfishness, or as theologians call it, the Fall, which prevents men from attaining a clear and persistent understanding of what constitutes right behaviour. And it is this which establishes the permanent need of Revelation, and places Christians in a privileged and especially responsible position.

The pattern of conduct which God has laid down for man is the same for all men. It is universally valid. When we speak of Christian ethics we do not mean that there is one law for Christians and another for non-Christians. We mean the Christian understanding and statement of the one common law for all men. Unbelievers also know or can be persuaded of that law or of part of it: Christians have a fuller and better knowledge. The reason for this is that Christians have by revelation a fuller and truer knowledge both of the nature of God Himself and of the nature of man. As has been well said, "Christian men, in order to learn what is the place of the Natural Law and its products in the economy of salvation, must look to the Bible as the witness of God's operations and as the record of God's supernatural destiny for man, to which the Natural Law is itself orientated and subordinated. Only with such a perspective, and with the will to purification of perception and purpose thereby created, will they be able to perceive or affirm the Natural Law in its completeness as an expression of the Lordship of Jesus Christ." (*Natural Law.* Edited by A. M. Vidler and W. A. Whitehouse. S.C.M. Press 1945. Page 24.)

The Revelation in the Bible plays a three-fold part. In the first place it recalls and restates in simple and even violent language fundamental moral judgements which men are always in danger of forgetting or explaining away. It thus provides a norm and standard of human behaviour in the broadest and simplest outline. Man's duty to worship God and love the truth, to respect lawful authority, to refrain from violence and robbery, to live in chastity, to be fair and even merciful in his dealings with his neighbour—and all this as the declared will of God, the way man *must* live if he would achieve his end—this is the constant theme of the Bible. The effect of it is not to reveal something new which men could not have found out for themselves, but to recall them to what they have forgotten or with culpable blindness have failed to perceive.

It is not easy to exaggerate the power of human self-deception nor man's ingenuity in persuading himself that black is white; manifest injustice can be depicted as justice, and unchastity acclaimed as "a venture of bold living." For example in times of shortages to exploit the needs and miseries of the poor by a strictly legal use of the markets may easily be represented as a perfectly proper use of one's opportunities, a quite legitimate advancement of oneself and one's family. The complacency born of such long and widespread practice is shattered by the violence of Revelation. "Thus saith the Lord: For three transgressions of Israel, and for four, I will not turn away the punishment thereof; because they sold the righteous for silver and the poor for a pair of shoes. . . ." (Amos ii, 6). This, then, is the first work of Revelation; it continuously sets forth the broad paths of right conduct. Lies are lies by whatever name you call them, and injustice is injustice however fairly screened and decked. They who read the Scriptures constantly and with attention cannot fail to ask themselves not only how far they have knowingly and wilfully transgressed the law of God, but also how far even that conduct which has seemed above question and reproach comes under divine condemnation.

And this leads to the second work of Revelation. The conduct which God demands of men, He demands out of His own Holiness and Righteousness. "Be ye perfect, as your Father in Heaven is perfect." Not the service of the lips but of the heart, not obedience in the letter but in the Spirit is commanded. The standard is too high: the Judge too all-seeing and just. The grandeur and majesty of the moral law proclaims the weakness and impotence of man. It shatters human pride and self-sufficiency: it overthrows that complacency with which the righteous regard the tattered robes of their partial virtues, and that satisfaction with which rogues rejoice to discover other men more evil than themselves. The revelation of the holiness of God and His Law, once struck home, drives men to confess their need of grace and brings them to Christ their Saviour.

Lastly, revelation, by the light which it throws on the nature of God and man, suggests new emphases and new precepts, a new scale of values which could not at all, or could not easily, have been perceived as part of the Natural Law for man without it. Thus it comes about that Christian ethics is at once old and new. It covers the same ground of human conduct as the law of the Old Testament and the "law of the Gentiles written in their hearts." Many of its precepts are the same precepts. Yet all is seen in a different light and in a new perspective—the perspective of God's love manifested in Christ. It will be worth while to give one or two illustrations of this.

Revelation throws into sharp relief the supreme value of each individual human being. Every man is an immortal soul created by God and designed for an eternal inheritance. The love of God effected by the Incarnation the restoration and renewal of fallen human nature in order that all men alike might benefit thereby. The Son of God showed particular care and concern for the fallen, the outcast, the weak and the despised. He came, not to call the righteous, but sinners to repentance. Like a good shepherd, He sought especially for the sheep which was lost. Moreover, the divine drama of Calvary which was the cost of man's redemption, the price necessary to give him again a clear picture of what human nature was designed to be and to provide him with the inspiration to strive towards it and the assurance that he is not irrevocably tied and bound to his sinful, selfish past, makes it equally clear that in the eyes of the Creator His creature man is of infinite worth and value.

The lesson is plain and clear: all men equally are the children of God, all men equally are the object of His love. In consequence of this, Christian ethics has always asserted that every man is a person possessed of certain inalienable rights, that he is an end in himself never to be used merely as a means to something else. And he is this in virtue of his being a man, no matter what his race or colour, no matter how well or poorly endowed with talents, no matter how primitive or developed. And further, since man is an end in himself, and that end transcends this world of time and space, being fully attained only in heaven, it follows that the individual takes precedence over society, in the sense that society exists for the good of its individual members, not those members for society. However much the good of the whole is greater than the good of any one of its parts, and whatever the duties each man owes to society, individual persons constitute the supreme value, and society itself exists only to promote the good of those persons.

This principle of the infinite worth of the individual is explicit in Scripture, and in the light of it all totalitarian doctrines of the State stand condemned. However, the implications of this principle for human living and for the organization of society are not explicit, but need to be perceived and worked out by the human conscience. How obtuse that conscience can be, even when illumined by revelation, is startlingly illustrated by the long centuries in which Christianity tolerated the institution of slavery. In view of the constant tendency of man to exploit his fellow men and use them as the instruments of his greed and selfishness, two things are certain. First, that the Scriptural revelation of the innate inalienable dignity and value of the individual is an indispensable bulwark of human freedom and growth. And second, that our knowledge of the implication of this revelation is far indeed from being perfect; there is constant need of further refinement of our moral perceptions, a refinement which can only emerge as the fruit of a deeper penetration of the Gospel of God's love into human life and thought.

Another illustration of the effect of Scripture upon ethics is given by the surrender of the principle of exact retribution in favour of the principle of mercy. Natural justice would seem to require exact retributive punishment, an eye for an eye, a tooth for a tooth. The codes of primitive peoples, and the long history of blood feuds show how the human conscience has approved of this concept. The revelation of the divine love and the explicit teaching of the Son of God have demonstrated the superiority of mercy, and have pointed the proper role of punishment as correction and not vengeance. Because of the revelation that in God justice is never unaccompanied by mercy, in Christian ethics there has always been an emphasis on the patient endurance of wrongs in imitation of Calvary, and on the suppression of all emotions of vindictive anger. As a means to soften human relations, as a restraint of human anger and cruelty, so easily disguised under the cloak of justice, the history of the world has nothing to show comparable to this Christian emphasis on patience and mercy, this insistence that even the just satisfaction of our wrongs yields to the divine example of forbearance. We are to be content with the reform or at least the restraint of the evil-doer, never to seek or demand vengeance.

It is well known how great a store Aristotle set by the "magnanimous" man, the man who holds himself to be intellectually and morally superior to his fellows, and is so. The concept of humility as a virtue is, I think, peculiar to the Christian code of ethics. It is inspired wholly by the example of the Son of God who came down from heaven and lived as man, and suffered the shameful death of the Cross. "The Son of Man came not to be ministered unto but to minister." "He that is greatest among you, let him be as one that serveth."

The duty of the great and highly placed not to seek their own advantage, but to devote themselves to the service of those over whom they bear rule: the conviction that all are equal in the sight of God, though different men have different functions: the recognition that all authority, power and wealth are from above, held in trust for God to whom account must one day be given: the understanding that respect, deference, prestige, rank are not things to be eagerly grasped at, but that, in imitation of Him who counted not His equality with God a prize to be snatched at, their surrender is nobler than their acquisition, their responsibility weightier than their privileges: these are insights not easily gained by the natural man, but plain in the Revelation and always emphasized in the Christian tradition. Humility in high and low alike is that virtue by which men are conscious of their own frailty and unworthiness, and grateful for the divine mercy and help upon which they constantly depend; by it they see in their own virtues only the triumph of God's grace and a divine commission to the service of others. This lovely quality is perhaps the noblest of all the gifts of Christianity to the human race.

Closely allied to humility is courtesy. Genuine good manners as distinct from conventional behaviour spring from consideration for others, and presuppose a readiness to sacrifice our own convenience and comfort together with a spontaneous concession of the equal dignity or greater need of others. They are the direct opposite of selfish and insensitive greed. They cover the whole range of human behaviour, have their place in every situation and are due to men of every rank and age and class. They are not capable of compressed definition: they are summed up in the behaviour of a Christian gentleman. They are rooted in the divine example of self-sacrifice and in the revelation of the divine care for the weak, outcast and wretched. They are shown in the Christian tradition of giving place to others, of offering assistance to the weak, of sympathy and respect for physical deformity, of endeavouring to alleviate pain and tend sickness. They cannot be taught or practised apart from the content of the divine command to love our neighbour and the divine example of the Son of Man. They become the instinctive and spontaneous behaviour of those to whom the Gospels are familiar and loved reading.

A last and familiar example of the corrective influence of Revelation upon the sin-darkened conscience of the human race is provided by the enhanced status of women in the Christian tradition. The certainty that women share equally with men in human nature and are therefore also of infinite value and worth, is implicit in the revelation which sternly forbids the use of them as mere instruments of male lust. Their physical weakness relative to men arouses the Christian impulse to defend and care for the weak. The conviction that though all have not the same office yet all are members of the one Body, all are equally the children of God, corrects the natural tendency to male superiority and prevents any permanent relegation of women to an inferior position. There is diversity of function, but essentially and in all that matters most equality of status. Above all, the taking by the Godhead of human flesh within the womb of our Lady has sanctified all motherhood and powerfully reinforced the natural human instinct of reverence for feminine chastity.

These are only a few of the matters on which the human conscience is enlightened by the revelation contained in the Christian tradition. Nor are all the implications of the Revelation anything like fully realized even now after nearly two thousand years. No doubt so long as humanity exists, among those who humbly and patiently seek to live under the Gospel there will develop an ever clearer and more delicate perception of what the divine pattern for human conduct is. It is certain that where the Revelation is ignored, the darkness of degeneracy and barbarism sets in. Sin-ridden man needs the Scriptures to rebuke his errors, to correct the distortion with which he perceives the natural law, to hold him firmly to its elementary principles and to lighten his eyes to its hidden depths. Christian ethics is the exposition of the moral truths implicit in the Revelation, and the application of them to human living. It interprets to man the natural law on the basis of that superior knowledge of the nature of God, of man and of the end for which man is created, which Revelation contains.

Euthyphro

Plato

PERSONS OF THE DIALOGUE: Socrates, Euthyphro.
SCENE: The Porch of the King Archon.

EUTHYPHRO

Why have you left the Lyceum, Socrates? and what are you doing in the Porch of the King Archon? Surely you cannot be concerned in a suit before the King, like myself?

SOCRATES

Not in a suit, Euthyphro; impeachment is the word which the Athenians use.

EUTHYPHRO

What! I suppose that some one has been prosecuting you, for I cannot believe that you are the prosecutor of another.

SOCRATES

Certainly not.

EUTHYPHRO

Then some one else has been prosecuting you?

SOCRATES

Yes.

EUTHYPHRO

And who is he?

SOCRATES

A young man who is little known, Euthyphro; and I hardly know him: his name is Meletus, and he is of the deme of Pitthis. Perhaps you may remember his appearance; he has a beak, and long straight hair, and a beard which is ill grown.

Plato, "Euthyphro," trans. Benjamin Jowett.

EUTHYPHRO

No, I do not remember him, Socrates. But what is the charge which he brings against you?

SOCRATES

What is the charge? Well, a very serious charge, which shows a good deal of character in the young man, and for which he is certainly not to be despised. He says he knows how the youth are corrupted and who are their corruptors. I fancy that he must be a wise man, and seeing that I am the reverse of a wise man, he has found me out, and is going to accuse me of corrupting his young friends. And of this our mother the state is to be the judge. Of all our political men he is the only one who seems to me to begin in the right way, with the cultivation of virtue in youth; like a good husbandman, he makes the young shoots his first care, and clears away us who are the destroyers of them. This is only the first step; he will afterwards attend to the elder branches; and if he goes on as he has begun, he will be a very great public benefactor.

EUTHYPHRO

I hope that he may; but I rather fear, Socrates, that the opposite will turn out to be the truth. My opinion is that in attacking you he is simply aiming a blow at the foundation of the state. But in what way does he say that you corrupt the young?

SOCRATES

He brings a wonderful accusation against me, which at first hearing excites surprise: he says that I am a poet or maker of gods, and that I invent new gods and deny the existence of old ones; this is the ground of his indictment.

EUTHYPHRO

I understand, Socrates; he means to attack you about the familiar sign which occasionally, as you say, comes to you. He thinks that you are a neologian, and he is going to have you up before the court for this. He knows that such a charge is readily received by the world, as I myself know too well; for when I speak in the assembly about divine things, and foretell the future to them, they laugh at me and think me a madman. Yet every word that I say is true. But they are jealous of us all; and we must be brave and go at them.

SOCRATES

Their laughter, friend Euthyphro, is not a matter of much consequence. For a man may be thought wise; but the Athenians, I suspect, do not much trouble themselves about him until he begins to impart his wisdom to others, and then for some reason or other, perhaps, as you say, from jealousy, they are angry.

EUTHYPHRO

I am never likely to try their temper in this way.

SOCRATES

I dare say not, for you are reserved in your behaviour, and seldom impart your wisdom. But I have a benevolent habit of pouring out myself to everybody, and would even pay for a listener, and I am afraid that the Athenians may think me too talkative. Now if, as I was saying, they would only laugh at me, as you say that they laugh at you, the time might pass gaily enough in the court; but perhaps they may be in earnest, and then what the end will be you soothsayers only can predict.

EUTHYPHRO

I dare say that the affair will end in nothing, Socrates, and that you will win your cause; and I think that I shall win my own.

SOCRATES

And what is your suit, Euthyphro? are you the pursuer or the defendant?

EUTHYPHRO

I am the pursuer.

SOCRATES

Of whom?

EUTHYPHRO

You will think me mad when I tell you.

SOCRATES

Why, has the fugitive wings?

EUTHYPHRO

Nay, he is not very volatile at his time of life.

SOCRATES

Who is he?

EUTHYPHRO

My father.

SOCRATES

Your father! my good man?

EUTHYPHRO

Yes.

SOCRATES

And of what is he accused?

EUTHYPHRO

Of murder, Socrates.

SOCRATES

By the powers, Euthyphro! how little does the common herd know of the nature of right and truth. A man must be an extraordinary man, and have made great strides in wisdom, before he could have seen his way to bring such an action.

EUTHYPHRO

Indeed, Socrates, he must.

SOCRATES

I suppose that the man whom your father murdered was one of your relatives—clearly he was; for if he had been a stranger you would never have thought of prosecuting him.

EUTHYPHRO

I am amused, Socrates, at your making a distinction between one who is a relation and one who is not a relation; for surely the pollution is the same in either case, if you knowingly associate with the murderer when you ought to clear yourself and him by proceeding against him. The real question is whether the murdered man has been justly slain. If justly, then your duty is to let the matter alone; but if unjustly, then even if the murderer lives under the same roof with you and eats at the same table, proceed against him. Now the man who is dead was a poor dependant of mine who worked for us as a field labourer on our farm in Naxos, and one day in a fit of drunken passion he got into a quarrel with one of our domestic servants and slew him. My father bound him hand and foot and threw him into a ditch, and then sent to Athens to ask of a diviner what he should do with him. Meanwhile he never attended to him and took no care about him, for he regarded him as a murderer; and thought that no great harm would be done even if he did die. Now this was just what happened. For such was the effect of cold and hunger and chains upon him, that before the messenger returned from the diviner, he was dead. And my father and family are angry with me for taking the part of the murderer and prosecuting my father. They say that he did not kill him, and that if he did, the dead man was but a murderer, and I ought not to take any notice, for that a son is impious who prosecutes a father. Which shows, Socrates, how little they know what the gods think about piety and impiety.

SOCRATES

Good heavens, Euthyphro! and is your knowledge of religion and of things pious and impious so very exact, that, supposing the circumstances to be as you state them, you are not afraid lest you too may be doing an impious thing in bringing an action against your father?

EUTHYPHRO

The best of Euthyphro, and that which distinguishes him, Socrates, from other men, is his exact knowledge of all such matters. What should I be good for without it?

SOCRATES

Rare friend! I think that I cannot do better than be your disciple. Then before the trial with Meletus comes on I shall challenge him, and say that I have always had a great interest in religious questions, and now, as he charges me with rash imaginations and innovations in religion, I have become your disciple. You, Meletus, as I shall say to him, acknowledge Euthyphro to be a great theologian, and sound in his opinions; and if you approve of him you ought to approve of me, and not have me into court; but if you disapprove, you should begin by indicting him who is my teacher, and who will be the ruin, not of the young, but of the old; that is to say, of myself whom he instructs, and of his old father whom he admonishes and chastises. And if Meletus refuses to listen to me, but will go on, and will not shift the indictment from me to you, I cannot do better than repeat this challenge in the court.

EUTHYPHRO

Yes, indeed, Socrates; and if he attempts to indict me I am mistaken if I do not find a flaw in him; the court shall have a great deal more to say to him than to me.

SOCRATES

And I, my dear friend, knowing this, am desirous of becoming your disciple. For I observe that no one appears to notice you—not even this Meletus; but his sharp eyes have found me out at once, and he has indicted me for impiety. And therefore, I adjure you to tell me the nature of piety and impiety, which you said that you knew so well, and of murder, and of other offences against the gods. What are they? Is not piety in every action always the same? and impiety, again—is it not always the opposite of piety, and also the same with itself, having, as impiety, one notion which includes whatever is impious?

EUTHYPHRO

To be sure, Socrates.

SOCRATES

And what is piety, and what is impiety?

EUTHYPHRO

Piety is doing as I am doing; that is to say, prosecuting any one who is guilty of murder, sacrilege, or of any similar crime—whether he be your father or mother, or whoever he may be—that makes no difference; and not to prosecute them is impiety. And please to consider, Socrates, what a notable proof I will give you of the truth of my words, a proof which

I have already given to others:—of the principle, I mean, that the impious, whoever he may be, ought not to go unpunished. For do not men regard Zeus as the best and most righteous of the gods?—and yet they admit that he bound his father (Cronos) because he wickedly devoured his sons, and that he too had punished his own father (Uranus) for a similar reason, in a nameless manner. And yet when I proceed against my father, they are angry with me. So inconsistent are they in their way of talking when the gods are concerned, and when I am concerned.

SOCRATES

May not this be the reason, Euthyphro, why I am charged with impiety—that I cannot [accept] with these stories about the gods? and therefore I suppose that people think me wrong. But, as you who are well informed about them approve of them, I cannot do better than assent to your superior wisdom. What else can I say, confessing as I do, that I know nothing about them? Tell me, for the love of Zeus, whether you really believe that they are true.

EUTHYPHRO

Yes, Socrates; and things more wonderful still, of which the world is in ignorance.

SOCRATES

And do you really believe that the gods fought with one another, and had dire quarrels, battles, and the like, as the poets say, and as you may see represented in the works of great artists? The temples are full of them; and notably the robe of Athene, which is carried up to the Acropolis at the great Panathenaea, is embroidered with them. Are all these tales of the gods true, Euthyphro?

EUTHYPHRO

Yes, Socrates; and, as I was saying, I can tell you, if you would like to hear them, many other things about the gods which would quite amaze you.

SOCRATES

I dare say; and you shall tell me them at some other time when I have leisure. But just at present I would rather hear from you a more precise answer, which you have not as yet given, my friend, to the question, What is 'piety'? When asked, you only replied, Doing as you do, charging your father with murder.

EUTHYPHRO

And what I said was true, Socrates.

SOCRATES

No doubt, Euthyphro; but you would admit that there are many other pious acts?

EUTHYPHRO

There are.

SOCRATES

Remember that I did not ask you to give me two or three examples of piety, but to explain the general idea which makes all pious things to be pious. Do you not recollect that there was one idea which made the impious impious, and the pious pious?

EUTHYPHRO

I remember.

SOCRATES

Tell me what is the nature of this idea, and then I shall have a standard to which I may look, and by which I may measure actions, whether yours or those of any one else, and then I shall be able to say that such and such an action is pious, such another impious.

EUTHYPHRO

I will tell you, if you like.

SOCRATES

I should very much like.

EUTHYPHRO

Piety, then, is that which is dear to the gods, and impiety is that which is not dear to them.

SOCRATES

Very good, Euthyphro; you have now given me the sort of answer which I wanted. But whether what you say is true or not I cannot as yet tell, although I make no doubt that you will prove the truth of your words.

EUTHYPHRO

Of course.

SOCRATES

Come, then, and let us examine what we are saying. That thing or person which is dear to the gods is pious, and that thing or person which is hateful to the gods is impious, these two being the extreme opposites of one another. Was not that said?

EUTHYPHRO

It was.

SOCRATES

And well said?

EUTHYPHRO

Yes, Socrates, I thought so; it was certainly said.

SOCRATES

And further, Euthyphro, the gods were admitted to have enmities and hatreds and differences?

EUTHYPHRO

Yes, that was also said.

SOCRATES

And what sort of difference creates enmity and anger? Suppose for example that you and I, my good friend, differ about a number; do differences of this sort make us enemies and set us at variance with one another? Do we not go at once to arithmetic, and put an end to them by a sum?

EUTHYPHRO

True.

SOCRATES

Or suppose that we differ about magnitudes, do we not quickly end the differences by measuring?

EUTHYPHRO

Very true.

SOCRATES

And we end a controversy about heavy and light by resorting to a weighing machine?

EUTHYPHRO

To be sure.

SOCRATES

But what differences are there which cannot be thus decided, and which therefore make us angry and set us at enmity with one another? I dare say the answer does not occur to you at the moment, and therefore I will suggest that these enmities arise when the matters of difference are the just and unjust, good and evil, honourable and dishonourable. Are not these the points about which men differ, and about which when we are unable satisfactorily to decide our differences, you and I and all of us quarrel, when we do quarrel? (Compare Alcib.)

EUTHYPHRO

Yes, Socrates, the nature of the differences about which we quarrel is such as you describe.

SOCRATES

And the quarrels of the gods, noble Euthyphro, when they occur, are of a like nature?

EUTHYPHRO

Certainly they are.

SOCRATES

They have differences of opinion, as you say, about good and evil, just and unjust, honourable and dishonourable: there would have been no quarrels among them, if there had been no such differences—would there now?

EUTHYPHRO

You are quite right.

SOCRATES

Does not every man love that which he deems noble and just and good, and hate the opposite of them?

EUTHYPHRO

Very true.

SOCRATES

But, as you say, people regard the same things, some as just and others as unjust,—about these they dispute; and so there arise wars and fightings among them.

EUTHYPHRO

Very true.

SOCRATES

Then the same things are hated by the gods and loved by the gods, and are both hateful and dear to them?

EUTHYPHRO

True.

SOCRATES

And upon this view the same things, Euthyphro, will be pious and also impious?

EUTHYPHRO

So I should suppose.

SOCRATES

Then, my friend, I remark with surprise that you have not answered the question which I asked. For I certainly did not ask you to tell me what action is both pious and impious: but now it would seem that what is loved by the gods is also hated by them. And therefore, Euthyphro, in thus chastising your father you may very likely be doing what is agreeable to Zeus but disagreeable to Cronos or Uranus, and what is acceptable to Hephaestus but unacceptable to [Hera], and there may be other gods who have similar differences of opinion.

EUTHYPHRO

But I believe, Socrates, that all the gods would be agreed as to the propriety of punishing a murderer: there would be no difference of opinion about that.

SOCRATES

Well, but speaking of men, Euthyphro, did you ever hear any one arguing that a murderer or any sort of evil-doer ought to be let off?

EUTHYPHRO

I should rather say that these are the questions which they are always arguing, especially in courts of law: they commit all sorts of crimes, and there is nothing which they will not do or say in their own defence.

SOCRATES

But do they admit their guilt, Euthyphro, and yet say that they ought not to be punished?

EUTHYPHRO

No; they do not.

SOCRATES

Then there are some things which they do not venture to say and do: for they do not venture to argue that the guilty are to be unpunished, but they deny their guilt, do they not?

EUTHYPHRO

Yes.

SOCRATES

Then they do not argue that the evil-doer should not be punished, but they argue about the fact of who the evil-doer is, and what he did and when?

EUTHYPHRO

True.

SOCRATES

And the gods are in the same case, if as you assert they quarrel about just and unjust, and some of them say while others deny that injustice is done among them. For surely neither God nor man will ever venture to say that the doer of injustice is not to be punished?

EUTHYPHRO

That is true, Socrates, in the main.

SOCRATES

But they join issue about the particulars—gods and men alike; and, if they dispute at all, they dispute about some act which is called in question, and which by some is affirmed to be just, by others to be unjust. Is not that true?

EUTHYPHRO

Quite true.

SOCRATES

Well then, my dear friend Euthyphro, do tell me, for my better instruction and information, what proof have you that in the opinion of all the gods a servant who is guilty of murder, and is put in chains by the master of the dead man, and dies because he is put in chains before he who bound him can learn from the interpreters of the gods what he ought to do with him, dies unjustly; and that on behalf of such an one a son ought to proceed against his father and accuse him of murder. How would you show that all the gods absolutely agree in approving of his act? Prove to me that they do, and I will applaud your wisdom as long as I live.

EUTHYPHRO

It will be a difficult task; but I could make the matter very clear indeed to you.

SOCRATES

I understand; you mean to say that I am not so quick of apprehension as the judges: for to them you will be sure to prove that the act is unjust, and hateful to the gods.

EUTHYPHRO

Yes indeed, Socrates; at least if they will listen to me.

SOCRATES

But they will be sure to listen if they find that you are a good speaker. There was a notion that came into my mind while you were speaking; I said to myself: 'Well, and what if Euthyphro does prove to me that all the gods regarded the death of the serf as unjust, how do I know anything more of the nature of piety and impiety? for granting that this action may be hateful to the gods, still piety and impiety are not adequately defined by these distinctions, for that which is hateful to the gods has been shown to be also pleasing and dear to them.' And therefore, Euthyphro, I do not ask you to prove this; I will suppose, if you like, that all the gods condemn and abominate such an action. But I will amend the definition so far as to say that what all the gods hate is impious, and what they love pious or holy; and what some of them love and others hate is both or neither. Shall this be our definition of piety and impiety?

EUTHYPHRO

Why not, Socrates?

SOCRATES

Why not! certainly, as far as I am concerned, Euthyphro, there is no reason why not. But whether this admission will greatly assist you in the task of instructing me as you promised, is a matter for you to consider.

EUTHYPHRO

Yes, I should say that what all the gods love is pious and holy, and the opposite which they all hate, impious.

SOCRATES

Ought we to enquire into the truth of this, Euthyphro, or simply to accept the mere statement on our own authority and that of others? What do you say?

EUTHYPHRO

We should enquire; and I believe that the statement will stand the test of enquiry.

SOCRATES

We shall know better, my good friend, in a little while. The point which I should first wish to understand is whether the pious or holy is beloved by the gods because it is holy, or holy because it is beloved of the gods.

EUTHYPHRO

I do not understand your meaning, Socrates.

SOCRATES

I will endeavour to explain: we, speak of carrying and we speak of being carried, of leading and being led, seeing and being seen. You know that in all such cases there is a difference, and you know also in what the difference lies?

EUTHYPHRO

I think that I understand.

SOCRATES

And is not that which is beloved distinct from that which loves?

EUTHYPHRO

Certainly.

SOCRATES

Well; and now tell me, is that which is carried in this state of carrying because it is carried, or for some other reason?

EUTHYPHRO

No; that is the reason.

SOCRATES

And the same is true of what is led and of what is seen?

EUTHYPHRO

True.

SOCRATES

And a thing is not seen because it is visible, but conversely, visible because it is seen; nor is a thing led because it is in the state of being led, or carried because it is in the state of being carried, but the converse of this. And now I think, Euthyphro, that my meaning will be intelligible; and my meaning is, that any state of action or passion implies previous action or passion. It does not become because it is becoming, but it is in a state of becoming because it becomes; neither does it suffer because it is in a state of suffering, but it is in a state of suffering because it suffers. Do you not agree?

EUTHYPHRO

Yes.

SOCRATES

Is not that which is loved in some state either of becoming or suffering?

EUTHYPHRO

Yes.

SOCRATES

> And the same holds as in the previous instances; the state of being loved follows the act of being loved, and not the act the state.

EUTHYPHRO

> Certainly.

SOCRATES

> And what do you say of piety, Euthyphro: is not piety, according to your definition, loved by all the gods?

EUTHYPHRO

> Yes.

SOCRATES

> Because it is pious or holy, or for some other reason?

EUTHYPHRO

> No, that is the reason.

SOCRATES

> It is loved because it is holy, not holy because it is loved?

EUTHYPHRO

> Yes.

SOCRATES

> And that which is dear to the gods is loved by them, and is in a state to be loved of them because it is loved of them?

EUTHYPHRO

> Certainly.

SOCRATES

> Then that which is dear to the gods, Euthyphro, is not holy, nor is that which is holy loved of God, as you affirm; but they are two different things.

EUTHYPHRO

> How do you mean, Socrates?

SOCRATES

> I mean to say that the holy has been acknowledged by us to be loved of God because it is holy, not to be holy because it is loved.

EUTHYPHRO

> Yes.

SOCRATES

> But that which is dear to the gods is dear to them because it is loved by them, not loved by them because it is dear to them.

EUTHYPHRO

> True.

SOCRATES

> But, friend Euthyphro, if that which is holy is the same with that which is dear to God, and is loved because it is holy, then that which is dear to God

would have been loved as being dear to God; but if that which is dear to God is dear to him because loved by him, then that which is holy would have been holy because loved by him. But now you see that the reverse is the case, and that they are quite different from one another. For one (the-ophiles) is of a kind to be loved cause it is loved, and the other (osion) is loved because it is of a kind to be loved. Thus you appear to me, Euthyphro, when I ask you what is the essence of holiness, to offer an attribute only, and not the essence—the attribute of being loved by all the gods. But you still refuse to explain to me the nature of holiness. And therefore, if you please, I will ask you not to hide your treasure, but to tell me once more what holiness or piety really is, whether dear to the gods or not (for that is a matter about which we will not quarrel); and what is impiety?

EUTHYPHRO

I really do not know, Socrates, how to express what I mean. For somehow or other our arguments, on whatever ground we rest them, seem to turn round and walk away from us.

SOCRATES

Your words, Euthyphro, are like the handiwork of my ancestor Daedalus; and if I were the sayer or propounder of them, you might say that my arguments walk away and will not remain fixed where they are placed because I am a descendant of his. But now, since these notions are your own, you must find some other gibe, for they certainly, as you yourself allow, show an inclination to be on the move.

EUTHYPHRO

Nay, Socrates, I shall still say that you are the Daedalus who sets arguments in motion; not I, certainly, but you make them move or go round, for they would never have stirred, as far as I am concerned.

SOCRATES

Then I must be a greater than Daedalus: for whereas he only made his own inventions to move, I move those of other people as well. And the beauty of it is, that I would rather not. For I would give the wisdom of Daedalus, and the wealth of Tantalus, to be able to detain them and keep them fixed. But enough of this. As I perceive that you are lazy, I will myself endeavour to show you how you might instruct me in the nature of piety; and I hope that you will not grudge your labour. Tell me, then—Is not that which is pious necessarily just?

EUTHYPHRO

Yes.

SOCRATES

And is, then, all which is just pious? or, is that which is pious all just, but that which is just, only in part and not all, pious?

EUTHYPHRO

I do not understand you, Socrates.

SOCRATES

And yet I know that you are as much wiser than I am, as you are younger. But, as I was saying, revered friend, the abundance of your wisdom makes you lazy. Please [do] exert yourself, for there is no real difficulty in understanding me. What I mean I may explain by an illustration of what I do not mean. The poet (Stasinus) sings—

'Of Zeus, the author and creator of all these things, You will not tell: for where there is fear there is also reverence.'

Now I disagree with this poet. Shall I tell you in what respect?

EUTHYPHRO

By all means.

SOCRATES

I should not say that where there is fear there is also reverence; for I am sure that many persons fear poverty and disease, and the like evils, but I do not perceive that they reverence the objects of their fear.

EUTHYPHRO

Very true.

SOCRATES

But where reverence is, there is fear; for he who has a feeling of reverence and shame about the commission of any action, fears and is afraid of an ill reputation.

EUTHYPHRO

No doubt.

SOCRATES

Then we are wrong in saying that where there is fear there is also reverence; and we should say, where there is reverence there is also fear. But there is not always reverence where there is fear; for fear is a more extended notion, and reverence is a part of fear, just as the odd is a part of number, and number is a more extended notion than the odd. I suppose that you follow me now?

EUTHYPHRO

Quite well.

SOCRATES

That was the sort of question which I meant to raise when I asked whether the just is always the pious, or the pious always the just; and whether there may not be justice where there is not piety; for justice is the more extended notion of which piety is only a part. Do you dissent?

EUTHYPHRO

No, I think that you are quite right.

SOCRATES

Then, if piety is a part of justice, I suppose that we should enquire what part? If you had pursued the enquiry in the previous cases; for instance, if you had asked me what is an even number, and what part of number the even is, I should have had no difficulty in replying, a number which represents a figure having two equal sides. Do you not agree?

EUTHYPHRO

Yes, I quite agree.

SOCRATES

In like manner, I want you to tell me what part of justice is piety or holiness, that I may be able to tell Meletus not to do me injustice, or indict me for impiety, as I am now adequately instructed by you in the nature of piety or holiness, and their opposites.

EUTHYPHRO

Piety or holiness, Socrates, appears to me to be that part of justice which attends to the gods, as there is the other part of justice which attends to men.

SOCRATES

That is good, Euthyphro; yet still there is a little point about which I should like to have further information, What is the meaning of 'attention'? For attention can hardly be used in the same sense when applied to the gods as when applied to other things. For instance, horses are said to require attention, and not every person is able to attend to them, but only a person skilled in horsemanship. Is it not so?

EUTHYPHRO

Certainly.

SOCRATES

I should suppose that the art of horsemanship is the art of attending to horses?

EUTHYPHRO

Yes.

SOCRATES

Nor is every one qualified to attend to dogs, but only the huntsman?

EUTHYPHRO

True.

SOCRATES

And I should also conceive that the art of the huntsman is the art of attending to dogs?

EUTHYPHRO

Yes.

SOCRATES

As the art of the oxherd is the art of attending to oxen?

EUTHYPHRO

Very true.

SOCRATES

In like manner holiness or piety is the art of attending to the gods?—that would be your meaning, Euthyphro?

EUTHYPHRO

Yes.

SOCRATES

And is not attention always designed for the good or benefit of that to which the attention is given? As in the case of horses, you may observe that when attended to by the horseman's art they are benefited and improved, are they not?

EUTHYPHRO

True.

SOCRATES

As the dogs are benefited by the huntsman's art, and the oxen by the art of the oxherd, and all other things are tended or attended for their good and not for their hurt?

EUTHYPHRO

Certainly, not for their hurt.

SOCRATES

But for their good?

EUTHYPHRO

Of course.

SOCRATES

And does piety or holiness, which has been defined to be the art of attending to the gods, benefit or improve them? Would you say that when you do a holy act you make any of the gods better?

EUTHYPHRO

No, no; that was certainly not what I meant.

SOCRATES

And I, Euthyphro, never supposed that you did. I asked you the question about the nature of the attention, because I thought that you did not.

EUTHYPHRO

You do me justice, Socrates; that is not the sort of attention which I mean.

SOCRATES

Good: but I must still ask what is this attention to the gods which is called piety?

EUTHYPHRO

It is such, Socrates, as servants show to their masters.

SOCRATES

I understand—a sort of ministration to the gods.

EUTHYPHRO

Exactly.

SOCRATES

Medicine is also a sort of ministration or service, having in view the attainment of some object—would you not say of health?

EUTHYPHRO

I should.

SOCRATES

Again, there is an art which ministers to the ship-builder with a view to the attainment of some result?

EUTHYPHRO

Yes, Socrates, with a view to the building of a ship.

SOCRATES

As there is an art which ministers to the house-builder with a view to the building of a house?

EUTHYPHRO

Yes.

SOCRATES

And now tell me, my good friend, about the art which ministers to the gods: what work does that help to accomplish? For you must surely know if, as you say, you are of all men living the one who is best instructed in religion.

EUTHYPHRO

And I speak the truth, Socrates.

SOCRATES

Tell me then, oh tell me—what is that fair work which the gods do by the help of our ministrations?

EUTHYPHRO

Many and fair, Socrates, are the works which they do.

SOCRATES

Why, my friend, and so are those of a general. But the chief of them is easily told. Would you not say that victory in war is the chief of them?

EUTHYPHRO

Certainly.

SOCRATES

Many and fair, too, are the works of the husbandman, if I am not mistaken; but his chief work is the production of food from the earth?

EUTHYPHRO

Exactly.

SOCRATES

And of the many and fair things done by the gods, which is the chief or principal one?

EUTHYPHRO

I have told you already, Socrates, that to learn all these things accurately will be very tiresome. Let me simply say that piety or holiness is learning how to please the gods in word and deed, by prayers and sacrifices. Such piety is the salvation of families and states, just as the impious, which is unpleasing to the gods, is their ruin and destruction.

SOCRATES

I think that you could have answered in much fewer words the chief question which I asked, Euthyphro, if you had chosen. But I see plainly that you are not disposed to instruct me—clearly not: else why, when we reached the point, did you turn aside? Had you only answered me I should have truly learned of you by this time the nature of piety. Now, as the asker of a question is necessarily dependent on the answerer, whither he leads I must follow; and can only ask again, what is the pious, and what is piety? Do you mean that they are a sort of science of praying and sacrificing?

EUTHYPHRO

Yes, I do.

SOCRATES

And sacrificing is giving to the gods, and prayer is asking of the gods?

EUTHYPHRO

Yes, Socrates.

SOCRATES

Upon this view, then, piety is a science of asking and giving?

EUTHYPHRO

You understand me capitally, Socrates.

SOCRATES

Yes, my friend; the reason is that I am a votary of your science, and give my mind to it, and therefore nothing which you say will be thrown away upon me. Please then to tell me, what is the nature of this service to the gods? Do you mean that we prefer requests and give gifts to them?

EUTHYPHRO

Yes, I do.

SOCRATES

Is not the right way of asking to ask of them what we want?

EUTHYPHRO

Certainly.

SOCRATES

And the right way of giving is to give to them in return what they want of us. There would be no meaning in an art which gives to any one that which he does not want.

EUTHYPHRO

Very true, Socrates.

SOCRATES

Then piety, Euthyphro, is an art which gods and men have of doing business with one another?

EUTHYPHRO

That is an expression which you may use, if you like.

SOCRATES

But I have no particular liking for anything but the truth. I wish, however, that you would tell me what benefit accrues to the gods from our gifts. There is no doubt about what they give to us; for there is no good thing which they do not give; but how we can give any good thing to them in return is far from being equally clear. If they give everything and we give nothing, that must be an affair of business in which we have very greatly the advantage of them.

EUTHYPHRO

And do you imagine, Socrates, that any benefit accrues to the gods from our gifts?

SOCRATES

But if not, Euthyphro, what is the meaning of gifts which are conferred by us upon the gods?

EUTHYPHRO

What else, but tributes of honour; and, as I was just now saying, what pleases them?

SOCRATES

Piety, then, is pleasing to the gods, but not beneficial or dear to them?

EUTHYPHRO

I should say that nothing could be dearer.

SOCRATES

Then once more the assertion is repeated that piety is dear to the gods?

EUTHYPHRO

Certainly.

SOCRATES

And when you say this, can you wonder at your words not standing firm, but walking away? Will you accuse me of being the Daedalus who makes them walk away, not perceiving that there is another and far greater artist than Daedalus who makes them go round in a circle, and he is yourself; for the argument, as you will perceive, comes round to the same point. Were we not saying that the holy or pious was not the same with that which is loved of the gods? Have you forgotten?

EUTHYPHRO

I quite remember.

SOCRATES

And are you not saying that what is loved of the gods is holy; and is not this the same as what is dear to them—do you see?

EUTHYPHRO

True.

SOCRATES

Then either we were wrong in our former assertion; or, if we were right then, we are wrong now.

EUTHYPHRO

One of the two must be true.

SOCRATES

Then we must begin again and ask, What is piety? That is an enquiry which I shall never be weary of pursuing as far as in me lies; and I entreat you not to scorn me, but to apply your mind to the utmost, and tell me the truth. For, if any man knows, you are he; and therefore I must detain you, like Proteus, until you tell. If you had not certainly known the nature of piety and impiety, I am confident that you would never, on behalf of a serf, have charged your aged father with murder. You would not have run such a risk of doing wrong in the sight of the gods, and you would have had too much respect for the opinions of men. I am sure, therefore, that you know the nature of piety and impiety. Speak out then, my dear Euthyphro, and do not hide your knowledge.

EUTHYPHRO

Another time, Socrates; for I am in a hurry, and must go now.

SOCRATES

Alas! my companion, and will you leave me in despair? I was hoping that you would instruct me in the nature of piety and impiety; and then I might have cleared myself of Meletus and his indictment. I would have told him that I had been enlightened by Euthyphro, and had given up rash innovations and speculations, in which I indulged only through ignorance, and that now I am about to lead a better life.

The *Torah*

1. Deuteronomy: 5:5–22; 6:5
   a. List the four commandments regarding duty to God and the six regarding duty to our neighbors.
   b. Do any of these commandments still seem reasonable as secular (not religious) moral commandments? If so, which ones and why?
   c. How much are we to love God?
2. Leviticus: 19:33–34; 23:22; 25:35–37; 26:18
   a. What do we learn regarding how we should treat foreigners in our own land?
   b. What do we learn about how we are to treat the poor? Should we profit from lending money or selling food to the poor?
   c. What do we learn about God's judgment on us if we disobey? Is this judgment finite or infinite?

The Christian *New Testament*

1. Mathew 5:21–22, 27–28, 31–32, 38–39; 19:16–24; 22:37–40
   a. What does Jesus suggest regarding murder, adultery, divorce, and revenge?
   b. What does Jesus suggest we must do in order to enter heaven?
   c. What two commandments does Jesus claim are the greatest?
2. Acts 10: 34–35: Does God show favoritism to one group? Explain.
3. Galatians: 3:26–29
   a. What is the theme of this section of Galatians?
   b. What sorts of things does this selection imply are immoral?

The *Qur'an*

1. Greater Sins: The Cow 2:275–76; Women 4:10; 4:36; The Table Spread 5:32; 5:90; The Spoils of War 8:15–16; The Light 24:23
   a. Explain the seven Greater Sins in Islam. (Reminder: polytheism, witchcraft, murder, mistreating orphans, usury, cowardice, and false accusations of adultery.)
   b. Compare these Greater Sins to the Jewish Ten Commandments.
2. Commandments regarding Evangelism: The Cow 2:256; The Bee 16:82; The Overwhelming Event 88: 21–22: Explain what the Qur'an teaches about the duty and limits of evangelism.

3. Hope: The family of Imran 3:31; The Table Spread 5:9; The Cow 2:62
   a. Explain what the Qur'an teaches about hope for Muslims and other religions.
   b. What two things must we do?

Mortimer, *Christian Ethics*

1. Why do we need to know what kind of "person" God is?
2. Why should we obey God?
3. Why is something right or wrong?
4. Mortimer claims the pattern of conduct God has decreed is universal. What does he mean?
5. Explain the three functions of revelation and how they lead to each other. (Hint: norm, grace & equality.)
   a. Which of these three functions is specifically Christian?
   b. How are these three functions illustrated in our sacred text selections?

Plato, *Euthyphro*

1. What is Euthyphro's first definition of piety? Why is it a poor definition?
2. What is Euthyphro's second definition of piety? Why is it a poor definition?
3. What is Euthyphro's third definition of piety? Why is it a poor definition?
4. Discussion: Are than any weaknesses in Socrates' criticism of the third definition of piety?

SUGGESTED READINGS

Adams, Robert Merrihew. "A Modified Divine Command Theory of Ethical Wrongness." In *Morality and the Good Life*, edited by Thomas L. Carson and Paul K. Moser. Oxford: Oxford University Press, 1997.

Alston, William. "Some Suggestions for Divine Command Theorists." In *Christian Theism and the Problems of Philosophy*, edited by Michael Beaty. Indiana: University of Notre Dame Press, 1990.

Arthur, John. "Morality, Religion, and Conscience" In *Morality and Moral Controversies: Readings in Moral, Social, and Political Philosophy*, edited by John Arthur. Upper Saddle River, NJ: Pearson, 2005.

Kretzmann, Norman. "Abraham, Isaac, and Euthyphro: God and the Basis of Morality." In *Hamarti, The Concept of Error in the Western Tradition: Essays in Honor of John M. Crossett*, edited by Donald V. Stump, James A. Arieti, Lloyd Gerson, and Eleonore Stump. New York: Edwin Mellen, 1982.

Quinn, Philip L. "Divine Command Ethics: A Causal Theory." In *Divine Command Morality: Historical and Contemporary Readings*, edited by Janine Idziak. New York: Edwin Mellen, 1979.

Natural Law Theory

INTRODUCTION TO NATURAL LAW THEORY

Natural law theory has its roots in the ethical theories of Plato and Aristotle as well as the Hellenistic philosophy of Stoicism and early modern thinkers such as Hugo Grotius. In its contemporary guises, the tradition of natural law thinking owes most to St. Thomas Aquinas (1225–1274), who synthesized the work of Aristotle and Christian theology, to which he was also committed. Now mostly associated with a long tradition of Catholic moral theology, natural law theory remains an important source of insights in both legal and moral philosophy independently of its associations with the Catholic church. It is important to note that adherents of natural law theory insist its principles and concepts can be arrived at through entirely rational means.

Aristotle begins *Nichomachean Ethics* by asking what kind of life is best for human beings, or what "the chief good" is for humans, and it is helpful to see St. Thomas Aquinas as asking similar questions, and indeed his debt to Aristotle is substantial. What Aquinas's Christianity enables him to add to Aristotle's picture of happiness as a life lived in accordance with virtue is a robust conception of law and a picture of morality as a system of laws telling us what we must do and, most importantly, what we must not do. While it may sound like divine command theory is in the offing when Aquinas begins by talking about God's eternal and divine laws, Aquinas defines laws as rules intended to direct those being governed by the law toward the good. A traffic law that makes the roads less safe and navigable is a bad law precisely because traffic laws should make things better—that is what laws are supposed to do. The natural law, then, is what tells us how to live so that we move toward what is truly good for us as rational beings. Importantly for Aquinas, God does this not as an act of pure will but as an expression of his rational nature. Because we share in that nature, reason alone can tell us what we are to do to advance our own flourishing.

This last move is critical because it allows the natural law tradition to bracket the theological components and point to reason itself as the normative force behind the natural law. For rational beings such as ourselves, the "First Precept of the Natural Law"—good is to be done and evil avoided—is self-evident, comparable to the epistemic principle that truth is to be believed and falsehood rejected. The epistemic precept is necessary for even minimal rationality when it comes to what we should believe, and for Aquinas the moral precept is needed for minimally rational behavior. Someone who knowingly pursues what she knows is destructive of her own flourishing is acting irrationally, just as much as someone who claims to believe what she knows to be false. Adding some detail, Aquinas identifies four basic or intrinsic goods—life, procreation, sociability, and knowledge—that are constitutive of our flourishing and that any rational person will recognize as inviolable.

Summa Theologica

St. Thomas Aquinas

∽

Question 91

Whether There Is an Eternal Law?
Objection 1: It would seem that there is no eternal law. Because every law is imposed on someone. But there was not someone from eternity on whom a law could be imposed: since God alone was from eternity. Therefore no law is eternal.

Obj. 2: Further, promulgation is essential to law. But promulgation could not be from eternity: because there was no one to whom it could be promulgated from eternity. Therefore no law can be eternal.

Obj. 3: Further, a law implies order to an end. But nothing ordained to an end is eternal: for the last end alone is eternal. Therefore no law is eternal.

On the contrary, Augustine says (De Lib. Arb. i, 6): "That Law which is the Supreme Reason cannot be understood to be otherwise than unchangeable and eternal."

I answer that, As stated above (Q. 90, A. 1, ad 2; AA. 3, 4), a law is nothing else but a dictate of practical reason emanating from the ruler who governs a perfect community. Now it is evident, granted that the world is ruled by Divine Providence, as was stated in the First Part (Q. 22, AA. 1, 2), that the whole community of the universe is governed by Divine Reason. Wherefore the very Idea of the government of things in God the Ruler of the universe, has the nature of a law. And since the Divine Reason's conception of things is

St. Thomas Aquinas, "Of Laws (Q91-94.2)," *Summa Theologica.*

not subject to time but is eternal, according to Prov. 8:23, therefore it is that this kind of law must be called eternal.

Reply Obj. 1: Those things that are not in themselves, exist with God, inasmuch as they are foreknown and preordained by Him, according to Rom. 4:17: "Who calls those things that are not, as those that are." Accordingly the eternal concept of the Divine law bears the character of an eternal law, in so far as it is ordained by God to the government of things foreknown by Him.

Reply Obj. 2: Promulgation is made by word of mouth or in writing; and in both ways the eternal law is promulgated: because both the Divine Word and the writing of the Book of Life are eternal. But the promulgation cannot be from eternity on the part of the creature that hears or reads.

Reply Obj. 3: The law implies order to the end actively, in so far as it directs certain things to the end; but not passively—that is to say, the law itself is not ordained to the end—except accidentally, in a governor whose end is extrinsic to him, and to which end his law must needs be ordained. But the end of the Divine government is God Himself, and His law is not distinct from Himself. Wherefore the eternal law is not ordained to another end.

Second Article [I-II, Q. 91, Art. 2]
Whether There Is in Us a Natural Law?
Objection 1: It would seem that there is no natural law in us. Because man is governed sufficiently by the eternal law: for Augustine says (De Lib. Arb. i) that "the eternal law is that by which it is right that all things should be most orderly." But nature does not abound in superfluities as neither does she fail in necessaries. Therefore no law is natural to man.

Obj. 2: Further, by the law man is directed, in his acts, to the end, as stated above (Q. 90, A. 2). But the directing of human acts to their end is not a function of nature, as is the case in irrational creatures, which act for an end solely by their natural appetite; whereas man acts for an end by his reason and will. Therefore no law is natural to man.

Obj. 3: Further, the more a man is free, the less is he under the law. But man is freer than all the animals, on account of his free-will, with which he is endowed above all other animals. Since therefore other animals are not subject to a natural law, neither is man subject to a natural law.

On the contrary, A gloss on Rom. 2:14: "When the Gentiles, who have not the law, do by nature those things that are of the law," comments as follows:

"Although they have no written law, yet they have the natural law, whereby each one knows, and is conscious of, what is good and what is evil."

I answer that, As stated above (Q. 90, A. 1, ad 1), law, being a rule and measure, can be in a person in two ways: in one way, as in him that rules and measures; in another way, as in that which is ruled and measured, since a thing is ruled and measured, in so far as it partakes of the rule or measure. Wherefore, since all things subject to Divine providence are ruled and measured by the eternal law, as was stated above (A. 1); it is evident that all things partake somewhat of the eternal law, in so far as, namely, from its being imprinted on them, they derive their respective inclinations to their proper acts and ends. Now among all others, the rational creature is subject to Divine providence in the most excellent way, in so far as it partakes of a share of providence, by being provident both for itself and for others. Wherefore it has a share of the Eternal Reason, whereby it has a natural inclination to its proper act and end: and this participation of the eternal law in the rational creature is called the natural law. Hence the Psalmist after saying (Ps. 4:6): "Offer up the sacrifice of justice," as though someone asked what the works of justice are, adds: "Many say, Who showeth us good things?" in answer to which question he says: "The light of Thy countenance, O Lord, is signed upon us": thus implying that the light of natural reason, whereby we discern what is good and what is evil, which is the function of the natural law, is nothing else than an imprint on us of the Divine light. It is therefore evident that the natural law is nothing else than the rational creature's participation of the eternal law.

Reply Obj. 1: This argument would hold, if the natural law were something different from the eternal law: whereas it is nothing but a participation thereof, as stated above.

Reply Obj. 2: Every act of reason and will in us is based on that which is according to nature, as stated above (Q. 10, A. 1): for every act of reasoning is based on principles that are known naturally, and every act of appetite in respect of the means is derived from the natural appetite in respect of the last end. Accordingly the first direction of our acts to their end must needs be in virtue of the natural law.

Reply Obj. 3: Even irrational animals partake in their own way of the Eternal Reason, just as the rational creature does. But because the rational creature partakes thereof in an intellectual and rational manner, therefore the participation of the eternal law in the rational creature is properly called a law, since a law is something pertaining to reason, as stated above (Q. 90, A. 1).

Irrational creatures, however, do not partake thereof in a rational manner, wherefore there is no participation of the eternal law in them, except by way of similitude.

QUESTION 92
Of The Effects of Law (In Two Articles)

We must now consider the effects of law; under which head there are two points of inquiry:

(1)   Whether an effect of law is to make men good?

(2)   Whether the effects of law are to command, to forbid, to permit, and to punish, as the Jurist states?

First Article [I-II, Q. 92, Art. 1]

Whether an Effect of Law Is to Make Men Good?

Objection 1: It seems that it is not an effect of law to make men good. For men are good through virtue, since virtue, as stated in *Ethic*, ii, 6 is "that which makes its subject good." But virtue is in man from God alone, because He it is Who "works it in us without us," as we stated above (Q. 55, A. 4) in giving the definition of virtue. Therefore the law does not make men good.

Obj. 2: Further, Law does not profit a man unless he obeys it. But the very fact that a man obeys a law is due to his being good. Therefore in man goodness is presupposed to the law. Therefore the law does not make men good.

Obj. 3: Further, Law is ordained to the common good, as stated above (Q. 90, A. 2). But some behave well in things regarding the community, who behave ill in things regarding themselves. Therefore it is not the business of the law to make men good.

Obj. 4: Further, some laws are tyrannical, as the Philosopher says (Polit. iii, 6). But a tyrant does not intend the good of his subjects, but considers only his own profit. Therefore law does not make men good.

On the contrary, The Philosopher says (Ethic, ii, 1) that the "intention of every lawgiver is to make good citizens."

I answer that, as stated above (Q. 90, A. 1, ad 2; AA. 3, 4), a law is nothing else than a dictate of reason in the ruler by whom his subjects are governed. Now the virtue of any subordinate thing consists in its being well subordinated to that by which it is regulated: thus we see that the virtue of the irascible and concupiscible faculties consists in their being obedient to reason; and accordingly "the virtue of every subject consists in his being well subjected to his ruler," as the Philosopher says (Polit. i). But every law aims at being obeyed by those who are subject to it. Consequently it is evident that the proper effect of law is to lead its subjects to their proper virtue: and since virtue is "that which makes its subject good," it follows that the proper effect of law is to make those to whom it is given, good, either simply or in some particular respect. For if the intention of the lawgiver is fixed on true good, which is the common good regulated according to Divine justice, it follows that the effect of the law is to make men good simply. If, however, the intention of the lawgiver is fixed on that which is not simply good, but useful or pleasurable to himself, or in opposition to Divine justice; then the law does not make men good simply, but in respect to that particular government. In this way good is found even in things that are bad of themselves: thus a man is called a good robber, because he works in a way that is adapted to his end.

Reply Obj. 1: Virtue is twofold, as explained above (Q. 63, A. 2), viz. acquired and infused. Now the fact of being accustomed to an action contributes to both, but in different ways; for it causes the acquired virtue; while it disposes to infused virtue, and preserves and fosters it when it already exists. And since law is given for the purpose of directing human acts; as far as human acts conduce to virtue, so far does law make men good. Wherefore the Philosopher says in the second book of the Politics (Ethic. ii) that "lawgivers make men good by habituating them to good works."

Reply Obj. 2: It is not always through perfect goodness of virtue that one obeys the law, but sometimes it is through fear of punishment, and sometimes from the mere dictates of reason, which is a beginning of virtue, as stated above (Q. 63, A. 1).

Reply Obj. 3: The goodness of any part is considered in comparison with the whole; hence Augustine says (Confess, iii) that "unseemly is the part that harmonizes not with the whole." Since then every man is a part of the state, it is impossible that a man be good, unless he be well proportionate to the common good: nor can the whole be well consistent unless its parts be proportionate to it. Consequently the common good of the state cannot flourish, unless the citizens be virtuous, at least those whose business it is to govern. But it is enough for the good of the community, that the other citizens be so far virtuous that they obey the commands of their rulers. Hence the Philosopher says (Polit. ii, 2) that "the virtue of a sovereign is the same as that of a good man, but the virtue of any common citizen is not the same as that of a good man."

Reply Obj. 4: A tyrannical law, through not being according to reason, is not a law, absolutely speaking, but rather a perversion of law; and yet in so far as it is something in the nature of a law, it aims at the citizens' being good. For all it has in the nature of a law consists in its being an ordinance made by a superior to his subjects, and aims at being obeyed by them, which is to make them good, not simply, but with respect to that particular government.

QUESTION 94
Of The Natural Law (In Six Articles)

We must now consider the natural law; concerning which there are six points of inquiry:
  (1) What is the natural law?
  (2) What are the precepts of the natural law?
  (3) Whether all acts of virtue are prescribed by the natural law?
  (4) Whether the natural law is the same in all?
  (5) Whether it is changeable?
  (6) Whether it can be abolished from the heart of man?

First Article [I–II, Q. 94, Art. 1]

Whether the Natural Law Is a Habit?

Objection 1: It would seem that the natural law is a habit. Because, as the Philosopher says (Ethic. ii, 5), "there are three things in the soul: power, habit, and passion." But the natural law is not one of the soul's powers: nor is it one of the passions; as we may see by going through them one by one. Therefore the natural law is a habit.

Obj. 2: Further, Basil [*Damascene, De Fide Orth. iv, 22] says that the conscience or *synderesis* "is the law of our mind"; which can only apply to the natural law. But the "synderesis" is a habit, as was shown in the First Part (Q. 79, A. 12). Therefore the natural law is a habit.

Obj. 3: Further, the natural law abides in man always, as will be shown further on (A. 6). But man's reason, which the law regards, does not always think about the natural law. Therefore the natural law is not an act, but a habit.

On the contrary, Augustine says (De Bono Conjug. xxi) that "a habit is that whereby something is done when necessary." But such is not the natural law: since it is in infants and in the damned who cannot act by it. Therefore the natural law is not a habit.

I answer that, A thing may be called a habit in two ways. First, properly and essentially: and thus the natural law is not a habit. For it has been stated above

(Q. 90, A. 1, ad 2) that the natural law is something appointed by reason, just as a proposition is a work of reason. Now that which a man does is not the same as that whereby he does it: for he makes a becoming speech by the habit of grammar. Since then a habit is that by which we act, a law cannot be a habit properly and essentially.

Secondly, the term habit may be applied to that which we hold by a habit: thus faith may mean that which we hold by faith. And accordingly, since the precepts of the natural law are sometimes considered by reason actually, while sometimes they are in the reason only habitually, in this way the natural law may be called a habit. Thus, in speculative matters, the indemonstrable principles are not the habit itself whereby we hold those principles, but are the principles the habit of which we possess.

Reply Obj. 1: The Philosopher proposes there to discover the genus of virtue; and since it is evident that virtue is a principle of action, he mentions only those things which are principles of human acts, viz. powers, habits and passions. But there are other things in the soul besides these three: there are acts; thus *to will* is in the one that wills; again, things known are in the knower; moreover its own natural properties are in the soul, such as immortality and the like.

Reply Obj. 2: *Synderesis* is said to be the law of our mind, because it is a habit containing the precepts of the natural law, which are the first principles of human actions.

Reply Obj. 3: This argument proves that the natural law is held habitually; and this is granted.

To the argument advanced in the contrary sense we reply that sometimes a man is unable to make use of that which is in him habitually, on account of some impediment: thus, on account of sleep, a man is unable to use the habit of science. In like manner, through the deficiency of his age, a child cannot use the habit of understanding of principles, or the natural law, which is in him habitually.

Second Article [I-II, Q. 94, Art. 2]

Whether the Natural Law Contains Several Precepts, or Only One?

Objection 1: It would seem that the natural law contains, not several precepts, but one only. For law is a kind of precept, as stated above (Q. 92, A. 2). If therefore there were many precepts of the natural law, it would follow that there are also many natural laws.

Obj. 2: Further, the natural law is consequent to human nature. But human nature, as a whole, is one; though, as to its parts, it is manifold. Therefore, either there is but one precept of the law of nature, on account of the unity of nature as a whole; or there are many, by reason of the number of parts of human nature. The result would be that even things relating to the inclination of the concupiscible faculty belong to the natural law.

Obj. 3: Further, law is something pertaining to reason, as stated above (Q. 90, A. 1). Now reason is but one in man. Therefore there is only one precept of the natural law.

On the contrary, The precepts of the natural law in man stand in relation to practical matters, as the first principles to matters of demonstration. But there are several first indemonstrable principles. Therefore there are also several precepts of the natural law.

I answer that, As stated above (Q. 91, A. 3), the precepts of the natural law are to the practical reason, what the first principles of demonstrations are to the speculative reason; because both are self-evident principles. Now a thing is said to be self-evident in two ways: first, in itself; secondly, in relation to us. Any proposition is said to be self-evident in itself, if its predicate is contained in the notion of the subject: although, to one who knows not the definition of the subject, it happens that such a proposition is not self-evident. For instance, this proposition, "Man is a rational being," is, in its very nature, self-evident, since who says "man," says "a rational being": and yet to one who knows not what a man is, this proposition is not self-evident. Hence it is that, as Boethius says (De Hebdom.), certain axioms or propositions are universally self-evident to all; and such are those propositions whose terms are known to all, as, "Every whole is greater than its part," and, "Things equal to one and the same are equal to one another." But some propositions are self-evident only to the wise, who understand the meaning of the terms of such propositions: thus to one who understands that an angel is not a body, it is self-evident that an angel is not circumscriptively in a place: but this is not evident to the unlearned, for they cannot grasp it.

Now a certain order is to be found in those things that are apprehended universally. For that which, before aught else, falls under apprehension, is *being,* the notion of which is included in all things whatsoever a man apprehends. Wherefore the first indemonstrable principle is that "the same thing cannot be affirmed and denied at the same time," which is based on the notion of *being* and *not-being:* and on this principle all others are based, as is stated in *Metaph.* iv, text. 9. Now as *being* is the first thing that falls under the apprehension simply, so *good* is the first thing that falls under the apprehension of the practical reason, which is directed to action: since every agent acts for an end under the aspect of good. Consequently the first principle of practical reason is one founded on the notion of good, viz. that "good is that which all things seek after." Hence this is the first precept of law, that "good is to be done and pursued, and evil is to be avoided." All other precepts of the natural law are based upon this: so that whatever the practical reason naturally apprehends as man's good (or evil) belongs to the precepts of the natural law as something to be done or avoided.

Since, however, good has the nature of an end, and evil, the nature of a contrary, hence it is that all those things to which man has a natural inclination, are naturally apprehended by reason as being good, and consequently as objects of pursuit, and their contraries as evil, and objects of avoidance. Wherefore according to the order of natural inclinations, is the order of the precepts of the natural law. Because in man there is first of all an inclination to good in accordance with the nature which he has in common with all substances: inasmuch as every substance seeks the preservation of its own being, according to its nature: and by reason of this inclination, whatever is a means of preserving human life, and of warding off its obstacles, belongs to the natural law. Secondly, there is in man an inclination to things that pertain to him more specially, according to that nature which he has in common with other animals: and in virtue of this inclination, those things are said to belong to the natural law, "which nature has taught to all animals" [*Pandect. Just. I, tit. i], such as sexual intercourse, education of offspring and so forth. Thirdly, there is in man an inclination to good, according to the nature of his reason, which nature is proper to him: thus man has a natural inclination to know the truth about God, and to live in society: and in this respect, whatever pertains to this inclination belongs to the natural law; for instance, to shun ignorance, to avoid offending those among whom one has to live, and other such things regarding the above inclination.

Reply Obj. 1: All these precepts of the law of nature have the character of one natural law, inasmuch as they flow from one first precept.

Reply Obj. 2: All the inclinations of any parts whatsoever of human nature, e.g. of the concupiscible and irascible parts, in so far as they are ruled by reason, belong to the natural law, and are reduced to one first precept, as stated above: so that the precepts of the natural law are many in themselves, but are based on one common foundation.

Reply Obj. 3: Although reason is one in itself, yet it directs all things regarding man; so that whatever can be ruled by reason, is contained under the law of reason.

∽

St. Thomas Aquinas, *Summa Theologica*

1. How does Aquinas define "law"? What are the differences between the eternal, divine, and natural laws?
2. Explain the First Precept of the Natural Law.
3. What are the basic tendencies that Aquinas uses to identify the basic goods? What would his list tell us are good things to do? What should we avoid?

SUGGESTIONS FOR FURTHER READING OR VIEWING

Finnis, John. *Natural Law and Natural Rights*. Oxford: Oxford University Press, 1980.

Natural Rights and the Social Contract

INTRODUCTION TO RIGHTS AND THE SOCIAL CONTRACT

This section introduces readings on two of the most important ideas in modern moral philosophy: the idea of the social contract and the idea of natural rights. Appealing to rights has become one of the most common and important ways to frame and debate moral issues. The language of human or natural rights features prominently in the stirring claims of the founding documents of modern democracies such as America's Declaration of Independence and France's Declaration of the Rights of Man. Contemporary international treaties such as the United Nations Universal Declaration of Human Rights build on these texts, as do conventions extending the recognition of rights to children, such as the United Nations Convention on the Rights of the Child. Similarly, since feminists first began to call attention to the mistreatment of and discrimination against women, the appeal to women's rights has been essential. Even those who would urge us to consider our moral duties to nonhuman animals frequently couch their appeals in the language of rights. In this chapter we present selections from three texts that have made lasting contributions to this moral tradition.

Talk of rights raises questions of the source and extent of those rights. On what basis can we claim that all humans share the same basic rights, and what rights can they claim? Our readings consider two ways in which these questions have been explored. One is by way of the important model of a social contract. Appearing first as a means of thinking about the source of legitimate political power, the social contract tradition derives our obligations to one another from agreements we would enter into as free and equal agents. A distinct tradition of thinking about rights draws on Utilitarianism.

We begin with selections from Thomas Hobbes' *Leviathan*. Hobbes (1588–1679) lived in England during unsettled times. Concerned that popular uprising against the king of England threatened the political stability of the British government, Hobbes looked to defend the absolute power of the monarchy.

While this may not seem like a promising start to a tradition devoted to human rights, Hobbes introduces some essential building blocks of modern social contract thinking. Specifically, Hobbes tries to show how the power of the state ultimately derives from the consent of those governed by conceiving it as an agreement that free persons enter into in order to escape a hostile "state of nature." Although we are free and equal in such a state, our security and well-being is always precarious, and there is little hope for the kind of cooperative endeavors that make life comfortable and rewarding. With this, Hobbes introduces the idea that our duties to one another turn on our being by nature free and equal—any rules we are bound by are ones we ourselves accept.

John Locke was also responding to events in England and, like Hobbes, was interested in discovering the true basis of legitimate political power. Adopting to his own purposes the idea of a state of nature in which humans are all free and equal, Locke departs from Hobbes by arguing that in fact we enjoy moral protections even before we agree to be governed by the state. Appealing to a version of natural law theory, Locke introduces the idea—familiar to anyone who has considered the most famous passage of the Declaration of Independence—that by nature we enjoy basic rights and freedom, and that it is the task of the state to protect those rights. With this comes a fundamental right to rebel against the government when it becomes a threat to our rights rather than a protector. Locke's vision of the state as a protector of our natural rights entails its legitimate reach is limited so that essential parts of our lives are beyond the proper control of the government. This idea of limited government constrains the reach of the state, allowing the individual complete control the private sphere. This is an early formulation of the idea, which we will also see in the work of Kant, that our rights derive from our autonomy as individuals.

As a Utilitarian, John Stuart Mill cannot appeal directly to the claim that by nature we enjoy basic rights. What he does argue in the selection here is that there is great utility granting individuals a significant degree of freedom from interference, either by the state or by individuals, as they live lives they choose for themselves. For Mill this means each of us should be free to do as we please so long as we do not harm others, a principle commonly referred to as the "harm principle." Adherence to the harm principle, Mill argues, will allow "experiments in living" that will ultimately benefit society as a whole.

Leviathan

Thomas Hobbes

CHAP. XIII

Of the NATURALL CONDITION of Mankind, as concerning their Felicity, and Misery

Men by nature NATURE hath made men so equall, in the faculties of body, and mind; as that
Equall though there bee found one man sometimes manifestly stronger in body, or of quicker mind then another; yet when all is reckoned together, the difference between man, and man, is not so considerable, as that one man can thereupon claim to himselfe any benefit, to which another may not pretend, as well as he. For as to the strength of body, the weakest has strength enough to kill the strongest, either by secret machination, or by confederacy with others, that are in the same danger with himselfe.

And as to the faculties of the mind, (setting aside the arts grounded upon words, and especially that skill of proceeding upon generall, and infallible rules, called Science; which very few have, and but in few things; as being not a native faculty, born with us; nor attained, (as Prudence,) while we look after somewhat els,) I find yet a greater equality amongst men, than that of strength. For Prudence, is but Experience; which equall time, equally bestowes on all men, in [61] those things they equally apply themselves unto. That which may perhaps make such equality incredible, is but a vain conceit of ones owne wisdome, which almost all men think they have in a greater degree, than the Vulgar; that is, than all men but themselves, and a few others, whom by Fame, or for concurring with themselves, they approve. For such is the nature of men, that howsoever they may acknowledge many others to be more witty, or more

Thomas Hobbes, Selections from *Leviathan*.

eloquent, or more learned; Yet they will hardly believe there be many so wise as themselves: For they see their own wit at hand, and other mens at a distance. But this proveth rather that men are in that point equall, than unequall. For there is not ordinarily a greater signe of the equall distribution of any thing, than that every man is contented with his share.

From this equality of ability, ariseth equality of hope in the attaining of our *From Equality* Ends. And therefore if any two men desire the same thing, which neverthelesse *proceeds Diffidence* they cannot both enjoy, they become enemies; and in the way to their End, (which is principally their owne conservation, and sometimes their delectation only,) endeavour to destroy, or subdue one an other. And from hence it comes to passe, that where an Invader hath no more to feare, than an other mans single power; if one plant, sow, build, or possesse a convenient Seat, others may probably be expected to come prepared with forces united, to dispossesse, and deprive him, not only of the fruit of his labour, but also of his life, or liberty. And the Invader again is in the like danger of another.

And from this diffidence of one another, there is no way for any man to *From Diffi-* secure himselfe, so reasonable, as Anticipation; that is, by force, or wiles, to *dence Warre* master the persons of all men he can, so long, till he see no other power great enough to endanger him: And this is no more than his own conservation requireth, and is generally allowed. Also because there be some, that taking pleasure in contemplating their own power in the acts of conquest, which they pursue farther than their security requires; if others, that otherwise would be glad to be at ease within modest bounds, should not by invasion increase their power, they would not be able, long time, by standing only on their defence, to subsist. And by consequence, such augmentation of dominion over men, being necessary to a mans conservation, it ought to be allowed him.

Againe, men have no pleasure, (but on the contrary a great deale of griefe) in keeping company, where there is no power able to over-awe them all. For every man looketh that his companion should value him, at the same rate he sets upon himselfe: And upon all signes of contempt, or undervaluing, naturally endeavours, as far as he dares (which amongst them that have no common power, to keep them in quiet, is far enough to make them destroy each other,) to extort a greater value from his contemners, by dommage; and from others, by the example.

So that in the nature of man, we find three principall causes of quarrell. First, Competition; Secondly, Diffidence; Thirdly, Glory.

[62] The first, maketh men invade for Gain; the second, for Safety; and the third, for Reputation. The first use Violence, to make themselves Masters of other mens persons, wives, children, and cattell; the second, to defend them; the third, for trifles, as a word, a smile, a different opinion, and any other signe of undervalue, either direct in their Persons, or by reflexion in their Kindred, their Friends, their Nation, their Profession, or their Name.

Out of Civil States, there is always Warre of every one against every one Hereby it is manifest, that during the time men live without a common Power to keep them all in awe, they are in that condition which is called WARRE; and such a warre, as is of every man, against every man. For Warre, consisteth not in Battell onely, or the act of fighting; but in a tract of time, wherein the Will to contend by Battell is sufficiently known: and therefore the notion of *Time*, is to be considered in the nature of Warre; as it is in the nature of Weather. For as the nature of Foule weather, lyeth not in a showre or two of rain; but in an inclination thereto of many dayes together: So the nature of War, consisteth not in actuall fighting; but in the known disposition thereto, during all the time there is no assurance to the contrary. All other time is PEACE.

The Incommodites of such a War Whatsoever therefore is consequent to a time of Warre, where every man is Enemy to every man; the same is consequent to the time, wherein men live without other security, than what their own strength, and their own invention shall furnish them withall. In such condition, there is no place for Industry; because the fruit thereof is uncertain: and consequently no Culture of the Earth; no Navigation, nor use of the commodities that may be imported by Sea; no commodious Building; no Instruments of moving, and removing such things as require much force; no Knowledge of the face of the Earth; no account of Time; no Arts; no Letters; no Society; and which is worst of all, continuall feare, and danger of violent death; And the life of man, solitary, poore, nasty, brutish, and short.

It may seem strange to some man, that has not well weighed these things; that Nature should thus dissociate, and render men apt to invade, and destroy one another: and he may therefore, not trusting to this Inference, made from the Passions, desire perhaps to have the same confirmed by Experience. Let him therefore consider with himselfe, when taking a journey, he armes himselfe, and seeks to go well accompanied; when going to sleep, he locks his dores; when even in his house he locks his chests; and this when he knows there bee Lawes, and publike Officers, armed, to revenge all injuries shall bee done him; what opinion he has of his fellow subjects, when he rides armed; of his fellow Citizens, when he locks his dores; and of his children, and servants, when he locks his chests. Does he not there as much accuse mankind by his actions, as I do by my words? But neither of us accuse mans nature in it. The Desires, and other Passions of man, are in themselves no Sin. No more are the Actions, that proceed from those Passions, till they know a Law that forbids them: which till Lawes be made they cannot know: nor can any Law be made, till they have agreed upon the Person that shall make it.

[63] It may peradventure be thought, there was never such a time, nor condition of warre as this; and I believe it was never generally so, over all the world: but there are many places, where they live so now. For the savage people in many places of *America*, except the government of small Families, the

concord whereof dependeth on naturall lust, have no government at all; and live at this day in that brutish manner, as I said before. Howsoever, it may be perceived what manner of life there would be, where there were no common Power to feare; by the manner of life, which men that have formerly lived under a peacefull government, use to degenerate into, in a civill Warre.

But though there had never been any time, wherein particular men were in a condition of warre one against another; yet in all times, Kings, and Persons of Soveraigne authority, because of their Independency, are in continuall jealousies, and in the state and posture of Gladiators; having their weapons pointing, and their eyes fixed on one another; that is, their Forts, Garrisons, and Guns upon the Frontiers of their Kingdomes; and continuall Spyes upon their neighbours; which is a posture of War. But because they uphold thereby, the Industry of their Subjects; there does not follow from it, that misery, which accompanies the Liberty of particular men.

To this warre of every man against every man, this also is consequent; that nothing can be Unjust. The notions of Right and Wrong, Justice and Injustice have there no place. Where there is no common Power, there is no Law: where no Law, no Injustice. Force, and Fraud, are in warre the two Cardinall vertues. Justice, and Injustice are none of the Faculties neither of the Body, nor Mind. If they were, they might be in a man that were alone in the world, as well as his Senses, and Passions. They are Qualities, that relate to men in Society, not in Solitude. It is consequent also to the same condition, that there be no Propriety, no Dominion, no *Mine* and *Thine* distinct; but onely that to be every mans that he can get; and for so long, as he can keep it. And thus much for the ill condition, which man by meer Nature is actually placed in; though with a possiblity to come out of it, consisting partly in the Passions, partly in his Reason. *In such a Warre, nothing is Unjust*

The Passions that encline men to Peace, are Feare of Death; Desire of such things as are necessary to commodious living; and a Hope by their Industry to obtain them. And Reason suggesteth convenient Articles of Peace, upon which men may be drawn to agreement. These Articles, are they, which otherwise are called the Lawes of Nature: whereof I shall speak more particularly, in the two following Chapters. [64] *The Passions that incline men to Peace*

CHAP. XIV

Of the first and second Naturall Lawes, and of Contracts

THE RIGHT OF NATURE, which Writers commonly call *Jus Naturale*, is the Liberty each man hath, to use his own power, as he will himselfe, for the preservation of his own Nature; that is to say, of his own Life; and consequently, of *Right of Nature what* doing any thing, which in his own Judgement, and Reason, hee shall conceive to be the aptest means thereunto.

Liberty what

By Liberty, is understood, according to the proper signification of the word, the absence of externall Impediments: which Impediments, may oft take away part of a mans power to do what hee would; but cannot hinder him from using the power left him, according as his judgement, and reason shall dictate to him.

A Law of Nature what

A Law Of Nature, (*Lex Naturalis,*) is a Precept, or generall Rule, found out by Reason, by which a man is forbidden to do, that, which is destructive of his life, or taketh away the means of preserving the same; and to omit, that, by which he thinketh it may be best preserved. For though they that speak of this subject, use to confound *Jus*, and *Lex, Right* and *Law*; yet they ought to be distinguished;

Difference of Right and Law

because Right, consisteth in liberty to do, or to forbeare; Whereas Law, determineth, and bindeth to one of them: so that Law, and Right, differ as much, as Obligation, and Liberty; which in one and the same matter are inconsistent.

Naturally every man has Right to everything

And because the condition of Man, (as hath been declared in the precedent Chapter) is a condition of Warre of every one against every one; in which case every one is governed by his own Reason; and there is nothing he can make use of, that may not be a help unto him, in preserving his life against his enemyes; It followeth, that in such a condition, every man has a Right to every thing; even to one anothers body. And therefore, as long as this naturall Right of every man to every thing endureth, there can be no security to any man, (how strong or wise soever he be,) of living out the time, which Nature ordinarily alloweth men to live. And consequently it is a precept, or generall

The Fundamentall Law of Nature

rule of Reason, *That every man, ought to endeavour Peace, as farre as he has hope of obtaining it; and when he cannot obtain it, that he may seek, and use, all helps, and advantages of Warre.* The first branch of which Rule, containeth the first, and Fundamentall Law of Nature; which is, *to seek Peace, and follow it.* The Second, the summe of the Right of Nature; which is, *By all means we can, to defend our selves.*

The second Law of Nature

From this Fundamentall Law of Nature, by which men are commanded to endeavour Peace, is derived this second Law; *That a man be willing, when others are so too, as farre-forth, as for Peace, and* [65] *defence of himselfe he shall think it necessary, to lay down this right to all things; and be contented with so much liberty against other men, as he would allow other men against himselfe.* For as long as every man holdeth this Right, of doing any thing he liketh; so long are all men in the condition of Warre. But if other men will not lay down their Right, as well as he; then there is no Reason for any one, to devest himselfe of his: For that were to expose himselfe to Prey, (which no man is bound to) rather than to dispose himselfe to Peace. This is that Law of the Gospel; *Whatsoever you require that others should do to you, that do ye to them.* And that Law of all men, *Quod tibi fieri non vis, alteri ne feceris.*

To *lay downe* a mans *Right* to any thing, is to *devest* himselfe of the *Liberty,* of hindring another of the benefit of his own Right to the same. For he that renounceth, or passeth away his Right, giveth not to any other man a Right which he had not before; because there is nothing to which every man had not Right by Nature: but onely standeth out of his way, that he may enjoy his own originall Right, without hindrance from him; not without hindrance from another. So that the effect which redoundeth to one man, by another mans defect of Right, is but so much diminution of impediments to the use of his own Right originall.

What it is to lay down a Right

OF COMMON-WEALTH
CHAP. XVII
Of the Causes, Generation, and Definition of a Common-Wealth

THE finall Cause, End, or Designe of men, (who naturally love Liberty, and Dominion over others,) in the introduction of that restraint upon themselves, (in which wee see them live in Common-wealths,) is the foresight of their own preservation, and of a more contented life thereby; that is to say, of getting themselves out from that miserable condition of Warre, which is necessarily consequent (as hath been shewn) to the naturall Passions of men, when there is no visible Power to keep them in awe, and tye them by feare of punishment to the performance of their Covenants, and observation of those Lawes of Nature set down in the fourteenth and fifteenth Chapters.

The End of Common-wealth, particular Security:

Chap. 13

For the Lawes of Nature (as *Justice, Equity, Modesty, Mercy,* and (in summe) *doing to others, as wee would be done to,*) of themselves, without the terrour of some Power, to cause them to be observed, are contrary to our naturall Passions, that carry us to Partiality, Pride, Revenge, and the like. And Covenants, without the Sword, are but Words, and of no strength to secure a man at all. Therefore notwithstanding the Lawes of Nature, (which every one hath then kept, when he has the will to keep them, when he can do it safely,) if there be no Power erected, or not great enough for our security; every man will and may lawfully rely on his own strength and art, for caution against all other men. And in all places, where men have lived by small Families, to robbe and spoyle one another, has been a Trade, and so farre from being reputed against the Law of Nature, that the greater spoyles they gained, the greater was their honour; and men observed no other Lawes therein, but the Lawes of Honour; that is, to abstain from cruelty, leaving to men their lives, and instruments of husbandry. And as small Familyes did then; so now do Cities and Kingdomes which are but greater Families (for their own security) enlarge their Dominions, upon all pretences of danger, and fear of Invasion, or assistance that may be

Which is not to be had from the Law of Nature:

given to Invaders, endeavour as much as they can, to subdue, or weaken their neighbours, by open force, and secret arts, for want of other Caution, justly; and are remembred for it in after ages with honour.

Nor from the conjunction of a few men or familyes: Nor is it the joyning together of a small number of men, that gives them this security; because in small numbers, small additions [86] on the one side or the other, make the advantage of strength so great, as is sufficient to carry the Victory; and therefore gives encouragement to an Invasion. The Multitude sufficient to confide in for our Security, is not determined by any certain number, but by comparison with the Enemy we feare; and is then sufficient, when the odds of the Enemy is not of so visible and conspicuous moment, to determine the event of warre, as to move him to attempt.

Nor from a great Multitude, unlesse directed by one judgement: And be there never so great a Multitude; yet if their actions be directed according to their particular judgements, and particular appetites, they can expect thereby no defence, nor protection, neither against a Common enemy, nor against the injuries of one another. For being distracted in opinions concerning the best use and application of their strength, they do not help, but hinder one another; and reduce their strength by mutuall opposition to nothing: whereby they are easily, not onely subdued by a very few that agree together; but also when there is no common enemy, they make warre upon each other, for their particular interests. For if we could suppose a great Multitude of men to consent in the observation of Justice, and other Lawes of Nature, without a common Power to keep them all in awe; we might as well suppose all Man-kind to do the same; and then there neither would be, nor need to be any Civill Government, or Common-wealth at all; because there would be Peace without subjection.

And that continually Nor is it enough for the security, which men desire should last all the time of their life, that they be governed, and directed by one judgement, for a limited time; as in one Battell, or one Warre. For though they obtain a Victory by their unanimous endeavour against a forraign enemy; yet afterwards, when either they have no common enemy, or he that by one part is held for an enemy, is by another part held for a friend, they must needs by the difference of their interests dissolve, and fall again into a Warre amongst themselves.

Why certain creatures without reason, or speech, do neverthelesse live in Society, without any coërcive Power It is true, that certain living creatures, as Bees, and Ants, live sociably one with another, (which are therefore by *Aristotle* numbred amongst Politicall creatures;) and yet have no other direction, than their particular judgements and appetites; nor speech, whereby one of them can signifie to another, what he thinks expedient for the common benefit: and therefore some man may perhaps desire to know, why Man-kind cannot do the same. To which I answer,

First, that men are continually in competition for Honour and Dignity, which these creatures are not; and consequently amongst men there ariseth on that ground, Envy and Hatred, and finally Warre; but amongst these not so.

Secondly, that amongst these creatures, the Common good differeth not from the Private; and being by nature enclined to their private, they procure thereby the common benefit. But man, whose Joy consisteth in comparing himselfe with other men, can relish nothing but what is eminent.

Thirdly, that these creatures, having not (as man) the use of reason, do not see, nor think they see any fault, in the administration of [87] their common businesse: whereas amongst men, there are very many, that thinke themselves wiser, and abler to govern the Publique, better than the rest; and these strive to reforme and innovate, one this way, another that way; and thereby bring it into Distraction and Civill warre.

Fourthly, that these creatures, though they have some use of voice, in making knowne to one another their desires, and other affections; yet they want that art of words, by which some men can represent to others, that which is Good, in the likenesse of Evill; and Evill, in the likenesse of Good; and augment, or diminish the apparent greatnesse of Good and Evill; discontenting men, and troubling their Peace at their pleasure.

Fiftly, irrationall creatures cannot distinguish betweene *Injury,* and *Dammage*; and therefore as long as they be at ease, they are not offended with their fellowes: whereas Man is then most troublesome, when he is most at ease: for then it is that he loves to shew his Wisdome, and controule the Actions of them that governe the Common-wealth.

Lastly, the agreement of these creatures is Naturall; that of men, is by Covenant only, which is Artificiall: and therefore it is no wonder if there be somewhat else required (besides Covenant) to make their Agreement constant and lasting; which is a Common Power, to keep them in awe, and to direct their actions to the Common Benefit.

Second Treatise on Government

John Locke

∽

CHAPTER. II.

Of The State of Nature.

Sect. 4. TO understand political power right, and derive it from its original, we must consider, what state all men are naturally in, and that is, a state of perfect freedom to order their actions, and dispose of their possessions and persons, as they think fit, within the bounds of the law of nature, without asking leave, or depending upon the will of any other man.

A state also of equality, wherein all the power and jurisdiction is reciprocal, no one having more than another; there being nothing more evident, than that creatures of the same species and rank, promiscuously born to all the same advantages of nature, and the use of the same faculties, should also be equal one amongst another without subordination or subjection, unless the lord and master of them all should, by any manifest declaration of his will, set one above another, and confer on him, by an evident and clear appointment, an undoubted right to dominion and sovereignty.

Sect. 6. But though this be a state of liberty, yet it is not a state of licence: though man in that state have an uncontroulable liberty to dispose of his person or possessions, yet he has not liberty to destroy himself, or so much as any creature in his possession, but where some nobler use than its bare preservation calls for it. The state of nature has a law of nature to govern it, which obliges every one: and reason, which is that law, teaches all mankind, who will but consult it, that being all equal and independent, no one ought to harm another in his life, health, liberty, or possessions: for men being all the workmanship of one

John Locke, Selections from *Second Treatise of Government*.

omnipotent, and infinitely wise maker; all the servants of one sovereign master, sent into the world by his order, and about his business; they are his property, whose workmanship they are, made to last during his, not one another's pleasure: and being furnished with like faculties, sharing all in one community of nature, there cannot be supposed any such subordination among us, that may authorize us to destroy one another, as if we were made for one another's uses, as the inferior ranks of creatures are for our's. Every one, as he is bound to preserve himself, and not to quit his station wilfully, so by the like reason, when his own preservation comes not in competition, ought he, as much as he can, to preserve the rest of mankind, and may not, unless it be to do justice on an offender, take away, or impair the life, or what tends to the preservation of the life, the liberty, health, limb, or goods of another.

Sect. 11. From these two distinct rights, the one of punishing the crime for restraint, and preventing the like offence, which right of punishing is in every body; the other of taking reparation, which belongs only to the injured party, comes it to pass that the magistrate, who by being magistrate hath the common right of punishing put into his hands, can often, where the public good demands not the execution of the law, remit the punishment of criminal offences by his own authority, but yet cannot remit the satisfaction due to any private man for the damage he has received. That, he who has suffered the damage has a right to demand in his own name, and he alone can remit: the damnified person has this power of appropriating to himself the goods or service of the offender, by right of self-preservation, as every man has a power to punish the crime, to prevent its being committed again, by the right he has of preserving all mankind, and doing all reasonable things he can in order to that end: and thus it is, that every man, in the state of nature, has a power to kill a murderer, both to deter others from doing the like injury, which no reparation can compensate, by the example of the punishment that attends it from every body, and also to secure men from the attempts of a criminal, who having renounced reason, the common rule and measure God hath given to mankind, hath, by the unjust violence and slaughter he hath committed upon one, declared war against all mankind, and therefore may be destroyed as a lion or a tyger, one of those wild savage beasts, with whom men can have no society nor security: and upon this is grounded that great law of nature, Whoso sheddeth man's blood, by man shall his blood be shed. And Cain was so fully convinced, that every one had a right to destroy such a criminal, that after the murder of his brother, he cries out, Every one that findeth me, shall slay me; so plain was it writ in the hearts of all mankind.

Sect. 13. To this strange doctrine, viz. That in the state of nature every one has the executive power of the law of nature, I doubt not but it will be objected, that it is unreasonable for men to be judges in their own cases, that self-love will make men partial to themselves and their friends: and on the other side, that ill nature, passion and revenge will carry them too far in punishing others; and hence nothing but confusion and disorder will follow, and that therefore God hath certainly appointed government to restrain the partiality and violence of men. I easily grant, that civil government is the proper remedy for the inconveniencies of the state of nature, which must certainly be great, where men may be judges in their own case, since it is easy to be imagined, that he who was so unjust as to do his brother an injury, will scarce be so just as to condemn himself for it: but I shall desire those who make this objection, to remember, that absolute monarchs are but men; and if government is to be the remedy of those evils, which necessarily follow from men's being judges in their own cases, and the state of nature is therefore not to be endured, I desire to know what kind of government that is, and how much better it is than the state of nature, where one man, commanding a multitude, has the liberty to be judge in his own case, and may do to all his subjects whatever he pleases, without the least liberty to any one to question or controul those who execute his pleasure? and in whatsoever he doth, whether led by reason, mistake or passion, must be submitted to? much better it is in the state of nature, wherein men are not bound to submit to the unjust will of another: and if he that judges, judges amiss in his own, or any other case, he is answerable for it to the rest of mankind.

CHAPTER. V.
Of Property.

Sect. 25. Whether we consider natural reason, which tells us, that men, being once born, have a right to their preservation, and consequently to meat and drink, and such other things as nature affords for their subsistence: or revelation, which gives us an account of those grants God made of the world to Adam, and to Noah, and his sons, it is very clear, that God, as king David says, Psal. cxv. 16. has given the earth to the children of men; given it to mankind in common. But this being supposed, it seems to some a very great difficulty, how any one should ever come to have a property in any thing: I will not content myself to answer, that if it be difficult to make out property, upon a supposition that God gave the world to Adam, and his posterity in common, it is impossible that any man, but one universal monarch, should have any property upon a supposition, that God gave the world to Adam, and his heirs in succession, exclusive of all the rest of his posterity. But I shall endeavour to shew, how men might come to have a property in several parts of that which God gave to mankind in common, and that without any express compact of all the commoners.

Sect. 26. God, who hath given the world to men in common, hath also given them reason to make use of it to the best advantage of life, and convenience. The earth, and all that is therein, is given to men for the support and comfort of their being. And tho' all the fruits it naturally produces, and beasts it feeds, belong to mankind in common, as they are produced by the spontaneous hand of nature; and no body has originally a private dominion, exclusive of the rest of mankind, in any of them, as they are thus in their natural state: yet being given for the use of men, there must of necessity be a means to appropriate them some way or other, before they can be of any use, or at all beneficial to any particular man. The fruit, or venison, which nourishes the wild Indian, who knows no enclosure, and is still a tenant in common, must be his, and so his, i.e. a part of him, that another can no longer have any right to it, before it can do him any good for the support of his life.

Sect. 27. Though the earth, and all inferior creatures, be common to all men, yet every man has a property in his own person: this no body has any right to but himself. The labour of his body, and the work of his hands, we may say, are properly his. Whatsoever then he removes out of the state that nature hath provided, and left it in, he hath mixed his labour with, and joined to it something that is his own, and thereby makes it his property. It being by him removed from the common state nature hath placed it in, it hath by this labour something annexed to it, that excludes the common right of other men: for this labour being the unquestionable property of the labourer, no man but he can have a right to what that is once joined to, at least where there is enough, and as good, left in common for others.

CHAPTER. VIII.
Of The Beginning of Political Societies.

Sect. 95. MEN being, as has been said, by nature, all free, equal, and independent, no one can be put out of this estate, and subjected to the political power of another, without his own consent. The only way whereby any one divests himself of his natural liberty, and puts on the bonds of civil society, is by agreeing with other men to join and unite into a community for their comfortable, safe, and peaceable living one amongst another, in a secure enjoyment of their properties, and a greater security against any, that are not of it. This any number of men may do, because it injures not the freedom of the rest; they are left as they were in the liberty of the state of nature. When any number of men have so consented to make one community or government, they are thereby presently incorporated, and make one body politic, wherein the majority have a right to act and conclude the rest.

Sect. 96. For when any number of men have, by the consent of every individual, made a community, they have thereby made that community one body, with a power to act as one body, which is only by the will and determination of the majority: for that which acts any community, being only the consent of the individuals of it, and it being necessary to that which is one body to move one way; it is necessary the body should move that way whither the greater force carries it, which is the consent of the majority: or else it is impossible it should act or continue one body, one community, which the consent of every individual that united into it, agreed that it should; and so every one is bound by that consent to be concluded by the majority. And therefore we see, that in assemblies, impowered to act by positive laws, where no number is set by that positive law which impowers them, the act of the majority passes for the act of the whole, and of course determines, as having, by the law of nature and reason, the power of the whole.

Sect. 97. And thus every man, by consenting with others to make one body politic under one government, puts himself under an obligation, to every one of that society, to submit to the determination of the majority, and to be concluded by it; or else this original compact, whereby he with others incorporates into one society, would signify nothing, and be no compact, if he be left free, and under no other ties than he was in before in the state of nature. For what appearance would there be of any compact? what new engagement if he were no farther tied by any decrees of the society, than he himself thought fit, and did actually consent to? This would be still as great a liberty, as he himself had before his compact, or any one else in the state of nature hath, who may submit himself, and consent to any acts of it if he thinks fit.

Sect. 98. For if the consent of the majority shall not, in reason, be received as the act of the whole, and conclude every individual; nothing but the consent of every individual can make any thing to be the act of the whole: but such a consent is next to impossible ever to be had, if we consider the infirmities of health, and avocations of business, which in a number, though much less than that of a commonwealth, will necessarily keep many away from the public assembly. To which if we add the variety of opinions, and contrariety of interests, which unavoidably happen in all collections of men, the coming into society upon such terms would be only like Cato's coming into the theatre, only to go out again. Such a constitution as this would make the mighty Leviathan of a shorter duration, than the feeblest creatures, and not let it outlast the day it was born in: which cannot be supposed, till we can think, that rational creatures should desire and constitute societies only to be dissolved: for where the majority cannot conclude the rest, there they cannot act as one body, and consequently will be immediately dissolved again.

Sect. 99. Whosoever therefore out of a state of nature unite into a community, must be understood to give up all the power, necessary to the ends for which they unite into society, to the majority of the community, unless they expresly agreed in any number greater than the majority. And this is done by barely agreeing to unite into one political society, which is all the compact that is, or needs be, between the individuals, that enter into, or make up a commonwealth. And thus that, which begins and actually constitutes any political society, is nothing but the consent of any number of freemen capable of a majority to unite and incorporate into such a society. And this is that, and that only, which did, or could give beginning to any lawful government in the world.

Sect. 100. To this I find two objections made. First, That there are no instances to be found in story, of a company of men independent, and equal one amongst another, that met together, and in this way began and set up a government.

Secondly, It is impossible of right, that men should do so, because all men being born under government, they are to submit to that, and are not at liberty to begin a new one.

CHAPTER. IX.
Of The Ends of Political Society
and Government.

Sect. 123. IF man in the state of nature be so free, as has been said; if he be absolute lord of his own person and possessions, equal to the greatest, and subject to no body, why will he part with his freedom? why will he give up this empire, and subject himself to the dominion and controul of any other power? To which it is obvious to answer, that though in the state of nature he hath such a right, yet the enjoyment of it is very uncertain, and constantly exposed to the invasion of others: for all being kings as much as he, every man his equal, and the greater part no strict observers of equity and justice, the enjoyment of the property he has in this state is very unsafe, very unsecure. This makes him willing to quit a condition, which, however free, is full of fears and continual dangers: and it is not without reason, that he seeks out, and is willing to join in society with others, who are already united, or have a mind to unite, for the mutual preservation of their lives, liberties and estates, which I call by the general name, property.

Sect. 221. There is therefore, secondly, another way whereby governments are dissolved, and that is, when the legislative, or the prince, either of them, act contrary to their trust. First, The legislative acts against the trust reposed in them, when they endeavour to invade the property of the subject, and to make themselves, or any part of the community, masters, or arbitrary disposers of the lives, liberties, or fortunes of the people.

Sect. 222. The reason why men enter into society, is the preservation of their property; and the end why they chuse and authorize a legislative, is, that there may be laws made, and rules set, as guards and fences to the properties of all the members of the society, to limit the power, and moderate the dominion, of every part and member of the society: for since it can never be supposed to be the will of the society, that the legislative should have a power to destroy that which every one designs to secure, by entering into society, and for which the people submitted themselves to legislators of their own making; whenever the legislators endeavour to take away, and destroy the property of the people, or to reduce them to slavery under arbitrary power, they put themselves into a state of war with the people, who are thereupon absolved from any farther obedience, and are left to the common refuge, which God hath provided for all men, against force and violence. Whensoever therefore the legislative shall transgress this fundamental rule of society; and either by ambition, fear, folly or corruption, endeavour to grasp themselves, or put into the hands of any other, an absolute power over the lives, liberties, and estates of the people; by this breach of trust they forfeit the power the people had put into their hands for quite contrary ends, and it devolves to the people, who have a right to resume their original liberty, and, by the establishment of a new legislative, (such as they shall think fit) provide for their own safety and security, which is the end for which they are in society. What I have said here, concerning the legislative in general, holds true also concerning the supreme executor, who having a double trust put in him, both to have a part in the legislative, and the supreme execution of the law, acts against both, when he goes about to set up his own arbitrary will as the law of the society. He acts also contrary to his trust, when he either employs the force, treasure, and offices of the society, to corrupt the representatives, and gain them to his purposes; or openly preengages the electors, and prescribes to their choice, such, whom he has, by sollicitations, threats, promises, or otherwise, won to his designs; and employs them to bring in such, who have promised before-hand what to vote, and what to enact. Thus to regulate candidates and electors, and new-model the ways of election, what is it but to cut up the government by the roots, and poison the very fountain of public security? for the people having reserved to themselves the choice of their representatives, as the fence to their properties, could do it for no other end, but that they might always be freely chosen, and so chosen, freely act, and advise, as the necessity of the commonwealth, and the public good should, upon examination, and mature debate, be judged to require. This, those who give their votes before they hear the debate, and have weighed the reasons on all sides, are not capable of doing. To prepare such an assembly as this, and endeavour to set up the declared abettors of his own will, for the true representatives of the people, and the law-makers of the society, is certainly as great a breach of trust, and as perfect a declaration of a design to subvert the government, as is possible to be met with. To which, if one shall add rewards and punishments visibly employed to the same end, and all the arts of perverted law made use of, to take off and destroy all that stand in the way of such a design, and will not comply and consent to betray the liberties of their country, it will be past doubt what is doing. What power they ought to have in the society, who thus employ it contrary to the trust went along with it in its first institution, is easy to determine; and one cannot but see, that he, who has once attempted any such thing as this, cannot any longer be trusted.

READING 3.10

On Liberty

by John Stuart Mill

The object of this Essay is to assert one very simple principle, as entitled to govern absolutely the dealings of society with the individual in the way of compulsion and control, whether the means used be physical force in the form of legal penalties, or the moral coercion of public opinion. That principle is, that the sole end for which mankind are warranted, individually or collectively in interfering with the liberty of action of any of their number, is self-protection. That the only purpose for which power can be rightfully exercised over any member of a civilized community, against his will, is to prevent harm to others. His own good, either physical or moral, is not a sufficient warrant. He cannot rightfully be compelled to do or forbear because it will be better for him to do so, because it will make him happier, because, in the opinions of others, to do so would be wise, or even right. These are good reasons for remonstrating with him, or reasoning with him, or persuading him, or entreating him, but not for compelling him, or visiting him with any evil, in case he do otherwise. To justify that, the conduct from which it is desired to deter him must be calculated to produce evil to some one else. The only part of the conduct of any one, for which he is amenable to society, is that which concerns others. In the part which merely concerns himself, his independence is, of right, absolute. Over himself, over his own body and mind, the individual is sovereign.

It is, perhaps, hardly necessary to say that this doctrine is meant to apply only to human beings in the maturity of their faculties. We are not speaking of children, or of young persons below the age which the law may fix as that of manhood or womanhood. Those who are still in a state to require being taken care of by others, must be protected against their own actions as well as against external injury. For the same reason, we may leave out of consideration those backward states of society in which the race itself may be considered as

John Stuart Mill, Selection from *On Liberty*.

in its nonage. The early difficulties in the way of spontaneous progress are so great, that there is seldom any choice of means for overcoming them; and a ruler full of the spirit of improvement is warranted in the use of any expedients that will attain an end, perhaps otherwise unattainable. Despotism is a legitimate mode of government in dealing with barbarians, provided the end be their improvement, and the means justified by actually effecting that end. Liberty, as a principle, has no application to any state of things anterior to the time when mankind have become capable of being improved by free and equal discussion. Until then, there is nothing for them but implicit obedience to an Akbar or a Charlemagne, if they are so fortunate as to find one. But as soon as mankind have attained the capacity of being guided to their own improvement by conviction or persuasion (a period long since reached in all nations with whom we need here concern ourselves), compulsion, either in the direct form or in that of pains and penalties for non-compliance, is no longer admissible as a means to their own good, and justifiable only for the security of others.

It is proper to state that I forego any advantage which could be derived to my argument from the idea of abstract right as a thing independent of utility. I regard utility as the ultimate appeal on all ethical questions; but it must be utility in the largest sense, grounded on the permanent interests of man as a progressive being. Those interests, I contend, authorize the subjection of individual spontaneity to external control, only in respect to those actions of each, which concern the interest of other people. If any one does an act hurtful to others, there is a prima facie case for punishing him, by law, or, where legal penalties are not safely applicable, by general disapprobation. There are also many positive acts for the benefit of others, which he may rightfully be compelled to perform; such as, to give evidence in a court of justice; to bear his fair share in the common defence, or in any other joint work necessary to the interest of the society of which he enjoys the protection; and to perform certain acts of individual beneficence, such as saving a fellow-creature's life, or interposing to protect the defenceless against ill-usage, things which whenever it is obviously a man's duty to do, he may rightfully be made responsible to society for not doing. A person may cause evil to others not only by his actions but by his inaction, and in neither case he is justly accountable to them for the injury. The latter case, it is true, requires a much more cautious exercise of compulsion than the former. To make any one answerable for doing evil to others, is the rule; to make him answerable for not preventing evil, is, comparatively speaking, the exception. Yet there are many cases clear enough and grave enough to justify that exception. In all things which regard the external relations of the individual, he is de jure amenable to those whose interests are concerned, and if need be, to society as their protector. There are often good reasons for not holding him to the responsibility; but these reasons must arise from the special expediencies of the case: either because it is a kind of case in which he is on the whole likely to act better, when left to his own discretion, than when controlled in any way in which society have it in their power to control him; or because the attempt to exercise control would produce other evils, greater than those which it would prevent. When such reasons as these preclude the enforcement of responsibility, the conscience of the agent himself should step into the vacant judgment-seat, and protect those interests of others which have no external protection; judging himself all the more rigidly, because the case does not admit of his being made accountable to the judgment of his fellow-creatures.

But there is a sphere of action in which society, as distinguished from the individual, has, if any, only an indirect interest; comprehending all that portion of a person's life and conduct which affects only himself, or, if it also affects others, only with their free, voluntary, and undeceived consent and participation. When I say only himself, I mean directly, and in the first instance: for whatever affects himself, may affect others through himself; and the objection which may be grounded on this contingency, will receive consideration in the sequel. This, then, is the appropriate region of human liberty. It comprises, first, the inward domain of consciousness; demanding liberty of conscience, in the most comprehensive sense; liberty of thought and feeling; absolute freedom of opinion and sentiment on all subjects, practical or speculative, scientific, moral, or theological. The liberty of expressing and publishing opinions may seem to fall under a different principle, since it belongs to that part of the conduct of an individual which concerns other people; but, being almost of as much importance as the liberty of thought itself, and resting in great part on the same reasons, is practically inseparable from it. Secondly, the principle requires liberty of tastes and pursuits; of framing the plan of our life to suit our own character; of doing as we like, subject to such consequences as may follow; without impediment from our fellow-creatures, so long as what we do does not harm them even though they should think our conduct foolish, perverse, or wrong. Thirdly, from this liberty of each individual, follows the liberty, within the same limits, of combination among individuals; freedom to unite, for any purpose not involving harm to others: the persons combining being supposed to be of full age, and not forced or deceived.

No society in which these liberties are not, on the whole, respected, is free, whatever may be its form of government; and none is completely free in which they do not exist absolute and unqualified. The only freedom which deserves the name, is that of pursuing our own good in our own way, so long as we do not attempt to deprive others of theirs, or impede their efforts to obtain it. Each is the proper guardian of his own health, whether bodily, or mental or spiritual. Mankind are greater gainers by suffering each other to live as seems good to themselves, than by compelling each to live as seems good to the rest.

Though this doctrine is anything but new, and, to some persons, may have the air of a truism, there is no doctrine which stands more directly opposed to the general tendency of existing opinion and practice. Society has expended fully as much effort in the attempt (according to its lights) to compel people to conform to its notions of personal, as of social excellence. The ancient commonwealths thought themselves entitled to practise, and the ancient philosophers counte-nanced, the regulation of every part of private conduct by public authority, on the ground that the State had a deep interest in the whole bodily and mental discipline of every one of its citizens, a mode of thinking which may have been admissible in small republics surrounded by powerful enemies, in constant peril of being subverted by foreign attack or internal commotion, and to which even a short interval of relaxed energy and self-command might so easily be fatal, that they could not afford to wait for the salutary permanent effects of freedom. In the modern world, the greater size of political communities, and above all, the separation between the spiritual and temporal authority (which placed the direction of men's consciences in other hands than those which controlled their worldly affairs), prevented so great an interference by law in the details of private life; but the engines of moral repression have been wielded more strenuously against divergence from the reigning opinion in self-regarding, than even in social matters; religion, the most powerful of the elements which have entered into the formation of moral feeling, having almost always been governed either by the ambition of a hierarchy, seeking control over every department of human conduct, or by the spirit of Puritanism. And some of those modern reformers who have placed themselves in strongest opposition to the religions of the past, have been noway behind either churches or sects in their assertion of the right of spiritual domination: M. Comte, in particular, whose social system, as unfolded in his Traite de Politique Positive, aims at establishing (though by moral more than by legal appliances) a despotism of society over the individual, surpassing anything contemplated in the political ideal of the most rigid disciplinarian among the ancient philosophers.

STUDY QUESTIONS FOR READINGS

Thomas Hobbes, *Leviathan*

1. How does Hobbes characterize the state of nature? What facts about human beings account for this?
2. According to Hobbes, why do we have an obligation to accept terms of peace so long as others do as well?
3. What does Hobbes think is necessary for the preservation of peace? What are the political implications of this?

John Locke, *The Second Treatise on Government*

1. How does Locke characterize the state of nature? How is this different than the state of nature as described by Hobbes?
2. According to Locke, why would the state of nature be a state of liberty and not license? What is the difference between the two?
3. Given his characterization of the state of nature, why does Locke think we would leave? What does this tell us about the purpose of the state?

John Stuart Mill, "On Liberty"

1. What is the "one simple principle" that Mill thinks should determine how much freedom individuals should enjoy?
2. What kinds of exceptions to this principle does Mill allow?
3. How does Mill seem to understand harm? Does he think we can cause harm by failing to act?

SUGGESTIONS FOR FURTHER READING OR VIEWING

Gauthier, David. *Morals by Agreement*. Oxford: Oxford University Press, 1986.

Nussbaum, Martha. *Creating Capabilities: The Human Development Approach*. Cambridge, MA: Harvard University Press, 2011.

Rawls, John. *Justice as Fairness: A Restatement*. Cambridge, MA: Belknap, 2001.

Kantianism

INTRODUCTION TO KANTIAN ETHICS

Introduction to Kantianism

Kant is widely admired as one of the greatest of western philosophers, rivaling the reputation of Plato and Aristotle. He was born in 1724 and died in 1804. Kant lived his entire life in Konigsberg, Prussia. (Konigsberg's is now Kaliningrad and is part of Russia.) Kant wrote many important works among which his most famous include his three Critiques: the *Critique of Pure Reason* (1781), the *Critique of Practical Reason* (1788), and the *Critique of the Power of Judgment* (1790).

Kant suggested that there are three questions reason should answer. The first is: "What can we know?" Much of Kant's writing is devoted to metaphysics and epistemology in an attempt to unravel this thorny question. The second is: "What should we do?" Kant's writings on ethics and law attempt to answer this question. The third is: "What can we hope for?" Kant's philosophy of religion attempts to wrestle with this question.

Kant's ethics are sometimes taught independent of his philosophy of religion and this is unfortunate. Knowing a little about Kant's philosophy of religion sheds light on his ethics.

A long quote from the conclusion of Kant's *Critique of Practical Reason* clarifies Kant's position on ethics, political life, and religion:

> Two things fill the mind with ever new and increasing admiration and awe, the oftener and the more steadily we reflect on them: the starry heavens above and the moral law within. I have not to search for them and conjecture them as though they were veiled in darkness or were in the transcendent region beyond my horizon; I see them before me and connect them directly with

the consciousness of my existence. The former begins from the place I occupy in the external world of sense, and enlarges my connection therein to an unbounded extent with worlds upon worlds and systems of systems, and moreover into limitless times of their periodic motion, its beginning and continuance. The second begins from my invisible self, my personality, and exhibits me in a world which has true infinity, but which is traceable only by the understanding, and with which I discern that I am not in a merely contingent but in a universal and necessary connection, as I am also thereby with all those visible worlds. The former view of a countless multitude of worlds annihilates as it were my importance as an animal creature, which after it has been for a short time provided with vital power, one knows not how, must again give back the matter of which it was formed to the planet it inhabits (a mere speck in the universe). The second, on the contrary, infinitely elevates my worth as an intelligence by my personality, in which the moral law reveals to me a life independent of animality and even of the whole sensible world, at least so far as may be inferred from the destination assigned to my existence by this law, a destination not restricted to conditions and limits of this life, but reaching into the infinite.

The first sentence of the above quote bears repeating: "Two things fill the mind with ever new and increasing admiration and awe, the oftener and the more steadily we reflect on them: the starry heavens above and the moral law within." The starry heavens above us are an awe-inspiring experience. Looking up at the stars of a midnight sky, while camping alone, can make a person feel small, insignificant, and unimportant in the vast, vast scheme of things. Some, like the Psalmist in Psalm 19, feel that the starry heavens declare the very glory of God. But when we look inside ourselves we find something equally awe inspiring. We find moral law. We find the thought that we should always do the right thing. Even if the right thing fails to personally benefit us, even if the right thing requires a sacrifice on our part, even if the right thing gets us killed. We feel inside our hearts the call to moral heroism. And this need to do the right thing makes us stand tall, makes our actions significant, and makes us important, even in the vast, vast scheme of things.

Kant once described the highest good as that state where happiness would be distributed among all persons based on their moral worth. Imagine a kingdom where the most moral people were the happiest and the most evil were miserable and you will have an idea of what Kant meant. But Kant recognized that in this life achieving the highest good is far, far from the norm. Many good people live lives of suffering and despair. Many bad people are never brought to justice for their crimes. (In the United States, for example, one of every three murders each year never even lead to an arrest, let alone a conviction.)

Perhaps that is why Kant believed that morality leads to religion. We place our faith in the highest good even though we do not see it in the violent, unjust world which surrounds us. For some of us, perhaps living in terrible times, we hope for the highest good in the next life, even if it cannot be achieved in this life. For others of us, perhaps living in better times, it is enough to hope that future generations will achieve the highest good, even if it cannot be achieved by us in this life. Even if one disagrees with Kant, consider this possibility: Knowing what we hope for sheds light on what we should do.

393

First Section

from *Groundwork for a Metaphysics of Morals*
by Immanuel Kant

Transition From The Ordinary

Rational Knowledge Of

Morality To The Philosophical

There is no possibility of thinking of anything at all in the world, or even out of it, which can be regarded as good without qualification, except a *good will.* Intelligence, wit, judgment, and whatever talents of the mind one might want to name are doubtless in many respects good and desirable, as are such qualities of temperament as courage, resolution, perseverance. But they can also become extremely bad and harmful if the will, which is to make use of these gifts of nature and which in its special constitution is called character, is not good. The same holds with gifts of fortune; power, riches, honor, even health, and that complete well-being and contentment with one's condition which is called happiness make for pride and often hereby even arrogance, unless there is a good will to correct their influence on the mind and herewith also to rectify the whole principle of action and make it universally conformable to its end. The sight of a being who is not graced by any touch of a pure and good will but who yet enjoys an uninterrupted prosperity can never delight a rational and impartial spectator. Thus a good will seems to constitute the indispensable condition of being even worthy of happiness.

 Some qualities are even conducive to this good will itself and can facilitate its
394 work. Nevertheless, they have no intrinsic unconditional worth; but they always presuppose, rather, a good will, which restricts the high esteem in which they are

otherwise rightly held, and does not permit them to be regarded as absolutely good. Moderation in emotions and passions, self-control, and calm deliberation are not only good in many respects but even seem to constitute part of the intrinsic worth of a person. But they are far from being rightly called good without qualification (however unconditionally they were commended by the ancients). For without the principles of a good will, they can become extremely bad; the coolness of a villain makes him not only much more dangerous but also immediately more abominable in our eyes than he would have been regarded by us without it.

A good will is good not because of what it effects or accomplishes, nor because of its fitness to attain some proposed end; it is good only through its willing, i.e., it is good in itself. When it is considered in itself, then it is to be esteemed very much higher than anything which it might ever bring about merely in order to favor some inclination, or even the sum total of all inclinations. Even if, by some especially unfortunate fate or by the niggardly provision of stepmotherly nature, this will should be wholly lacking in the power to accomplish its purpose; if with the greatest effort it should yet achieve nothing, and only the good will should remain (not, to be sure, as a mere wish but as the summoning of all the means in our power), yet would it, like a jewel, still shine by its own light as something which has its full value in itself. Its usefulness or fruitlessness can neither augment nor diminish this value. Its usefulness would be, as it were, only the setting to enable us to handle it in ordinary dealings or to attract to it the attention of those who are not yet experts, but not to recommend it to real experts or to determine its value.

But there is something so strange in this idea of the absolute value of a mere will, in which no account is taken of any useful results, that in spite of all the agreement received even from ordinary reason, yet there must arise the suspicion that such an idea may perhaps have as its hidden basis merely some high-flown fancy, and that we may have misunderstood the purpose of nature in assigning to reason the governing of our will. Therefore, this idea will be 395 examined from this point of view.

In the natural constitution of an organized being, i.e., one suitably adapted to the purpose of life, let us take as a principle that in such a being no organ is to be found for any end unless it be the most fit and the best adapted for that end. Now if that being's preservation, welfare, or in a word its happiness, were the real end of nature in the case of a being having reason and will, then nature would have hit upon a very poor arrangement in having the reason of the creature carry out this purpose. For all the actions which such a creature has to perform with this purpose in view, and the whole rule of his conduct would have been prescribed much more exactly by instinct; and the purpose in question could have been attained much more certainly by instinct than it ever can be by reason. And if in addition reason had been imparted to this favored creature, then it would have had to serve him only to contemplate the happy constitution of his nature, to admire that nature, to rejoice in it, and to feel grateful to the cause that bestowed it; but reason would not have served him to subject his faculty of desire to its weak and delusive guidance nor would it have served him to meddle incompetently with the purpose of nature. In a word, nature would have taken care that reason did not strike out into a practical use nor presume, with its weak insight, to think out for itself a plan for happiness and the means for attaining it. Nature would have taken upon herself not only the choice of ends but also that of the means, and would with wise foresight have entrusted both to instinct alone.

And, in fact, we find that the more a cultivated reason devotes itself to the aim of enjoying life and happiness, the further does man get away from true contentment. Because of this there arises in many persons, if only they are candid enough to admit it, a certain degree of misology, i.e., hatred of reason. This is especially so in the case of those who are the most experienced in the use of reason, because after calculating all the advantages they derive, I say not from the invention of all the arts of common luxury, but even from the sciences (which in the end seem to them to be also a luxury of the understanding), they yet find 396 that they have in fact only brought more trouble on their heads than they have gained in happiness. Therefore, they come to envy, rather than despise, the more common run of men who are closer to the guidance of mere natural instinct and who do not allow their reason much influence on their conduct. And we must admit that the judgment of those who would temper, or even reduce below zero, the boastful eulogies on behalf of the advantages which reason is supposed to provide as regards the happiness and contentment of life is by no means morose or ungrateful to the goodness with which the world is governed. There lies at the root of such judgments, rather, the idea that existence has another and much more worthy purpose, for which, and not for happiness, reason is quite properly intended, and which must, therefore, be regarded as the supreme condition to which the private purpose of men must, for the most part, defer.

Reason, however, is not competent enough to guide the will safely as regards its objects and the satisfaction of all our needs (which it in part even multiplies); to this end would an implanted natural instinct have led much more certainly. But inasmuch as reason has been imparted to us as a practical faculty, i.e., as one which is to have influence on the will, its true function must be to produce a will which is not merely good as a means to some further end, but is good in itself. To produce a will good in itself reason was absolutely necessary, inasmuch as nature in distributing her capacities has everywhere gone to work in a purposive manner. While such a will may not indeed be the sole and complete good, it must, nevertheless, be the highest good and the condition of all the rest, even of the desire for happiness. In this case there is nothing inconsistent with the wisdom of nature that the cultivation of reason, which is requisite for the first and unconditioned purpose, may in many ways restrict, at least in this life, the attainment of the second purpose, viz., happiness, which is always conditioned. Indeed happiness can even be reduced to less than nothing, without nature's failing thereby in her purpose; for reason recognizes as its highest practical function the establishment of a good will, whereby in the attainment of this end reason is capable only of its own kind of satisfaction, viz., that of fulfilling a purpose which is in turn determined only by reason, even though such fulfilment were often to interfere with the purposes of inclination.

The concept of a will estimable in itself and good without regard to any further 397 end must now be developed. This concept already dwells in the natural sound understanding and needs not so much to be taught as merely to be elucidated. It always holds first place in estimating the total worth of our actions and constitutes the condition of all the rest. Therefore, we shall take up the concept of *duty*, which includes that of a good will, though with certain subjective restrictions and hindrances, which far from hiding a good will or rendering it unrecognizable, rather bring it out by contrast and make it shine forth more brightly.

I here omit all actions already recognized as contrary to duty, even though they may be useful for this or that end; for in the case of these the question does not arise at all as to whether they might be done from duty, since they even conflict with duty. I also set aside those actions which are really in accordance with duty, yet to which men have no immediate inclination, but perform them because they are impelled thereto by some other inclination. For in this [second] case to decide whether the action which is in accord with duty has been done from duty or from some selfish purpose is easy. This difference is far more difficult to note in the [third] case where the action accords with duty and the subject has in addition an immediate inclination to do the action. For example,[1] that a dealer should not overcharge an inexperienced purchaser certainly accords with duty; and where there is much commerce, the prudent merchant does not overcharge but keeps to a fixed price for everyone in general, so that a child may buy from him just as well as everyone else may. Thus customers are honestly served, but this is not nearly enough for making us believe that the merchant has acted this way from duty and from principles of honesty; his own advantage required him to do it. He cannot, however, be assumed to have in addition [as in the third case] an immediate inclination toward his buyers, causing him, as it were, out of love to give no one as far as price is concerned any advantage over another. Hence the action was done neither from duty nor from immediate inclination, but merely for a selfish purpose.

---

1 [The ensuing example provides an illustration of the second case.]

On the other hand,[2] to preserve one's life is a duty; and, furthermore, everyone has also an immediate inclination to do so. But on this account the often
anxious care taken by most men for it has no intrinsic worth, and the maxim
398 of their action has no moral content. They preserve their lives, to be sure, in
accordance with duty, but not from duty. On the other hand,[3] if adversity and
hopeless sorrow have completely taken away the taste for life, if an unfortunate
man, strong in soul and more indignant at his fate than despondent or dejected,
wishes for death and yet preserves his life without loving it—not from inclination or fear, but from duty—then his maxim indeed has a moral content.[4]

To be beneficent where one can is a duty; and besides this, there are many
persons who are so sympathetically constituted that, without any further motive
of vanity or self-interest, they find an inner pleasure in spreading joy around them
and can rejoice in the satisfaction of others as their own work. But I maintain
that in such a case an action of this kind, however dutiful and amiable it may
be, has nevertheless no true moral worth.[5] It is on a level with such actions as
arise from other inclinations, e.g., the inclination for honor, which if fortunately
directed to what is in fact beneficial and accords with duty and is thus honorable,
deserves praise and encouragement, but not esteem; for its maxim lacks the moral
content of an action done not from inclination but from duty. Suppose then the
mind of this friend of mankind to be clouded over with his own sorrow so that
all sympathy with the lot of others is extinguished, and suppose him still to have

---

2 [This next example illustrates the third case.]

3 [The ensuing example illustrates the fourth case.]

4 [Four different cases have been distinguished in the two foregoing paragraphs. Case 1 involves those
actions which are contrary to duty (lying, cheating, stealing, etc.). Case 2 involves those which accord
with duty but for which a person perhaps has no immediate inclination. though he does have a mediate
inclination thereto (one pays his taxes not because he likes to but in order to avoid the penalties set for
delinquents, one treats his fellows well not because he really likes them but because he wants their votes
when at some future time he runs for public office, etc.). A vast number of so-called "morally good"
actions actually belong to this case 2—they accord with duty because of self-seeking inclinations. Case 3
involves those which accord with duty and for which a person does have an immediate inclination (one
docs not commit suicide because all is going well with him, one does not commit adultery because he
considers his wife to be the most desirable creature in the whole world, etc.). Case 4 involves those
actions which accord with duty but are contary to some immediate inclination (one does not commit
suicide even when he is in dire distress, one does not commit adultery even though his wife has turned
out to be an impossible shrew, etc.). Now case 4 is the crucial test case of the will's possible goodness—
but Kant does not claim that one should lead his life in such a way as to encounter as many such cases
as possible in order constantly to test his virtue (deliberately marry a shrew so as to be able to resist
the temptation to commit adultery). Life itself forces enough such cases upon a person without his
seeking them out. But when there is a conflict between duty and inclination, duty should always be
followed. Case 3 makes for the easiest living and the greatest contentment, and anyone would wish
that life might present him with far more of these cases than with cases 2 or 4. But yet one should not
arrange his life in such a way as to avoid case 4 at all costs and to seek out case 3 as much as possible
(become a recluse so as to avoid the possible rough and tumble involved with frequent association with
one's fellows, avoid places where one might encounter the sick and the poor so as to spare oneself
the pangs of sympathy and the need to exercise the virtue of benefiting those in distress, etc.). For the
purpose of philosophical analysis Kant emphasizes case 4 as being the test case of the will's possible
goodness, but he is not thereby advocating puritanism.]

5 5 [This is an example of case 3.]

the power to benefit others in distress, even though he is not touched by their trouble because he is sufficiently absorbed with his own; and now suppose that, even though no inclination moves him any longer, he nevertheless tears himself from this deadly insensibility and performs the action without any inclination at all, but solely from duty—then for the first time his action has genuine moral worth.[6] Further still, if nature has put little sympathy in this or that man's heart, if (while being an honest man in other respects) he is by temperament cold and indifferent to the sufferings of others, perhaps because as regards his own sufferings he is endowed with the special gift of patience and fortitude and expects or even requires that others should have the same; if such a man (who would truly not be nature's worst product) had not been exactly fashioned by her to be a philanthropist, would he not yet find in himself a source from which he might give himself a worth far higher than any that a good-natured temperament might have? By all means, because just here does the worth of the character come out; this worth is moral and incomparably the highest of all, viz., that he is beneficent, not from inclination, but from duty.[7]

To secure one's own happiness is a duty (at least indirectly); for discontent with one's condition under many pressing cares and amid unsatisfied wants might easily become a great temptation to transgress one's duties. But here also do men of themselves already have, irrespective of duty, the strongest and deepest inclination toward happiness, because just in this idea are all inclinations combined into a sum total.[8] But the precept of happiness is often so constituted as greatly to interfere with some inclinations, and yet men cannot form any definite and certain concept of the sum of satisfaction of all inclinations that is called happiness. Hence there is no wonder that a single inclination which is determinate both as to what it promises and as to the time within which it can be satisfied may outweigh a fluctuating idea; and there is no wonder that a man, e.g., a gouty patient, can choose to enjoy what he likes and to suffer what he may, since by his calculation he has here at least not sacrificed the enjoyment of the present moment to some possibly groundless expectations of the good fortune that is supposed to be found in health. But even in this case, if the universal inclination to happiness did not determine his will and if health, at least for him, did not figure as so necessary an element in his calculations; there still remains here, as in all other cases, a law, viz., that he should promote his happiness not from inclination but from duty, and thereby for the first time does his conduct have real moral worth.[9]

399

---

6 [This is an example of case 4.]

7 [This is an even more extreme example of case 4.]

8 [This is an example of case 3.]

9 [This example is a weak form of case 4; the action accords with duty but is not contrary to some immediate inclination.]

Undoubtedly in this way also are to be understood those passages of Scripture which command us to love our neighbor and even our enemy. For love as an inclination cannot be commanded; but beneficence from duty, when no inclination impels us[10] and even when a natural and unconquerable aversion opposes such beneficence,[11] is practical, and not pathological, love. Such love resides in the will and not in the propensities of feeling, in principles of action and not in tender sympathy; and only this practical love can be commanded.

The second proposition[12] is this: An action done from duty has its moral worth, not in the purpose that is to be attained by it, but in the maxim according to which the action is determined. The moral worth depends, therefore,
400 not on the realization of the object of the action, but merely on the principle of volition according to which, without regard to any objects of the faculty of desire, the action has been done. From what has gone before it is clear that the purposes which we may have in our actions, as well as their effects regarded as ends and incentives of the will, cannot give to actions any unconditioned and moral worth. Where, then, can this worth lie if it is not to be found in the will's relation to the expected effect? Nowhere but in the principle of the will, with no regard to the ends that can be brought about through such action. For the will stands, as it were, at a crossroads between its a priori principle, which is formal, and its a posteriori incentive, which is material; and since it must be determined by something, it must be determined by the formal principle of volition, if the action is done from duty—and in that case every material principle is taken away from it.

The third proposition, which follows from the other two, can be expressed thus: Duty is the necessity of an action done out of respect for the law. I can indeed have an inclination for an object as the effect of my proposed action; but I can never have respect for such an object, just because it is merely an effect and is not an activity of the will. Similarly, I can have no respect for inclination as such, whether my own or that of another. I can at most, if my own inclination, approve it; and, if that of another, even love it, i.e., consider it to be favorable to my own advantage. An object of respect can only be what is connected with my will solely as ground and never as effect—something that does not serve my inclination but, rather, outweighs it, or at least excludes it from consideration when some choice is made—in other words, only the law itself can be an object of respect and hence can be a command. Now an action done from duty must altogether exclude the influence of inclination and therewith every object of the will. Hence there is nothing left which can

10 [This is case 4 in its weak form.]

11 [This is case 4 in its strong form.]

12 [The first proposition of morality says that an action must be done from duty in order to have any moral worth. It is implicit in the preceding examples but was never explicitly stated.]

determine the will except objectively the law and subjectively pure respect for this practical law, i.e., the will can be subjectively determined by the maxim[13] that I should follow such a law even if all my inclinations are thereby thwarted. 401

Thus the moral worth of an action does not lie in the effect expected from it nor in any principle of action that needs to borrow its motive from this expected effect. For all these effects (agreeableness of one's condition and even the furtherance of other people's happiness) could have been brought about also through other causes and would not have required the will of a rational being, in which the highest and unconditioned good can alone be found. Therefore, the pre-eminent good which is called moral can consist in nothing but the representation of the law in itself, and such a representation can admittedly be found only in a rational being insofar as this representation, and not some expected effect, is the determining ground of the will. This good is already present in the person who acts according to this representation, and such good need not be awaited merely from the effect.[14]

But what sort of law can that be the thought of which must determine the 402 will without reference to any expected effect, so that the will can be called absolutely good without qualification? Since I have deprived the will of every impulse that might arise for it from obeying any particular law, there is nothing left to serve the will as principle except the universal conformity of its actions to law as such, i.e., I should never act except in such a way that I can also will that my maxim should become a universal law.[15] Here mere conformity to law as such (without having as its basis any law determining particular actions) serves the will as principle and must so serve it if duty is not to be a

---

13 A maxim is the subjective principle of volition. The objective principle (i.e., one which would serve all rational beings also subjectively as a practical principle if reason had full control over the faculty of desire) is the practical law. [See below Kant's footnote at Ak. 420-21.]

14 There might be brought against me here an objection that I take refuge behind the word "respect" in an obscure feeling, instead of giving a clear answer to the question by means of a concept of reason. But even though respect is a feeling, it is not one received through any outside influence but is, rather, one that is self-produced by means of a rational concept; hence it is specifically different from all feelings of the first kind, which can all be reduced to inclination or fear. What I recognize immediately as a law for me, I recognize with respect; this means merely the consciousness of the subordination of my will to a law without the mediation of other influences upon my sense. The immediate determination of the will by the law, and the consciousness thereof, is called respect, which is hence regarded as the effect of the law upon the subject and not as the cause of the law. Respect is properly the representation of a worth that thwarts my self-love. Hence respect is something that is regarded as an object of neither inclination nor fear, although it has at the same time something analogous to both. The object of respect is, therefore, nothing but the law—indeed that very law which we impose on ourselves and yet recognize as necessary in itself. As law, we are subject to it without consulting self-love; as imposed on us by ourselves, it is a consequence of our will. In the former aspect, it is analogous to fear; in the latter, to inclination. All respect for a person is properly only respect for the law (of honesty, etc.) of which the person provides an example. Since we regard the development of our talents as a duty, we think of a man of talent as being also a kind of example of the law (the law of becoming like him by practice), and that is what constitutes our respect for him. All so-called moral interest consists solely in respect for the law.

15 [This is the first time in the *Grounding* that the categorical imperative is stated.]

vain delusion and a chimerical concept. The ordinary reason of mankind in its practical judgments agrees completely with this, and always has in view the aforementioned principle.

For example, take this question. When I am in distress, may I make a promise with the intention of not keeping it? I readily distinguish here the two meanings which the question may have; whether making a false promise conforms with prudence or with duty. Doubtless the former can often be the case. Indeed I clearly see that escape from some present difficulty by means of such a promise is not enough. In addition I must carefully consider whether from this lie there may later arise far greater inconvenience for me than from what I now try to escape. Furthermore, the consequences of my false promise are not easy to forsee, even with all my supposed cunning; loss of confidence in me might prove to be far more disadvantageous than the misfortune which I now try to avoid. The more prudent way might be to act according to a universal maxim and to make it a habit not to promise anything without intending to keep it. But that such a maxim is, nevertheless, always based on nothing but a fear of consequences becomes clear to me at once. To be truthful from duty is, however, quite different from being truthful from fear of disadvantageous consequences; in the first case the concept of the action itself contains a law for me, while in the second I must first look around elsewhere to see what are the results for me that might be connected with
403 the action. For to deviate from the principle of duty is quite certainly bad; but to abandon my maxim of prudence can often be very advantageous for me, though to abide by it is certainly safer. The most direct and infallible way, however, to answer the question as to whether a lying promise accords with duty is to ask myself whether I would really be content if my maxim (of extricating myself from difficulty by means of a false promise) were to hold as a universal law for myself as well as for others, and could I really say to myself that everyone may promise falsely when he finds himself in a difficulty from which he can find no other way to extricate himself. Then I immediately become aware that I can indeed will the lie but can not at all will a universal law to lie. For by such a law there would really be no promises at all, since in vain would my willing future actions be professed to other people who would not believe what I professed, or if they over-hastily did believe, then they would pay me back in like coin. Therefore, my maxim would necessarily destroy itself just as soon as it was made a universal law.[16]

Therefore, I need no far-reaching acuteness to discern what I have to do in order that my will may be morally good. Inexperienced in the course of the world and incapable of being prepared for all its contingencies, I only ask myself

---

16 [This means that when you tell a lie, you merely take exception to the general rule that says everyone should always tell the truth and believe that what you are saying is true. When you lie, you do not thereby will that everyone else lie and not believe that what you are saying is true, because in such a case your lie would never work to get you what you want.]

whether I can also will that my maxim should become a universal law. If not, then the maxim must be rejected, not because of any disadvantage accruing to me or even to others, but because it cannot be fitting as a principle in a possible legislation of universal law, and reason exacts from me immediate respect for such legislation. Indeed I have as yet no insight into the grounds of such respect (which the philosopher may investigate). But I at least understand that respect is an estimation of a worth that far outweighs any worth of what is recommended by inclination, and that the necessity of acting from pure respect for the practical law is what constitutes duty, to which every other motive must give way because duty is the condition of a will good in itself, whose worth is above all else.

Thus within the moral cognition of ordinary human reason we have arrived at its principle. To be sure, such reason does not think of this principle abstractly in its universal form, but does always have it actually in view and does use it as the standard of judgment. It would here be easy to show how ordinary reason, 404 with this compass in hand, is well able to distinguish, in every case that occurs, what is good or evil, in accord with duty or contrary to duty, if we do not in the least try to teach reason anything new but only make it attend, as Socrates did, to its own principle—and thereby do we show that neither science nor philosophy is needed in order to know what one must do to be honest and good, and even wise and virtuous. Indeed we might even have conjectured beforehand that cognizance of what every man is obligated to do, and hence also to know, would be available to every man, even the most ordinary. Yet we cannot but observe with admiration how great an advantage the power of practical judgment has over the theoretical in ordinary human understanding. In the theoretical, when ordinary reason ventures to depart from the laws of experience and the perceptions of sense, it falls into sheer inconceivabilities and self-contradictions, or at least into a chaos of uncertainty, obscurity, and instability. In the practical, however, the power of judgment first begins to show itself to advantage when ordinary understanding excludes all sensuous incentives from practical laws. Such understanding then becomes even subtle, whether in quibbling with its own conscience or with other claims regarding what is to be called right, or whether in wanting to determine correctly for its own instruction the worth of various actions. And the most extraordinary thing is that ordinary understanding in this practical case may have just as good a hope of hitting the mark as that which any philosopher may promise himself. Indeed it is almost more certain in this than even a philosopher is, because he can have no principle other than what ordinary understanding has, but he may easily confuse his judgment by a multitude of foreign and irrelevant considerations and thereby cause it to swerve from the right way. Would it not, therefore, be wiser in moral matters to abide by the ordinary rational judgment or at most to bring in philosophy merely for the purpose of rendering the system of morals more complete and intelligible and of presenting its rules in a way that is more convenient for use (especially in disputation), but not for the purpose of leading ordinary human understanding away from its happy simplicity in practical matters and of bringing it by means of philosophy into a new path of inquiry and instruction?

405   Innocence is indeed a glorious thing; but, unfortunately, it does not keep very well and is easily led astray. Consequently, even wisdom—which consists more in doing and not doing than in knowing—needs science, not in order to learn from it, but in order that wisdom's precepts may gain acceptance and permanence. Man feels within himself a powerful counterweight to all the commands of duty, which are presented to him by reason as being so pre-eminently worthy of respect; this counterweight consists of his needs and inclinations, whose total satisfaction is summed up under the name of happiness. Now reason irremissibly commands its precepts, without thereby promising the inclinations anything; hence it disregards and neglects these impetuous and at the same time so seemingly plausible claims (which do not allow themselves to be suppressed by any command). Hereby arises a natural dialectic, i.e., a propensity to quibble with these strict laws of duty, to cast doubt upon their validity, or at least upon their purity and strictness, and to make them, where possible, more compatible with our wishes and inclinations. Thereby are such laws corrupted in their very foundations and their whole dignity is destroyed—something which even ordinary practical reason cannot in the end call good.

Thus is ordinary human reason forced to go outside its sphere and take a step into the field of practical philosophy, not by any need for speculation (which never befalls such reason so long as it is content to be mere sound reason) but on practical grounds themselves. There it tries to obtain information and clear instruction regarding the source of its own principle and the correct determination of this principle in its opposition to maxims based on need and inclination, so that reason may escape from the perplexity of opposite claims and may avoid the risk of losing all genuine moral principles through the ambiguity into which it easily falls. Thus when ordinary practical reason cultivates itself, there imperceptibly arises in it a dialectic which compels it to seek help in philosophy. The same thing happens in reason's theoretical use; in this case, just as in the other, peace will be found only in a thorough critical examination of our reason.

READING 3.12

Second Section
406

from *Groundwork for a Metaphysics of Morals*
by Immanuel Kant

Transition From Popular

Moral Philosophy To

A Metaphysics Of Morals

If we have so far drawn our concept of duty from the ordinary use of our practical reason, one is by no means to infer that we have treated it as a concept of
experience. On the contrary, when we pay attention to our experience of the
way human beings act, we meet frequent and—as we ourselves admit—justified
complaints that there cannot be cited a single certain example of the disposition
to act from pure duty; and we meet complaints that although much may be done
that is in accordance with what duty commands, yet there are always doubts
as to whether what occurs has really been done from duty and so has moral
worth. Hence there have always been philosophers who have absolutely denied
the reality of this disposition in human actions and have ascribed everything
to a more or less refined self-love. Yet in so doing they have not cast doubt
upon the rightness of the concept of morality. Rather, they have spoken with
sincere regret as to the frailty and impurity of human nature, which they think
is noble enough to take as its precept an idea so worthy of respect but yet is
too weak to follow this idea: reason, which should legislate for human nature,
is used only to look after the interest of inclinations, whether singly or, at best,
in their greatest possible harmony with one another.

407   In fact there is absolutely no possibility by means of experience to make out
with complete certainty a single case in which the maxim of an action that may

in other respects conform to duty has rested solely on moral grounds and on the representation of one's duty. It is indeed sometimes the case that after the keenest self-examination we can find nothing except the moral ground of duty that could have been strong enough to move us to this or that good action and to such great sacrifice. But there cannot with certainty be at all inferred from this that some secret impulse of self-love, merely appearing as the idea of duty, was not the actual determining cause of the will. We like to flatter ourselves with the false claim to a more noble motive; but in fact we can never, even by the strictest examination, completely plumb the depths of the secret incentives of our actions. For when moral value is being considered, the concern is not with the actions, which are seen, but rather with their inner principles, which are not seen.

Moreover, one cannot better serve the wishes of those who ridicule all morality as being a mere phantom of human imagination getting above itself because of self-conceit than by conceding to them that the concepts of duty must be drawn solely from experience (just as from indolence one willingly persuades himself that such is the case as regards all other concepts as well). For by so conceding, one prepares for them a sure triumph. I am willing to admit out of love for humanity that most of our actions are in accordance with duty; but if we look more closely at our planning and striving, we everywhere come upon the dear self, which is always turning up, and upon which the intent of our actions is based rather than upon the strict command of duty (which would often require self-denial). One need not be exactly an enemy of virtue, but only a cool observer who does not take the liveliest wish for the good to be straight off its realization, in order to become doubtful at times whether any true virtue is actually to be found in the world. Such is especially the case when years increase and one's power of judgment is made shrewder by experience and keener in observation. Because of these things nothing can protect us from a complete falling away from our ideas of duty and preserve in the

408 soul a well-grounded respect for duty's law except the clear conviction that, even if there never have been actions springing from such pure sources, the question at issue here is not whether this or that has happened but that reason of itself and independently of all experience commands what ought to happen. Consequently, reason unrelentingly commands actions of which the world has perhaps hitherto never provided an example and whose feasibility might well be doubted by one who bases everything upon experience; for instance, even though there might never yet have been a sincere friend, still pure sincerity in friendship is nonetheless required of every man, because this duty, prior to all experience, is contained as duty in general in the idea of a reason that determines the will by means of a priori grounds.

There may be noted further that unless we want to deny to the concept of morality all truth and all reference to a possible object, we cannot but admit that the moral law is of such widespread significance that it must hold not merely for men but for all rational beings generally, and that it must be valid not merely under contingent conditions and with exceptions but must be absolutely necessary. Clearly, therefore, no experience can give occasion for inferring even the possibility of such apodeictic laws. For with what right could we bring into unlimited respect as a universal precept for every rational nature what is perhaps valid only under the contingent conditions of humanity? And how could laws for the determination of our will be regarded as laws for the determination of a rational being in general and of ourselves only insofar as we are rational beings, if these laws were merely empirical and did not have their source completely a priori in pure, but practical, reason?

Moreover, worse service cannot be rendered morality than that an attempt be made to derive it from examples. For every example of morality presented to me must itself first be judged according to principles of morality in order to see whether it is fit to serve as an original example, i.e., as a model. But in no way can it authoritatively furnish the concept of morality. Even the Holy One of the gospel must first be compared with our ideal of moral perfection before he is recognized as such. Even he says of himself, "Why do you call me (whom you see) good? None is good (the archetype of the good) except God only (whom you do not see)." But whence have we the concept of God as the highest good? Solely from the idea of moral perfection, which reason frames a priori and connects inseparably with the concept of a free will. Imitation has no place at all in moral matters. And examples serve only for encouragement, i.e., they put beyond doubt the feasibility of what the law commands and they make visible what the practical rule expresses more generally. But examples can never justify us in setting aside their true original, which lies in reason, and letting ourselves be guided by them.

If there is then no genuine supreme principle of morality which does not rest on pure reason alone, independent of all experience, I think it is unnecessary even to ask whether it is a good thing to exhibit these concepts generally *(in abstracto)*, which, along with the principles that belong to them, hold a priori, so far as the knowledge involved is to be distinguished from ordinary knowledge and is to be called philosophical. But in our times it may well be necessary to do so. For if one were to take a vote as to whether pure rational knowledge separated from everything empirical, i.e., metaphysics of morals, or whether popular practical philosophy is to be preferred, one can easily guess which side would be preponderant.

This descent to popular thought is certainly very commendable once the ascent to the principles of pure reason has occurred and has been satisfactorily accomplished. That would mean that the doctrine of morals has first been grounded on metaphysics and that subsequently acceptance for morals has been won by giving it a popular character after it has been firmly established. But it is quite absurd to try for popularity in the first inquiry, upon which depends the total correctness of the principles. Not only can such a procedure never lay claim to the very rare merit of a true philosophical popularity, inasmuch as there is really no art involved at all in being generally intelligible if one thereby renounces all basic insight, but such a procedure turns out a disgusting mishmash of patchwork observations and half-reasoned principles in which shallowpates revel because all this is something quite useful for the chitchat of everyday life. Persons of insight, on the other hand, feel confused by all this and turn their eyes away with a dissatisfaction which they nevertheless cannot cure.

410 Yet philosophers, who quite see through the delusion, get little hearing when they summon people for a time from this pretended popularity in order that they may be rightfully popular only after they have attained definite insight.

One need only look at the attempts to deal with morality in the way favored by popular taste. What he will find in an amazing mixture is at one time the particular constitution of human nature (but along with this also the idea of a rational nature in general), at another time perfection, at another happiness; here moral feeling, and there the fear of God; something of this, and also something of that. But the thought never occurs to ask whether the principles of morality are to be sought at all in the knowledge of human nature (which can be had only from experience). Nor does the thought occur that if these principles are not to be sought here but to be found, rather, completely a priori and free from everything empirical in pure rational concepts only, and are to be found nowhere else even to the slightest extent—then there had better be adopted the plan of undertaking this investigation as a separate inquiry, i.e., as pure practical philosophy or (if one may use a name so much decried) as a metaphysics[1] of morals. It is better to bring this investigation to full completeness entirely by itself and to bid the public, which demands popularity, to await the outcome of this undertaking.

But such a completely isolated metaphysics of morals, not mixed with any anthropology, theology, physics, or hyperphysics, and still less with occult qualities (which might be called hypophysical), is not only an indispensable substratum of all theoretical and precisely defined knowledge of duties, but is at the same time a desideratum of the highest importance for the actual fulfillment of their precepts. For the pure thought of duty and of the moral law generally, unmixed with any extraneous addition of empirical inducements, has by the way of reason alone (which first becomes aware hereby that it can of itself be

---

1 Pure philosophy of morals (metaphysics) may be distinguished from the applied (viz., applied to human nature) just as pure mathematics is distinguished from applied mathematics and pure logic from applied logic. By this designation one is also immediately reminded that moral principles are not grounded on the peculiarities of human nature but must subsist a priori of themselves, and that from such principles practical rules must be derivable for every rational nature, and accordingly for human nature.

practical) an influence on the human heart so much more powerful than all other incentives[2] which may be derived from the empirical field that reason in the consciousness of its dignity despises such incentives and is able gradually to become their master. On the other hand, a mixed moral philosophy, compounded both of incentives drawn from feelings and inclinations and at the same time of rational concepts, must make the mind waver between motives that cannot be brought under any principle and that can only by accident lead to the good but often can also lead to the bad. 411

It is clear from the foregoing that all moral concepts have their seat and origin completely a priori in reason, and indeed in the most ordinary human reason just as much as in the most highly speculative. They cannot be abstracted from any empirical, and hence merely contingent, cognition. In this purity of their origin lies their very worthiness to serve us as supreme practical principles; and to the extent that something empirical is added to them, just so much is taken away from their genuine influence and from the absolute worth of the corresponding actions. Moreover, it is not only a requirement of the greatest necessity from a theoretical point of view, when it is a question of speculation, but also of the greatest practical importance, to draw these concepts and laws from pure reason, to present them pure and unmixed, and indeed to determine the extent of this entire practical and pure rational cognition, i.e., to determine the whole faculty of pure practical reason. The principles should not be made 412 to depend on the particular nature of human reason, as speculative philosophy may permit and even sometimes finds necessary; but, rather, the principles should be derived from the universal concept of a rational being in general, since moral laws should hold for every rational being as such. In this way all morals, which require anthropology in order to be applied to humans, must be entirely expounded at first independently of anthropology as pure philosophy, i.e., as metaphysics (which can easily be done in such distinct kinds of knowledge). One knows quite well that unless one is in possession of such a metaphysics, then the attempt is futile, I shall not say to determine exactly for speculative judgment the moral element of duty in all that accords with duty, but that the attempt is impossible, even in ordinary and practical usage, especially in that

---

2 I have a letter from the late excellent Sulzer [Johann Georg Sulzer (1720-1779), an important Berlin savant, who translated Hume's *Inquiry Concerning the Principles of Morals* into German in 1755] in which he asks me why it is that moral instruction accomplishes so little, even though it contains so much that is convincing to reason. My answer was delayed so that I might make it complete. But it is just that the teachers themselves have not purified their concepts: since they try to do too well by looking everywhere for motives for being morally good, they spoil the medicine by trying to make it really strong. For the most ordinary observation shows that when a righteous act is represented as being done with a steadfast soul and sundered from all view to any advantage in this or another world, and even under the greatest temptations of need or allurement, it far surpasses and eclipses any similar action that was in the least affected by any extraneous incentive; it elevates the soul and inspires the wish to be able to act in this way. Even moderately young children feel this impression, and duties should never be represented to them in any other way.

of moral instruction, to ground morals on their genuine principles and thereby to produce pure moral dispositions and engraft them on men's minds for the promotion of the highest good in the world.

In this study we must advance by natural stages not merely from ordinary moral judgment (which is here ever so worthy of respect) to philosophical judgment, as has already been done, but also from popular philosophy, which goes no further than it can get by groping about with the help of examples, to metaphysics (which does not permit itself to be held back any longer by what is empirical, and which, inasmuch as it must survey the whole extent of rational knowledge of this kind, goes right up to ideas, where examples themselves fail us). In order to make such an advance, we must follow and clearly present the practical faculty of reason from its universal rules of determination to the point where the concept of duty springs from it.

Everything in nature works according to laws. Only a rational being has the power to act according to his conception of laws, i.e., according to principles, and thereby has he a will. Since the derivation of actions from laws requires reason, the will is nothing but practical reason. If reason infallibly determines the will, then in the case of such a being actions which are recognized to be objectively necessary are also subjectively necessary, i.e., the will is a faculty of choosing only that which reason, independently of inclination, recognizes as being practically necessary, i.e., as good. But if reason of itself does not sufficiently determine the 413 will, and if the will submits also to subjective conditions (certain incentives) which do not always agree with objective conditions; in a word, if the will does not in itself completely accord with reason (as is actually the case with men), then actions which are recognized as objectively necessary are subjectively contingent, and the determination of such a will according to objective laws is necessitation. That is to say that the relation of objective laws to a will not thoroughly good is represented as the determination of the will of a rational being by principles of reason which the will does not necessarily follow because of its own nature.

The representation of an objective principle insofar as it necessitates the will is called a command (of reason), and the formula of the command is called an imperative.

All imperatives are expressed by an *ought* and thereby indicate the relation of an objective law of reason to a will that is not necessarily determined by this law because of its subjective constitution (the relation of necessitation). Imperatives say that something would be good to do or to refrain from doing, but they say it to a will that does not always therefore do something simply because it has been represented to the will as something good to do. That is practically good which determines the will by means of representations of reason and hence not by subjective causes, but objectively, i.e., on grounds valid for every rational being as such. It is distinguished from the pleasant as that which influences the will only by means of sensation from merely subjective causes, which hold only for this or that person's senses but do not hold as a principle of reason valid for everyone.[3]

A perfectly good will would thus be quite as much subject to objective 414 laws (of the good), but could not be conceived as thereby necessitated to act in conformity with law, inasmuch as it can of itself, according to its subjective constitution, be determined only by the representation of the good. Therefore no imperatives hold for the divine will, and in general for a holy will; the *ought* is here out of place, because the *would* is already of itself necessarily in agreement with the law. Consequently, imperatives are only formulas for expressing the relation of objective laws of willing in general to the subjective imperfection of the will of this or that rational being, e.g., the human will.

Now all imperatives command either hypothetically or categorically. The former represent the practical necessity of a possible action as a means for attaining something else that one wants (or may possibly want). The categorical imperative would be one which represented an action as objectively necessary in itself, without reference to another end.

Every practical law represents a possible action as good and hence as necessary for a subject who is practically determinable by reason; therefore all imperatives are formulas for determining an action which is necessary according to the principle of a will that is good in some way. Now if the action would be good merely as a means to something else, so is the imperative hypothetical. But if the action is represented as good in itself, and hence as necessary in a will which of itself conforms to reason as the principle of the will, then the imperative is categorical.

An imperative thus says what action possible by me would be good, and it presents the practical rule in relation to a will which does not forthwith perform an action simply because it is good, partly because the subject does not always know that the action is good and partly because (even if he does know it is good) his maxims might yet be opposed to the objective principles of practical reason.

---

3 The dependence of the faculty of desire on sensations is called inclination, which accordingly always indicates a need. The dependence of a contingently determinable will on principles of reason, however, is called interest. Therefore an interest is found only in a dependent will which is not of itself always in accord with reason; in the divine will no interest can be thought. But even the human will can take an interest in something without thereby acting from interest. The former signifies practical interest in the action, while the latter signifies pathological interest in the object of the action. The former indicates only dependence of the will on principles of reason by itself, while the latter indicates the will's dependence on principles of reason for the sake of inclination, i.e., reason merely gives the practical rule for meeting the need of inclination. In the former case the action interests me, while in the latter case what interests me is the object of the action (so far as this object is pleasant for me). In the First Section we have seen that in the case of an action done from duty regard must be given not to the interest in the object, but only to interest in the action itself and in its rational principle (viz., the law).

A hypothetical imperative thus says only that an action is good for some
415 purpose, either possible or actual. In the first case it is a problematic practical
principle; in the second case an assertoric one. A categorical imperative, which
declares an action to be of itself objectively necessary without reference to any
purpose, i.e., without any other end, holds as an apodeictic practical principle.

Whatever is possible only through the powers of some rational being can be
thought of as a possible purpose of some will. Consequently, there are in fact
infinitely many principles of action insofar as they are represented as necessary
for attaining a possible purpose achievable by them. All sciences have a practical part consisting of problems saying that some end is possible for us and of
imperatives telling us how it can be attained. These can, therefore, be called in
general imperatives of skill. Here there is no question at all whether the end
is reasonable and good, but there is only a question as to what must be done
to attain it. The prescriptions needed by a doctor in order to make his patient
thoroughly healthy and by a poisoner in order to make sure of killing his victim
are of equal value so far as each serves to bring about its purpose perfectly.
Since there cannot be known in early youth what ends may be presented to us
in the course of life, parents especially seek to have their children learn many
different kinds of things, and they provide for skill in the use of means to all
sorts of arbitrary ends, among which they cannot determine whether any one
of them could in the future become an actual purpose for their ward, though
there is always the possibility that he might adopt it. Their concern is so great
that they commonly neglect to form and correct their children's judgment
regarding the worth of things which might be chosen as ends.

There is, however, one end that can be presupposed as actual for all rational beings (so far as they are dependent beings to whom imperatives apply);
and thus there is one purpose which they not merely can have but which can
certainly be assumed to be such that they all do have by a natural necessity,
and this is happiness. A hypothetical imperative which represents the practical
necessity of an action as means for the promotion of happiness is assertoric.
416 It may be expounded not simply as necessary to an uncertain, merely possible
purpose, but as necessary to a purpose which can be presupposed a priori and
with certainty as being present in everyone because it belongs to his essence.
Now skill in the choice of means to one's own greatest well-being can be called
prudence[4] in the narrowest sense. And thus the imperative that refers to the
choice of means to one's own happiness, i.e., the precept of prudence, still

---

4 The word "prudence" is used in a double sense: firstly, it can mean worldly wisdom, and, secondly,
private wisdom. The former is the skill of someone in influencing others so as to use them for his own
purposes. The latter is the sagacity to combine all these purposes for his own lasting advantage. The
value of the former is properly reduced to the latter, and it might better be said of one who is prudent
in the former sense but not in the latter that he is clever and cunning, but on the whole imprudent.

remains hypothetical; the action is commanded not absolutely but only as a means to a further purpose.

Finally, there is one imperative which immediately commands a certain conduct without having as its condition any other purpose to be attained by it. This imperative is categorical. It is not concerned with the matter of the action and its intended result, but rather with the form of the action and the principle from which it follows; what is essentially good in the action consists in the mental disposition, let the consequences be what they may. This imperative may be called that of morality.

Willing according to these three kinds of principles is also clearly distinguished by dissimilarity in the necessitation of the will. To make this dissimilarity clear I think that they are most suitably named in their order when they are said to be either *rules of skill, counsels of prudence,* or *commands (laws) of morality.* For law alone involves the concept of a necessity that is unconditioned and indeed objective and hence universally valid, and commands are laws which must be obeyed, i.e., must be followed even in opposition to inclination. Counsel does indeed involve necessity, but involves such necessity as is valid only under a subjectively contingent condition, viz., whether this or that man counts this or that as belonging to his happiness. On the other hand, the categorical imperative is limited by no condition, and can quite properly be called a command since it is absolutely, though practically, necessary. The first kind of imperatives might also be called technical (belonging to art), the 417 second kind pragmatic[5] (belonging to welfare), the third kind moral (belonging to free conduct as such, i.e., to morals).

The question now arises: how are all of these imperatives possible?[6] This question does not seek to know how the fulfillment of the action commanded by the imperative can be conceived, but merely how the necessitation of the will expressed by the imperative in setting a task can be conceived. How an imperative of skill is possible requires no special discussion. Whoever wills the end, wills (so far as reason has decisive influence on his actions) also the means that are indispensably necessary to his actions and that lie in his power. This proposition, as far as willing is concerned, is analytic. For in willing an object as my effect there is already thought the causality of myself as an acting cause, i.e., the use of means. The imperative derives the concept of actions necessary to this end from the concept of willing this end. (Synthetic propositions are indeed

---

5 It seems to me that the proper meaning of the word "pragmatic" could be defined most accurately in this way. For those sanctions are called pragmatic which properly flow not from the law of states as necessary enactments but from provision for the general welfare. A history is pragmatically written when it teaches prudence, i.e., instructs the world how it can provide for its interests better than, or at least as well as, has been done in former times.

6 [That is, why should one let his actions be determined at various times by one or the other of these three kinds of imperatives?]

required for determining the means to a proposed end; but such propositions are concerned not with the ground, i.e., the act of the will, but only with the way to realize the object of the will.) Mathematics teaches by nothing but synthetic propositions that in order to bisect a line according to a sure principle I must from each of its extremities draw arcs such that they intersect. But when I know that the proposed result can come about only by means of such an action, then the proposition (if I fully will the effect, then I also will the action required for it) is analytic. For it is one and the same thing to conceive of something as an effect that is possible in a certain way through me and to conceive of myself as acting in the same way with regard to the aforesaid effect.

If it were only as easy to give a determinate concept of happiness, then the imperatives of prudence would exactly correspond to those of skill and would 418 be likewise analytic. For there could be said in this case just as in the former that whoever wills the end also wills (necessarily according to reason) the sole means thereto which are in his power. But, unfortunately, the concept of happiness is such an indeterminate one that even though everyone wishes to attain happiness, yet he can never say definitely and consistently what it is that he really wishes and wills. The reason for this is that all the elements belonging to the concept of happiness are unexceptionally empirical, i.e., they must be borrowed from experience, while for the idea of happiness there is required an absolute whole, a maximum of well-being in my present and in every future condition. Now it is impossible for the most insightful and at the same time most powerful, but nonetheless finite, being to frame here a determinate concept of what it is that he really wills. Does he want riches? How much anxiety, envy, and intrigue might he not thereby bring down upon his own head! Or knowledge and insight? Perhaps these might only give him an eye that much sharper for revealing that much more dreadfully evils which are at present hidden but are yet unavoidable, or such an eye might burden him with still further needs for the desires which already concern him enough. Or long life? Who guarantees that it would not be a long misery? Or health at least? How often has infirmity of the body kept one from excesses into which perfect health would have allowed him to fall, and so on? In brief, he is not able on any principle to determine with complete certainty what will make him truly happy, because to do so would require omniscience. Therefore, one cannot act according to determinate principles in order to be happy, but only according to empirical counsels, e.g., of diet, frugality, politeness, reserve, etc., which are shown by experience to contribute on the average the most to wellbeing. There follows from this that imperatives of prudence, strictly speaking, cannot command at all, i.e., present actions objectively as practically necessary. They are to be taken as counsels (*consilia*) rather than as commands (*praecepta*) of reason. The problem of determining certainly and universally what action will promote the happiness of a rational being is completely insoluble. Therefore, regarding such action no imperative that in the strictest sense could command what is to be done to make one happy is possible, inasmuch as happiness is not an ideal of reason but of imagination. Such an ideal rests merely on empirical grounds; 419 in vain can there be expected that such grounds should determine an action whereby the totality of an infinite series of consequences could be attained. This imperative of prudence would, nevertheless, be an analytic practical proposition if one assumes that the means to happiness could with certainty be assigned; for it differs from the imperative of skill only in that for it the end is given while for the latter the end is merely possible. Since both, however, command only the means to what is assumed to be willed as an end, the imperative commanding him who wills the end to will likewise the means thereto is in both cases analytic. Hence there is also no difficulty regarding the possibility of an imperative of prudence.

On the other hand, the question as to how the imperative of morality is possible is undoubtedly the only one requiring a solution. For it is not at all hypothetical; and hence the objective necessity which it presents cannot be based on any pre-supposition, as was the case with the hypothetical imperatives. Only there must never here be forgotten that no example can show, i.e., empirically, whether there is any such imperative at all. Rather, care must be taken lest all imperatives which are seemingly categorical may nevertheless be covertly hypothetical. For instance, when it is said that you should not make a false promise, the assumption is that the necessity of this avoidance is no mere advice for escaping some other evil, so that it might be said that you should not make a false promise lest you ruin your credit when the falsity comes to light. But when it is asserted that an action of this kind must be regarded as bad in itself, then the imperative of prohibition is therefore categorical. Nevertheless, it cannot with certainty be shown by means of an example that the will is here determined solely by the law without any other incentive, even though such may seem to be the case. For it is always possible that secretly there is fear of disgrace and perhaps also obscure dread of other dangers; such fear and dread may have influenced the will. Who can prove by experience that a cause is not present? Experience only shows that a cause is not perceived. But in such a case the so-called moral imperative, which as such appears to be categorical and unconditioned, would actually be only a pragmatic precept which makes us pay attention to our own advantage and merely teaches us to take such advantage into consideration.

We shall, therefore, have to investigate the possibility of a categorical imperative entirely a priori, inasmuch as we do not here have the advantage of having its reality given in experience and consequently of thus being obligated merely to 420 explain its possibility rather than to establish it. In the meantime so much can be seen for now: the categorical imperative alone purports to be a practical law, while all the others may be called principles of the will but not laws. The reason for this is that whatever is necessary merely in order to attain some arbitrary purpose can be regarded as in itself contingent, and the precept can always be ignored once the purpose is abandoned. Contrariwise, an unconditioned command does not leave the will free to choose the opposite at its own liking. Consequently, only such a command carries with it that necessity which is demanded from a law.

Secondly, in the case of this categorical imperative, or law of morality, the reason for the difficulty (of discerning its possibility) is quite serious. The categorical imperative is an a priori synthetic practical proposition;[7] and since discerning the possibility of propositions of this sort involves so much difficulty in theoretic knowledge, there may readily be gathered that there will be no less difficulty in practical knowledge.

In solving this problem, we want first to inquire whether perhaps the mere concept of a categorical imperative may not also supply us with the formula containing the proposition that can alone be a categorical imperative. For even when we know the purport of such an absolute command, the question as to how it is possible will still require a special and difficult effort, which we postpone to the last section.[8]

If I think of a hypothetical imperative in general, I do not know beforehand what it will contain until its condition is given. But if I think of a categorical imperative, I know immediately what it contains. For since, besides the law, the imperative contains only the necessity that the maxim[9] should accord with this

421 law, while the law contains no condition to restrict it, there remains nothing but the universality of a law as such with which the maxim of the action should conform. This conformity alone is properly what is represented as necessary by the imperative.

Hence there is only one categorical imperative and it is this: Act only according to that maxim whereby you can at the same time will that it should become a universal law.[10]

Now if all imperatives of duty can be derived from this one imperative as their principle, then there can at least be shown what is understood by the concept of duty and what it means, even though there is left undecided whether what is called duty may not be an empty concept.

---

7 I connect a priori, and therefore necessarily, the act with the will without presupposing any condition taken from some inclination (though I make such a connection only objectively, i.e., under the idea of a reason having full power over all subjective motives). Hence this is a practical proposition which does not analytically derive the willing of an action from some other willing already presupposed (for we possess no such perfect will) but which connects the willing of an action immediately with the concept of the will of a rational being as something which is not contained in this concept.

8 [See below Ak. 446–63.]

9 A maxim is the subjective principle of acting and must be distinguished from the objective principle, viz., the practical law. A maxim contains the practical rule which reason determines in accordance with the conditions of the subject (often his ignorance or his inclinations) and is thus the principle according to which the subject does act. But the law is the objective principle valid for every rational being, and it is the principle according to which he ought to act, i.e., an imperative.

10 [This formulation of the categorical imperative is often referred to as the formula of universal law.]

The universality of law according to which effects are produced constitutes what is properly called nature in the most general sense (as to form), i.e., the existence of things as far as determined by universal laws. Accordingly, the universal imperative of duty may be expressed thus: Act as if the maxim of your action were to become through your will a universal law of nature.[11]

We shall now enumerate some duties, following the usual division of them into duties to ourselves and to others and into perfect and imperfect duties.[12]

1. A man reduced to despair by a series of misfortunes feels sick of life but is still so far in possession of his reason that he can ask himself whether taking his own life would not be contrary to his duty to himself.[13] Now he asks whether the maxim of his action could become a universal law of nature. But his maxim is this: from self-love I make as my principle to shorten my life when its continued duration threatens more evil than it promises satisfaction. There only remains the question as to whether this principle of self-love can become a universal law of nature. One sees at once a contradiction in a system of nature whose law would destroy life by means of the very same feeling that acts so as to stimulate the furtherance of life, and hence there could be no existence as a system of nature. Therefore, such a maxim cannot possibly hold as a universal law of nature and is, consequently, wholly opposed to the supreme principle of all duty.

2. Another man in need finds himself forced to borrow money. He knows well that he won't be able to repay it, but he sees also that he will not get any loan unless he firmly promises to repay it within a fixed time. He wants to make such a promise, but he still has conscience enough to ask himself whether it is not permissible and is contrary to duty to get out of difficulty in this way. Suppose, however, that he decides to do so. The maxim of his action would then be expressed as follows: when I believe myself to be in need of money, I will borrow money and promise to pay it back, although I know that I can never do so. Now this principle of self-love or personal advantage may perhaps be quite compatible with one's entire future welfare, but the question is now whether it is right.[14] I then transform the requirement of self-love into a universal law and put the question thus: how would things stand if my maxim were to become a universal law? He then sees at once that such a maxim could never hold as

422

---

11 [This is often called the formula of the law of nature.]

12 There should be noted here that I reserve the division of duties for a future *Metaphysics of Morals* [in Part II of the *Metaphysics of Morals,* entitled *The Metaphysical Principles of Virtue,* Ak. 417–474]. The division presented here stands as merely an arbitrary one (in order to arrange my examples). For the rest, I understand here by a perfect duty one which permits no exception in the interest of inclination. Accordingly, I have perfect duties which are external [to others], while other ones are internal [to oneself], This classification runs contrary to the accepted usage of the schools, but I do not intend to justify it here, since there is no difference for my purpose whether this classification is accepted or not.

13 [Not committing suicide is an example of a perfect duty to oneself. See *Metaphysical Principles of Virtue,* Ak. 422–24.]

14 [Keeping promises is an example of a perfect duty to others. See *ibid.,* Ak. 423–31.]

a universal law of nature and be consistent with itself, but must necessarily be self-contradictory. For the universality of a law which says that anyone believing himself to be in difficulty could promise whatever he pleases with the intention of not keeping it would make promising itself and the end to be attained thereby quite impossible, inasmuch as no one would believe what was promised him but would merely laugh at all such utterances as being vain pretenses.

3. A third finds in himself a talent whose cultivation could make him a man useful in many respects. But he finds himself in comfortable circumstances and prefers to indulge in pleasure rather than to bother himself about broadening and improving his fortunate natural aptitudes. But he asks himself further whether his maxim of neglecting his natural gifts, besides agreeing of itself with his propensity to indulgence, might agree also with what is called duty.[15] He then sees that a system of nature could indeed always subsist according to such a universal law, even though every man (like South Sea Islanders) should let his talents rust and resolve to devote his life entirely to idleness, indulgence, propagation, and, in a word, to enjoyment. But he cannot possibly will that this should become a universal law of nature or be implanted in us as such a law by a natural instinct. For as a rational being he necessarily wills that all his faculties should be developed, inasmuch as they are given him for all sorts of possible purposes.

4. A fourth man finds things going well for himself but sees others (whom he could help) struggling with great hardships; and he thinks: what does it matter to me? Let everybody be as happy as Heaven wills or as he can make himself; I shall take nothing from him nor even envy him; but I have no desire to contribute anything to his well-being or to his assistance when in need. If such a way of thinking were to become a universal law of nature, the human race admittedly could very well subsist and doubtless could subsist even better than when everyone prates about sympathy and benevolence and even on occasion exerts himself to practice them but, on the other hand, also cheats when he can, betrays the rights of man, or otherwise violates them. But even though it is possible that a universal law of nature could subsist in accordance with that maxim, still it is impossible to will that such a principle should hold everywhere as a law of nature.[16] For a will which resolved in this way would contradict itself, inasmuch as cases might often arise in which one would have need of the love and sympathy of others and in which he would deprive himself, by such a law of nature springing from his own will, of all hope of the aid he wants for himself.

These are some of the many actual duties, or at least what are taken to be such, whose derivation from the single principle cited above is clear. We must be able 424

---

15 [Cultivating one's talents is an example of an imperfect duty to oneself. See *ibid.*, Ak. 444–46.]

16 [Benefiting others is an example of an imperfect duty to others. See *ibid.*, Ak. 452–54.]

to will that a maxim of our action become a universal law; this is the canon for morally estimating any of our actions. Some actions are so constituted that their maxims cannot without contradiction even be thought as a universal law of nature, much less be willed as what should become one. In the case of others this internal impossibility is indeed not found, but there is still no possibility of willing that their maxim should be raised to the universality of a law of nature, because such a will would contradict itself. There is no difficulty in seeing that the former kind of action conflicts with strict or narrow [perfect] (irremissible) duty, while the second kind conflicts only with broad [imperfect] (meritorious) duty.[17] By means of these examples there has thus been fully set forth how all duties depend as regards the kind of obligation (not the object of their action) upon the one principle.

If we now attend to ourselves in any transgression of a duty, we find that we actually do not will that our maxim should become a universal law—because this is impossible for us—but rather that the opposite of this maxim should remain a law universally.[18] We only take the liberty of making an exception to the law for ourselves (or just for this one time) to the advantage of our inclination. Consequently, if we weighed up everything from one and the same standpoint, namely, that of reason, we would find a contradiction in our own will, viz., that a certain principle be objectively necessary as a universal law and yet subjectively not hold universally but should admit of exceptions. But since we at one moment regard our action from the standpoint of a will wholly in accord with reason and then at another moment regard the very same action from the standpoint of a will affected by inclination, there is really no contradiction here. Rather, there is an opposition *(antagonismus)* of inclination to the precept of reason, whereby the universality *(universalitas)* of the principle is changed into a mere generality *(generalitas)* so that the practical principle of reason may meet the maxim halfway. Although this procedure cannot be justified in our own impartial judgment, yet it does show that we actually acknowledge the validity of the categorical imperative and (with all respect for it) merely allow ourselves a few exceptions which, as they seem to us, are unimportant and forced upon us.

We have thus at least shown that if duty is a concept which is to have sig- 425 nificance and real legislative authority for our actions, then such duty can be expressed only in categorical imperatives but not at all in hypothetical ones. We have also—and this is already a great deal—exhibited clearly and definitely for every application what is the content of the categorical imperative, which must contain the principle of all duty (if there is such a thing at all). But we have not

---

17   [Compare *ibid.*, Ak. 390–94, 410–11, 421–51.]

18   [This is to say, for example, that when you tell a lie, you do so on the condition that others are truthful and believe that what you are saying is true, because otherwise your lie will never work to get you what you want. When you tell a lie, you simply take exception to the general rule that says everyone should always tell the truth.]

yet advanced far enough to prove a priori that there actually is an imperative of this kind, that there is a practical law which of itself commands absolutely and without any incentives, and that following this law is duty.

In order to attain this proof there is the utmost importance in being warned that we must not take it into our mind to derive the reality of this principle from the special characteristics of human nature. For duty has to be a practical, unconditioned necessity of action; hence it must hold for all rational beings (to whom alone an imperative is at all applicable) and for this reason only can it also be a law for all human wills. On the other hand, whatever is derived from the special natural condition of humanity, from certain feelings and propensities, or even, if such were possible, from some special tendency peculiar to human reason and not holding necessarily for the will of every rational being—all of this can indeed yield a maxim valid for us, but not a law. This is to say that such can yield a subjective principle according to which we might act if we happen to have the propensity and inclination, but cannot yield an objective principle according to which we would be directed to act even though our every propensity, inclination, and natural tendency were opposed to it. In fact, the sublimity and inner worth of the command are so much the more evident in a duty, the fewer subjective causes there are for it and the more they oppose it; such causes do not in the least weaken the necessitation exerted by the law or take away anything from its validity.

Here philosophy is seen in fact to be put in a precarious position, which should be firm even though there is neither in heaven nor on earth anything upon which it depends or is based. Here philosophy must show its purity as author of its laws, and not as the herald of such laws as are whispered to it by an implanted sense or by who knows what tutelary nature. Such laws may be better than nothing 426 at all, but they can never give us principles dictated by reason. These principles must have an origin that is completely a priori and must at the same time derive from such origin their authority to command. They expect nothing from the inclination of men but, rather, expect everything from the supremacy of the law and from the respect owed to the law. Without the latter expectation, these principles condemn man to self-contempt and inward abhorrence.

Hence everything empirical is not only quite unsuitable as a contribution to the principle of morality, but is even highly detrimental to the purity of morals. For the proper and inestimable worth of an absolutely good will consists precisely in the fact that the principle of action is free of all influences from contingent grounds, which only experience can furnish. This lax or even mean way of thinking which seeks its principle among empirical motives and laws cannot too much or too often be warned against, for human reason in its weariness is glad to rest upon this pillow. In a dream of sweet illusions (in which not Juno but a cloud is embraced) there is substituted for morality some bastard patched up from limbs of quite varied ancestry and looking like anything one wants to see in it but not looking like virtue to him who has once beheld her in her true form.[19]

Therefore, the question is this: is it a necessary law for all rational beings always to judge their actions according to such maxims as they can themselves will that such should serve as universal laws? If there is such a law, then it must already be connected (completely a priori) with the concept of the will of a rational being in general. But in order to discover this connection we must, however reluctantly, take a step into metaphysics, although into a region of it different from speculative philosophy, i.e., we must enter the metaphysics of morals. In practical philosophy the concern is not with accepting grounds for 427 what happens but with accepting laws of what ought to happen, even though it never does happen—that is, the concern is with objectively practical laws. Here there is no need to inquire into the grounds as to why something pleases or displeases, how the pleasure of mere sensation differs from taste, and whether taste differs from a general satisfaction of reason, upon what does the feeling of pleasure and displeasure rest, and how from this feeling desires and inclinations arise, and how, finally, from these there arise maxims through the cooperation of reason. All of this belongs to an empirical psychology, which would consti- tute the second part of the doctrine of nature, if this doctrine is regarded as the philosophy of nature insofar as this philosophy is grounded on empirical laws. But here the concern is with objectively practical laws, and hence with the relation of a will to itself insofar as it is determined solely by reason. In this case everything related to what is empirical falls away of itself, because if reason entirely by itself determines conduct (and the possibility of such determination we now wish to investigate), then reason must necessarily do so a priori.

The will is thought of as a faculty of determining itself to action in accordance with the representation of certain laws, and such a faculty can be found only in rational beings. Now what serves the will as the objective ground of its self- determination is an end; and if this end is given by reason alone, then it must be equally valid for all rational beings. On the other hand, what contains merely the ground of the possibility of the action, whose effect is an end, is called the means. The subjective ground of desire is the incentive; the objective ground of volition is the motive. Hence there arises the distinction between subjective ends, which rest on incentives, and objective ends, which depend on motives valid for every rational being. Practical principles are formal when they abstract from all subjective ends; they are material, however, when they are founded upon subjective ends, and hence upon certain incentives. The ends which a rational

---

19 To behold virtue in her proper form is nothing other than to present morality stripped of all admixture of what is sensuous and of every spurious adornment of reward or self-love. How much she then eclipses all else that appears attractive to the inclinations can be easily seen by everyone with the least effort of his reason, if it be not entirely ruined for all abstraction.

being arbitrarily proposes to himself as effects of this action (material ends) are all merely relative, for only their relation to a specially constituted faculty of desire in the subject gives them their worth. Consequently, such worth cannot provide any universal principles, which are valid and necessary for all rational beings and, furthermore, are valid for every volition, i.e., cannot provide any practical laws. Therefore, all such relative ends can be grounds only for hypothetical imperatives.

But let us suppose that there were something whose existence has in itself an absolute worth, something which as an end in itself could be a ground of determinate laws. In it, and in it alone, would there be the ground of a possible categorical imperative, i.e., of a practical law.

Now I say that man, and in general every rational being, exists as an end in himself and not merely as a means to be arbitrarily used by this or that will. He must in all his actions, whether directed to himself or to other rational beings, always be regarded at the same time as an end. All the objects of inclinations have only a conditioned value; for if there were not these inclinations and the needs founded on them, then their object would be without value. But the inclinations themselves, being sources of needs, are so far from having an absolute value such as to render them desirable for their own sake that the universal wish of every rational being must be, rather, to be wholly free from them. Accordingly, the value of any object obtainable by our action is always conditioned. Beings whose existence depends not on our will but on nature have, nevertheless, if they are not rational beings, only a relative value as means and are therefore called things. On the other hand, rational beings are called persons inasmuch as their nature already marks them out as ends in themselves, i.e., as something which is not to be used merely as means and hence there is imposed thereby a limit on all arbitrary use of such beings, which are thus objects of respect. Persons are, therefore, not merely subjective ends, whose existence as an effect of our actions has a value for us; but such beings are objective ends, i.e., exist as ends in themselves. Such an end is one for which there can be substituted no other end to which such beings should serve merely as means, for otherwise nothing at all of absolute value would be found anywhere. But if all value were conditioned and hence contingent, then no supreme practical principle could be found for reason at all.

If then there is to be a supreme practical principle and, as far as the human will is concerned, a categorical imperative, then it must be such that from the conception of what is necessarily an end for everyone because this end is an end in itself it constitutes an objective principle of the will and can hence serve as a practical law. The ground of such a principle is this: rational nature exists as an end in itself. In this way man necessarily thinks of his own existence; thus far is it a subjective principle of human actions. But in this way also does every other rational being think of his existence on the same rational ground that holds also for me;[20] hence it is at the same time an objective principle, from which, as a supreme practical ground, all laws of the will must be able to be derived. The practical imperative will therefore be the following: Act in such a way that you treat humanity, whether in your own person or in the person of another, always at the same time as an end and never simply as a means.[21] We now want to see whether this can be carried out in practice.

Let us keep to our previous examples.[22]

First, as regards the concept of necessary duty to oneself, the man who contemplates suicide will ask himself whether his action can be consistent with the idea of humanity as an end in itself. If he destroys himself in order to escape from a difficult situation, then he is making use of his person merely as a means so as to maintain a tolerable condition till the end of his life. Man, however, is not a thing and hence is not something to be used merely as a means; he must in all his actions always be regarded as an end in himself. Therefore, I cannot dispose of man in my own person by mutilating, damaging, or killing him. (A more exact determination of this principle so as to avoid all misunderstanding, e.g., regarding the amputation of limbs in order to save oneself, or the exposure of one's life to danger in order to save it, and so on, must here be omitted; such questions belong to morals proper.)

Second, as concerns necessary or strict duty to others, the man who intends to make a false promise will immediately see that he intends to make use of another man merely as a means to an end which the latter does not likewise hold. For the man whom I want to use for my own purposes by such a promise cannot possibly concur with my way of acting toward him and hence cannot himself hold the end of this action. This conflict with the principle of duty to others becomes even clearer when instances of attacks on the freedom and property of others are considered. For then it becomes clear that a transgressor of the rights of men intends to make use of the persons of others merely as a means, without taking into consideration that, as rational beings, they should always be esteemed at the same time as ends, i.e., be esteemed only as beings who must themselves be able to hold the very same action as an end.[23]

430

---

20 This proposition I here put forward as a postulate. The grounds for it will be found in the last section. [See below Ak. 446–63.]

21 [This oft-quoted version of the categorical imperative is usually referred to as the formula of the end in itself.]

22 [See above Ak. 422–23.]

23 Let it not be thought that the trivial *quod tibi non vis fieri, etc.* [do not do to others what you do not want done to yourself] can here serve as a standard or principle. For it is merely derived from our principle, although with several limitations. It cannot be a universal law, for it contains the ground neither of duties to oneself nor of duties of love toward others (for many a man would gladly consent that others should not benefit him, if only he might be excused from benefiting them). Nor, finally, does it contain the ground of strict duties toward others, for the criminal would on this ground be able to dispute with the judges who punish him; and so on.

Third, with regard to contingent (meritorious) duty to oneself, it is not enough that the action does not conflict with humanity in our own person as an end in itself; the action must also harmonize with this end. Now there are in humanity capacities for greater perfection which belong to the end that nature has in view as regards humanity in our own person. To neglect these capacities might perhaps be consistent with the maintenance of humanity as an end in itself, but would not be consistent with the advancement of this end.

Fourth, concerning meritorious duty to others, the natural end that all men have is their own happiness. Now humanity might indeed subsist if nobody contributed anything to the happiness of others, provided he did not intentionally impair their happiness. But this, after all, would harmonize only negatively and not positively with humanity as an end in itself, if everyone does not also strive, as much as he can, to further the ends of others. For the ends of any subject who is an end in himself must as far as possible be my ends also, if that conception of an end in itself is to have its full effect in me.

431 This principle of humanity and of every rational nature generally as an end in itself is the supreme limiting condition of every man's freedom of action. This principle is not borrowed from experience, first, because of its universality, inasmuch as it applies to all rational beings generally, and no experience is capable of determining anything about them; and, secondly, because in experience (subjectively) humanity is not thought of as the end of men, i.e., as an object that we of ourselves actually make our end which as a law ought to constitute the supreme limiting condition of all subjective ends (whatever they may be); and hence this principle must arise from pure reason [and not from experience]. That is to say that the ground of all practical legislation lies objectively in the rule and in the form of universality, which (according to the first principle) makes the rule capable of being a law (say, for example, a law of nature). Subjectively, however, the ground of all practical legislation lies in the end; but (according to the second principle) the subject of all ends is every rational being as an end in himself. From this there now follows the third practical principle of the will as the supreme condition of the will's conformity with universal practical reason, viz., the idea of the will of every rational being as a will that legislates universal law.[24]

According to this principle all maxims are rejected which are not consistent with the will's own legislation of universal law. The will is thus not merely subject to the law but is subject to the law in such a way that it must be regarded also as legislating for itself and only on this account as being subject to the law (of which it can regard itself as the author).

---

24 [This is usually called the formula of autonomy.]

STUDY GUIDE QUESTIONS FOR READINGS

1. What is the only thing that is good without qualification? Why aren't things like intelligence, perseverance, and wealth good without qualification?
2. What can an impartial, rational spectator take no pleasure in seeing? Why? What quality must one have to be worthy of being happy?
3. What is the difference between a hypothetical imperative and a categorical imperative?
4. What is the first formulation of the Categorical Imperative?
5. Explain how we can use the second formulation of the categorical imperative to arrive at the same conclusions as the first for each of Kant's four examples.

SUGGESTIONS FOR FURTHER READING OR VIEWING

Kant, Immanuel. *The Critique of Practical Reason.* Translated by Mary Gregor. Cambridge: University of Cambridge Press, 2015. Of particular interest are the sections "The Existence of God as a Postulate of Pure Practical Reason" and "Methodology of Pure Practical Reason."

"Kant's Moral Philosophy." In *The Stanford Encyclopedia of Philosophy*, edited by Edward N. Zalta. Stanford University, 2016. https://plato.stanford.edu/entries/kant-moral/.

"Kant's Philosophy of Religion." In *The Stanford Encyclopedia of Philosophy, edited by Edward N. Zalta. Stanford University,* 2014. http://plato.stanford.edu/entries/kant-religion/.

Utilitarianism

INTRODUCTION TO UTILITARIANISM

Utilitarianism is a normative ethical theory that defines morality in terms of happiness production for all affected. There are a couple of key ideas that are essential to thinking about morality in this respect. First, utilitarianism is consequentialist, meaning that morality is evaluated in terms of end results, and those results are the most significant consideration in determining what is right or wrong and how people ought to act. At some level, all forms of utilitarianism use a hedonistic calculus or cost/benefit analysis as a decision procedure for determining what is moral. Secondly, the happiness that determines morality is not merely individual happiness but rather that of all affected. Utilitarianism is egalitarian in this respect meaning that everyone's happiness counts equally with no one's happiness having more significance than anyone else's happiness. Furthermore, everyone's happiness includes that of any sentient being, that is, any creature capable of feeling pleasure or pain and thus having an interest.

Utilitarianism in its modern form was introduced and popularized by Jeremy Bentham and John Stuart Mill in the nineteenth century; however, its roots go back to ancient times. Philosophical ideas stemming from the works of Aristotle and Epicurus are very influential on modern utilitarianism. Modern utilitarianism is often connected to and associated with hedonism, the view that pleasure and the absence of pain are the sole objects of inherent value. Both Bentham and Mill define happiness in terms of pleasure and the absence of pain. While pleasure constitutes a common way of thinking about happiness, there are problems that arise for such a view and some utilitarians offer different accounts of what happiness is, including possibilities such as preference satisfaction or a more general sense of welfare or well-being.

Utilitarianism holds that morality is objective. The main principle that utilitarians subscribe to is known as the principle of utility or the greatest happiness principle. According to this principle, something is right insofar as it produces happiness/reduces unhappiness for all affected and something is wrong insofar as it produces unhappiness/minimizes happiness for all affected. Thus, a thing is right or wrong regardless of what anyone happens to think. Rather, morality is determined by relevant facts about the universe which in this case would have to do with happiness production. It is worth noting that while all utilitarians endorse the principle of utility as the supreme principle of morality, not all utilitarians apply it in the same way. One significant distinction is that which is drawn between act utilitarians and rule utilitarians. Act utilitarians apply the principle of utility directly to actions and in doing so, evaluate each individual case in terms of the specific consequences of that case. On the other hand, rule utilitarians evaluate individual actions in terms of more general social rules of whose consequences increase happiness beyond that of alternative social rules. In other words, rule utilitarians use the principle of utility to determine which rules we use to evaluate the morality of individual actions. The distinction between act and rule utilitarians postdates the work of Bentham and Mill, although many scholars now interpret their views in light of this distinction.

John Stuart Mill's *Utilitarianism* introduces the theory and defends it against several criticisms. In the chapters found here, Mill attempts to prove utilitarianism in two ways, although he admits that "proof" in the strict sense of the term is not possible, meaning it cannot be established conclusively through reasoning. Instead, Mill first explains how utilitarianism has been criticized, constructing arguments as to why such criticisms do not hold. Second, Mill offers affirmative reasons why utilitarianism offers a plausible account of morality. He also discusses the relationship between utilitarianism and virtue.

Kai Nielsen's article "Against Moral Conservativism" considers hypothetical cases that present variations of a common type of objection that consequentialist theories face due to their emphasis on outcome as the central concern in assessing morality. Nielsen argues against alternative ethical theories that take a more conservative approach to such problems and defends the plausibility of consequentialist theories in responding to such ethically challenging circumstances.

Utilitarianism

John Stuart Mill

∾

Chapter II. What Utilitarianism Is.

A passing remark is all that needs be given to the ignorant blunder of supposing that those who stand up for utility as the test of right and wrong, use the
term in that restricted and merely colloquial sense in which utility is opposed
to pleasure. An apology is due to the philosophical opponents of utilitarianism, for even the momentary appearance of confounding them with any
one capable of so absurd a misconception; which is the more extraordinary,
inasmuch as the contrary accusation, of referring everything to pleasure,
and that too in its grossest form, is another of the common charges against
utilitarianism: and, as has been pointedly remarked by an able writer, the
same sort of persons, and often the very same persons, denounce the theory
"as impracticably dry when the word utility precedes the word pleasure, and
as too practically voluptuous when the word pleasure precedes the word
utility." Those who know anything about the matter are aware that every
writer, from Epicurus to Bentham, who maintained the theory of utility,
meant by it, not something to be contradistinguished from pleasure, but
pleasure itself, together with exemption from pain; and instead of opposing
the useful to the agreeable or the ornamental, have always declared that the
useful means these, among other things. Yet the common herd, including
the herd of writers, not only in newspapers and periodicals, but in books
of weight and pretension, are perpetually falling into this shallow mistake.
Having caught up the word utilitarian, while knowing nothing whatever about
it but its sound, they habitually express by it the rejection, or the neglect, of

John Stuart Mill, "What Utilitarianism Is," *Utilitarianism*.

pleasure in some of its forms; of beauty, of ornament, or of amusement. Nor is the term thus ignorantly misapplied solely in disparagement, but occasionally in compliment; as though it implied superiority to frivolity and the mere pleasures of the moment. And this perverted use is the only one in which the word is popularly known, and the one from which the new generation are acquiring their sole notion of its meaning. Those who introduced the word, but who had for many years discontinued it as a distinctive appellation, may well feel themselves called upon to resume it, if by doing so they can hope to contribute anything towards rescuing it from this utter degradation.[A]

The creed which accepts as the foundation of morals, Utility, or the Greatest Happiness Principle, holds that actions are right in proportion as they tend to promote happiness, wrong as they tend to produce the reverse of happiness. By happiness is intended pleasure, and the absence of pain; by unhappiness, pain, and the privation of pleasure. To give a clear view of the moral standard set up by the theory, much more requires to be said; in particular, what things it includes in the ideas of pain and pleasure; and to what extent this is left an open question. But these supplementary explanations do not affect the theory of life on which this theory of morality is grounded—namely, that pleasure, and freedom from pain, are the only things desirable as ends; and that all desirable things (which are as numerous in the utilitarian as in any other scheme) are desirable either for the pleasure inherent in themselves, or as means to the promotion of pleasure and the prevention of pain.

Now, such a theory of life excites in many minds, and among them in some of the most estimable in feeling and purpose, inveterate dislike. To suppose that life has (as they express it) no higher end than pleasure—no better and nobler object of desire and pursuit—they designate as utterly mean and grovelling; as a doctrine worthy only of swine, to whom the followers of Epicurus were, at a very early period, contemptuously likened; and modern holders of the doctrine are occasionally made the subject of equally polite comparisons by its German, French, and English assailants.

When thus attacked, the Epicureans have always answered, that it is not they, but their accusers, who represent human nature in a degrading light; since the accusation supposes human beings to be capable of no pleasures except those of which swine are capable. If this supposition were true, the charge could not be gainsaid, but would then be no longer an imputation; for if the sources of pleasure were precisely the same to human beings and to swine, the rule of life which is good enough for the one would be good enough for the other. The comparison of the Epicurean life to that of beasts is felt as degrading, precisely because a beast's pleasures do not satisfy a human being's conceptions of happiness. Human beings have faculties more elevated than the animal appetites, and when once made conscious of them, do not regard anything as happiness which does not include their gratification. I do not, indeed, consider the Epicureans to have been by any means faultless in drawing out their scheme of consequences from the utilitarian principle. To do this in any sufficient manner, many Stoic, as well as Christian elements require to be included. But there is no known Epicurean theory of life which does not assign to the pleasures of the intellect; of the feelings and imagination, and of the moral sentiments, a much higher value as pleasures than to those of mere sensation. It must be admitted, however, that utilitarian writers in general have placed the superiority of mental over bodily pleasures chiefly in the greater permanency, safety, uncostliness, &c., of the former—that is, in their circumstantial advantages rather than in their intrinsic nature. And on all these points utilitarians have fully proved their case; but they might have taken the other, and, as it may be called, higher ground, with entire consistency. It is quite compatible with the principle of utility to recognise the fact, that some _kinds_ of pleasure are more desirable and more valuable than others. It would be absurd that while, in estimating all other things, quality is considered as well as quantity, the estimation of pleasures should be supposed to depend on quantity alone.

If I am asked, what I mean by difference of quality in pleasures, or what makes one pleasure more valuable than another, merely as a pleasure, except its being greater in amount, there is but one possible answer. Of two pleasures, if there be one to which all or almost all who have experience of both give a decided preference, irrespective of any feeling of moral obligation to prefer it, that is the more desirable pleasure. If one of the two is, by those who are competently acquainted with both, placed so far above the other that they prefer it, even though knowing it to be attended with a greater amount of discontent, and would not resign it for any quantity of the other pleasure which their nature is capable of, we are justified in ascribing to the preferred enjoyment a superiority in quality, so far outweighing quantity as to render it, in comparison, of small account.

Now it is an unquestionable fact that those who are equally acquainted with, and equally capable of appreciating and enjoying, both, do give a most marked preference to the manner of existence which employs their higher faculties. Few human creatures would consent to be changed into any of the lower animals, for a promise of the fullest allowance of a beast's pleasures; no intelligent human being would consent to be a fool, no instructed person would be an ignoramus, no person of feeling and conscience would be selfish and base, even though they should be persuaded that the fool, the dunce, or the rascal is better satisfied with his lot than they are with theirs. They would not resign what they possess more than he, for the most complete satisfaction of all the desires which they have in common with him. If they ever fancy they would, it is only in cases of unhappiness so extreme, that to escape from it they would exchange their lot for almost any other, however undesirable in their own eyes. A being of higher faculties requires more to make him happy, is capable probably of more acute suffering, and is certainly accessible to it at more points, than one of an inferior type; but in spite of these liabilities, he can never really wish to sink into what he feels to be a lower grade of existence. We may give what explanation we please of this unwillingness; we may attribute it to pride, a name which is given indiscriminately to some of the most and to some of the least estimable feelings of which mankind are capable; we may refer it to the love of liberty and personal independence, an appeal to which was with the Stoics one of the most effective means for the inculcation of it; to the love of power, or to the love of excitement, both of which do really enter into and contribute to it: but its most appropriate appellation is a sense of dignity, which all human beings possess in one form or other, and in some, though by no means in exact, proportion to their higher faculties, and which is so essential a part of the happiness of those in whom it is strong, that nothing which conflicts with it could be, otherwise than momentarily, an object of desire to them. Whoever supposes that this preference takes place at a sacrifice of happiness-that the superior being, in anything like equal circumstances, is not happier than the inferior-confounds the two very different ideas, of happiness, and content. It is indisputable that the being whose capacities of enjoyment are low, has the greatest chance of having them fully satisfied; and a highly-endowed being will always feel that any happiness which he can look for, as the world is constituted, is imperfect. But he can learn to bear its imperfections, if they are at all bearable; and they will not make him envy the being who is indeed unconscious of the imperfections, but only because he feels not at all the good which those imperfections qualify. It is better to be a human being dissatisfied than a pig satisfied; better to be Socrates dissatisfied than a fool satisfied. And if the fool, or the pig, is of a different opinion, it is because they only know their own side of the question. The other party to the comparison knows both sides.

It may be objected, that many who are capable of the higher pleasures, occasionally, under the influence of temptation, postpone them to the lower. But this is quite compatible with a full appreciation of the intrinsic superiority of the higher. Men often, from infirmity of character, make their election for the nearer good, though they know it to be the less valuable; and this no less when the choice is between two bodily pleasures, than when it is between bodily and mental. They pursue sensual indulgences to the injury of health, though perfectly aware that health is the greater good. It may be further objected, that many who begin with youthful enthusiasm for everything noble, as they advance in years sink into indolence and selfishness. But I do not believe that those who undergo this very common change, voluntarily choose the lower description of pleasures in preference to the higher. I believe that before they devote themselves exclusively to the one, they have already become incapable of the other. Capacity for the nobler feelings is in most natures a very tender plant, easily killed, not only by hostile influences, but by mere want of sustenance; and in the majority of young persons it speedily dies away if the occupations to which their position in life has devoted them, and the society into which it has thrown them, are not favourable to keeping that higher capacity in exercise. Men lose their high aspirations as they lose their intellectual tastes, because they have not time or opportunity for indulging them; and they addict themselves to inferior pleasures, not because they deliberately prefer them, but because they are either the only ones to which they have access, or the only ones which they are any longer capable of enjoying. It may be questioned whether any one who has remained equally susceptible to both classes of pleasures, ever knowingly and calmly preferred the lower; though many, in all ages, have broken down in an ineffectual attempt to combine both.

From this verdict of the only competent judges, I apprehend there can be no appeal. On a question which is the best worth having of two pleasures, or which of two modes of existence is the most grateful to the feelings, apart from its moral attributes and from its consequences, the judgment of those who are qualified by knowledge of both, or, if they differ, that of the majority among them, must be admitted as final. And there needs be the less hesitation to accept this judgment respecting the quality of pleasures, since there is no other tribunal to be referred to even on the question of quantity. What means are there of determining which is the acutest of two pains, or the intensest of two pleasurable sensations, except the general suffrage of those who are familiar with both? Neither pains nor pleasures are homogeneous, and pain is always heterogeneous with pleasure. What is there to decide whether a particular pleasure is worth purchasing at the cost of a particular pain, except the feelings and judgment of the experienced? When, therefore, those feelings and judgment declare the pleasures derived from the higher faculties to be preferable _in kind_, apart from the question of intensity, to those of which the animal nature, disjoined from the higher faculties, is susceptible, they are entitled on this subject to the same regard.

I have dwelt on this point, as being a necessary part of a perfectly just conception of Utility or Happiness, considered as the directive rule of human conduct. But it is by no means an indispensable condition to the acceptance of the utilitarian standard; for that standard is not the agent's own greatest happiness, but the greatest amount of happiness altogether; and if it may possibly be doubted whether a noble character is always the happier for its nobleness, there can be no doubt that it makes other people happier, and that the world in general is immensely a gainer by it. Utilitarianism, therefore, could only attain its end by the general cultivation of nobleness of character, even if each individual were only benefited by the nobleness of others, and his own, so far as happiness is concerned, were a sheer deduction from the benefit. But the bare enunciation of such an absurdity as this last, renders refutation superfluous.

According to the Greatest Happiness Principle, as above explained, the ultimate end, with reference to and for the sake of which all other things are desirable (whether we are considering our own good or that of other people), is an existence exempt as far as possible from pain, and as rich as possible in enjoyments, both in point of quantity and quality; the test of quality, and the rule for measuring it against quantity, being the preference felt by those who, in their opportunities of experience, to which must be added their habits of self-consciousness and self-observation, are best furnished with the means of comparison. This, being, according to the utilitarian opinion, the end of human action, is necessarily also the standard of morality; which may accordingly be defined, the rules and precepts for human conduct, by the observance of which an existence such as has been described might be, to the greatest extent possible, secured to all mankind; and not to them only, but, so far as the nature of things admits, to the whole sentient creation.

Against this doctrine, however, arises another class of objectors, who say that happiness, in any form, cannot be the rational purpose of human life and action; because, in the first place, it is unattainable: and they contemptuously ask, What right hast thou to be happy? a question which Mr. Carlyle clenches by the addition, What right, a short time ago, hadst thou even _to be_? Next, they say, that men can do _without_ happiness; that all noble human beings have felt this, and could not have become noble but by learning the lesson of Entsagen, or renunciation; which lesson, thoroughly learnt and submitted to, they affirm to be the beginning and necessary condition of all virtue.

The first of these objections would go to the root of the matter were it well founded; for if no happiness is to be had at all by human beings, the attainment of it cannot be the end of morality, or of any rational conduct. Though, even in that case, something might still be said for the utilitarian theory; since utility includes not solely the pursuit of happiness, but the prevention or mitigation of unhappiness; and if the former aim be chimerical, there will be all the greater scope and more imperative need for the latter, so long at least as mankind think fit to live, and do not take refuge in the simultaneous act of suicide recommended under certain conditions by Novalis. When, however, it is thus positively asserted to be impossible that human life should be happy, the assertion, if not something like a verbal quibble, is at least an exaggeration. If by happiness be meant a continuity of highly pleasurable excitement, it is evident enough that this is impossible. A state of exalted pleasure lasts only moments, or in some cases, and with some intermissions, hours or days, and is the occasional brilliant flash of enjoyment, not its permanent and steady flame. Of this the philosophers who have taught that happiness is the end of life were as fully aware as those who taunt them. The happiness which they meant was not a life of rapture, but moments of such, in an existence made up of few and transitory pains, many and various pleasures, with a decided predominance of the active over the passive, and having as the foundation of the whole, not to expect more from life than it is capable of bestowing. A life thus composed, to those who have been fortunate enough to obtain it, has always appeared worthy of the name of happiness. And such an existence is even now the lot of many, during some considerable portion of their lives. The present wretched education, and wretched social arrangements, are the only real hindrance to its being attainable by almost all.

The objectors perhaps may doubt whether human beings, if taught to consider happiness as the end of life, would be satisfied with such a moderate share of it. But great numbers of mankind have been satisfied with much less. The main constituents of a satisfied life appear to be two, either of which by itself is often found sufficient for the purpose: tranquillity, and excitement. With much tranquillity, many find that they can be content with very little pleasure: with much excitement, many can reconcile themselves to a considerable quantity of pain. There is assuredly no inherent impossibility in enabling even the mass of mankind to unite both; since the two are so far from being incompatible that they are in natural alliance, the prolongation of either being a preparation for, and exciting a wish for, the other. It is only those in whom indolence amounts to a vice, that do not desire excitement after an interval of repose; it is only those in whom the need of excitement is a disease, that feel the tranquillity which follows excitement dull and insipid, instead of pleasurable in direct proportion to the excitement which preceded it. When people who are tolerably fortunate in their outward lot do not find in life sufficient enjoyment to make it valuable to them, the cause generally is, caring for nobody but themselves. To those who have neither public nor private affections, the excitements of life are much curtailed, and in any case dwindle in value as the time approaches when all selfish interests must be terminated by death: while those who leave after them objects of personal affection, and especially those who have also cultivated a fellow-feeling with the collective interests of mankind, retain as lively an interest in life on the eve of death as in the vigour of youth and health. Next to selfishness, the principal cause which makes life unsatisfactory, is want of mental cultivation. A cultivated mind—I do not mean that of a philosopher, but any mind to which the fountains of knowledge have been opened, and which has been taught, in any tolerable degree, to exercise its faculties—finds sources of inexhaustible interest in all that surrounds it; in the objects of nature, the achievements of art, the imaginations of poetry, the incidents of history, the ways of mankind past and present, and their prospects in the future. It is possible, indeed, to become indifferent to all this, and that too without having exhausted a thousandth part of it; but only when one has had from the beginning no moral or human interest in these things, and has sought in them only the gratification of curiosity.

Now there is absolutely no reason in the nature of things why an amount of mental culture sufficient to give an intelligent interest in these objects of contemplation, should not be the inheritance of every one born in a civilized country. As little is there an inherent necessity that any human being should be a selfish egotist, devoid of every feeling or care but those which centre in his own miserable individuality. Something far superior to this is sufficiently common even now, to give ample earnest of what the human species may be made. Genuine private affections, and a sincere interest in the public good, are possible, though in unequal degrees, to every rightly brought-up human being. In a world in which there is so much to interest, so much to enjoy, and so much also to correct and improve, every one who has this moderate amount of moral and intellectual requisites is capable of an existence which may be called enviable; and unless such a person, through bad laws, or subjection to the will of others, is denied the liberty to use the sources of happiness within his reach, he will not fail to find this enviable existence, if he escape the positive evils of life, the great sources of physical and mental suffering—such as indigence, disease, and the unkindness, worthlessness, or premature loss of objects of affection. The main stress of the problem lies, therefore, in the contest with these calamities, from which it is a rare good fortune entirely to escape; which, as things now are, cannot be obviated, and often cannot be in any material degree mitigated. Yet no one whose opinion deserves a moment's consideration can doubt that most of the great positive evils of the world are in themselves removable, and will, if human affairs continue to improve, be in the end reduced within narrow limits. Poverty, in any sense implying suffering, may be completely extinguished by the wisdom of society, combined with the good sense and providence of individuals. Even that most intractable of enemies, disease, may be indefinitely reduced in dimensions by good physical and moral education, and proper control of noxious influences; while the progress of science holds out a promise for the future of still more direct conquests over this detestable foe. And every advance in that direction relieves us from some, not only of the chances which cut short our own lives, but, what concerns us still more, which deprive us of those in whom our happiness is wrapt up. As for vicissitudes of fortune, and other disappointments connected with worldly circumstances, these are principally the effect either of gross imprudence, of ill-regulated desires, or of bad or imperfect social institutions. All the grand sources, in short, of human suffering are in a great degree, many of them almost entirely, conquerable by human care and effort; and though their removal is grievously slow—though a long succession of generations will perish in the breach before the conquest is completed, and this world becomes all that, if will and knowledge were not wanting, it might easily be made— yet every mind sufficiently intelligent and generous to bear a part, however small and unconspicuous, in the endeavour, will draw a noble enjoyment from the contest itself, which he would not for any bribe in the form of selfish indulgence consent to be without.

And this leads to the true estimation of what is said by the objectors concerning the possibility, and the obligation, of learning to do without happiness. Unquestionably it is possible to do without happiness; it is done involuntarily by nineteen-twentieths of mankind, even in those parts of our present world which are least deep in barbarism; and it often has to be done voluntarily by the hero or the martyr, for the sake of something which he prizes more than his individual happiness. But this something, what is it, unless the happiness of others, or some of the requisites of happiness? It is noble to be capable of resigning entirely one's own portion of happiness, or chances of it: but, after all, this self-sacrifice must be for some end; it is not its own end; and if we are told that its end is not happiness, but virtue, which is better than happiness, I ask, would the sacrifice be made if the hero or martyr did not believe that it would earn for others immunity from similar sacrifices? Would it be made, if he thought that his renunciation of happiness for himself would produce no fruit for any of his fellow creatures, but to make their lot like his, and place them also in the condition of persons who have renounced happiness? All honour to those who can abnegate for themselves the personal enjoyment of life, when by such renunciation they contribute worthily to increase the amount of happiness in the world; but he who does it, or professes to do it, for any other purpose, is no more deserving of admiration than the ascetic mounted on his pillar. He may be an inspiriting proof of what men _can_ do, but assuredly not an example of what they _should_.

Though it is only in a very imperfect state of the world's arrangements that any one can best serve the happiness of others by the absolute sacrifice of his own, yet so long as the world is in that imperfect state, I fully acknowledge that the readiness to make such a sacrifice is the highest virtue which can be found in man. I will add, that in this condition of the world, paradoxical as the assertion may be, the conscious ability to do without happiness gives the best prospect of realizing such happiness as is attainable. For nothing except that consciousness can raise a person above the chances of life, by making him feel that, let fate and fortune do their worst, they have not power to subdue him: which, once felt, frees him from excess of anxiety concerning the evils of life, and enables him, like many a Stoic in the worst times of the Roman Empire, to cultivate in tranquillity the sources of satisfaction accessible to him, without concerning himself about the uncertainty of their duration, any more than about their inevitable end.

Meanwhile, let utilitarians never cease to claim the morality of self-devotion as a possession which belongs by as good a right to them, as either to the Stoic or to the Transcendentalist. The utilitarian morality does recognise in human beings the power of sacrificing their own greatest good for the good of others. It only refuses to admit that the sacrifice is itself a good. A sacrifice which does not increase, or tend to increase, the sum total of happiness, it considers as wasted. The only self-renunciation which it applauds, is devotion to the happiness, or to some of the means of happiness, of others; either of mankind collectively, or of individuals within the limits imposed by the collective interests of mankind.

I must again repeat, what the assailants of utilitarianism seldom have the justice to acknowledge, that the happiness which forms the utilitarian standard of what is right in conduct, is not the agent's own happiness, but that of all concerned. As between his own happiness and that of others, utilitarianism requires him to be as strictly impartial as a disinterested and benevolent spectator. In the golden rule of Jesus of Nazareth, we read the complete spirit of the ethics of utility. To do as one would be done by, and to love one's neighbour as oneself, constitute the ideal perfection of utilitarian morality. As the means of making the nearest approach to this ideal, utility would enjoin, first, that laws and social arrangements should place the happiness, or (as speaking practically it may be called) the interest, of every individual, as nearly as possible in harmony with the interest of the whole; and secondly, that education and opinion, which have so vast a power over human character, should so use that power as to establish in the mind of every individual an indissoluble association between his own happiness and the good of the whole; especially between his own happiness and the practice of such modes of conduct, negative and positive, as regard for the universal happiness prescribes: so that not only he may be unable to conceive the possibility of happiness to himself, consistently with conduct opposed to the general good, but also that a direct impulse to promote the general good may be in every individual one of the habitual motives of action, and the sentiments connected therewith may fill a large and prominent place in every human being's sentient existence. If the impugners of the utilitarian morality represented it to their own minds in this its true character, I know not what recommendation possessed by any other morality they could possibly affirm to be wanting to it: what more beautiful or more exalted developments of human nature any other ethical system can be supposed to foster, or what springs of action, not accessible to the utilitarian, such systems rely on for giving effect to their mandates.

The objectors to utilitarianism cannot always be charged with representing it in a discreditable light. On the contrary, those among them who entertain anything like a just idea of its disinterested character, sometimes find fault with its standard as being too high for humanity. They say it is exacting too much to require that people shall always act from the inducement of promoting the general interests of society. But this is to mistake the very meaning of a standard of morals, and to confound the rule of action with the motive of it. It is the business of ethics to tell us what are our duties, or by what test we may know them; but no system of ethics requires that the sole motive of all we do shall be a feeling of duty; on the contrary, ninety-nine hundredths of all our actions are done from other motives, and rightly so done, if the rule of duty does not condemn them. It is the more unjust to utilitarianism that this particular misapprehension should be made a ground of objection to it, inasmuch as utilitarian moralists have gone beyond almost all others in affirming that the motive has nothing to do with the morality of the action, though much with the worth of the agent. He who saves a fellow creature from drowning does what is morally right, whether his motive be duty, or the hope of being paid for his trouble: he who betrays the friend that trusts him, is guilty of a crime, even if his object be to serve another friend to whom he is under greater obligations.[B] But to speak only of actions done from the motive of duty, and in direct obedience to principle: it is a misapprehension of the utilitarian mode of thought, to conceive it as implying that people should fix their minds upon so wide a generality as the world, or society at large. The great majority of good actions are intended, not for the benefit of the world, but for that of individuals, of which the good of the world is made up; and the thoughts of the most virtuous man need not on these occasions travel beyond the particular persons concerned, except so far as is necessary to assure himself that in benefiting them he is not violating the rights—that is, the legitimate and authorized expectations—of any one else. The multiplication of happiness is, according to the utilitarian ethics, the object of virtue: the occasions on which any person (except one in a thousand) has it in his power to do this on an extended scale, in other words, to be a public benefactor, are but exceptional; and on these occasions alone is he called on to consider public utility; in every other case, private utility, the interest or happiness of some few persons, is all he has to attend to. Those alone the influence of whose actions extends to society in general, need concern themselves habitually about so large an object. In the case of abstinences indeed—of things which people forbear to do, from moral considerations, though the consequences in the particular case might be beneficial—it would be unworthy of an intelligent agent not to be consciously aware that the action is of a class which, if practised generally, would be generally injurious, and that this is the ground of the obligation to abstain from it. The amount of regard for the public interest implied in this recognition, is no greater than is demanded by every system of morals; for they all enjoin to abstain from whatever is manifestly pernicious to society.

The same considerations dispose of another reproach against the doctrine of utility, founded on a still grosser misconception of the purpose of a standard of morality, and of the very meaning of the words right and wrong. It is often affirmed that utilitarianism renders men cold and unsympathizing; that it chills their moral feelings towards individuals; that it makes them regard only the dry and hard consideration of the consequences of actions, not taking into their moral estimate the qualities from which those actions emanate. If the assertion means that they do not allow their judgment respecting the rightness or wrongness of an action to be influenced by their opinion of the qualities of the person who does it, this is a complaint not against utilitarianism, but against having any standard of morality at all; for certainly no known ethical standard decides an action to be good or bad because it is done by a good or a bad man, still less because done by an amiable, a brave, or a benevolent man or the contrary. These considerations are relevant, not to the estimation of actions, but of persons; and there is nothing in the utilitarian theory inconsistent with the fact that there are other things which interest us in persons besides the rightness and wrongness of their actions. The Stoics, indeed, with the paradoxical misuse of language which was part of their system, and by which they strove to raise themselves above all concern about anything but virtue, were fond of saying that he who has that has everything; that he, and only he, is rich, is beautiful, is a king. But no claim of this description is made for the virtuous man by the utilitarian doctrine. Utilitarians are quite aware that there are other desirable possessions and qualities besides virtue, and are perfectly willing to allow to all of them their full worth. They are also aware that a right action does not necessarily indicate a virtuous character, and that actions which are blameable often proceed from qualities entitled to praise. When this is apparent in any particular case, it modifies their estimation, not certainly of the act, but of the agent. I grant that they are, notwithstanding, of opinion, that in the long run the best proof of a good character is good actions; and resolutely refuse to consider any mental disposition as good, of which the predominant tendency is to produce bad conduct. This makes them unpopular with many people; but it is an unpopularity which they must share with every one who regards the distinction between right and wrong in a serious light; and the reproach is not one which a conscientious utilitarian need be anxious to repel.

If no more be meant by the objection than that many utilitarians look on the morality of actions, as measured by the utilitarian standard, with too exclusive a regard, and do not lay sufficient stress upon the other beauties of character which go towards making a human being loveable or admirable, this may be admitted. Utilitarians who have cultivated their moral feelings, but not their sympathies nor their artistic perceptions, do fall into this mistake; and so do all other moralists under the same conditions. What can be said in excuse for other moralists is equally available for them, namely, that if there is to be any error, it is better that it should be on that side. As a matter of fact, we may affirm that among utilitarians as among adherents of other systems, there is every imaginable degree of rigidity and of laxity in the application of their standard: some are even puritanically rigorous, while others are as indulgent as can possibly be desired by sinner or by sentimentalist. But on the whole, a doctrine which brings prominently forward the interest that mankind have in the repression and prevention of conduct which violates the moral law, is likely to be inferior to no other in turning the sanctions of opinion against such violations. It is true, the question, What does violate the moral law? is one on which those who recognise different standards of morality are likely now and then to differ. But difference of opinion on moral questions was not first introduced into the world by utilitarianism, while that doctrine does supply, if not always an easy, at all events a tangible and intelligible mode of deciding such differences.

* * * * *

It may not be superfluous to notice a few more of the common misapprehensions of utilitarian ethics, even those which are so obvious and gross that it might appear impossible for any person of candour and intelligence to fall into them: since persons, even of considerable mental endowments, often give themselves so little trouble to understand the bearings of any opinion against which they entertain a prejudice, and men are in general so little conscious of this voluntary ignorance as a defect, that the vulgarest misunderstandings of ethical doctrines are continually met with in the deliberate writings of persons of the greatest pretensions both to high principle and to philosophy. We not uncommonly hear the doctrine of utility inveighed against as a _godless_ doctrine. If it be necessary to say anything at all against so mere an assumption, we may say that the question depends upon what idea we have formed of the moral character of the Deity. If it be a true belief that God desires, above all things, the happiness of his creatures, and that this was his purpose in their creation, utility is not only not a godless doctrine, but more profoundly religious than any other. If it be meant that utilitarianism does not recognise the revealed will of God as the supreme law of morals, I answer, that an utilitarian who believes in the perfect goodness and wisdom of God, necessarily believes that whatever God has thought fit to reveal on the subject of morals, must fulfil the requirements of utility in a supreme degree. But others besides utilitarians have been of opinion that the Christian revelation was intended, and is fitted, to inform the hearts and minds of mankind with a spirit which should enable them to find for themselves what is right, and incline them to do it when found, rather than to tell them, except in a very general way, what it is: and that we need a doctrine of ethics, carefully followed out, to _interpret_ to us the will of God. Whether this opinion is correct or not, it is superfluous here to discuss; since whatever aid religion, either natural or revealed, can afford to ethical investigation, is as open to the utilitarian moralist as to any other. He can use it as the testimony of God to the usefulness or hurtfulness of any given course of action, by as good a right as others can use it for the indication of a transcendental law, having no connexion with usefulness or with happiness.

Again, Utility is often summarily stigmatized as an immoral doctrine by giving it the name of Expediency, and taking advantage of the popular use of that term to contrast it with Principle. But the Expedient, in the sense in which it is opposed to the Right, generally means that which is expedient for the particular interest of the agent himself: as when a minister sacrifices the interest of his country to keep himself in place. When it means anything better than this, it means that which is expedient for some immediate object, some temporary purpose, but which violates a rule whose observance is expedient in a much higher degree. The Expedient, in this sense, instead of being the same thing with the useful, is a branch of the hurtful. Thus, it would often be expedient, for the purpose of getting over some momentary embarrassment, or attaining some object immediately useful to ourselves or others, to tell a lie. But inasmuch as the cultivation in ourselves of a sensitive feeling on the subject of veracity, is one of the most useful, and the enfeeblement of that feeling one of the most hurtful, things to which our conduct can be instrumental; and inasmuch as any, even unintentional, deviation from truth, does that much towards weakening the trustworthiness of human assertion, which is not only the principal support of all present social well-being, but the insufficiency of which does more than any one thing that can be named to keep back civilisation, virtue, everything on which human happiness on the largest scale depends; we feel that the violation, for a present advantage, of a rule of such transcendent expediency, is not expedient, and that he who, for the sake of a convenience to himself or to some other individual, does what depends on him to deprive mankind of the good, and inflict upon them the evil, involved in the greater or less reliance which they can place in each other's word, acts the part of one of their worst enemies. Yet that even this rule, sacred as it is, admits of possible exceptions, is acknowledged by all moralists; the chief of which is when the withholding of some fact (as of information from a male-factor, or of bad news from a person dangerously ill) would preserve some one (especially a person other than oneself) from great and unmerited evil, and when the withholding can only be effected by denial. But in order that the exception may not extend itself beyond the need, and may have the least possible effect in weakening reliance on veracity, it ought to be recognized, and, if possible, its limits defined; and if the principle of utility is good for anything, it must be good for weighing these conflicting utilities against one another, and marking out the region within which one or the other preponderates.

Again, defenders of utility often find themselves called upon to reply to such objections as this—that there is not time, previous to action, for calculating and weighing the effects of any line of conduct on the general happiness. This is exactly as if any one were to say that it is impossible to guide our conduct by Christianity, because there is not time, on every occasion on which anything has to be done, to read through the Old and New Testaments. The answer to the objection is, that there has been ample time, namely, the whole past duration of the human species. During all that time mankind have been learning by experience the tendencies of actions; on which experience all the prudence, as well as all the morality of life, is dependent. People talk as if the commencement of this course of experience had hitherto been put off, and as if, at the moment when some man feels tempted to meddle with the property or life of another, he had to begin considering for the first time whether murder and theft are injurious to human happiness. Even then I do not think that he would find the question very puzzling; but, at all events, the matter is now done to his hand. It is truly a whimsical supposition, that if mankind were agreed in considering utility to be the test of morality, they would remain without any agreement as to what is useful, and would take no measures for having their notions on the subject taught to the young, and enforced by law and opinion. There is no difficulty in proving any ethical standard whatever to work ill, if we suppose universal idiocy to be conjoined with it, but on any hypothesis short of that, mankind must by this time have acquired positive beliefs as to the effects of some actions on their happiness; and the beliefs which have thus come down are the rules of morality for the multitude, and for the philosopher until he has succeeded in finding better. That philosophers might easily do this, even now, on many subjects; that the received code of ethics is by no means of divine right; and that mankind have still much to learn as to the effects of actions on the general happiness, I admit, or rather, earnestly maintain. The corollaries from the principle of utility, like the precepts of every practical art, admit of indefinite improvement, and, in a progressive state of the human mind, their improvement is perpetually going on. But to consider the rules of morality as improvable, is one thing; to pass over the intermediate generalizations entirely, and endeavour to test each individual action directly by the first principle, is another. It is a strange notion that the acknowledgment of a first principle is inconsistent with the admission of secondary ones. To inform a traveller respecting the place of his ultimate destination, is not to forbid the use of landmarks and direction-posts on the way. The proposition that happiness is the end and aim of morality, does not mean that no road ought to be laid down to that goal, or that persons going thither should not be advised to take one direction rather than another. Men really ought to leave off talking a kind of nonsense on this subject, which they would neither talk nor listen to on other matters of practical concernment. Nobody argues that the art of navigation is not founded on astronomy, because sailors cannot wait to calculate the Nautical Almanack. Being rational creatures, they go to sea with it ready calculated; and all rational creatures go out upon the sea of life with their minds made up on the common questions of right and wrong, as well as on many of the far more difficult questions of wise and foolish. And this, as long as foresight is a human quality, it is to be presumed they will continue to do. Whatever we adopt as the fundamental principle of morality, we require subordinate principles to apply it by: the impossibility of doing without them, being common to all systems, can afford no argument against any one in particular: but gravely to argue as if no such secondary principles could be had, and as if mankind had remained till now, and always must remain, without drawing any general conclusions from the experience of human life, is as high a pitch, I think, as absurdity has ever reached in philosophical controversy.

The remainder of the stock arguments against utilitarianism mostly consist in laying to its charge the common infirmities of human nature, and the general difficulties which embarrass conscientious persons in shaping their course through life. We are told that an utilitarian will be apt to make his own particular case an exception to moral rules, and, when under temptation, will see an utility in the breach of a rule, greater than he will see in its observance. But is utility the only creed which is able to furnish us with excuses for evil doing, and means of cheating our own conscience? They are afforded in abundance by all doctrines which recognise as a fact in morals the existence of conflicting considerations; which all doctrines do, that have been believed by sane persons. It is not the fault of any creed, but of the complicated nature of human affairs, that rules of conduct cannot be so framed as to require no exceptions, and that hardly any kind of action can safely be laid down as either always obligatory or always condemnable. There is no ethical creed which does not temper the rigidity of its laws, by giving a certain latitude, under the moral responsibility of the agent, for accommodation to peculiarities of circumstances; and under every creed, at the opening thus made, self-deception and dishonest casuistry get in. There exists no moral system under which there do not arise unequivocal cases of conflicting obligation. These are the real difficulties, the knotty points both in the theory of ethics, and in the conscientious guidance of personal conduct. They are overcome practically with greater or with less success according to the intellect and virtue of the individual; but it can hardly be pretended that any one will be the less qualified for dealing with them, from possessing an ultimate standard to which conflicting rights and duties can be referred. If utility is the ultimate source of moral obligations, utility may be invoked to decide between them when their demands are incompatible. Though the application of the standard may be difficult, it is better than none at all: while in other systems, the moral laws all claiming independent authority, there is no common umpire entitled to interfere between them; their claims to precedence one over another rest on little better than sophistry, and unless determined, as they generally are, by the unacknowledged influence of considerations of utility, afford a free scope for the action of personal desires and partialities. We must remember that only in these cases of conflict between secondary principles is it requisite that first principles should be appealed to. There is no case of moral obligation in which some secondary principle is not involved; and if only one, there can seldom be any real doubt which one it is, in the mind of any person by whom the principle itself is recognized.

Footnotes

[Footnote A: The author of this essay has reason for believing himself to be the first person who brought the word utilitarian into use. He did not invent it, but adopted it from a passing expression in Mr. Galt's _Annals of the Parish_. After using it as a designation for several years, he and others abandoned it from a growing dislike to anything resembling a badge or watchword of sectarian distinction. But as a name for one single opinion, not a set of opinions—to denote the recognition of utility as a standard, not any particular way of applying it—the term supplies a want in the language, and offers, in many cases, a convenient mode of avoiding tiresome circumlocution.]

[Footnote B: An opponent, whose intellectual and moral fairness it is a pleasure to acknowledge (the Rev. J. Llewellyn Davis), has objected to this passage, saying, "Surely the rightness or wrongness of saving a man from drowning does depend very much upon the motive with which it is done. Suppose that a tyrant, when his enemy jumped into the sea to escape from him, saved him from drowning simply in order that he might inflict upon him more exquisite tortures, would it tend to clearness to speak of that rescue as 'a morally right action?' Or suppose again, according to one of the stock illustrations of ethical inquiries, that a man betrayed a trust received from a friend, because the discharge of it would fatally injure that friend himself or some one belonging to him, would utilitarianism compel one to call the betrayal 'a crime' as much as if it had been done from the meanest motive?"

I submit, that he who saves another from drowning in order to kill him by torture afterwards, does not differ only in motive from him who does the same thing from duty or benevolence; the act itself is different. The rescue of the man is, in the case supposed, only the necessary first step of an act far more atrocious than leaving him to drown would have been. Had Mr. Davis said, "The rightness or wrongness of saving a man from drowning does depend very much"—not upon the motive, but—"upon the _intention_" no utilitarian would have differed from him. Mr. Davis, by an oversight too common not to be quite venial, has in this case confounded the very different ideas of Motive and Intention. There is no point which utilitarian thinkers (and Bentham preeminently) have taken more pains to illustrate than this. The morality of the action depends entirely upon the intention—that is, upon what the agent _wills to do_. But the motive, that is, the feeling which makes him will so to do, when it makes no difference in the act, makes none in the morality: though it makes a great difference in our moral estimation of the agent, especially if it indicates a good or a bad habitual _disposition_—a bent of character from which useful, or from which hurtful actions are likely to arise.]

READING 3.14

Of What Sort of Proof the Principle of Utility is Susceptible

John Stuart Mill

It has already been remarked, that questions of ultimate ends do not admit of proof, in the ordinary acceptation of the term. To be incapable of proof by reasoning is common to all first principles; to the first premises of our knowledge, as well as to those of our conduct. But the former, being matters of fact, may be the subject of a direct appeal to the faculties which judge of fact—namely, our senses, and our internal consciousness. Can an appeal be made to the same faculties on questions of practical ends? Or by what other faculty is cognizance taken of them?

Questions about ends are, in other words, questions what things are desirable. The utilitarian doctrine is, that happiness is desirable, and the only thing desirable, as an end; all other things being only desirable as means to that end. What ought to be required of this doctrine—what conditions is it requisite that the doctrine should fulfil—to make good its claim to be believed?

The only proof capable of being given that an object is visible, is that people actually see it. The only proof that a sound is audible, is that people hear it: and so of the other sources of our experience. In like manner, I apprehend, the sole evidence it is possible to produce that anything is desirable, is that people do actually desire it. If the end which the utilitarian doctrine proposes to itself were not, in theory and in practice, acknowledged to be an end, nothing could ever convince any person that it was so. No reason can be given why the general happiness is desirable, except that each person, so far as he believes it to be attainable, desires his own happiness. This, however, being a fact, we have not only all the proof which the case admits of, but all which it is possible to require, that happiness is a good: that each person's happiness is a good to that person, and the general happiness, therefore, a good to the aggregate of all persons. Happiness has made out its title as _one_ of the ends of conduct, and consequently one of the criteria of morality.

John Stuart Mill, "Of What Sort of Proof the Principle of Utility is Susceptible," *Utilitarianism*, pp. 22-26.

But it has not, by this alone, proved itself to be the sole criterion. To do that, it would seem, by the same rule, necessary to show, not only that people desire happiness, but that they never desire anything else. Now it is palpable that they do desire things which, in common language, are decidedly distinguished from happiness. They desire, for example, virtue, and the absence of vice, no less really than pleasure and the absence of pain. The desire of virtue is not as universal, but it is as authentic a fact, as the desire of happiness. And hence the opponents of the utilitarian standard deem that they have a right to infer that there are other ends of human action besides happiness, and that happiness is not the standard of approbation and disapprobation.

But does the utilitarian doctrine deny that people desire virtue, or maintain that virtue is not a thing to be desired? The very reverse. It maintains not only that virtue is to be desired, but that it is to be desired disinterestedly, for itself. Whatever may be the opinion of utilitarian moralists as to the original conditions by which virtue is made virtue; however they may believe (as they do) that actions and dispositions are only virtuous because they promote another end than virtue; yet this being granted, and it having been decided, from considerations of this description, what _is_ virtuous, they not only place virtue at the very head of the things which are good as means to the ultimate end, but they also recognise as a psychological fact the possibility of its being, to the individual, a good in itself, without looking to any end beyond it; and hold, that the mind is not in a right state, not in a state conformable to Utility, not in the state most conducive to the general happiness, unless it does love virtue in this manner—as a thing desirable in itself, even although, in the individual instance, it should not produce those other desirable consequences which it tends to produce, and on account of which it is held to be virtue. This opinion is not, in the smallest degree, a departure from the Happiness principle. The ingredients of happiness are very various, and each of them is desirable in itself, and not merely when considered as swelling an aggregate. The principle of utility does not mean that any given pleasure, as music, for instance, or any given exemption from pain, as for example health, are to be looked upon as means to a collective something termed happiness, and to be desired on that account. They are desired and desirable in and for themselves; besides being means, they are a part of the end. Virtue, according to the utilitarian doctrine, is not naturally and originally part of the end, but it is capable of becoming so; and in those who love it disinterestedly it has become so, and is desired and cherished, not as a means to happiness, but as a part of their happiness.

To illustrate this farther, we may remember that virtue is not the only thing, originally a means, and which if it were not a means to anything else, would be and remain indifferent, but which by association with what it is a means to, comes to be desired for itself, and that too with the utmost intensity. What, for example, shall we say of the love of money? There is nothing originally more desirable about money than about any heap of glittering pebbles. Its worth is solely that of the things which it will buy; the desires for other things than itself, which it is a means of gratifying. Yet the love of money is not only one of the strongest moving forces of human life, but money is, in many cases, desired in and for itself; the desire to possess it is often stronger than the desire to use it, and goes on increasing when all the desires which point to ends beyond it, to be compassed by it, are falling off. It may be then said truly, that money is desired not for the sake of an end, but as part of the end. From being a means to happiness, it has come to be itself a principal ingredient of the individual's conception of happiness. The same may be said of the majority of the great objects of human life—power, for example, or fame; except that to each of these there is a certain amount of immediate pleasure annexed, which has at least the semblance of being naturally inherent in them; a thing which cannot be said of money. Still, however, the strongest natural attraction, both of power and of fame, is the immense aid they give to the attainment of our other wishes; and it is the strong association thus generated between them and all our objects of desire, which gives to the direct desire of them the intensity it often assumes, so as in some characters to surpass in strength all other desires. In these cases the means have become a part of the end, and a more important part of it than any of the things which they are means to. What was once desired as an instrument for the attainment of happiness, has come to be desired for its own sake. In being desired for its own sake it is, however, desired as part of happiness. The person is made, or thinks he would be made, happy by its mere possession; and is made unhappy by failure to obtain it. The desire of it is not a different thing from the desire of happiness, any more than the love of music, or the desire of health. They are included in happiness. They are some of the elements of which the desire of happiness is made up. Happiness is not an abstract idea, but a concrete whole; and these are some of its parts. And the utilitarian standard sanctions and approves their being so. Life would be a poor thing, very ill provided with sources of happiness, if there were not this provision of nature, by which things originally indifferent, but conducive to, or otherwise associated with, the satisfaction of our primitive desires, become in themselves sources of pleasure more valuable than the primitive pleasures, both in permanency, in the space of human existence that they are capable of covering, and even in intensity. Virtue, according to the utilitarian conception, is a good of this description. There was no original desire of it, or motive to it, save its conduciveness to pleasure, and especially to protection from pain. But through the association thus formed, it may be felt a good in itself, and desired as such with as great intensity as any other good; and with this difference between it and the love of money, of power, or of fame, that all of these may, and often do, render the individual noxious to the other members of the society to which he belongs, whereas there is nothing which makes him so much a blessing to them as the cultivation of the disinterested, love of virtue. And consequently, the utilitarian standard, while it tolerates and approves those other acquired desires, up to the point beyond which they would be more injurious to the general happiness than promotive of it, enjoins and requires the cultivation of the love of virtue up to the greatest strength possible, as being above all things important to the general happiness.

It results from the preceding considerations, that there is in reality nothing desired except happiness. Whatever is desired otherwise than as a means to some end beyond itself, and ultimately to happiness, is desired as itself a part of happiness, and is not desired for itself until it has become so. Those who desire virtue for its own sake, desire it either because the consciousness of it is a pleasure, or because the consciousness of being without it is a pain, or for both reasons united; as in truth the pleasure and pain seldom exist separately, but almost always together, the same person feeling pleasure in the degree of virtue attained, and pain in not having attained more. If one of these gave him no pleasure, and the other no pain, he would not love or desire virtue, or would desire it only for the other benefits which it might produce to himself or to persons whom he cared for.

We have now, then, an answer to the question, of what sort of proof the principle of utility is susceptible. If the opinion which I have now stated is psychologically true—if human nature is so constituted as to desire nothing which is not either a part of happiness or a means of happiness, we can have no other proof, and we require no other, that these are the only things desirable. If so, happiness is the sole end of human action, and the promotion of it the test by which to judge of all human conduct; from whence it necessarily follows that it must be the criterion of morality, since a part is included in the whole.

And now to decide whether this is really so; whether mankind do desire nothing for itself but that which is a pleasure to them, or of which the absence is a pain; we have evidently arrived at a question of fact and experience, dependent, like all similar questions, upon evidence. It can only be determined by practised self-consciousness and self-observation, assisted by observation of others. I believe that these sources of evidence, impartially consulted, will declare that desiring a thing and finding it pleasant, aversion to it and thinking of it as painful, are phenomena entirely inseparable, or rather two parts of the same phenomenon; in strictness of language, two different modes of naming the same psychological fact: that to think of an object as desirable (unless for the sake of its consequences), and to think of it as pleasant, are one and the same thing; and that to desire anything, except in proportion as the idea of it is pleasant, is a physical and metaphysical impossibility.

So obvious does this appear to me, that I expect it will hardly be disputed: and the objection made will be, not that desire can possibly be directed to anything ultimately except pleasure and exemption from pain, but that the will is a different thing from desire; that a person of confirmed virtue, or any other person whose purposes are fixed, carries out his purposes without any thought of the pleasure he has in contemplating them, or expects to derive from their fulfilment; and persists in acting on them, even though these pleasures are much diminished, by changes in his character or decay of his passive sensibilities, or are outweighed by the pains which the pursuit of the purposes may bring upon him. All this I fully admit, and have stated it elsewhere, as positively and emphatically as any one. Will, the active phenomenon, is a different thing from desire, the state of passive sensibility, and though originally an offshoot from it, may in time take root and detach itself from the parent stock; so much so, that in the case of an habitual purpose, instead of willing the thing because we desire it, we often desire it only because we will it. This, however, is but an instance of that familiar fact, the power of habit, and is nowise confined to the case of virtuous actions. Many indifferent things, which men originally did from a motive of some sort, they continue to do from habit. Sometimes this is done unconsciously, the consciousness coming only after the action: at other times with conscious volition, but volition which has become habitual, and is put into operation by the force of habit, in opposition perhaps to the deliberate preference, as often happens with those who have contracted habits of vicious or hurtful indulgence. Third and last comes the case in which the habitual act of will in the individual instance is not in contradiction to the general intention prevailing at other times, but in fulfilment of it; as in the case of the person of confirmed virtue, and of all who pursue deliberately and consistently any determinate end. The distinction between will and desire thus understood, is an authentic and highly important psychological fact; but the fact consists solely in this—that will, like all other parts of our constitution, is amenable to habit, and that we may will from habit what we no longer desire for itself, or desire only because we will it. It is not the less true that will, in the beginning, is entirely produced by desire; including in that term the repelling influence of pain as well as the attractive one of pleasure. Let us take into consideration, no longer the person who has a confirmed will to do right, but him in whom that virtuous will is still feeble, conquerable by temptation, and not to be fully relied on; by what means can it be strengthened? How can the will to be virtuous, where it does not exist in sufficient force, be implanted or awakened? Only by making the person _desire_ virtue—by making him think of it in a pleasurable light, or of its absence in a painful one. It is by associating the doing right with pleasure, or the doing wrong with pain, or by eliciting and impressing and bringing home to the person's experience the pleasure naturally involved in the one or the pain in the other, that it is possible to call forth that will to be virtuous, which, when confirmed, acts without any thought of either pleasure or pain. Will is the child of desire, and passes out of the dominion of its parent only to come under that of habit. That which is the result of habit affords no presumption of being intrinsically good; and there would be no reason for wishing that the purpose of virtue should become independent of pleasure and pain, were it not that the influence of the pleasurable and painful associations which prompt to virtue is not sufficiently to be depended on for unerring constancy of action until it has acquired the support of habit. Both in feeling and in conduct, habit is the only thing which imparts certainty; and it is because of the importance to others of being able to rely absolutely on one's feelings and conduct, and to oneself of being able to rely on one's own, that the will to do right ought to be cultivated into this habitual independence. In other words, this state of the will is a means to good, not intrinsically a good; and does not contradict the doctrine that nothing is a good to human beings but in so far as it is either itself pleasurable, or a means of attaining pleasure or averting pain.

But if this doctrine be true, the principle of utility is proved. Whether it is so or not, must now be left to the consideration of the thoughtful reader.

Against Moral Conservativism

Kai Nielson

I

It is sometimes claimed that any consequentialist view of ethics has monstrous implications which make such a conception of morality untenable. What we must do—so the claim goes—is reject all forms of consequentialism and accept what has been labeled 'conservativism' or 'moral absolutism.' By 'conservativism' is meant, here, a normative ethical theory which maintains that there is a privileged moral principle or cluster of moral principles, prescribing determinate actions, with which it would always be wrong not to act in accordance no matter what the consequences. A key example of such a principle is the claim that it is always wrong to kill an innocent human, whatever the consequences of not doing so.

I will argue that such moral conservativism is itself unjustified and, indeed, has morally unacceptable consequences, while consequentialism does not have implications which are morally monstrous and does not contain evident moral mistakes.

A consequentialist maintains that actions, rules, policies, practices, and moral principles are ultimately to be judged by certain consequences: to wit (for a very influential kind of consequentialism), by whether doing them more than, or at least as much as doing anything else, or acting in accordance with them more than or at least as much as acting in accordance with alternative policies, practices, rules or principles, tends, on the whole, and for *everyone* involved, to maximize satisfaction and minimize dissatisfaction. The states of affairs to be sought are those which maximize these things to the greatest extent possible for all mankind. But while this all sounds very humane and

Kai Nielsen, "Against Moral Conversativism," *Ethics, vol. 82*, no. 3, pp. 219-225, 227-231. Copyright © 1972 by University of Chicago Press. Reprinted with permission.

humanitarian, when its implications are thought through, it has been force-fully argued, it will be seen actually to have inhumane and morally intolerable implications. Circumstances could arise in which one holding such a view would have to assert that one was justified in punishing, killing, torturing, or deliberately harming the innocent, and such a consequence is, morally speaking, unacceptable.[1] As Anscombe has put it, anyone who "really thinks, *in advance,* that it is open to question whether such an action as procuring the judicial execution of the innocent should be quite excluded from con-sideration—I do not want to argue with him; he shows a corrupt mind."[2]

At the risk of being thought to exhibit a corrupt mind and a shallow con-sequentialist morality, I should like to argue that things are not as simple and straightforward as Anscombe seems to believe.

Surely, every moral man must be appalled at the judicial execution of the innocent or at the punishment, torture, and killing of the innocent. Indeed, being appalled by such behavior partially defines what it is to be a moral agent. And a consequentialist has very good utilitarian grounds for being so appalled, namely, that it is always wrong to inflict pain for its own sake. But this does not get to the core considerations which divide a conservative position such as Anscombe's from a consequentialist view. There are a series of tough cases that need to be taken to heart and their implications thought through by any reflective person, be he a conservative or a consequentialist. By doing this, we can get to the heart of the issue between conservativism and consequentialism. Consider this clash between conservativism and consequentialism arising over the problem of a 'just war.'

If we deliberately bomb civilian targets, we do not pretend that civilians are combatants in any simple fashion, but argue that this bombing will terminate hostilities more quickly, and will minimize all around suffering. It is hard to see how any brand of utilitarian will escape Miss Anscombe's objections. We are certainly killing the innocent . . . we are not killing them for the sake of killing them, but to save the lives of other innocent persons. Utilitarians, I think, grit their teeth and put up with this as part of the logic of total war; Miss Anscombe and anyone who thinks like her surely has to either redescribe the situation to ascribe guilt to the civilians or else she has to refuse to accept this sort of military tactics as simply wrong.[3]

It is indeed true that we cannot but feel the force of Anscombe's objections here. But is it the case that anyone shows a corrupt mind if he defends such

---

1   Alan Donagan, "Is There a Credible Form of Utilitarianism?" and H. J. McCloskey, "A Non-Utilitarian Approach to Punishment," both in *Contemporary Utilitarianism,* ed. Michael D. Bayles (Garden City, N.Y.: Doubleday & Co., 1968).

2   Elizabeth Anscombe, "Modern Moral Philosophy," *Philosophy* 23 (January 1957): 16–17.

3   Alan Ryan, "Review of Jan Narveson's *Morality and Utility,*" *Philosophical Books* 9, no. 3 (October 1958): 14.

bombing when, horrible as it is, it will quite definitely lessen appreciably the total amount of suffering and death in the long run, and if he is sufficiently nonevasive not to rationalize such a bombing of civilians into a situation in which all the putatively innocent people—children and all—are somehow in some measure judged guilty? Must such a man exhibit a corrupt moral sense if he refuses to hold that such military tactics are never morally justified? Must this be the monstrous view of a fanatical man devoid of any proper moral awareness? It is difficult for me to believe that this must be so.

Consider the quite parallel actions of guerrilla fighters and terrorists in wars of national liberation. In certain almost unavoidable circumstances, they must deliberately kill the innocent. We need to see some cases in detail here to get the necessary contextual background, and for this reason the motion picture *The Battle of Algiers* can be taken as a convenient point of reference. There we saw Algerian women—gentle, kindly women with children of their own and plainly people of moral sensitivity—with evident heaviness of heart, plant bombs which they had every good reason to believe would kill innocent people, including children; and we also saw a French general, also a human being of moral fiber and integrity, order the torture of Arab terrorists and threaten the bombing of houses in which terrorists were concealed but which also contained innocent people, including children. There are indeed many people involved in such activities who are cruel, sadistic beasts, or simply morally indifferent or, in important ways, morally uncomprehending. But the characters I have referred to from *The Battle of Algiers* were not of that stamp. They were plainly moral agents of a high degree of sensitivity, and yet they deliberately killed or were prepared to kill the innocent. And, with inessential variations, this is a recurrent phenomenon of human living in extreme situations. Such cases are by no means desert-island or esoteric cases.

It is indeed arguable whether such actions are always morally wrong—whether anyone should ever act as the Arab women or French general acted. But what could not be reasonably maintained, *pace* Anscombe, by any stretch of the imagination, is that the characters I described from *The Battle of Algiers* exhibited corrupt minds. Possibly morally mistaken, yes; guilty of moral corruption, no.

Dropping the charge of moral corruption but sticking with the moral issue about what actions are right, is it not the case that my consequentialist position logically forces me to conclude that under some circumstances—where the good to be achieved is great enough—I must not only countenance but actually advocate such violence toward the innocent? But is it not always, no matter what the circumstances or consequences, wrong to countenance, advocate, or engage in such violence? To answer such a question affirmatively is to commit oneself to the kind of moral absolutism or conservativism which Anscombe advocates. But, given the alternatives, should not one be such a conservative or at least hold that certain deontological principles must never be overridden?

I will take, so to speak, the papal bull by the horns and answer that there are circumstances when such violence must be reluctantly assented to or even taken to be something that one, morally speaking, must do. But, *pace* Anscombe, this very much needs arguing, and I shall argue it; but first I would like to set out some further but simpler cases which have a similar bearing. They are, by contrast, artificial cases. I use them because, in their greater simplicity, by contrast with my above examples, there are fewer variables to control and I can more coveniently make the essential conceptual and moral points. But, if my argument is correct for these simpler cases, the line of reasoning employed is intended to be applicable to those more complex cases as well.

II

Consider the following cases embedded in their exemplary tales;

1. The Case of the Innocent Fat Man

Consider the story (well known to philosophers) of the fat man stuck in the mouth of a cave on a coast. He was leading a group of people out of the cave when he got stuck in the mouth of the cave and in a very short time high tide will be upon them, and unless he is promptly unstuck, they all will be drowned except the fat man, whose head is out of the cave. But, fortunately or unfortunately, someone has with him a stick of dynamite. The short of the matter is, either they use the dynamite and blast the poor innocent fat man out of the mouth of the cave or everyone else drowns. Either one life or many lives. Our conservative presumably would take the attitude that it is all in God's hands and say that he ought never to blast the fat man out, for it is always wrong to kill the innocent. Must or should a moral man come to that conclusion? I shall argue that he should not.

My first exemplary tale was designed to show that our normal, immediate, rather absolutistic, moral reactions need to be questioned along with such principles as 'The direct intention of the death of an innocent person is never justifiable.' I have hinted (and later shall argue) that we should *beware* of our moral outrage here—our naturally conservative and unreflective moral reactions—for here the consequentialist has a strong case for what I shall call 'moral radicalism.' But, before turning to a defense of that, I want to tell another story taken from Phillipa Foot but used for my own purposes.[4] This tale, I shall argue,

---

4   Phillipa Foot, "The Problem of Abortion and the Doctrine of the Double Effect," *Oxford Review*, no. 5 (Trinity 1967), pp. 5–15.

has a different import than our previous tale. Here our unrehearsed, common-sense moral reactions will stand up under moral scrutiny. But, I shall also argue when I consider them in Section III, that our commonsense moral reactions here, initial expectations to the contrary notwithstanding, can be shown to be justified on consequentialist grounds. The thrust of my argument for this case is that we are not justified in opting for a theistic and/or deontological absolutism or in rejecting consequentialism.

2. The Magistrate and the Threatening Mob

A magistrate or judge is faced with a very real threat from a large and uncontrollable mob of rioters demanding a culprit for a crime. Unless the criminal is produced, promptly tried, and executed, they will take their own bloody revenge on a much smaller and quite vulnerable section of the community (a kind of frenzied pogrom). The judge knows that the real culprit is unknown and that the authorities do not even have a good clew as to who he may be. But he also knows that there is within easy reach a disreputable, thoroughly disliked, and useless man, who, though innocent, could easily be framed so that the mob would be quite convinced that he was guilty and would be pacified if he were promptly executed. Recognizing that he can prevent the occurrence of extensive carnage only by framing some innocent person, the magistrate has him framed, goes through the mockery of a trial, and has him executed. Most of us regard such a framing and execution of such a man in such circumstances as totally unacceptable.[5] There are some who would say that it is categorically wrong—morally inexcusable—*whatever the circumstances.* Indeed, such a case remains a problem for the consequentialist, but here again, I shall argue, one can consistently remain a consequentialist and continue to accept commonsense moral convictions about such matters.

My storytelling is at an end. The job is to see what the stories imply. We must try to determine whether thinking through their implications should lead a clearheaded and morally sensitive man to abandon consequentialism and to adopt some form of theistic absolutism and/or deontological absolutism. I shall argue that it does not.

III

I shall consider the last case first because there are good reasons why the consequentialist should stick with commonsense moral convictions for such cases. I shall start by giving my rationale for that claim. If the magistrate were a

---

5 Later, I shall show that there are desert-island circumstances—i.e., highly improbable situations—in which such judicial railroading might be a moral necessity. But I also shall show what little force desert-island cases have in the articulation and defense of a normative ethical theory.

tough-minded but morally conscientious consequentialist, he could still, on straightforward consequentialist grounds, refuse to frame and execute the innocent man, even knowing that this would unleash the mob and cause much suffering and many deaths. The rationale for his particular moral stand would be that, by so framing and then executing such an innocent man, he would, in the long run, cause still more suffering through the resultant corrupting effect on the institution of justice. That is, in a case involving such extensive general interest in the issue—without that, there would be no problem about preventing the carnage or call for such extreme measures—knowledge that the man was framed, that the law had prostituted itself, would, surely, eventually leak out. This would encouarge mob action in other circumstances, would lead to an increased skepticism about the incorruptibility or even the reliability of the judicial process, and would set a dangerous precedent for less clearheaded or less scrupulously humane magistrates. Given such a potential for the corruption of justice, a utilitarian or consequentialist judge or magistrate could, on good utilitarian or consequentialist grounds, argue that it was morally wrong to frame an innocent man. If the mob must rampage if such a sacrificial lamb is not provided, then the mob must rampage.

Must a utilitarian or consequentialist come to such a conclusion? The answer is no. It is the conclusion which is, as things stand, the most reasonable conclusion, but that he *must* come to it is far too strong a claim. A consequentialist could *consistently*—I did not say successfully—argue that, in taking the above tough-minded utilitarian position, we have overestimated the corrupting effects of such judicial railroading. His circumstance was an extreme one: a situation not often to be repeated even if, instead of acting as he did, he had set a precedent by such an act of judicial murder. A utilitarian rather more skeptical than most utilitarians about the claims of commonsense morality might reason that the lesser evil here is the judicial murder of an innocent man, vile as it is. He would persist in his moral iconoclasm by standing on the consequentialist rock that the lesser evil is always to be preferred to the greater evil.

The short of it is that utilitarians could disagree, as other consequentialists could disagree, about what is morally required of us in that case. The disagreement here between utilitarians or consequentialists of the same type is not one concerning fundamental moral principles but a disagreement about the empirical facts, about what course of action would in the long run produce the least suffering and the most happiness for *everyone* involved.[6]

However, considering the effect advocating the deliberate judicial killing of an innocent man would have on the reliance people put on commonsense

---

6 'Everyone' here is used distributively; i.e., I am talking about the interests of each and every one. In that sense, everyone's interests need to be considered.

moral beliefs of such a ubiquitous sort as the belief that the innocent must not be harmed, a utilitarian who defended the centrality of commonsense moral beliefs would indeed have a strong utilitarian case here. But the most crucial thing to recognize is that, to regard such judicial bowing to such a threatening mob as unqualifiedly wrong, as morally intolerable, one need not reject utilitarianism and accept some form of theistic or deontological absolutism. …

IV

So far, I have tried to show with reference to the case of the magistrate and the threatening mob how consequentialists can reasonably square their normative ethical theories with an important range of commonsense moral convictions. Now, I wish by reference to the case of the innocent fat man to establish that there is at least a serious question concerning whether such fundamental commonsense moral convictions should always function as 'moral facts' or a kind of moral ground to test the adequacy of normative ethical theories or positions. I want to establish that careful attention to such cases shows that we are not justified in taking the principles embodied in our commonsense moral reasoning about such cases as normative for all moral decisions. That a normative ethical theory is incompatible with some of our 'moral intuitions' (moral feelings or convictions) does not refute the normative ethical theory. What I will try to do here is to establish that this case, no more than the case examined in Section III, gives us adequate grounds for abandoning consequentialism and for adopting moral conservativism.

Forget the levity of the example and consider the case of the innocent fat man. If there really is no other way of unsticking our fat man and if plainly, without blasting him out, everyone in the cave will drown, then, innocent or not, he should be blasted out. This indeed overrides the principle that the innocent should never be deliberately killed, but it does not reveal a callousness toward life, for the people involved are caught in a desperate situation in which, if such extreme action is not taken, many lives will be lost and far greater misery will obtain. Moreover, the people who do such a horrible thing or acquiesce in the doing of it are not likely to be rendered more callous about human life and human suffering as a result. Its occurrence will haunt them for the rest of their lives and is as likely as not to make them more rather than less morally sensitive. It is not even correct to say that such a desperate act shows a lack of respect for persons. We are not treating the fat man merely as a means. The fat man's person—his interests and rights—are not ignored. Killing him is something which is undertaken with the greatest reluctance. It is only when it is quite certain that there is no other way to save the lives of the others that such a violent course of action is justifiably undertaken.

Alan Donagan, arguing rather as Anscombe argues, maintains that "to use any innocent man ill for the sake of some public good is directly to degrade him to being a mere means" and to do this is of course to violate a principle essential to morality, that is, that human beings should never merely be treated as means but should be treated as ends in themselves (as persons worthy of respect).[7] But, as my above remarks show, it need not be the case, and in the above situation it is not the case, that in killing such an innocent man we are treating him *merely* as a means. The action is universalizable, all alternative actions which would save his life are duly considered, the blasting out is done only as a last and desperate resort with the minimum of harshness and indifference to his suffering and the like. It indeed sounds ironical to talk this way, given what is done to him. But if such a terrible situation were to arise, there would always be more or less humane ways of going about one's grim task. And in acting in the more humane ways toward the fat man, as we do what we must do and would have done to ourselves were the roles reversed, we show a respect for his person.[8]

In so treating the fat man—not just to further the public good but to prevent the certain death of a whole group of people (that is to prevent an even greater evil than his being killed in this way)—the claims of justice are not overidden either, for each individual involved, if he is reasoning correctly, should realize that if he were so stuck rather than the fat man, he should in such situations be blasted out. Thus, there is no question of being unfair. Surely we must choose between evils here, but is there anything more reasonable, more morally appropriate, than choosing the lesser evil when doing or allowing some evil cannot be avoided? That is, where there is no avoiding both and where our actions can determine whether a greater or lesser evil obtains, should we not plainly always opt for the lesser evil? And is it not obviously a greater evil that all those other innocent people should suffer and die than that the fat man should suffer and die? Blowing up the fat man is indeed monstrous. But letting him remain stuck while the whole group drowns is still more monstrous.

The consequentialist is on strong moral ground here, and, if his reflective moral convictions do not square either with certain unrehearsed or with certain reflective particular moral convictions of human beings, so much the worse for such commonsense moral convictions. One could even usefully and relevantly adapt here—though for a quite different purpose—an argument of Donagan's. Consequentialism of the kind I have been arguing for provides so persuasive

7 Alan Donagan (n. 1 above), pp. 199–200.

8 Again, I am not asserting that we would have enough fortitude to assent to it were the roles actually reversed. I am making a conceptual remark about what as moral beings we must try to do and not a psychological observation about what we can do.

"a theoretical basis for common morality that when it contradicts some moral intuition, it is natural to suspect that intuition, not theory, is corrupt."[9] Given the comprehensiveness, plausibility, and overall rationality of consequentialism, it is not unreasonable to override even a deeply felt moral conviction if it does not square with such a theory, though, if it made no sense or overrode the bulk of or even a great many of our considered moral convictions, that would be another matter indeed.

Anticonsequentialists often point to the inhumanity of people who will sanction such killing of the innocent, but cannot the compliment be returned by speaking of the even greater inhumanity, conjoined with evasiveness, of those who will allow even more death and far greater misery and then excuse themselves on the ground that they did not intend the death and misery but merely forbore to prevent it? In such a context, such reasoning and such forbearing to prevent seems to me to constitute a moral evasion. I say it is evasive because rather than steeling himself to do what in normal circumstances would be a horrible and vile act but in this circumstance is a harsh moral necessity, he allows, when he has the power to prevent it, a situation which is still many times worse. He tries to keep his 'moral purity' and avoid 'dirty hands' at the price of utter moral failure and what Kierkegaard called 'double-mindedness.' It is understandable that people should act in this morally evasive way but this does not make it right.

My consequentialist reasoning about such cases as the case of the innocent fat man is very often resisted on the grounds that it starts a very dangerous precedent. People rationalize wildly and irrationally in their own favor in such situations. To avoid such rationalization, we must stubbornly stick to our deontological principles and recognize as well that very frequently, if people will put their wits to work or just endure, such admittedly monstrous actions done to prevent still greater evils will turn out to be unnecessary.

The general moral principles surrounding bans on killing the innocent are strong and play such a crucial role in the ever-floundering effort to humanize the savage mind—savage as a primitive and savage again as a contemporary in industrial society—that it is of the utmost social utility, it can be argued, that such bans against killing the innocent not be called into question in any practical manner by consequentialist reasoning.

However, in arguing in this way, the moral conservative has plainly shifted his ground, and he is himself arguing on consequentialist grounds that we must treat certain nonconsequentialist moral principles as absolute (as principles which can never *in fact,* from a reasonable moral point of view, be overriden

---

9   Alan Donagan (n. 1 above), p. 198.

for it would be just too disastrous to do so).[10] But now he is on my home court, and my reply is that there is no good evidence at all that in the circumstances I characterized, overriding these deontological principles would have this disastrous effect. I am aware that a bad precedent could be set. Such judgments must not be made for more doubtful cases. But my telling my two stories in some detail, and my contrasting them, was done in order to make evident the type of situation, with its attendant rationale, in which the overriding of those deontological principles can be seen clearly to be justified and the situations in which this does not obtain and why. My point was to specify the situations in which we ought to override our commonsense moral convictions about those matters, and the contexts in which we are not so justified or at least in which it is not clear which course of action is justified.[11]

If people are able to be sufficiently clearheaded about these matters, they can see that there are relevant differences between the two sorts of cases. But I was also carefully guarding against extending such 'moral radicalism'—if such it should be called—to other and more doubtful cases. Unless solid empirical evidence can be given that such a 'moral radicalism' would—if it were to gain a toehold in the community—overflow destructively and inhumanely into the other doubtful and positively unjustifiable situations, nothing has been said to undermine the correctness of my consequentialist defense of 'moral radicalism' in the contexts in which I defended it.[12]

---

10 Jonathan Bennett, "Whatever the Consequences," *Analysis,* vol. 26 (1966), has shown that this is a very common equivocation for the conservative and makes, when unnoticed, his position seem more plausible than it actually is.

11 I have spoken, conceding this to the Christian absolutist for the sake of the discussion, as if (1) it is fairly evident what our commonsense moral convictions are here and (2) that they are deontological principles taken to hold no matter what the consequences. But that either (1) or (2) is clearly so seems to me very much open to question.

12 I do not mean to suggest that I am giving a blanket defense to our commonsense morality; that is one of the last things I would want to do. Much of what we or any other tribe take to be commonsense morality is little better than a set of magical charms to deal with our social environment. But I was defending the importance of such cross-culturally ubiquitous moral principles as that one ought not to harm the innocent or that promises ought to be kept. However, against Christian absolutists of the type I have been discussing, I take them to be prima facie obligations. This means that they always hold *ceteris paribus;* but the *ceteris paribus* qualification implies that they can be overridden on occasion. On my account, appeal to consequences and considerations about justice and respect for persons determines when they should on a given occasion be overridden.

Mill, *Utilitarianism,* Chapter 2

1. What role does happiness play in relation to ethics according to Mill? How does Mill define happiness?
2. Why do critics consider utilitarianism to be a doctrine fit for swine? How does Mill respond to this critique?
3. Is utilitarianism a selfish theory of morality? Explain.
4. Why do people think utilitarianism is too demanding? Does Mill agree? Explain.

Mill, *Of What Sort of Proof the Principle of Utility is Susceptible*

1. Why does Mill think the Principle of Utility is not capable of proof in the strict sense? What alternative "proof" does Mill offer? How compelling is his account?
2. Explain Mill's discussion of virtue and its relationship to happiness. Compare and contrast Mill's view with Aristotelian Virtue Ethics.

Nielsen, *Against Moral Conservativism*

1. What sort of criticisms are raised against consequentialist theories based on examples like The Innocent Fat Man and the Magistrate and the Mob? Explain these cases and why they seem to pose problems for consequentialism.
2. How does Nielsen argue against moral conservativism and, rather, defend consequentialism in dealing with situations like the aforementioned cases? Is Nielsen's perspective compelling? Explain.

SUGGESTIONS FOR FURTHER READING OR VIEWING

Bentham, Jeremy. *Principles of Morals and Legislation.* New York: Prometheus, 1988.

Crisp, Roger. *Routledge Philosophy Guidebook to Mill on Utilitarianism.* New York: Routledge, 1997.

Driver, Julia. *Consequentialism: New Problems of Philosophy.* New York: Routledge, 1997.

Eggleston, Ben, and Dale E. Miller, eds. *The Cambridge Companion to Utilitarianism.* Cambridge: Cambridge University Press, 2014.

Hooker, Brad. *Ideal Code, Real World.* Oxford: Oxford University Press, 2000.

Smart, J. J. C., and Bernard Williams. *Utilitarianism For & Against.* Cambridge: Cambridge University Press, 1973.

Feminist Ethics

INTRODUCTION TO FEMINIST ETHICS

This section introduces two readings on feminist ethics, one of the more dynamic and important movements in contemporary philosophy. One reading is from a classic work of feminist philosophy, Mary Wollstone-craft's *Vindication of the Rights of Woman*, originally published in 1792, while the second is an excerpt from a recent book by care ethicist Nel Noddings called *The Maternal Factor: Two Paths to Morality*.

Mary Wollstonecraft (1759–1797) lived during the tumultuous period of European history that produced both the American War of Independence and the French Revolution, a time when the rationalist, scientific, and egalitarian ideals of the Enlightenment were in full bloom. On one level, Wollstonecraft's *Vindication of the Rights of Woman* can be understood as appealing to the political goals of the emerging liberal tradition on behalf of women. At the time, women were systematically denied, in both theory and practice, the litany of rights claimed on behalf of "all men" in documents such as the Declaration of Independence and the Declaration of the Rights of Man. Anticipating the now familiar distinction between sex and gender, Wollstonecraft argues that by nature women are as capable of men in pursuing virtuous and autonomous lives while conceding that as they are currently educated, women tend to prefer lives of subservience in gilded cages. Rather than being taught to think and take part in public affairs, the women of her time, Wollstonecraft claims, are more typically taught to leverage their attractiveness to men for trivial pleasures and physical comfort.

Wollstonecraft's criticism of the women of her time, who she compares to wealthy men in being more concerned with comfort than virtue, is controversial. Later feminists came to see her stance as depreciating women by disregarding the value and importance of the domestic work women have traditionally been compelled to do. As important as it is that women take their proper place in the worlds of politics and business, contemporary feminists do not want to disparage the critical work of child-rearing and caregiving traditionally assigned to women. Care ethics, a movement in modern ethical thinking spearheaded by Nel Noddings, Carol Gilligan, and Sara Ruddick, begins by celebrating the sensibilities traditionally associated with women—empathy, sensitivity to the needs of others, and a moral focus on the importance of human relations. In the selection from *The Maternal Factor*, Noddings covers the basics of her version of care ethics by explaining key concepts such as caring relations, the difference between natural and ethical care, and the role of sentiment and spontaneous responses to the needs of others in our best moral thinking. In this more recent work she adds—and this itself is controversial—an appeal to evolutionary psychology to suggest such foundational moral sentiments may come more naturally to women.

READING 3.16

Vindication of the Rights of Women

Mary Wollstonecraft

∿

Chap. IV. Observations on the State of Degradation to Which Woman Is Reduced by Various Causes.

That woman is naturally weak, or degraded by a concurrence of circumstances, is, I think, clear. But this position I shall simply contrast with a conclusion, which I have frequently heard fall from sensible men in favour of an aristocracy: that the mass of mankind cannot be any thing, or the obsequious slaves, who patiently allow themselves to be penned up, would feel their own consequence, and spurn their chains. Men, they further observe, submit every where to oppression, when they have only to lift up their heads to throw off the yoke; yet, instead of asserting their birthright, they quietly lick the dust, and say, let us eat and drink, for to-morrow we die. Women, I argue from analogy, are degraded by the same propensity to enjoy the present moment; and, at last, despise the freedom which they have not sufficient virtue to struggle to attain. But I must be more explicit.   1

With respect to the culture of the heart, it is unanimously allowed that sex is out of the question; but the line of subordination in the mental powers is never to be passed over. 1 Only 'absolute in loveliness,' the portion of rationality granted to woman, is indeed very scanty; for, denying her genius and judgment, it is scarcely possible to divine what remains to characterize intellect.   2

The stamina of immortality, if I may be allowed the phrase is the perfectibility of human reason: for, was man created perfect, or did a flood of knowledge break in upon him, when he arrived at maturity, that precluded error, I should doubt whether his existence would be continued after the dissolution of the body. But, in the present state of things, every difficulty in morals that escapes from human discussion, and equally baffles the investigation of profound thinking,

Mary Wollstonecraft, "Observations on the State of Degradation to Which Woman Is Reduced by Various Causes," *Vindication of the Rights of Women*.

and the lightning glance of genius, is an argument on which I build my belief of the immortality of the soul. Reason is, consequentially, the simple power of improvement; or, more properly speaking, of discerning truth. Every individual is in this respect a world in itself. More or less may be conspicuous in one being than another; but the nature of reason must be the same in all, if it be an emanation of divinity, the tie that connects the creature with the Creator; for, can that soul be stamped with the heavenly image, that is not perfected by the exercise of its own reason? 2 Yet outwardly ornamented with elaborate care, and so adorned to delight man, 'that with honour he may love,' 3 the soul of woman is not allowed to have this distinction, and man, ever placed between her and reason, she is always represented as only created to see through a gross medium, and to take things on trust. But, dismissing these fanciful theories, and considering woman as a whole, let it be what it will, instead of a part of man, the inquiry is whether she has reason or not. If she has, which, for a moment, I will take for granted, she was not created merely to be the solace of man, and

3   the sexual should not destroy the human character.

Into this error men have, probably, been led by viewing education in a false light; not considering it as the first step to form a being advancing gradually towards perfection; 4 but only as a preparation for life. On this sensual error, for I must call it so, has the false system of female manners been reared, which robs the whole sex of its dignity, and classes the brown and fair with the smiling flowers that only adorns the land. This has ever been the language of men, and the fear of departing from a supposed sexual character, has made even women of superior sense adopt the same sentiments. 5 Thus understanding, strictly speaking, has been denied to woman; and instinct, sublimated into wit and

4   cunning, for the purposes of life, has been substituted in its stead.

The power of generalizing ideas, of drawing comprehensive conclusions from individual observations, is the only acquirement, for an immortal being, that really deserves the name of knowledge. Merely to observe, without endeavouring to account for any thing, may (in a very incomplete manner) serve as the common sense of life; but where is the store laid up that is to clothe the

5   soul when it leaves the body?

This power has not only been denied to women; but writers have insisted that it is inconsistent, with a few exceptions, with their sexual character. Let men prove this, and I shall grant that woman only exists for man. I must, however, previously remark, that the power of generalizing ideas, to any great extent, is not very common amongst men or women. But this exercise is the true cultivation of the understanding; and every thing conspires to render the cultivation of the understanding more difficult in the female than the

6   male world.

I am naturally led by this assertion to the main subject of the present chapter, and shall now attempt to point out some of the causes that degrade the sex, and prevent women from generalizing their observations.

I shall not go back to the remote annals of antiquity to trace the history of woman; it is sufficient to allow that she has always been either a slave, or a despot, and to remark, that each of these situations equally retards the progress of reason. The grand source of female folly and vice has ever appeared to me to arise from narrowness of mind; and the very constitution of civil governments has put almost insuperable obstacles in the way to prevent the cultivation of the female understanding:—yet virtue can be built on no other foundation! The same obstacles are thrown in the way of the rich, and the same consequences ensue.

Necessity has been proverbially termed the mother of invention—the aphorism may be extended to virtue. It is an acquirement, and an acquirement to which pleasure must be sacrificed—and who sacrifices pleasure when it is within the grasp, whose mind has not been opened and strengthened by adversity, or the pursuit of knowledge goaded on by necessity?—Happy is it when people have the cares of life to struggle with; for these struggles prevent their becoming a prey to enervating vices, merely from idleness! But, if from their birth men and women are placed in a torrid zone, with the meridian sun of pleasure darting directly upon them, how can they sufficiently brace their minds to discharge the duties of life, or even to relish the affections that carry them out of themselves?

Pleasure is the business of woman's life, according to the present modification of society, and while it continues to be so, little can be expected from such weak beings. Inheriting, in a lineal descent from the first fair defect in nature, the sovereignty of beauty, they have, to maintain their power, resigned the natural rights, which the exercise of reason might have procured them, and chosen rather to be short-lived queens than labour to obtain the sober pleasures that arise from equality. Exalted by their inferiority (this sounds like a contradiction) they constantly demand homage as women, though experience should teach them that the men who pride themselves upon paying this arbitrary insolent respect to the sex, with the most scrupulous exactness, are most inclined to tyrannize over, and despise, the very weakness they cherish. Often do they repeat Mr. Hume's sentiments; when, comparing the French and Athenian character, he alludes to women. 'But what is more singular in this whimsical nation, say I to the Athenians, is, that a frolick of yours during the Saturnalia, when the slaves are served by their masters, is, seriously, continued by them through the whole year, and through the whole course of their lives; accompanied too with some circumstances, which still further augment the absurdity and ridicule. Your sport only elevates for a few days those whom fortune has thrown down, and whom she too, in sport, may really elevate for

ever above you. But this nation gravely exalts those, whom nature has subjected to them, and whose inferiority and infirmities are absolutely incurable. The
10 women, though without virtue, are their masters and sovereigns.'

Ah! why do women, I write with affectionate solicitude, condescend to receive a degree of attention and respect from strangers, different from that reciprocation of civility which the dictates of humanity and the politeness of civilization authorise between man and man? And, why do they not discover, when 'in the noon of beauty's power,' that they are treated like queens only to be deluded by hollow respect, till they are led to resign, or not assume, their natural prerogatives? Confined then in cages like the feathered race, they have nothing to do but to plume themselves, and stalk with mock majesty from perch to perch. It is true they are provided with food and raiment, for which they neither toil nor spin; but health, liberty, and virtue, are given in exchange. But, where, amongst mankind has been found sufficient strength of mind to enable a being to resign these adventitious prerogatives; one who, rising with the calm dignity of reason above opinion, dared to be proud of the privileges inherent in man? And it is vain to expect it whilst hereditary power chokes the
11 affections and nips reason in the bud.

The passions of men have thus placed women on thrones, and, till mankind become more reasonable, it is to be feared that women will avail themselves of the power which they attain with the least exertion, and which is the most indisputable. They will smile,—yes, they will smile, though told that—

'In beauty's empire is no mean,
And woman, either slave or queen,
Is quickly scorn'd when not ador'd.'

12 But the adoration comes first, and the scorn is not anticipated.

Lewis the XIVth, in particular, spread factitious manners, and caught, in a specious way, the whole nation in his toils; for, establishing an artful chain of despotism, he made it the interest of the people at large, individually to respect his station and support his power. And women, whom he flattered by a puerile attention to the whole sex, obtained in his reign that prince-like distinction so
13 fatal to reason and virtue.

A king is always a king—and a woman always a woman: <u>6</u> his authority and her sex, ever stand between them and rational converse. With a lover, I grant, she should be so, and her sensibility will naturally lead her to endeavour to excite emotion, not to gratify her vanity, but her heart. This I do not allow to be coquetry, it is the artless impulse of nature, I only exclaim against the sexual
14 desire of conquest when the heart is out of the question.

This desire is not confined to women; 'I have endeavoured,' says Lord Chesterfield, 'to gain the hearts of twenty women, whose persons I would not have given a fig for.' The libertine, who, in a gust of passion, takes advantage of unsuspecting tenderness, is a saint when compared with this cold-hearted rascal; for I like to use significant words. Yet only taught to please, women are always on the watch to please, and with true heroic ardour endeavour to gain hearts merely to resign, or spurn them, when the victory is decided, and conspicuous. 15

I must descend to the minutiæ of the subject. 16

I lament that women are systematically degraded by receiving the trivial attentions, which men think it manly to pay to the sex, when, in fact, they are insultingly supporting their own superiority. It is not condescension to bow to an inferiour. So ludicrous, in fact, do these ceremonies appear to me, that I scarcely am able to govern my muscles, when I see a man start with eager, and serious solicitude to lift a handkerchief, or shut a door, when the *lady* could have done it herself, had she only moved a pace or two. 17

A wild wish has just flown from my heart to my head, I will not stifle it though it may excite a horse-laugh.—I do earnestly wish to see the distinction of sex confounded in society, unless where love animates the behaviour. For this distinction is, I am firmly persuaded, the foundation of the weakness of character ascribed to woman; is the cause why the understanding is neglected, whilst accomplishments are acquired with sedulous care: and the same cause accounts for their preferring the graceful before the heroic virtues. 18

Mankind, including every description, wish to be loved and respected for *something;* and the common herd will always take the nearest road to the completion of their wishes. The respect paid to wealth and beauty is the most certain, and unequivocal; and, of course, will always attract the vulgar eye of common minds. Abilities and virtues are absolutely necessary to raise men from the middle rank of life into notice; and the natural consequence is notorious; the middle rank contains most virtue and abilities. Men have thus, in one station, at least, an opportunity of exerting themselves with dignity, and of rising by the exertions which really improve a rational creature; but the whole female sex are, till their character is formed, in the same condition as the rich: for they are born, I now speak of a state of civilization, with certain sexual privileges, and whilst they are gratuitously granted them, few will ever think of works of supererogation, to obtain the esteem of a small number of superiour people. 19

When do we hear of women who, starting out of obscurity, boldly claim respect on account of their great abilities or daring virtues? Where are they to be found?—'To be observed, to be attended to, to be taken notice of with sympathy, complacency, and approbation, are all the advantages which they seek.'—True! my male readers will probably exclaim; but let them, before they draw any conclusion, recollect that this was not written originally as descriptive of women, but of the rich. In Dr. Smith's Theory of Moral Sentiments, I have found a general character of people of rank and fortune, that, in my opinion, might with the greatest propriety be applied to the female sex. I refer the sagacious reader to the whole comparison; but must be allowed to quote a passage to enforce an argument that I mean to insist on, as the one most conclusive against a sexual character. For if, excepting warriors, no great men, of any denomination, have ever appeared amongst the nobility, may it not be fairly inferred that their local situation swallowed up the man, and produced a character similar to that of women, who are *localized,* if I may be allowed the word, by the rank they are placed in, by *courtesy*? Women, commonly called Ladies, are not to be contradicted in company, are not allowed to exert any manual strength; and from them the negative virtues only are expected, when any virtues are expected, patience, docility, good-humour, and flexibility; virtues incompatible with any vigorous exertion of intellect. Besides, by living more with each other, and being seldom absolutely alone, they are more under the influence of sentiments than passions. Solitude and reflection are necessary to give to wishes the force of passions, and to enable the imagination to enlarge the object, and make it the most desirable. The same may be said of the rich; they do not sufficiently deal in general ideas, collected by impassioned thinking, or calm investigation, to acquire that strength of character on which great resolves

20 are built. But hear what an acute observer says of the great.

'Do the great seem insensible of the easy price at which they may acquire the publick admiration; or do they seem to imagine that to them, as to other men, it must be the purchase either of sweat or of blood? By what important accomplishments is the young nobleman instructed to support the dignity of his rank, and to render himself worthy of that superiority over his fellow-citizens, to which the virtue of his ancestors had raised them? Is it by knowledge, by industry, by patience, by self-denial, or by virtue of any kind? As all his words, as all his motions are attended to, he learns an habitual regard to every circumstance of ordinary behaviour, and studies to perform all those small duties with the most exact propriety. As he is conscious how much he is observed, and how much mankind are disposed to favour all his inclinations, he acts, upon the most indifferent occasions with that freedom and elevation which the thought of this naturally inspires. His air, his manner, his deportment, all mark that elegant and graceful sense of his own superiority, which those who are born to inferiour station can hardly ever arrive at. These are the arts by which he proposes to make mankind more easily submit to his authority, and to govern their inclinations according to his own pleasure: and in this he is seldom disappointed. These arts, supported by rank and pre-eminence, are, upon ordinary occasions, sufficient to govern the world. Lewis XIV. during the greater part of his reign, was regarded, not only in France, but over all Europe, as the most perfect model of a great prince. But what were the talents and virtues by which he acquired this great reputation? Was it by the scrupulous and inflexible justice of all his undertakings, by the immense dangers and difficulties with which they were attended, or by the unwearied and unrelenting application with which he pursued them? Was it by his extensive knowledge, by his exquisite judgment, or by his heroic valour? It was by none of these qualities. But he was, first of all, the most powerful prince in Europe, and consequently held the highest rank among kings; and then, says his historian, "he surpassed all his courtiers in the gracefulness of his shape, and the majestic beauty of his features. The sound of his voice, noble and affecting, gained those hearts which his presence intimidated. He had a step and a deportment which could suit only him and his rank, and which would have been ridiculous in any other person. The embarrassment which he occasioned to those who spoke to him, flattered that secret satisfaction with which he felt his own superiority." 'These frivolous accomplishments, supported by his rank, and, no doubt too, by a degree of other talents and virtues, which seems, however, not to have been much above mediocrity, established this prince in the esteem of his own age, and have drawn, even from posterity, a good deal of respect for his memory. Compared with these, in his own times, and in his own presence, no other virtue, it seems, appeared to have any merit. Knowledge, industry, valour, and beneficence, trembled, were abashed, and lost all dignity before them.' 21

Woman also thus 'in herself complete,' by possessing all these *frivolous* accomplishments, so changes the nature of things

———'That what she wills to do or say
Seems wisest, virtuousest, discreetest, best;
All higher knowledge in *her presence* falls
Degraded. Wisdom in discourse with her
Loses discountenanc'd, and, like Folly, shows;
Authority and Reason on her wait.'—
And all this is built on her loveliness! 22

Note 1 Into what inconsistencies do men fall when they argue without the compass of principles. Women, weak women, are compared with angels; yet, a superiour order of beings should be supposed to possess more intellect than man; or, in what does their superiority consist? In the same style, to drop the sneer, they are allowed to possess more goodness of heart, piety, and benevolence.—I doubt the fact, though it be courteously brought forward, unless ignorance be allowed to be the mother of devotion; for I am firmly persuaded that, on an average, the proportion between virtue and knowledge, is more upon a par than is commonly granted. [back]

Note 2 'The brutes,' says Lord Monboddo, 'remain in the state in which nature has placed them, except in so far as their natural instinct is improved by the culture *we* bestow upon them.' [back]

Note 3 Vide Milton. [back]

Note 4 This word is not strictly just, but I cannot find a better. [back]

Note 5

'Pleasure's the portion of th' *inferiour* kind;
But glory, virtue, Heaven for *man* design'd.'

After writing these lines, how could Mrs. Barbauld write the following ignoble comparison?

'*To a Lady, with some* painted flowers.'
'Flowers to the fair: to you these flowers I bring,
And strive to greet you with an earlier spring.
Flowers, SWEET, *and gay, and* DELICATE LIKE YOU;
Emblems of innocence, and beauty too.
With flowers the Graces bind their yellow hair,
And flowery wreaths consenting lovers wear.
Flowers, the sole luxury which nature knew,
In Eden's pure and guiltless garden grew.
To loftier forms are rougher tasks assign'd;
The sheltering oak resists the stormy wind,
The tougher yew repels invading foes,
And the tall pine for future navies grows;
But this soft family, to cares unknown,
Were born for pleasure and delight ALONE.
Gay without toil, and lovely without art,
They spring to CHEER *the sense, and* GLAD *the heart,*
Nor blush, my fair, to own you copy these;
Your BEST, *your* SWEETEST *empire is*—to PLEASE.'

So the men tell us; but virtue must be acquired by *rough* toils, and useful struggles with worldly *cares*.

Note 6 And a wit, always a wit, might be added; for the vain fooleries of wits and beauties to obtain attention, and make conquests, are much upon a par.

Care Ethics

selection from *The Maternal Factor*
by Nel Noddings

༄

The Caring Relation

Many feminist philosophers view human beings as relational selves—selves constituted by the relations in which they are embedded.[1] For care theorists, the *caring relation* is morally basic, and it is the purpose of this chapter to describe its development from the original caring relation established by maternal instinct to natural caring. The last section of the chapter will explore how we might best prepare people to establish and maintain caring relations.

Instinctive and Natural Caring

In exploring a path to morality rooted in maternal caring, we must look at instinctive caring, natural caring, and ethical caring, but these should not be considered stages in moral development. Certainly natural caring has incorporated instinctive caring and, because it seems to have evolved from instinct, it represents a next step. But ethical caring, which again builds on natural caring, is not necessarily better than natural caring. It becomes morally necessary when natural caring fails in its usual settings or when the setting has become too large for natural caring to function. In the latter case, it seems reasonable to many that we should switch from caring to justice. But a concept of justice may be guided by the fundamental ideas of caring. The best approach for policymakers might then be to choose a theory of justice that aims to establish or restore conditions in which natural caring might flourish rather than to invoke

Nel Noddings, "The Caring Relation," *The Maternal Factor: Two Paths to Morality,* pp. 33-66, 254-256. Copyright © 2010 by University of California Press. Reprinted with permission.

an entirely different moral approach or to attempt caring directly. Throughout the discussion, the use of *caring* will have to be clarified repeatedly.

Every human being is born into, takes shape in, relation. For the embryo and fetus, life exists only in relation. Physical separation at birth initiates a caring relation once maintained almost entirely by instinct. Since the emergence of recognized human life, the whole process has been overlaid with practices developed in cultural evolution and, as part of cognitive evolution, with the conscious attention of mothers capable of thoughtful planning and reflection.[2]

The dyadic connection consisting of mother and child was originally one of instinctive caring. We might think of this caring relation between mother and child as "naturally normative," in the language of Philippa Foot.[3] Today, a woman who does not wish to bear children is not—and should not be—thought to be somehow defective, but a mother who does not care for her child might be considered as having a defect in the sense that she lacks an instinct or trait considered essential for the survival of the human species. By today's standards, such a woman is nevertheless—and I think rightly—regarded as fully human, because she possesses other qualities characteristic of the human species. Neither would we regard her as a "defective female," although we acknowledge this one defect. Cases of this sort underscore why so many feminists reject essentialism. Too much has been loaded onto one trait. However, if a significant number of females were to lack the characteristic of maternal caring, not only would that lack be labeled a defect in the individuals; the whole group would be seen as violating a natural norm—a defect that would predict the extinction of the species.

In this brief discussion of maternal instinct, we see that complete rejection of essentialism may not be possible. On the one hand, maternal instinct is not an essential characteristic of human females, one that separates fully human females from "unnatural" females; on the other hand, it is an essential characteristic of human females as a class in that it is clearly essential to the survival of their species. Humans are complex creatures, and we have learned to avoid labeling any infant born to a human mother "defective" because of some lack or anomaly. A child born with four arms, for example, is still human, and the anomaly (deviation from the natural norm) may be corrected. A severe mental deviation (what was once called idiocy or imbecility) is not correctable, but we point to other qualities that such a child shares with fellow humans. Again, if this deviation were widespread in a group, we would have to label it a severe violation of natural normativity because the group lacks a characteristic (normal human intelligence) essential to the continuation of human life.

The characteristic attitude of caring (we'll say much more about what this is) is manifested in love for the child—an almost fierce love inherited from its beginnings in maternal instinct. This first caring relation is important not only because human reproduction depends on it but also because it represents a prototype of caring. Except in rare cases when a mother emotionally rejects her infant, no moral imperative is involved in the mother's decision to care for her child. The caring is *natural* in this sense—that it is practiced out of love or inclination. Recall that, in Kant's ethical theory, acts done from love or inclination have no moral worth. To have moral worth, from Kant's perspective, an act must be chosen in obedience to an ethical principle. Mothers do not refer to a moral principle in deciding to feed their babies. They *want* to do so. Does their love or instinctive inclination have no moral worth?

I agree with Kant that there is a difference between natural caring and ethical caring, but I will argue that both have moral worth. We should distinguish between informal or everyday morality and formal morality. When I say that natural caring represents a moral approach to life, I am referring to an informal morality, a way of interacting with others that does not require explicit attention to moral criteria such as duty, principle, God's will, or the exercise of virtue. In a climate of natural caring, our attention is on identifying and satisfying needs, maintaining or establishing caring relations, keeping open the channels of sympathy, and promoting this way of life among the young. In care theory, we are concerned with the full scope of moral life, not only with ethical decisions and their justification. Natural caring is, in some ways, superior to ethical caring. Consider how we would feel if a friend were to visit us while we were ill and tell us frankly that he was doing so because it is his duty. We might well feel hurt. We might even wish he would simply go home. In almost all close relationships, many of the most important acts and attitudes are governed by inclination, not duty. Often, as we shall see, the purpose of ethical caring is to establish or restore natural caring. If natural caring never failed, if it could be extended without limit to all others, we would have no need for ethical caring.

The first caring relation is our original condition. The infant does not choose to be born and does not choose the family or community into which she or he is born. The child will eventually make choices, and this capacity to choose has led liberal philosophers (and some existentialists) to exaggerate the human capacity to choose. In the usual course of life, people do not choose their sex, race, or ethnicity. They do not choose their stature, physical strength, or susceptibility to disease. Indeed, few choose their religion, and many do not even choose their occupational way of life. It is extremely difficult to make choices in opposition to one's immediate culture. The liberal emphasis on the individual and individual choice has begun to give way, thanks to evolutionary studies, to an acknowledgment of the group or society as a unit that functions in much the way a "population" does in nonhuman species.[5] The social group is primary, and individuals are both developed and limited by it.

Evolutionary studies are having effects across the disciplines. Not only is emphasis shifting from the individual to social units in biology, anthropology, and psychology, but history is moving well beyond the "great man" as a center of interest.[5] Jean Piaget noted forty years ago that such thinking should change: "The great man who at any time seems to be launching some new line of thought is simply the point of intersection or synthesis of ideas which have been elaborated by a continuous process of cooperation, and, even if he is opposed to current opinions, he represents a response to underlying needs which arise outside himself. This is why the social environment is able to do so effectively for the intelligence what genetic recombinations of the population did for evolutionary variation or the transindividual cycle of the instincts."[6]

Natural caring is "natural" in the sense that it is exercised with no need for reference to moral principles or direct reasoning from such principles. Perhaps the easiest way to get an initial grasp on the difference between natural caring as a way of moral life and the body of thought traditionally associated with moral philosophy or ethics is to reflect on the "different voice" identified by Carol Gilligan. Instead of drawing on principles and rules, the female participants in Gilligan's study concentrated on relationships and response.[7] I am trying here to describe this alternative mode of moral life more fully.

Natural caring is not a stage—either historical or developmental—on the road to a "higher" morality. It has always been present and active in human life but largely unarticulated and overwhelmed by male-dominated theories of morality. These theories have concentrated on fundamental principles, often entirely separated from real (biological/social) life, ostensibly "anchored" in a mysterious entity or entities beyond that real life. Or they have depended on customs and rules developed in various occupations, practices, and traditions—all defined in terms of male experience. The development of male moral theories has tended toward the abstract with little attention to the facts of biological life. At the extreme, moral theory has become a sophisticated linguistic/mathematical game entirely foreign to the everyday social life of human beings. Indeed, because natural caring is visible in the actual lived world, it might be (has been) identified with "isness." In contrast, traditional philosophers have described ethical conduct (formal morality) in terms of "oughtness."

It has been that way from the beginning of male moral thought. Consider the culture in which classical Greek thought emerged. It was a culture constantly at war, and many of its virtues were defined as qualities of the warrior. It supported slavery, and its moral rules, customs, and virtues were tightly connected to social/political status. It denigrated women and women's contributions to family life, and it even made an attempt (through Plato) to show that family life was unnecessary. Where something practical was acknowledged and described (as in Aristotle), it arose in and was elaborated through male experience.

This is not to say that centuries of male thought on moral life have been useless. There are beautiful, inspiring ideas that continue to excite thought. My complaint is that they have had relatively little effect on actual human conduct. Instead of effecting an end to war, they have constructed elaborate schemes for the "moral" conduct of war. They have condemned slavery and contributed to its formal elimination in much of the world, but human trafficking continues, and millions still exist in slavelike conditions. Male philosophies still denigrate women by ignoring the contributions women have made *as women*. Forced by their own theories of justice to accept women as equals, they implicitly reemphasize the dominant status of men by inviting women to become more like men.

In his interesting exploration of the evolution of morality, Marc Hauser argues—as I do in this book—that we need to pay more attention to the natural origins of morality and to the moral feelings he calls "intuitions," but he then decides to move away from empirical reality in human life: "To understand our moral psychology, I will *not* explore all the ways in which we use it in our daily interactions with others. In the same way that linguists in the Chomskyan tradition sidestep issues of language use, focusing instead on the unconscious knowledge that gives each of us the competence to express and judge a limitless number of sentences, I adopt a similarly narrow focus with respect to morality. The result is a richly detailed explanation of how an unconscious and universal moral grammar underlies our judgments of right and wrong."[8] The result, from the perspective of care theory, is unnaturally narrow. Hauser does not mention female experience or maternal instinct. When he writes about the nurture of infants, he speaks of "parenting"—as though males and females play similar and equal roles. There is no reference at all to work in feminist psychology or philosophy. What is explained in absorbing detail is a notion of reciprocity that concentrates on the expectation of compensation or giving back. When a person does something for another, the expectation is that the other—perhaps at a later time—will "reciprocate"— do something helpful in return.

This way of looking at the origins of moral life is part of a parallel (and enormously powerful) philosophical tradition that puts the individual at the center of moral thought and action, building a system of ethics on the foundation of self-interest. The resulting description of moral life seems accurate when we look at the way things operate in the male-dominated world.

But *think*. Reciprocity in female experience often involves no expectation of compensatory action. A mother hopes for *response* from her infant, but there is nothing in her conduct that corresponds to contractual reciprocity—"you scratch my back, I'll scratch yours." Right from the start, we are talking about relation and, in the mother-child relation, the child comes first in the mother's thinking. In many of the interactions characteristic of female experience, the so-called conditions of reciprocal altruism do not apply. Mothers have not negotiated small costs for their giving, looking for great benefits in return, nor have they made giving contingent upon receiving.

The Golden Rule, heralded as a universal judgment, is admirable, but it too might be thought of as a male universal because, again, it puts the individual moral agent at the center: Do unto others as you would have done unto you. If we look at female life and experience, we might enunciate a somewhat different rule: Do unto others as they would have done unto them. This way of response requires many of the attitudes and skills described in an account of natural caring.

In later chapters, I'll discuss how care theory can provide guidance for social policy. Of course, in liberal democracies, we want to educate people so that they can make intelligent choices, but—even more important—we should work toward a society in which the original condition of every child is one in which natural caring can flourish.

Natural caring starts in the settings influenced by maternal instinct. The mother's care is lavished upon children, children are taught to care for one another, and the biological tendency to care for blood relations is augmented by social customs. However, natural caring is not limited to families. Wherever people come together out of common interests, we are likely to find natural caring—forms of address and response not motivated by rule or principle. Once again, I must emphasize that we may certainly detect and describe behavior that seems to be guided by rule or custom. It is descriptively correct to say that people in such communities behave in ways that can be predicted by descriptive principles. It would be a mistake, however, to say that these people refer to these rules before acting. Circles of common interest, guided by natural caring, can provide a foundation for a care-driven approach to justice, and I will say more about this in a later chapter.

Just as the entities we call *individuals* are initially defined by relations in the home, they continue to be shaped in various groups of common interest. In settings characterized by natural caring, people do not consciously refer to rules or principles to guide their behavior. Loved, or at least accepted, people go about their daily lives without recourse to explicit moral thought. They use reason, of course, primarily in means-ends analysis. How can I accomplish this end I seek? How can I reshape the mistaken goals of the cared-for?

A setting characterized by natural caring is widely (perhaps universally) regarded as *good*. It is thought *good* to be safe, to have one's needs met, to expect and receive response to one's overtures. The appreciation of natural caring is rooted deeply in our evolutionary past, but it is still an important feature of ordinary contemporary life. To return home after a hectic day's public work, kick off one's shoes, settle back with a sigh, cuddle a loved child (or pet), close one's eyes in recognition that one is safely situated in a circle of caring is to realize a basic human good.

Evaluating the conditions of natural caring as *good* gives rise to what we now think of as moral thought. If something goes wrong, how can I restore the conditions necessary to sustain relations of natural caring? When we ask the moral question, What ought I to do? we are usually asking what we would do if we were at our best as caring selves and if this other were one we naturally care for. In most such cases, there is no need to consult abstract rules and principles.

Although natural caring grows out of instinctive caring, it is clearly not merely instinctive. All mammalian females are capable of some rudimentary thought, and they exercise it in seeking an appropriate place to give birth, in choosing relatively safe times to search for food, and in deciding who may or may not approach their young. But human females are capable of fully human cognition. Moral reasoning is not involved in the decision to care, but reasoning is employed in deciding how best to satisfy the inclination to care.

Female humans, like virtually all mammalian females, have had and continue to have major responsibility for mothering, but human female thinking is not confined to the tasks of mothering. I argue in this book that it is reasonable to suppose that female and male minds have evolved somewhat differently, but I do not suppose that one is generally superior to the other. However, one may be better adapted than the other to certain tasks. This is a risky claim because, as many feminists have warned, admission of difference in the past has almost always resulted in a declaration of superiority favoring the male.[9] That arrogant conclusion is to be deplored, but it should not lead us to deny that differences exist. Rather, we should ask how best to acknowledge and use the differences to benefit everyone. In some cases, it might be beneficial to reduce the differences. *If* a difference exists between the sexes in mathematical ability, for example, should we work to reduce the difference? Why? *If* a difference exists in the capacity for empathy, should we work to reduce that difference?

Some care theorists concentrate on caring as a virtue and deemphasize care as a relation.[10] From an evolutionary perspective, however, the caring relation is primary. Indeed, it may be considered the incubator of virtue—phylogenetically, of the virtues associated with maternal care, ontogenetically, of the virtues developed in interaction between mother and child. This is not to deny other possible sources of virtue such as cooperative hunting and pathfinding among males. But the original caring relation is almost certainly a major source of empathy and the virtues associated with it.

The original caring relation is not chosen; it happens. Other caring relations may be constructed, and that possibility will occupy much of what follows. What can we say, for example, of the earliest male-female bondings? We know little about these. Why did females enter such relations? The relation itself (a mere association over some time) might not initially have been one of caring. As suggested earlier, the female's motive might have been concern for the survival of her young. However, the relation—dyadic interaction—might well give rise to caring in either partner. Males might become genuinely concerned with the welfare of their female partners and, secondarily but less intensely, with the survival of their offspring. Females, learning of necessity to read their male partners, might begin to care for them. From the merely instrumental, caring relations might develop. It seems more likely that females, with the growing capacity for empathy engendered by maternal experience, would nurture the transition from instrumental relation to caring relation. Or it just might happen that the female begins to feel something for her mate, and so what started as instrumental caregiving becomes natural caring. Neither instrumental caregiving nor natural caring requires reference to a principle.

Natural caring is "natural" in that it exists prior to formal moral thought; it is there, in the empirical world. It is found in families and in other face-to-face circles of interaction. As an organic system, it is characterized by mutual protectiveness, cooperation, response to one another's needs, and support for one another's projects. I am not talking about a moral utopia here. Although natural caring is usually found in family and small group situations, there are such groups (usually on their way to extinction) in which natural caring is absent, and in most groups natural caring sometimes fails. We might call groups that regularly fail to exhibit natural caring defective; they are lacking in essential human qualities. When natural caring fails episodically in groups that usually live by it, it is sorely missed. Everyone is thrown off balance, perhaps even deeply unhappy. On these occasions, ethical caring is required to restore natural caring.

Relational care theories recognize that the "individual" extolled by liberal philosophies is a myth. Life begins and develops in relation. The quality and quantity of interactions steer cultural evolution. Without denying other sources of morality, it seems reasonable to suggest that one powerful source is the maternal instinct that, with cognitive development, grew into natural caring and the virtues often associated with it. Right from the start, we are relational beings. As the relation is basic to biological life, the caring relation is basic to moral life. But how should this caring relation be described? What are its elements and what virtues are associated with it?

Carer and Cared-For

We may identify two parties in a caring relation: a carer and a cared-for. Each contributes distinctively to the relation. Note that this marks an important difference between care theory and traditional moral philosophy, which usually concentrates on the individual moral agent and the agent's connection to principle or to the agent's own virtue. The original caring relation is what Martin Buber described as an *unequal* relation; that is, it is one in which the parties cannot exchange positions.[11] In this relation, the mother is necessarily the one caring (or the carer) and the infant the one cared-for. The same sort of inequality characterizes formally defined relationships such as physician-patient, teacher-student, and lawyer-client.

In most adult relationships, however, we expect mutuality; the parties exchange places as the situation within which the relation exists changes. Indeed, we often judge the health of long-term relationships by the number and appropriateness of these exchanges. It should not be expected that, in a female-male relationship, the female will always serve as carer and the male as cared-for. Some feminists have expressed worry that acceptance of care ethics might contribute to the long-standing exploitation of women—that women will fall into or fail to escape from the "caring trap."

This worry has some legitimacy, but the legitimacy rests on two mistakes: first, that "carer" applies permanently to a person by virtue of her gender, and second, that *caring* as it is used in care theory is identical with caregiving. If we eliminate these two misunderstandings, there should be no fear that care theory will set a trap for women. Notice that I do not deny the reality of a caring trap, and we'll have to discuss how it was set and how it continues to be baited.[12] But I do deny that care theory, properly understood, contributes to the maintenance of the trap.

Let's use the original caring relation as a setting in which to analyze the contributions of carer and cared-for. The carer must first of all be attentive to the expressed needs of the cared-for. These needs are not always expressed verbally. Obviously, an infant does not express itself in words, and there are many other situations in which needs are expressed with body language. The carer's task is to discern correctly what is being expressed. [...] For now, it should be enough to note that a carer must exercise receptive attention—to listen and watch.

Analysis of receptive attention has been relatively scarce in philosophy. Simone Weil discussed this form of attention and its place in moral life. The basic attitude of one exercising receptive attention is captured in the question asked (explicitly or implicitly) by carers: What are you going through? Weil writes: "This way of looking is first of all attentive. The soul empties itself of all its own contents in order to receive the being it is looking at, just as he is, in all his truth."[13]

In *Caring,* I used the word *engrossment* to name this form of attention, but the word has been too often misinterpreted.[14] I did not intend to suggest that an individual (carer) should be engrossed in another individual (cared-for) as a lover might be engrossed in the beloved. What I meant to suggest is that the carer is engrossed in (or receptively attentive to) the needs expressed in an encounter. In the case of maternal caring, the attention is continual; engrossment may be the right word. But in the momentary encounters we regularly experience—for example, being asked by a stranger for directions—we are engrossed or completely attentive just long enough to hear the request; we respond, and the moment passes. At these moments, as Buber put it, the other "fills the firmament."[15] But the stranger fills the firmament briefly; the infant fills the firmament often and not only when immediately present.

When one engages in receptive attention, the result is often motivational displacement; that is, the motive energy of the carer flows toward the needs of the cared-for. Temporarily, the carer's own projects are set aside. A teacher may feel her own fingers twitching as though they were holding a pencil as she gets ready to respond to a student's struggle with a math problem, and many parents have experienced a similar bodily reaction when watching a child's first wobbly performance on a bicycle. But motivational displacement is not always revealed in bodily reactions. Its fundamental character is a shift in the direction of motive energy.

Then, of course, the one-caring must do something. Decisions on how to respond—what to do—depend not only on the expressed need but also on the competence of the carer and the resources she has at her disposal.

An incipient caring encounter may be disrupted or aborted at any stage: the carer may fail to engage in receptive attention, the expressed need may not trigger motivational displacement, or the carer's response may not be recognized as caring by the cared-for. To qualify as a caring encounter, the cared-for must contribute to the relation; the cared-for must show in some way that the caring has been received. This response completes the caring relation. Without it, we may acknowledge a carer's effort to care, but the encounter, episode, or relation cannot be said to be one of caring. However, acknowledgment of the carer's efforts need not take the form of gratitude. An infant's smile, eye contact, and extended arms all represent acknowledgment. Similarly, a patient's release from pain or a student's renewed energy in pursuing a learning objective conveys to the carer that the caring has been received. Further, the response of the cared-for supplies more information for the carer to use in the next encounter. The response is vital to the caring relation. Requiring a response of recognition from the cared-for makes care ethics distinct from virtue ethics. We need not interpret the infant's smile, the patient's sigh of relief, or the student's perseverance as virtuous, but we recognize that these responses contribute to the caring relation and, more generally, to moral life. In care ethics, *caring* more often points to the quality of relation than to a virtue in the one caring.

I should clarify use of the words *encounter, episode,* and *relation.* All three point to dyadic interactions. An *encounter* might be thought of as a minimal relation (A, B) in which A acts as carer and B as cared-for. B expresses some need—for example, for directions or help in lifting a heavy package—and A responds by meeting the need or, at least, by explaining regretfully why she cannot do so. A may, for example, reply, "I'm a stranger here myself," or "I'm just recovering from a back injury," and may help by trying to enlist a third person's aid. A has been attentive, felt the desire to help, and responded with an expression of concern; B has recognized A's effort as caring. The encounter is rightly called a (minimal) caring relation.

By *episode,* I mean an encounter or set of encounters within a longer-term relation. A long-term relation such as mother-child is a caring relation if most of the episodes within it are caring and the growing child acknowledges the continuing relation as caring. Such relations are also characterized by continuing interest or concern between encounters. Mothers do not forget about their children when they are not interacting directly with them, nor do good teachers abandon concern for their students between classes. Carers in long-term caring relations maintain a disposition to care; they are prepared to care. In the last section of this chapter, we'll examine this idea more closely. How is it that some people approach the world "prepared to care," and how do we cultivate this attitude?

Discussion of being prepared to care necessitates examination of another important distinction—that between *caring for* and *caring about. Caring for* requires direct interaction with the cared-for, the criteria of caring already laid out, and the expectation of response from the cared-for showing the caring has been received. In contrast, *caring about* is characterized by concern, perhaps about people at a distance or about groups of people at some risk. Although we are not always in a position to *care for* people, when we sincerely *care about* them, we may contribute to a charity, vote in a way thought to improve their condition, or moderate our own way of life in an effort to conserve resources.

Caring about may provide one foundation for a theory of justice. (Another, of course, is self-interest.) We cannot care for everyone; that is physically impossible. When there is no provision for direct encounter and reception of the all-important response of the cared-for, we try to employ some form of justice in our policies. Justice does not become irrelevant when we embrace an ethic of care. However, care theory counsels that whatever is done in the name of justice be guided in part by the spirit of caring. Instead of imposing rules and practices derived from our own conception of justice, we ask how we might help to establish conditions in which caring relations can flourish in the society or culture that will receive our care/justice. Thus the caring relation and caring-for remain basic in both theory and practice.

Often in caring about, as in caring for, we are moved by empathy, but the intensity of feeling is not usually so strong. We contribute something to overseas needs, but we continue to give most of our attention to those close to us. Occasionally, when feeling is very strong, a person may drop everything else and seek a way to establish direct encounters with those cared about. Stories about people who do this excite considerable public interest, but we recognize that few people are in a position to do this. However, we note that *caring about* may inspire *caring for*.

Notes

1. See the summary in Virginia Held, *The Ethics of Care: Personal, Political, and Global* (Oxford: Oxford University Press, 2006).

2. On maternal thinking, see Sara Ruddick, *Maternal Thinking: Toward a Politics of Peace* (Boston: Beacon Press, 1989).

3. See Philippa Foot, *Natural Goodness* (Oxford: Oxford University Press, 2001).

4. See Daniel Lord Smail, *On Deep History and the Brain* (Berkeley and Los Angeles: University of California Press, 2007).

5. Ibid.

6. Jean Piaget, *Biology and Knowledge* (Chicago: University of Chicago Press, 1971), 368.

7. Carol J. Gilligan, *In a Different Voice* (Cambridge, MA: Harvard University Press, 1982).

8. Marc D. Hauser, *Moral Minds* (New York: Harper Collins, 2006), xviii.

9. See Catherine A. MacKinnon, *Feminism Unmodified* (Cambridge, MA: Harvard University Press, 1987). But on neurogenic and hormonal differences, see Sarah Blaffer Hrdy, *Mothers and Others* (Cambridge, MA: Belknap Press of Harvard University Press, 2009).

10. See, for example, Michael Slote, *The Ethics of Care and Empathy* (New York: Routledge, 2007).

11. See Martin Buber, *I and Thou*, trans. Walter Kaufmann (New York: Charles Scribner's Sons, 1970). I also discuss unequal relations at some length in Nel Noddings, *Caring: A Feminine Approach to Ethics and Moral Education* (Berkeley and Los Angeles: University of California Press, 1984).

12. For discussion of the role of mothering in the "care trap," see Nancy Chodorow, *The Reproduction of Mothering* (Berkeley and Los Angeles: University of California Press, 1978).

13. Simone Weil, *Simone Weil Reader,* ed. George A. Panichas (Mt. Kisco, NY: Moyer Bell Limited, 1977), 51.

14. See Noddings, *Caring.*

15. Buber, *I and Thou,* 59.

16. Weil, *Simone Weil Reader,* 44–52.

17. Ibid., 313–39.

18. Iris Murdoch, *The Sovereignty of Good* (London: Routledge & Kegan Paul, 1970), 28.

19. William W. Ickes writes about empathic accuracy. See his *Empathic Accuracy* (New York: Guilford, 1997).

20. Murdoch, *Sovereignty of Good,* 17.

21. Ibid., 23.

22. Michael Stocker, *Valuing Emotions* (Cambridge: Cambridge University Press, 1996), 216–17.

23. See the chapters on Murdoch (chaps. 1 and 2) in Lawrence A. Blum, *Moral Perception and Particularity* (Cambridge: Cambridge University Press, 1994).

24. This possibility is described in some depth in Ruddick, *Maternal Thinking.* However, Ruddick considers men as well as women capable of maternal thinking. See also Hrdy, *Mothers and Others,* on this.

25. See Jon Entine, *Abraham's Children: Race, Identity, and the DNA of the Chosen People* (New York: Grand Central, 2007); also Sean B. Carroll, *The Making of the Fittest* (New York: W. W. Norton, 2006).

26. I have described such cases more fully in Noddings, *Starting at Home: Caring and Social Policy* (Berkeley and Los Angeles: University of California Press, 2002), using as illustrative the case of Theobald and Ernest in Samuel Butler's *The Way of All Flesh* (Garden City, NY: Doubleday, 1944).

27. Martin Hoffman, *Empathy and Moral Development* (New York: Cambridge University Press, 2000), 143.

28. Ruddick, *Maternal Thinking,* 104.

29. See Ruddick, *Maternal Thinking,* for a wide-ranging discussion of the issues that arise in dialogue.

30. James Terry White, *Character Lessons in American Biography* (New York: Character Development League, 1909).

31. See Hoffman, *Empathy,* on induction and transgressive guilt.

32. Hoffman, *Empathy*, 119.

33. For more on confirmation in moral education, see Noddings, *Educating Moral People* (New York: Teachers College Press, 2002).

Wollstonecraft, *Vindication of the Rights of Woman*

1. How does Wollstonecraft characterize the purpose of our lives? In what ways do both women and the wealthy fail to pursue good lives?
2. According to Wollstonecraft, what kind of power are women able to achieve in the world? How do they get such power? Why does she think this kind of influence "systematically degrading"?
3. What is the "wild wish" that Wollstonecraft considers a remedy to women's current state?

Noddings, *The Maternal Factor*

1. Explain what Nodding means by a "caring relation." How is this illustrated in the case of mothers and children?
2. Explain the difference between natural and ethical caring. How does each differ from caregiving?
3. How does Nodding understand the "maternal instinct"? In what sense is she willing to accept a version of "essentialism"?

SUGGESTIONS FOR FURTHER READING OR VIEWING

Card, Claudia. "Care and Evil." *Hypatia* 5 (1990): 101–108..

Cudd, Ann, and Robin Andreason, eds. *Feminist Theory: A Philosophical Anthropology.* Hoboken, NJ: Wiley-Blackwell, 2005.

Gilligan, Carol. *In a Difference Voice: Psychological Theory and Women's Development.* Cambridge, MA: Harvard University Press, 1993.

Ruddick, Sara. *Maternal Thinking: Towards a Politics of Peace.* Boston: Beacon, 1995.

PART 4

Applied Ethics

THINKING THROUGH CONTEMPORARY CONTROVERSIES

The readings of the previous sections have all focused on the kinds of theoretical questions that occupy moral philosophers. It is time now to put all this theory to work in examining the kinds of concrete moral concerns that worry us as members of a broader world to see if ethics has anything to say there. Applied ethics examines concerns we often encounter first as political controversies or legal uncertainties:

- How should we as a society defend ourselves against our worst criminals?

- Should we allow women to choose to have an abortion in at least some circumstances?

- Is it right that we live in ways that bring such enormous suffering to animals and damage to the environment?

- What should we do to address the extreme poverty so many around the world live in?

- Is the brutality of war justified if we fight for the right things?

- Should we allow doctors to hasten the deaths of those suffering horribly?

All these questions are the topics of discussions in law and social policy, but philosophers can contribute a lot that is unique and important. Armed with the carefully worked-out normative theories we have considered, those working in applied ethics illuminate the practical implications of common moral assumptions, identify inconsistencies in commonly offered arguments, and point to overlooked and unexplored lines of reasoning that lead to surprising—and frequently quite controversial—conclusions. We invite you to consider this last set of readings with a willingness to be challenged on matters you may have thought settled.

Capital Punishment

INTRODUCTION TO CAPITAL PUNISHMENT

The practice of capital punishment—here understood as the state-sanctioned execution of convicted criminals—raises a lot of difficult moral questions and has long been a subject of philosophical debate. It is helpful to situate these controversies within some thoughts about the ethics of punishment more broadly. Punishment poses ethical problems because it typically involves treating people in ways that are normally impermissible. When we forcibly take away the freedom of criminals, or take away substantial amounts of their money, or (as is still done in many places) beat them, or—the ultimate punishment—deliberately kill them, we are doing things we usually judge to be immoral, and indeed typically our behavior itself would be seen as criminal. So, a basic question is why in the case of punishing criminals are these so often seen as permissible. And, to ask the philosophical question, are they really permissible—how can punishment be *justified*?

A long tradition of debate about the moral justification for punishment has tended to focus on two ideas. One is that punishment is justified because it is deserved. In other words, as it seems to most of us without much reflection, it just seems right that if we do something bad—particularly if it harms others or violates important and fair rules—we deserve something bad in return. This intuition lies at the heart of what is known as the retributive theory of punishment. Immanuel Kant is a particularly strong advocate of this position.

A different way to think about justifying punishment looks at its possible beneficial effects, and here philosophers are able to marshal powerful intuitions. Surely, we want good things to come from punishment, lest it looks too much like simple vengeance. What good might punishment do? Some philosophers point to a potential communicative or educational function—punishment helps us to convey to the one being punished our collective disapproval of their behavior and encourages reform or moral improvement. A more popular argument, however, is that punishment is justified because it acts as a deterrent by giving both the person being punished and those who are aware that wrong doing is reliably punished ample reason to avoid criminal behavior in the future. The deterrent theory of punishment, then, is essentially consequentialist in nature, and is defended by utilitarians such as John Stuart Mill.

Debates about capital punishment reflect disagreements about these basic strategies for defending punishment. The finality of execution and its ties to deeper issues about the morality of taking human life add additional layers of complexity to the controversy. Although opponents such as Bedau push back against both retributive and deterrent arguments in favor of the practice, on a deeper level it is the very idea of empowering the state to end the lives of its citizens that is at issue. Before considering what philosophers have to say about the topic, here are some general questions you might consider.

Is capital punishment morally permissible for the state to engage in but not morally praiseworthy for the state to engage in? Is capital punishment permissible for heinous or truly vicious murderers but not morally permissible for all acts of murder? If so, when is murder heinous enough to warrant capital punishment? Is capital punishment morally impermissible because it is analogous to murder? Is capital punishment morally permissible if it is not analogous to murder? (Or, is capital punishment morally impermissible even if it is not analogous to murder?) Does capital punishment morally corrupt people who must engage in the "dirty work" of putting convicted criminals to death? Are there crimes, other than murder, that capital punishment seems appropriate for?

READING 4.1

The Principles of Public Right

selection from *The Philosophy of Law*
by Immanuel Kant

Judicial or Juridical Punishment (*pœna forensis*) is to be distinguished from Natural Punishment (*pœna naturalis*), in which Crime as Vice punishes itself, and does not as such come within the cognizance of the Legislator. Juridical Punishment can never be administered merely as a means for promoting another Good either with regard to the Criminal himself or to Civil Society, but must in all cases be imposed only because the individual on whom it is inflicted *has committed a Crime.* For one man ought never to be dealt with merely as a means subservient to the purpose of another, nor be mixed up with the subjects of Real Right. Against such treatment his Inborn Personality has a Right to protect him, even although he may be condemned to lose his Civil Personality. He must first be found guilty and *punishable,* before there can be any thought of drawing from his Punishment any benefit for himself or his fellow-citizens. The Penal Law is a Categorical Imperative; and woe to him who creeps through the serpent-windings of Utilitarianism to discover some advantage that may discharge him from the Justice of Punishment, or even from the due measure of it, according to the Pharisaic maxim: 'It is better that *one* man should die than that the whole people should perish.' For if Justice and Righteousness perish, human life would no longer have any value in the world.—What, then, is to be said of such a proposal as to keep a Criminal alive who has been condemned to death, on his being given to understand that if he agreed to certain dangerous experiments being performed upon him, he would be allowed to survive if he came happily through them? It is argued that Physicians might thus obtain new information that would *be* of value to the Commonweal. But a Court of Justice would repudiate with scorn any proposal

Immanuel Kant, Selection from "The Principles of Public Right," *The Philosophy of Law: An Exposition of The Fundamental Principles of Jurisprudence as the Science of Right*, ed. William Hastie, pp. 195-198.

of this kind if made to it by the Medical Faculty; for Justice would cease to be Justice, if it were bartered away for any consideration whatever.

But what is the mode and measure of Punishment which Public Justice takes as its Principle and Standard? It is just the Principle of Equality, by which the pointer of the Scale of Justice is made to incline no more to the one side than the other. It may be rendered by saying that the undeserved evil which any one commits on another, is to be regarded as perpetrated on himself. Hence it may be said: 'If you slander another, you slander yourself; if you steal from another, you steal from yourself; if you strike another, you strike yourself; if you kill another, you kill yourself.' This is the Right of RETALIATION (*jus talionis*); and properly understood, it is the only Principle which in regulating a Public Court, as distinguished from mere private judgment, can definitely assign both the quality and the quantity of a just penalty. All other standards are wavering and uncertain; and on account of other considerations involved in them, they contain no principle conformable to the sentence of pure and strict Justice. It may appear, however, that difference of social status would not admit the application of the Principle of Retaliation, which is that of 'Like with Like.' But although the application may not in all cases be possible according to the letter, yet as regards the effect it may always be attained in practice, by due regard being given to the disposition and sentiment of the parties in the higher social sphere. Thus a pecuniary penalty on account of a verbal injury, may have no direct proportion to the injustice of slander; for one who is wealthy may be able to indulge himself in this offence for his own gratification. Yet the attack committed on the honour of the party aggrieved may have its equivalent in the pain inflicted upon the pride of the aggressor, especially if he is condemned by the judgment of the Court, not only to retract and apologize, but to submit to some meaner ordeal, as kissing the hand of the injured person. In like manner, if a man of the highest rank has violently assaulted an innocent citizen of the lower orders, he may be condemned not only to apologize but to undergo a solitary and painful imprisonment, whereby, in addition to the discomfort endured, the vanity of the offender would be painfully affected, and the very shame of his position would constitute an adequate Retaliation after the principle of 'Like with Like.' But how then would we render the statement: 'If you *steal* from another, you steal from yourself'? In this way, that whoever steals anything makes the property of all insecure; he therefore robs himself of all security in property, according to the Right of Retaliation. Such a one has nothing, and can acquire nothing, but he has the Will to live; and this is only possible by others supporting him. But as the State should not do this gratuitously, he must for this purpose yield his powers to the State to be used in penal labour; and thus he falls for a time, or it may be for life, into a condition of slavery.—But whoever has committed Murder, must *die*. There is, in this case, no juridical substitute or surrogate, that can be given or taken for the satisfaction of Justice. There is no *Likeness* or proportion between Life, however painful, and Death; and therefore there is no Equality between the crime of Murder and the retaliation of it but what is judicially accomplished by the execution of the Criminal. His death, however, must be kept free from all maltreatment that would make the humanity suffering in his Person loathsome or abominable. Even if a Civil Society resolved to dissolve itself with the consent of all its members—as might be supposed in the case of a People inhabiting an island resolving to separate and scatter themselves throughout the whole world—the last Murderer lying in the prison ought to be executed before the resolution was carried out. This ought to be done in order that every one may realize the desert of his deeds, and that bloodguiltiness may not remain upon the people; for otherwise they might all be regarded as participators in the murder as a public violation of Justice.

How to Argue About
the Death Penalty

Hugo Bedau

I

Argument over the death penalty—especially in the United States during the
past generation—has been concentrated in large part on trying to answer various disputed *questions of fact*. Among them two have been salient: Is the death
penalty a better deterrent to crime (especially murder) than the alternative of
imprisonment? Is the death penalty administered in a discriminatory way, and,
in particular, are black or other nonwhite offenders (or offenders whose victims
are white) more likely to be tried, convicted, sentenced to death, and executed
than whites (or offenders whose victims are nonwhite)? Other questions of fact
have also been explored, including these two: What is the risk that an innocent
person could actually be executed for a crime he did not commit? What is the
risk that a person convicted of a capital felony but not executed will commit
another capital felony?

Earlier versions of this paper were read to audiences at Hampshire College and Dartmouth College
in 1987, and the Jerusalem Conference on Justice and Punishment in 1988. I am grateful for the
stimulus these audiences provided. Comments by Jay L. Garfield prompted a major revision in
section IV, and written criticisms by Walter Sinnott-Armstrong led to many improvements. Con-
stance Putnam has my gratitude for helping me to improve clarity of expression in many places.

Varying degrees of effort have been expended in trying to answer these questions. Although I think the current answers are capable of further refinement, I also think anyone who studies the evidence today must conclude that the best current answers to these four questions are as follows. (1) There is little or no evidence that the death penalty is a better deterrent to murder than is imprisonment; on the contrary, most evidence shows that these two punishments are about equally (in)effective as deterrents to murder. Furthermore, as long as the death penalty continues to be used relatively rarely, there is no prospect of gaining more decisive evidence on the question (Klein et al., 1978). (2) There is evidence that the death penalty has been and continues to be administered, whether intentionally or not, in a manner that produces arbitrary and racially discriminatory results in death sentencing. At the very least, this is true in those jurisdictions where the question has been investigated in recent years (Baldus et al., 1986). (3) It is impossible to calculate the risk that an innocent person will be executed, but the risk is not zero, as the record of convicted, sentenced, and executed innocents shows (Bedau and Radelet, 1987). (4) Recidivism data show that some murderers have killed after a conviction and prison sentence for murder; so there is a risk that others will do so as well (Bedau, 1982: 173–80).

Let us assume that my summary of the results of research on these four questions is correct, and that further research will not significantly change these answers. The first thing to notice is that even if everyone agreed on these answers, this would not by itself settle the dispute over whether to keep, expand, reduce, or abolish the death penalty. Knowing these empirical truths about the administration and effects of the death penalty in our society does not entail knowing whether one should support its retention or abolition. This would still be true even if we knew with finality the answers to *all* the factual questions that can be asked about it.

There are two reasons for this. The facts as they currently stand and as seen from the abolitionist perspective do not point strongly and overwhelmingly to the futility of the death penalty or to the harm it does, at least as long as it continues to be used only in the limited and restricted form of the past decade: confined to the crime of murder, with trial courts empowered to exercise "guided discretion" in sentencing, with defense counsel able to introduce anything as mitigating evidence, and with automatic review of both conviction and sentence by some appellate court *(Gregg v. Georgia,* 428 U.S. 153 [1976]; *Proffitt v. Florida,* 428 U.S. 242 [1976]; *Jurek v. Texas,* 428 U.S. 262 [1976]). Nor do the facts show that the alternative of life imprisonment is on balance a noticeably superior punishment. For example, the evidence of racial discrimination in the administration of the death penalty, while incontestable, may be no worse than the racial discrimination that occurs where lesser crimes and punishments are concerned. No one who has studied the data thinks that the administration of justice for murder approaches the level of racial discrimination reached a generation ago in the South by the administration of justice for rape (Wolfgang and Riedel, 1976). Besides, it is always possible to argue that such discrimination is diminishing, or will diminish over time, and that, in any case, since the fault does not lie in the capital statutes themselves—they are color-blind on their face—the remedy does not lie in repealing them.

But the marginal impact of the empirical evidence is not the major factor in explaining why settling disputes over matters of fact does not and cannot settle the larger controversy over the death penalty itself. As a matter of sheer logic, it is not possible to deduce a policy conclusion (such as the desirability of abolishing the death penalty) from any set of factual premises, however general and well supported. Any argument intended to recommend continuing or reforming current policy on the death penalty must include among its premises one or more normative propositions. Unless disputants over the death penalty can agree about these normative propositions, their agreement on the general facts will never suffice to resolve their dispute.

II

Accordingly, the course of wisdom for those interested in arguing about the death penalty is to focus attention on the normative propositions crucial to the dispute, in the hope that some headway may be made in narrowing disagreement over their number, content, and weight.

If this is to be done effectively, the context of these norms in general political ideology needs to be fixed. Suffice it to say here that I proceed from within the context of liberal pluralistic constitutional democracy and the conception of punishment appropriate therein (see Hart, 1968; Rawls, 1971).

Logically prior to the idea of punishment is the idea of a crime. What counts as a criminal harm depends in part on our conception of persons as bearers of rights deserving respect and protection. In this setting, liability to punishment and its actual infliction serve the complex function of reinforcing compliance with a set of laws deemed necessary to protect the fundamental equal rights of all members of society. The normative propositions relevant to the death penalty controversy are interwoven with the basic purposes and principles of liberal society, including the recognition and protection of individual rights to life and liberty, and to security of person and property.

These norms can be divided into two groups: those that express relevant and desirable *social goals* or *purposes,* and those that express relevant and respectable *moral principles.* Punishment is thus a practice or institution defined through various policies—such as the death penalty for murder—and intended to be the means or instrument whereby certain social goals are achieved within the constraints imposed by acknowledged moral principles (cf. Dworkin, 1977:22–23, 169–71).

Reduction of crime, or at least prevention of an increase in crime, is an example of such a goal. This goal influences the choice of punishments because of their impact (hypothesized or verified) on the crime rate. No one, except for purists of a retributive stripe, would dissent from the view that this goal is relevant to the death penalty controversy. Because of its relevance, there is continuing interest in the outcome of research on the differential deterrent efficacy of death versus imprisonment. The only questions normally in dispute are what that research shows (I have summarized it above) and how important this goal is (some regard it as decisive).

Similarly, that no one should be convicted and sentenced to death without a fair trial (i.e., in violation of "due process of law") is a principle of law and morality generally respected. Its general acceptance explains the considerable reformation in the laws governing the death penalty in the United States that have been introduced since 1972 by the Supreme Court *(Furman v. Georgia,* 408 U.S. 238 [1972]). The Court argued that capital trials and death sentencing were in practice unfair (in constitutional jargon, they were in violation of the Eighth and Fourteenth Amendments, which bar "cruel and unusual punishments" and require "equal protection of the laws," respectively). State legislatures and thoughtful observers agreed. Here again the only questions concern how important it is to comply with this principle (some regard it as decisive) and the extent to which the death penalty currently violates it (I have remarked on this point above, too).

The chief use of a moral principle in the present setting is to constrain the methods used in pursuit of policy (as when respect for "due process" rules out curbstone justice as a tactic in crime fighting). However, identifying the relevant goals, acknowledging the force of the relevant principles, and agreeing on the relevant general facts will still not suffice to resolve the dispute. The relative importance of achieving a given goal and the relative weight of a given principle remain to be settled, and disagreement over these matters is likely to show up in disagreement over the justification of the death penalty itself.

If this is a correct sketch of the structural character of debate and disagreement over the death penalty, then (as I noted earlier) the best hope for progress may lie in looking more carefully at the non-factual normative ingredients so far isolated in the dispute. Ideally, we would identify and evaluate the policy goals relevant to punishment generally, as well as the moral principles that constrain the structure and content of the penalty schedule. We would also settle the proper relative weights to attach to these goals and constraints, if not in general, then at least for their application in the present context. Then, with whatever relevant general facts are at our disposal, we would be in a position to draw the appropriate inferences and resolve the entire dispute, confident that we have examined and duly weighed everything that reason and morality can bring to bear on the problem.

As an abstract matter, therefore, the question is whether the set of relevant policies and principles, taken in conjunction with the relevant facts, favors reduction (even complete abolition) of the death penalty, or whether it favors retention (or even extension) of the death penalty. Lurking in the background, of course, is the troubling possibility that the relevant norms and facts underdetermine the resolution of the dispute. But let us not worry about sharks on dry land, not yet.

III

Where choice of punishments is concerned, the relevant social goals, I suggest, are few. Two in particular generally commend themselves:

(G 1) Punishment should contribute to the reduction of crime; accordingly, the punishment for a crime should not be so idle a threat or so slight a deprivation that it has no deterrent or incapacitative effects; and it certainly should not contribute to an increase in crime.

(G 2) Punishments should be "economical"—they should not waste valuable social resources in futile or unnecessarily costly endeavors.

The instrumental character of these purposes and goals is evident. They reflect the fact that society does not institute and maintain the practice of punishment for its own sake, as though it were a good in itself. Rather, punishment is and is seen to be a means to an end or ends. The justification of a society's punitive policies and practices must therefore involve two steps: first, it must be shown that these ends are desirable; second, it must be shown that the practice of punishment is the best means to these ends. What is true of the justification of punishment generally is true a fortiori of justifying the death penalty.

Endorsement of these two policy goals tends to encourage support for the death penalty. Opponents of capital punishment need not reject these goals, however, and its defenders cannot argue that accepting these goals vindicates their preferred policy. Traditionally, it is true, the death penalty has often been supported on the ground that it provides the best social defense and is extremely cheap to administer. But since the time of Beccaria and Bentham, these empirical claims have been challenged (see Bedau, 1983), and rightly so. If support for the death penalty today in a country such as the United States rests on the high priority placed on these goals, then there is much (some would say com-pelling) evidence to undermine this support. The most that can be said solely by reference to these goals is that recognition of their importance can always be counted on to kindle interest in capital punishment, and to that extent put its opponents on the defensive.

Whether punishment is intended to serve only the two goals so far identified is disputable. An argument can be made that there are two or three further goals:

(G 3) Punishment should rectify the harm and injustice caused by crime.
(G 4) Punishment should serve as a recognized channel for the release of public indignation and anger at the offender.
(G 5) Punishment should make convicted offenders into better persons rather than leave them as they are or make them worse.

Obviously, anyone who accepts the fifth goal must reject the death penalty. I shall not try here to argue the merits of this goal, either in itself or relative to the other goals of punishment. Whatever its merits, this goal is less widely sought than the others, and for that reason alone is less useful in trying to develop rational agreement over the death penalty. Its persuasive power for those not already persuaded against the death penalty on other grounds is likely to be slight to zero. Although I am unwilling to strike it from the list of goals that punishment in general is and should be practiced to achieve, it would be unreasonable to stress its pre-eminence in the present context.

The proposed third goal is open to the objection that rectification of injustice is not really a goal of punishment, even if it is a desirable goal in other settings. (Indeed, it is widely believed that rectification is not a goal of punishment but of noncriminal tort judgments.) But even if it is a goal of punishment generally, it seems irrelevant to the death penalty controversy, because neither death nor imprisonment (as practiced in the United States) rectifies anything. Nonetheless, this goal may be indirectly important for the death penalty controversy. To the extent that one believes punishments ought to serve this goal, and that there is no possible way to rectify the crime of murder, one may come to believe that the fourth goal is of even greater importance than would otherwise be the case. Indeed, striving to achieve this fourth goal and embracing the death penalty as a consequence is quite parallel to striving to achieve the fifth goal and consequently embracing its abolition.

Does this fourth goal have a greater claim on our support than I have allowed is true of the fifth goal, so obviously incompatible with it? Many would say that it does. Some would even argue that it is this goal, not any of the others, that is the paramount purpose of punishment under law (Berns, 1979). Whatever else punishment does, its threat and infliction are to be seen as the expression of social indignation at deliberate harm to the innocent. Preserving a socially acceptable vehicle for the expression of anger at offenders is absolutely crucial to the health of a just society.

There are in principle three ways to respond to this claim insofar as it is part of an argument for capital punishment. One is to reject it out of hand as a false proposition from start to finish. A second is to concede that the goal of providing a visible and acceptable channel for the emotion of anger is legitimate, but to argue that this goal could at best justify the death penalty only in a very small number of cases (the occasional Adolf Eichmann, for example), since otherwise its importance would be vastly exaggerated. A third response is to concede both the legitimacy and the relative importance of this goal, but to point out that its pursuit, like that of all other goals, is nonetheless constrained by moral principles (yet to be examined), and that once these principles are properly employed, the death penalty ceases to be a permissible method of achieving this goal. I think both the second and third objections are sound, and a few further words here about each are appropriate.

First of all, anger is not the same as resentment or indignation, since the latter feeling or emotion can be aroused only through the perceived violation of some moral principle, whereas the former does not have this constraint. But whether the feeling aroused by a horrible murder is really only anger rather than indignation is just the question whether the principles of morality have been violated or not. Knowing that the accused offender has no legal excuse or justification for his criminal conduct is not enough to warrant the inference that he and his conduct are appropriate objects of our unqualified moral hostility. More about the context of the offense and its causation must be supplied; it may well be that in ordinary criminal cases one rarely or never knows enough to reach such a condemnatory judgment with confidence. Even were this not so, one has no reason to suppose that justified anger at offenders is of overriding importance, and that all countervailing considerations must yield to its pre-eminence. For one thing, the righteous anger needed for that role is simply not available in a pluralistic secular society. Even if it were, we have been assured from biblical times that it passes all too easily into self-righteous and hypocritical repression by some sinners of others.

Quite apart from such objections, there is a certain anomaly, even irony, in the defense of the death penalty by appeal to this goal. On the one hand, we are told of the importance of a publicly recognized ritual for extermination of convicted murderers as a necessary vent for otherwise unchanneled disruptive public emotions. On the other hand, our society scrupulously rejects time-honored methods of execution that truly do express hatred and anger at offenders: beheading, crucifixion, dismemberment, and even hanging and the electric chair are disappearing. Execution by lethal injection, increasingly the popular option, hardly seems appropriate as the outlet of choice for such allegedly volatile energies! And is it not ironic that this technique, invented to facilitate life-saving surgery, now turns out to be the preferred channel for the expression of moral indignation?

IV

If the purposes or goals of punishment lend a utilitarian quality to the practice of punishment, the moral principles relevant to the death penalty operate as deontological constraints on their pursuit. Stating all and only the principles relevant to the death penalty controversy is not easy, and the list that follows is no more than the latest approximation to the task (for my previous attempts, see Bedau, 1980:159–60, 1987:24). With some overlap here and there, these principles are six:

(P 1) No one should deliberately and intentionally take another's life where there is a feasible alternative.

(P 2) The more severe a penalty is, the more important it is that it be imposed only on those who truly deserve it.

(P 3) The more severe a penalty is, the weightier the justification required to warrant its imposition on anyone.

(P 4) Whatever the criminal offense, the accused and convicted offender does not forfeit all his rights and dignity as a person. Accordingly, there is an upper limit to the severity—cruelty, destructiveness, finality—of permissible punishments, regardless of the offense.

(P 5) Fairness requires that punishments should be graded in their severity according to the gravity of the offense.

(P 6) If human lives are to be risked, the risk should fall more heavily on wrong-doers (the guilty) than on others (the innocent).

I cannot argue here for all these principles, but they really need no argument from me. Each is recognized implicitly or explicitly in our practice; each can be seen to constrain our conduct as individuals and as officers in democratic institutions. Outright repudiation or cynical disregard of any of these principles would disqualify one from engaging in serious discourse and debate over punishment in a liberal society. All can be seen as corollaries or theorems of the general proposition that life, limb, and security of person—of *all* persons—are of paramount value. Thus, only minimal interference (in the jargon of the law, "the least restrictive means") is warranted with anyone's life, limb, and security in order to protect the rights of others.

How do these principles direct or advise us in regard to the permissibility or desirability of the death penalty? The first thing to note is that evidently none directly rules it out. I know of no moral principle that is both sufficiently rigid and sufficiently well established for us to point to it and say: "The practice of capital punishment is flatly contradictory to the requirements of this moral principle." (Of course, we could invent a principle that would have this consequence, but that is hardly to the point.) This should not be surprising; few if any of the critics or the defenders of the death penalty have supposed otherwise. Second, several of these principles do reflect the heavy burden that properly falls on anyone who advocates that certain human beings be deliberately killed by others, when those to be killed are not at the time a danger to anyone. For example, whereas the first principle may permit lethal force in self-defense, it directly counsels against the death penalty in *all* cases without exception. The second and third principles emphasize the importance of "due process" and "equal protection" as the finality and incompensability of punishments increase. The fourth principle draws attention to the nature and value of persons, even those convicted of terrible crimes. It reminds us that even if crimes know no upper limit in their wantonness, cruelty, destructiveness, and horror, punishments under law in a civilized society cannot imitate crimes in this regard. Punishment does operate under limits, and these limits are not arbitrary.

The final two principles, however, seem to be exceptions to the generalization that the principles as a group tend to favor punishments other than death. The fifth principle seems to entail that if murder is the gravest crime, then it should receive the severest punishment. This does not, of course, *require* a society to invoke the death penalty for murder—unless one accepts *lex talionis* ("a life for a life, an eye for an eye") in a singularly literal-minded manner. Since *lex talionis* is not a sound principle on which to construct the penalty schedule generally, appealing to this interpretation of the fifth principle here simply begs the question. Nevertheless, the principle that punishments should be graded to fit the crime does encourage consideration of the death penalty, especially if it seems that there is no other way to punish murder with the utmost permissible severity.

Of rather more interest is the sixth principle. Some make it the cornerstone of their defense of the death penalty (van den Haag, 1986: 1665). They argue that it is better to execute all convicted murderers, lest on a future occasion any of them murder again, than it is to execute none of them, thereby averting the risk of executing any who may be innocent. A policy of complete abolition—at least in the United States today—would result in thousands of convicted killers (only a few of whom are innocent) being held behind bars for life. This cohort would constitute a permanent risk to the safety of many millions of innocent citizens. The sole gain to counterbalance this risk is the guarantee that no lives (innocent or guilty) will be lost through legal executions. The practice of executions thus protects far more innocent citizens than the same practice puts in jeopardy.

This argument is far less conclusive than it may at first seem. Even if we grant it full weight, it is simply unreasonable to use it (or any other argument) as a way of dismissing the relevance of principles that counsel a different result, or as a tactic to imply the subordinate importance of those other principles. If used in this manner, the sixth principle would be thoroughly transformed. It has become a disguised version of the first policy goal (viz., Reduce crime!) and in effect would elevate that goal to pre-eminence over every competing and constraining consideration. The argument also fosters the illusion that we can in fact reasonably estimate, if not actually calculate, the number of lives risked by a policy of abolition as opposed to a policy of capital punishment. This is false; we do not and cannot reasonably hope to know what the risk is of convicting the innocent (see Bedau and Radelet, 1987:78–81, 83–85), even if we could estimate the risk of recidivist murder. We therefore cannot really compare the two risks with any precision. Finally, the argument gains whatever strength it appears to have by tacitly ignoring the following dilemma. If the policy of killing the convicted in order to reduce risk to the innocent is to achieve maximum effect, then death must be the *mandatory* penalty for everyone convicted of murder (never mind other crimes). But such a policy cannot really be carried out. It flies in the face of two centuries of political reality, which demonstrates the impossibility of enforcing truly mandatory death penalties for murder and other crimes against the person. The only realistic policy alternative is some version of a *discretionary* death penalty. However, every version of this policy actually tried has proved vulnerable to criticism on grounds of inequity in its administration, as critic after critic has shown (e.g., Amsterdam, 1987; Baldus et al., 1986; Bedau, 1987:164–84; Gradess, 1987; Tabak, 1986; Weisberg, 1984). Meanwhile, history tells us that our society is unable to avoid all risk of recidivist murder.

The upshot is that we today run both the risk of executing the innocent and the risk of recidivist murder, even though it is necessary to run only one of these risks.

V

What has our examination of the relevant goals and principles shown about the possibility of resolving the death penalty controversy on rational grounds? First, the death penalty is primarily a means to one or more ends or goals, but it is not the only (and arguably not the best) means to them. Second, several principles of relevance to sound punitive policy in general favor (although they do not demand) abolition of the death penalty. Third, there is no goal or principle that constitutes a conclusive reason favoring either side in the dispute. Unless, of course, some one goal or principle is interpreted or weighted in such a manner (cf. the fifth goal, or the fifth principle). But in that case, one side or the other will refuse to accept it. Finally, the several goals and principles of punishment that have been identified have no obvious rank order or relative weighting. As they stand, these goals and principles do indeed underdetermine the policy dispute over capital punishment. Perhaps such a ranking could be provided by some comprehensive socioethical theory. But the failure of every known such theory to secure general acceptance so far does not bode well for prompt and rational resolution of the controversy along these lines.

Despite the absence of any conclusive reasons or decisive ranking of principles, we may take refuge in the thought (as I have done elsewhere; see Bedau, 1987:44–45, 238–47) that a preponderance of reasons does favor one side rather than the other. Such a preponderance emerges, however, only when the relevant goals and principles of punishment are seen in a certain light, or from a particular angle of vision. Perhaps this amounts to one rather than another weighting of goals and principles but without conscious reliance upon any manifest theory. In any case, I shall mention three such considerations that are important in my assessment of the moral objections to the death penalty.

The first and by far the most important concerns the role and function of *power* in the hands of government. It is in general preferable, *ceteris paribus,* that such power over individuals should shrink rather than expand. Where such power must be used, then let it be devoted to constructive rather than destructive purposes, thus enhancing the autonomy and liberty of those directly affected. But the death penalty contradicts this concern; it is government power used in a dramatically destructive manner upon individuals in the absence of any compelling social necessity. No wonder it is the ultimate symbol of such power.

Another consideration that shapes my interpretation of the goals and principles of evaluation is an orientation to the *future* rather than to the past. We cannot do anything for the dead victims of crime. (How many of those who oppose the death penalty would continue to do so if, *mirabile dictu,* executing the murderer brought the victim back to life?) But we can—or at least we can try to—do something for the living: we can protect the innocent, prevent illegitimate violence, and help those in despair over their own victimization. None of these constructive tasks involves punishing anyone for expressive, vindictive, or retributive reasons. The more we stress these factors in our choice of punishments, the more we orient our punitive policies toward the past—toward trying to use government power over the lives of a few as a socially approved instrument of moral bookkeeping.

Finally, the death penalty projects a false and misleading picture of man and society. Its professed message for those who support it is this: justice requires killing the convicted murderer. So we focus on the death that all murderers supposedly deserve and overlook our inability to give a rational account of why so few actually get it. Hence, the lesson taught by the practice of capital punishment is really quite different. Far from being a symbol of justice, it is a symbol of brutality and stupidity. Perhaps if we lived in a world of autonomous Kantian moral agents, where all the criminals freely expressed their rational will in the intention to kill others without their consent or desert, then death for the convicted murderer might be just (as even Karl Marx was inclined to think; see Marx, 1853). But a closer look at the convicts who actually are on our death rows shows that these killers are a far cry from the rational agents of Kant's metaphysical imagination. We fool ourselves if we think a system of ideal retributive justice designed for such persons is the appropriate model for the penal system in our society.

Have I implicitly conceded that argument over the death penalty is irrational? If I am right that the death penalty controversy does not really turn on controversial social goals or controversial moral principles, any more than it does on disputed general facts, but instead turns on how all three are to be balanced or weighed, does it follow that reason alone cannot resolve the controversy, because reason alone cannot determine which weighting or balancing is the correct one? Or can reason resolve this problem, perhaps by appeal to further theory, theory that would deepen our appreciation of what truly underlies a commitment to liberal institutions and a belief in the possibilities for autonomy of all persons (Bedau, 1987: 123–28)? I think it can—but this is the right place to end the present investigation because we have reached the launching platform for another one.

References

Amsterdam, Anthony G. 1987. "The Supreme Court and Capital Punishment." *Human Rights* 14 (Winter): 14–17, 49–60.

Baldus, David C.; Charles A. Pulaski, Jr.; and George Woodworth. 1986. "Arbitrariness and Discrimination in the Administration of the Death Penalty: A Challenge to State Supreme Courts." *Stetson Law Review* 15:133–261.

Bedau, Hugo Adam. 1980. "Capital Punishment." Pp. 147-82 in *Matters of Life and Death,* edited by Tom Regan. New York: Random House.

_____. 1982. *The Death Penalty in America.* 3d ed. New York: Oxford University Press.

_____. 1983. "Bentham's Utilitarian Critique of the Death Penalty." *Journal of Criminal Law and Criminology* 74:1033–66. Reprinted at pp. 64–91 of H. A. Bedau, *Death Is Different: Studies in the Morality, Law, and Politics of Capital Punishment.* Boston: Northeastern University Press, 1987.

_____. 1987. *Death Is Different: Studies in the Morality, Law, and Politics of Capital Punishment.* Boston: Northeastern University Press.

Bedau, Hugo Adam, and Michael L. Radelet. 1987. "Miscarriages of Justice in Potentially Capital Cases." *Stanford Law Review* 40:21–179.

Berns, Walter. 1979. *For Capital Punishment: Crime and the Morality of the Death Penalty.* New York: Basic Books.

Dworkin, Ronald. 1977. *Taking Rights Seriously.* Cambridge: Harvard University Press.

Gradess, Jonathan F. 1987. "The Road From Scottsboro." *Criminal Justice* 2 (2): 2–4, 44–47.

Hart, H. L. A. 1968. *Punishment and Responsibility: Essays in the Philosophy of Law.* New York: Oxford University Press.

Klein, Lawrence R.; Brian Forst; and Victor Filatov. 1978. "The Deterrent Effect of Capital Punishment: An Assessment of the Evidence." Pp. 336–60 in *Deterrence and Incapacitation: Estimating the Effects of Criminal Sanctions on Crime Rates,* edited by Alfred Blumstein, Jacqueline Cohen, and Daniel Nagin. Washington, D.C.: National Academy of Sciences.

Marx, Karl. 1853. "Capital Punishment." Pp. 485–86 in *Basic Writings on Politics and Philosophy: Karl Marx and Frederick Engels,* edited by Lewis Feuer. Garden City, N.Y.: Doubleday Anchor, 1959.

Rawls, John. 1971. *A Theory of Justice.* Cambridge: Harvard University Press.

Tabak, Ronald J. 1986. "The Death of Fairness: The Arbitrary and Capricious Imposition of the Death Penalty in the 1980's." *New York University Review of Law and Social Change* 4:797–848.

van den Haag, Ernest. 1986. "The Ultimate Punishment: A Defense." *Harvard Law Review* 99:1662–69.

Weisberg, Robert. 1984. "Deregulating Death." *Supreme Court Review* 8 (1983):305–95.

Wolfgang, Marvin E., and Marc Riedel. 1976. "Rape, Racial Discrimination, and the Death Peanlty." Pp. 99–121 in *Capital Punishment in the United States,* edited by Hugo Adam Bedau and Chester M. Pierce. New York: AMS Press.

Cases Cited

Furman v. Georgia, 408 U.S. 238 (1972).

Gregg v. Georgia, 428 U.S. 153 (1976).

Jurek v. Texas, 428 U.S. 262 (1976).

Proffitt v. Florida, 428 U.S. 242 (1976).

Kant, *The Principles of Public Right*

1. According to Kant, what is the difference between judicial punishment and natural punishment? What is a vice? Do we need judicial punishments for vices?

2. According to Kant, what should never be our motive for inflicting judicial punishment? Why? What should our motive be?

3. Explain Kant's "right of retaliation" and how it applies to his examples of slander, (assault), theft, and murder.

4. Explain Kant's final comment about "blood-guilt."

Bedau, How to Argue about the Death Penalty

1. How does Bedau summarize the empirical research into the death penalty? Why does he say that this research cannot itself settle the moral questions about capital punishment?

2. Explain the two goals of punishment that Bedau thinks are reasonable in a liberal, democratic state. What goals does he think would be unreasonable?

3. What are the deontological principles that Bedau identifies as relevant to the debate over capital punishment? Would Kant agree with this list?

4. What does Bedau think is the role of government in our lives that gives him a reason to be opposed to the death penalty?

SUGGESTIONS FOR FURTHER READING OR VIEWING

Dead Man Walking. 1996. A film about capital punishment loosely based on a true story.

Hampton, Jean. "The Moral Education Theory of Punishment." *Philosophy & Public Affairs* 13, no. 3 (1984).

Euthanasia

INTRODUCTION TO EUTHANASIA

Euthanasia is the practice of deliberately killing a person for what is believed to be their own good, where this usually means the person otherwise faces prolonged, unrelieved suffering or they face a life judged not worth living. The most familiar kinds of cases are medical, involving terminally ill patients in protracted physical pain or patients who have permanently lost consciousness. Strictly speaking, euthanasia takes place when another person, typically a doctor, kills the patient, but many of the moral issues euthanasia raises apply to doctor-assisted suicide as well. This is when a doctor provides the means by which a patient kills herself. At their core, the moral issues here come at the intersection of questions about the value of human life and the wrongness of killing, our duty to respect the autonomous choices of others, and the duty to avoid causing or tolerating unnecessary suffering.

It is useful to distinguish different types of euthanasia along two axes. One is the degree to which the decision to end the patient's life belongs to the patient herself. In what is commonly known as voluntary euthanasia, a mentally competent patient expressly conveys a desire to die. In nonvoluntary euthanasia, the patient has neither consented to nor expressed a desire to die and is unable to do either. This would be the case, for example, with a patient who has permanently lost consciousness without having ever clearly indicated a preference for how she would want to be treated in such a condition. Involuntary euthanasia would be when a patient is killed against her competently expressed will. Most debates about whether euthanasia should be legal are about whether voluntary euthanasia should be legal, and the emphasis on ensuring that the patient is making the choice also adds greater plausibility to doctor-assisted suicide. Some philosophers, including Peter Singer in the reading included here, are willing to argue on utilitarian grounds for the permissibility of nonvoluntary euthanasia. One would be hard pressed, however, to find advocates of involuntary euthanasia.

A separate distinction is often made between active and passive euthanasia. In active euthanasia the doctor brings about the patient's death by doing something that is immediately responsible for her death, such as giving a lethal injection. Passive euthanasia, however, happens when death comes because either the doctor chooses not to pursue some course of treatment that would prolong life, or when life-preserving measures are deliberately ended. Choosing not to give a terminally ill cancer patient an additional round of chemotherapy or choosing to remove a respirator from a patient unable to breathe on her own, would count as passive euthanasia if the intent is to bring about death for benevolent reasons. James Rachels is a prominent voice on the side of those who argue that there is no morally interesting difference between these two forms of euthanasia because there is no morally interesting difference between killing someone and deliberately allowing them to die. Others, such as Daniel Callahan, insist there is a moral difference here. Others will argue further that if the intent in withholding treatment is not to bring about death but to spare a patient from medical treatment that will not benefit her all things considered, it is a mistake to call her death euthanasia.

As noted, the theme of autonomy is a prominent one in debates about euthanasia, and it largely common ground that a mentally competent person has the right to refuse medical treatment. For Singer and Rachels, it is a short step from this to recognizing a right to die. By contrast, Callahan insists a patient's right to make her own medical decisions does not rightly translate into a right to empower another to kill her.

Some questions you might consider in thinking about these complex issues: Both avoiding suffering and respecting human life seem to be important values. How should they be weighed when they seem to come into conflict? What ultimately is the purpose of medical treatment? Is death to be avoided for as long as possible? If euthanasia can be justified in cases of extreme physical suffering, is it also permissible in cases of extreme mental anguish? If doctor-assisted suicide is justified on the basis of relieving suffering, should we allow suicide in nonclinical settings as well? Will euthanasia be truly voluntary if we come to have societal expectations that the old and infirm will choose to die? Are such expectations likely if we come to embrace euthanasia as a normal part of medical practice?

Justifying Voluntary Euthanasia

Peter Singer

We have seen that it is possible to justify ending the life of a human being who lacks the capacity to consent. We must now ask in what way the ethical issues are different when the being is capable of consenting, and does in fact consent.

Let us return to the general principles about killing proposed in the chapter "What's Wrong with Killing?" I argued there that killing a self-conscious being is a more serious matter than killing a merely conscious being. I gave four distinct grounds on which this could be argued:

1. The classical utilitarian claim that since self-conscious beings are capable of fearing their own death, killing them has worse effects on others.
2. The preference utilitarian calculation that counts the thwarting of the victim's desire to go on living as an important reason against killing.
3. A theory of rights according to which to have a right one must have the ability to desire that to which one has a right, so that to have a right to life one must be able to desire one's own continued existence.
4. Respect for the autonomous decisions of rational agents.

Now suppose we have a situation in which a person suffering from a painful and incurable disease wishes to die. If the individual were not a person—not rational or self-conscious—euthanasia would, as I have said, be justifiable. Do any of the four grounds for holding that it is normally worse to kill a person provide reasons against killing when the individual is a person who wants to die?

The classical utilitarian objection does not apply to killing that takes place only with the genuine consent of the person killed. That people are killed under these conditions would have no tendency to spread fear or insecurity, since we have no cause to be fearful of being killed with our own genuine consent.

Peter Singer, "Justifying Voluntary Euthanasia," *Practical Ethics.* Cambridge University Press. Copyright © 1993 by Peter Singer. Reprinted with permission.

If we do not wish to be killed, we simply do not consent. In fact, the argument from fear points in favor of voluntary euthanasia, for if voluntary euthanasia is not permitted we may, with good cause, be fearful that our deaths will be unnecessarily drawn out and distressing. In the Netherlands, a nationwide study commissioned by the government found that "Many patients want an assurance that their doctor will assist them to die should suffering become unbearable." Often, having received this assurance, the patients made no persistent request for euthanasia. The availability of euthanasia brought comfort without euthanasia having to be provided.

Preference utilitarianism also points in favor of, not against, voluntary euthanasia. Just as preference utilitarianism must count a desire to go on living as a reason against killing, so it must count a desire to die as a reason for killing.

According to the theory of rights we have considered, it is an essential feature of a right that one can waive one's rights if one so chooses. I may have a right to privacy; but I can, if I wish, film every detail of my daily life and invite the neighbors to my home movies. Neighbors sufficiently intrigued to accept my invitation could do so without violating my right to privacy, since the right has on this occasion been waived. Similarly, to say that I have a right to life is not to say that it would be wrong for my doctor to end my life, if she does so at my request. In making this request I waive my right to life.

Last, the principle of respect for autonomy tells us to allow rational agents to live their own lives according to their own autonomous decisions, free from coercion or interference; but if rational agents should autonomously choose to die, then respect for autonomy will lead us to assist them to do as they choose.

So, although there are reasons for thinking that killing a self-conscious being is normally worse than killing any other kind of being, in the special case of voluntary euthanasia most of these reasons count for euthanasia rather than against it. Surprising as this result might at first seem, it really does no more than reflect the fact that what is special about self-conscious beings is that they can know that they exist over time and will, unless they die, continue to exist. Normally this continued existence is fervently desired; when the foreseeable continued existence is dreaded rather than desired however, the desire to die may take the place of the normal desire to live, reversing the reasons against killing based on the desire to live. Thus the case for voluntary euthanasia is arguably much stronger than the case for nonvoluntary euthanasia.

Some opponents of the legalisation of voluntary euthanasia might concede that all this follows, if we have a genuinely free and rational decision to die: but, they add, we can never be sure that a request to be killed is the result of a free and rational decision. Will not the sick and elderly be pressured by their relatives to end their lives quickly? Will it not be possible to commit outright murder by pretending that a person has requested euthanasia? And even if there is no pressure of falsification, can anyone who is ill, suffering pain, and very probably in a drugged and confused state of mind make a rational decision about whether to live or die?

These questions raise technical difficulties for the legalisation of voluntary euthanasia, rather than objections to the underlying ethical principles; but they are serious difficulties nonetheless. The guidelines developed by the courts in the Netherlands have sought to meet them by proposing that euthanasia is acceptable only if

- It is carried out by a physician.
- The patient has explicitly requested euthanasia in a manner that leaves no doubt of the patient's desire to die.
- The patient's decision is well-informed, free, and durable.
- The patient has an irreversible condition causing protracted physical or mental suffering that the patient finds unbearable.
- There is no reasonable alternative (reasonable from the patient's point of view) to alleviate the patient's suffering.
- The doctor has consulted another independent professional who agrees with his or her judgment.

Euthanasia in these circumstances is strongly supported by the Royal Dutch Medical Association, and by the general public in the Netherlands. The guidelines make murder in the guise of euthanasia rather farfetched, and there is no evidence of an increase in the murder rate in the Netherlands.

It is often said, in debates about euthanasia, that doctors can be mistaken. In rare instances patients diagnosed by two competent doctors as suffering from an incurable condition have survived and enjoyed years of good health. Possibly the legalization of voluntary euthanasia would, over the years, mean the deaths of a few people who would otherwise have recovered from their immediate illness and lived for some extra years. This is not, however, the knockdown argument against euthanasia that some imagine it to be. Against a very small number of unnecessary deaths that might occur if euthanasia is legalized we must place the very large amount of pain and distress that will be suffered if euthanasia is not legalized, by patients who really are terminally ill. Longer life is not such a supreme good that it outweighs all other considerations. (If it were, there would be many more effective ways of saving life—such as a ban on smoking, or a reduction of speed limits to 25 miles per hour—than prohibiting voluntary euthanasia.) The possibility that two doctors may make a mistake means that the person who opts for euthanasia is deciding on the balance of probabilities and giving up a very slight chance of survival in order to avoid suffering that will almost certainly end in death. This may be a perfectly rational choice. Probability is the guide of life, and of death, too. Against this, some will reply that improved care for the terminally ill has eliminated pain and made voluntary euthanasia unnecessary. Elisabeth Kübler-Ross, whose *On Death and Dying* is perhaps the best-known book on care for the dying, has claimed that none of her patients request euthanasia. Given personal attention and the right medication, she says, people come to accept their death and die peacefully without pain.

Kübler-Ross may be right. It may be possible, now, to eliminate pain. In almost all cases, it may even be possible to do it in a way that leaves patients in possession of their rational faculties and free from vomiting, nausea, or other distressing side effects. Unfortunately, only a minority of dying patients now receive this kind of care. Nor is physical pain the only problem. There can also be other distressing conditions, like bones so fragile they fracture at sudden movements, uncontrollable nausea and vomiting, slow starvation due to a cancerous growth, inability to control one's bowels or bladder, difficulty in breathing, and so on.

Dr. Timothy Quill, a doctor from Rochester, New York, has described how he prescribed barbiturate sleeping pills for "Diane," a patient with a severe form of leukemia, knowing that she wanted the tablets in order to be able to end her life. Dr. Quill had known Diane for many years, and he admired her courage in dealing with previous serious illnesses. In an article in the *New England Journal of Medicine,* Dr. Quill wrote:

> It was extraordinarily important to Diane to maintain control of herself and her own dignity during the time remaining to her. When this was no longer possible, she clearly wanted to die. As a former director of a hospice program, I know how to use pain medicines to keep patients comfortable and lessen suffering. I explained the philosophy of comfort care, which I strongly believe in. Although Diane understood and appreciated this, she had known of people lingering in what was called relative comfort, and she wanted no part of it. When the time came, she wanted to take her life in the least painful way possible. Knowing of her desire for independence and her decision to stay in control, I thought this request made perfect sense. . . . In our discussion it became clear that preoccupation with her fear of a lingering death would interfere with Diane's getting the most out of the time she had left until she found a safe way to ensure her death.

Not all dying patients who wish to die are fortunate enough to have a doctor like Timothy Quill. Betty Rollin has described, in her moving book *Last Wish,* how her mother developed ovarian cancer that spread to other parts of her body. One morning her mother said to her:

> I've had a wonderful life, but now it's over, or it should be. I'm not afraid to die, but I am afraid of this illness, what it's doing to me. . . . There's never any relief from it now. Nothing but nausea and this pain. . . . There won't be any more chemotherapy. There's no treatment anymore. So what happens to me now? I know what happens. I'll die slowly. . . . I don't want that. . . . Who does it benefit if I die slowly? If it benefits my children I'd be willing. But it's not going to do you any good. . . . There's no point in a slow death, none. I've never liked doing things with no point. I've got to end this.

Betty Rollin found it very difficult to help her mother to carry out her desire: "Physician after physician turned down our pleas for help (How many pills? What kind?)." After her book about her mother's death was published, she received hundreds of letters, many from people, or close relatives of people, who had tried to die, failed, and suffered even more. Many of these people were denied help from doctors, because although suicide is legal in most jurisdictions, assisted suicide is not.

Perhaps one day it will be possible to treat all terminally ill and incurable patients in such a way that no one requests euthanasia and the subject becomes a nonissue; but this is now just a utopian ideal, and no reason at all to deny euthanasia to those who must live and die in far less comfortable conditions. It is, in any case, highly paternalistic to tell dying patients that they are now so well looked after that they need not be offered the option of euthanasia. It would be more in keeping with respect for individual freedom and autonomy to legalize euthanasia and let patients decide whether their situation is bearable.

Do these arguments for voluntary euthanasia perhaps give too much weight to individual freedom and autonomy? After all, we do not allow people free choices on matters like, for instance, the taking of heroin. This is a restriction of freedom but, in the view of many, one that can be justified on paternalistic grounds. If preventing people from becoming heroin addicts is justifiable paternalism, why isn't preventing people from having themselves killed?

The question is a reasonable one, because respect for individual freedom can be carried too far. John Stuart Mill thought that the state should never interfere with the individual except to prevent harm to others. The individual's own good, Mill thought, is not a proper reason for state intervention.

But Mill may have had too high an opinion of the rationality of a human being. It may occasionally be right to prevent people from making choices that are obviously not rationally based and that we can be sure they will later regret. The prohibition of voluntary euthanasia cannot be justified on paternalistic grounds, however, for voluntary euthanasia is an act for which good reasons exist. Voluntary euthanasia occurs only when, to the best of medical knowledge, a person is suffering from an incurable and painful or extremely distressing condition. In these circumstances one cannot say that to choose to die quickly is obviously irrational. The strength of the case for voluntary euthanasia lies in this combination of respect for the preferences, or autonomy, of those who decide for euthanasia, and in the clear rational basis of the decision itself.

Active and Passive Euthanasia

by James Rachels

Abstract The traditional distinction between active and passive euthanasia requires critical analysis. The conventional doctrine is that there is such an important moral difference between the two that, although the latter is sometimes permissible, the former is always forbidden. This doctrine may be challenged for several reasons. First of all, active euthanasia is in many cases more humane than passive euthanasia. Secondly, the conventional doctrine leads to decisions concerning life and death on irrelevant grounds. Thirdly, the doctrine rests on a distinction between killing and letting die that itself has no moral importance. Fourthly, the most common arguments in favor of the doctrine are invalid. I therefore suggest that the American Medical Association policy statement that endorses this doctrine is unsound. (N Engl J Med 292:78-80, 1975)

The distinction between active and passive euthanasia is thought to be crucial for medical ethics. The idea is that it is permissible, at least in some cases, to withhold treatment and allow a patient to die, but it is never permissible to take any direct action designed to kill the patient. This doctrine seems to be accepted by most doctors, and it is endorsed in a statement adopted by the House of Delegates of the American Medical Association on December 4, 1973:

> The intentional termination of the life of one human being by another—mercy killing—is contrary to that for which the medical profession stands and is contrary to the policy of the American Medical Association.
>
> The cessation of the employment of extraordinary means to prolong the life of the body when there is irrefutable evidence that

biological death is imminent is the decision of the patient and/or his immediate family. The advice and judgment of the physician should be freely available to the patient and/or his immediate family.

However, a strong case can be made against this doctrine. In what follows I will set out some of the relevant arguments, and urge doctors to reconsider their views on this matter.

To begin with a familiar type of situation, a patient who is dying of incurable cancer of the throat is in terrible pain, which can no longer be satisfactorily alleviated. He is certain to die within a few days, even if present treatment is continued, but he does not want to go on living for those days since the pain is unbearable. So he asks the doctor for an end to it, and his family joins in the request.

Suppose the doctor agrees to withhold treatment, as the conventional doctrine says he may. The justification for his doing so is that the patient is in terrible agony, and since he is going to die anyway, it would be wrong to prolong his suffering needlessly. But now notice this. If one simply withholds treatment, it may take the patient longer to die, and so he may suffer more than he would if more direct action were taken and a lethal injection given. This fact provides strong reason for thinking that, once the initial decision not to prolong his agony has been made, active euthanasia is actually preferable to passive euthanasia, rather than the reverse. To say otherwise is to endorse the option that leads to more suffering rather than less, and is contrary to the humanitarian impulse that prompts the decision not to prolong his life in the first place.

Part of my point is that the process of being "allowed to die" can be relatively slow and painful, whereas being given a lethal injection is relatively quick and painless. Let me give a different sort of example. In the United States about one in 600 babies is born with Down's syndrome. Most of these babies are otherwise healthy—that is, with only the usual pediatric care, they will proceed to an otherwise normal infancy. Some, however, are born with congenital defects such as intestinal obstructions that require operations if they are to live. Sometimes, the parents and the doctor will decide not to operate, and let the infant die. Anthony Shaw describes what happens then:

> ...When surgery is denied [the doctor] must try to keep the infant from suffering while natural forces sap the baby's life away. As a surgeon whose natural inclination is to use the scalpel to fight off death, standing by and watching a salvageable baby die is the most emotionally exhausting experience I know. It is easy at a conference, in a theoretical discussion, to decide that such infants should be allowed to die. It is altogether different to stand by in

the nursery and watch as dehydration and infection wither a tiny being over hours and days. This is a terrible ordeal for me and the hospital staff—much more so than for the parents who never set foot in the nursery.*

I can understand why some people are opposed to all euthanasia, and insist that such infants must be allowed to live. I think I can also understand why other people favor destroying these babies quickly and painlessly. But why should anyone favor letting "dehydration and infection wither a tiny being over hours and days?" The doctrine that says that a baby may be allowed to dehydrate and wither, but may not be given an injection that would end its life without suffering, seems so patently cruel as to require no further refutation. The strong language is not intended to offend, but only to put the point in the clearest possible way.

My second argument is that the conventional doctrine leads to decisions concerning life and death made on irrelevant grounds.

Consider again the case of the infants with Down's syndrome who need operations for congenital defects unrelated to the syndrome to live. Sometimes, there is no operation, and the baby dies, but when there is no such defect, the baby lives on. Now, an operation such as that to remove an intestinal obstruction is not prohibitively difficult. The reason why such operations are not performed in these cases is, clearly, that the child has Down's syndrome and the parents and doctor judge that because of that fact it is better for the child to die.

But notice that this situation is absurd, no matter what view one takes of the lives and potentials of such babies. If the life of such an infant is worth preserving, what does it matter if it needs a simple operation? Or, if one thinks it better that such a baby should not live on, what difference does it make that it happens to have an unobstructed intestinal tract? In either case, the matter of life and death is being decided on irrelevant grounds. It is the Down's syndrome, and not the intestines, that is the issue. The matter should be decided, if at all, on that basis, and not be allowed to depend on the essentially irrelevant question of whether the intestinal tract is blocked.

What makes this situation possible, of course, is the idea that when there is an intestinal blockage, one can "let the baby die," but when there is no such defect there is nothing that can be done, for one must not "kill" it. The fact that this idea leads to such results as deciding life or death on irrelevant grounds is another good reason why the doctrine should be rejected.

One reason why so many people think that there is an important moral difference between active and passive euthanasia is that they think killing

* Shaw A: 'Doctor, Do We Have a Choice?' The New York Times Magazine, January 30, 1972, p 54

someone is morally worse than letting someone die. But is it? Is killing, in itself, worse than letting die? To investigate this issue, two cases may be considered that are exactly alike except that one involves killing whereas the other involves letting someone die. Then, it can be asked whether this difference makes any difference to the moral assessments. It is important that the cases be exactly alike, except for this one difference, since otherwise one cannot be confident that it is this difference and not some other that accounts for any variation in the assessments of the two cases. So, let us consider this pair of cases:

In the first, Smith stands to gain a large inheritance if anything should happen to his six-year-old cousin. One evening while the child is taking his bath, Smith sneaks into the bathroom and drowns the child, and then arranges things so that it will look like an accident.

In the second, Jones also stands to gain if anything should happen to his six-year-old cousin. Like Smith, Jones sneaks in planning to drown the child in his bath. However, just as he enters the bathroom Jones sees the child slip and hit his head, and fall face down in the water. Jones is delighted; he stands by, ready to push the child's head back under if it is necessary, but it is not necessary. With only a little thrashing about, the child drowns all by himself, "accidentally," as Jones watches and does nothing.

Now Smith killed the child, whereas Jones "merely" let the child die. That is the only difference between them. Did either man behave better, from a moral point of view? If the difference between killing and letting die were in itself a morally important matter, one should say that Jones's behavior was less reprehensible than Smith's. But does one really want to say that? I think not. In the first place, both men acted from the same motive, personal gain, and both had exactly the same end in view when they acted. It may be inferred from Smith's conduct that he is a bad man, although that judgment may be withdrawn or modified if certain further facts are learned about him—for example, that he is mentally deranged. But would not the very same thing be inferred about Jones from his conduct? And would not the same further considerations also be relevant to any modification of this judgment? Moreover, suppose Jones pleaded, in his own defense, "After all, I didn't do anything except just stand there and watch the child drown. I didn't kill him; I only let him die." Again, if letting die were in itself less bad than killing, this defense should have at least some weight. But it does not. Such a "defense" can only be regarded as a grotesque perversion of moral reasoning. Morally speaking, it is no defense at all.

Now, it may be pointed out, quite properly, that the cases of euthanasia with which doctors are concerned are not like this at all. They do not involve personal gain or the destruction of normal healthy children. Doctors are concerned only with cases in which the patient's life is of no further use to him, or in which the patient's life has become or will soon become a terrible burden. However, the point is the same in these cases: the bare difference between killing and letting die does not, in itself, make a moral difference. If a doctor lets a patient die, for humane reasons, he is in the same moral position as if he had given the patient a lethal injection for humane reasons. If his decision was wrong—if, for example, the patient's illness was in fact curable—the decision would be equally regrettable no matter which method was used to carry it out. And if the doctor's decision was the right one, the method used is not in itself important.

The AMA policy statement isolates the crucial issue very well; the crucial issue is "the intentional termination of the life of one human being by another." But after identifying this issue, and forbidding "mercy killing," the statement goes on to deny that the cessation of treatment is the intentional termination of a life. This is where the mistake comes in, for what is the cessation of treatment, in these circumstances, if it is not "the intentional termination of the life of one human being by another?" Of course it is exactly that, and if it were not, there would be no point to it.

Many people will find this judgment hard to accept. One reason, I think, is that it is very easy to conflate the question of whether killing is, in itself, worse than letting die, with the very different question of whether most actual cases of killing are more reprehensible than most actual cases of letting die. Most actual cases of killing are clearly terrible (think, for example, of all the murders reported in the newspapers), and one hears of such cases every day. On the other hand, one hardly ever hears of a case of letting die, except for the actions of doctors who are motivated by humanitarian reasons. So one learns to think of killing in a much worse light than of letting die. But this does not mean that there is something about killing that makes it in itself worse than letting die, for it is not the bare difference between killing and letting die that makes the difference in these cases. Rather, the other factors—the murderer's motive of personal gain, for example, contrasted with the doctor's humanitarian motivation—account for different reactions to the different cases.

I have argued that killing is not in itself any worse than letting die; if my contention is right, it follows that active euthanasia is not any worse than passive euthanasia. What arguments can be given on the other side? The most common, I believe, is the following:

"The important difference between active and passive euthanasia is that, in passive euthanasia, the doctor does not do anything to bring about the patient's death. The doctor does nothing, and the patient dies of whatever ills already afflict him. In active euthanasia, however, the doctor does something to bring about the patient's death: he kills him. The doctor who gives the patient with cancer a lethal injection has himself caused his patient's death; whereas if he merely ceases treatment, the cancer is the cause of the death."

A number of points need to be made here. The first is that it is not exactly correct to say that in passive euthanasia the doctor does nothing, for he does do one thing that is very important: he lets the patient die. "Letting someone die" is certainly different, in some respects, from other types of action—mainly in that it is a kind of action that one may perform by way of not performing certain other actions. For example, one may let a patient die by way of not giving medication, just as one may insult someone by way of not shaking his hand. But for any purpose of moral assessment, it is a type of action nonetheless. The decision to let a patient die is subject to moral appraisal in the same way that a decision to kill him would be subject to moral appraisal: it may be assessed as wise or unwise, compassionate or sadistic, right or wrong. If a doctor deliberately let a patient die who was suffering from a routinely curable illness, the doctor would certainly be to blame for what he had done, just as he would be to blame if he had needlessly killed the patient. Charges against him would then be appropriate. If so, it would be no defense at all for him to insist that he didn't "do anything." He would have done something very serious indeed, for he let his patient die.

Fixing the cause of death may be very important from a legal point of view, for it may determine whether criminal charges are brought against the doctor. But I do not think that this notion can be used to show a moral difference between active and passive euthanasia. The reason why it is considered bad to be the cause of someone's death is that death is regarded as a great evil—and so it is. However, if it has been decided that euthanasia—even passive euthanasia—is desirable in a given case, it has also been decided that in this instance death is no greater an evil than the patient's continued existence. And if this is true, the usual reason for not wanting to be the cause of someone's death simply does not apply.

Finally, doctors may think that all of this is only of academic interest—the sort of thing that philosophers may worry about but that has no practical bearing on their own work. After all, doctors must be concerned about the legal consequences of what they do, and active euthanasia is clearly forbidden by the law. But even so, doctors should also be concerned with the fact that the law is forcing upon them a moral doctrine that may well be indefensible, and has a considerable effect on their practices. Of course, most doctors are not now in the position of being coerced in this matter, for they do not regard themselves as merely going along with what the law requires. Rather, in statements such as the AMA policy statement that I have quoted, they are endorsing this doctrine as a central point of medical ethics. In that statement, active euthanasia is condemned not merely as illegal but as "contrary to that for which the medical profession stands," whereas passive euthanasia is approved. However, the preceding considerations suggest that there is really no moral difference between the two, considered in themselves (there may be important moral differences in some cases in their *consequences,* but, as I pointed out, these differences may make active euthanasia, and not passive euthanasia, the morally preferable option). So, whereas doctors may have to discriminate between active and passive euthanasia to satisfy the law, they should not do any more than that. In particular, they should not give the distinction any added authority and weight by writing it into official statements of medical ethics.

READING 4.5

When Self-Determination Runs Amok

Daniel Callahan

The euthanasia debate is not just another moral debate, one in a long list of arguments in our pluralistic society. It is profoundly emblematic of three important turning points in Western thought The first is that of the legitimate conditions under which one person can kill another. The acceptance of voluntary active euthanasia would morally sanction what can only be called "consenting adult killing." By that term I mean the killing of one person by another in the name of their mutual right to be killer and killed if they freely agree to play those roles. This turn flies in the face of a longstanding effort to limit the circumstances under which one person can take the life of another, from efforts to control the free flow of guns and arms, to abolish capital punishment, and to more tightly control warfare. Euthanasia would add a whole new category of killing to a society that already has too many excuses to indulge itself in that way.

The second turning point lies in the meaning and limits of self-determination. The acceptance of euthanasia would sanction a view of autonomy holding that individuals may, in the name of their own private, idiosyncratic view of the good life, call upon others, including such institutions as medicine, to help them pursue that life, even at the risk of harm to the common good. This works against the idea that the meaning and scope of our own right to lead our own lives must be conditioned by, and be compatible with, the good of the community, which is more than an aggregate of self-directing individuals.

Daniel Callahan, "When Self-Determination Runs Amok," *The Hastings Center Report*, vol. 22, no. 2, pp. 52-55. Copyright © 1992 by John Wiley & Sons, Inc. Reprinted with permission.

Daniel Callahan *is the director of The Hastings Center*

The third turning point is to be found in the claim being made upon medicine: it should be prepared to make its skills available to individuals to help them achieve their private vision of the good life. This puts medicine in the business of promoting the individualistic pursuit of general human happiness and well-being. It would overturn the traditional belief that medicine should limit its domain to promoting and preserving human health, redirecting it instead to the relief of that suffering which stems from life itself, not merely from a sick body.

I believe that, at each of these three turning points, proponents of euthanasia push us in the wrong direction. Arguments in favor of euthanasia fall into four general categories, which I will take up in turn: (1) the moral claim of individual self-determination and wellbeing; (2) the moral irrelevance of the difference between killing and allowing to die; (3) the supposed paucity of evidence to show likely harmful consequences of legalized euthanasia; and (4) the compatibility of euthanasia and medical practice.

Self-Determination

Central to most arguments for euthanasia is the principle of self-determination. People are presumed to have an interest in deciding for themselves, according to their own beliefs about what makes life good, how they will conduct their lives. That is an important value, but the question in the euthanasia context is, What does it mean and how far should it extend? If it were a question of suicide, where a person takes her own life without assistance from another, that principle might be pertinent, at least for debate. But euthanasia is not that limited a matter. The self-determination in that case can only be effected by the moral and physical assistance of another. Euthanasia is thus no longer a matter only of self-determination, but of a mutual, social decision between two people, the one to be killed and the other to do the killing.

How are we to make the moral move from my right of self-determination to some doctor's right to kill me—from *my* right to *his* right? Where does the doctor's moral warrant to kill come from? Ought doctors to be able to kill anyone they want as long as permission is given by competent persons? Is our right to life just like a piece of property, to be given away or alienated if the price (happiness, relief of suffering) is right? And then to be destroyed with our permission once alienated?

In answer to all those questions, I will say this: I have yet to hear a plausible argument why it should be permissible for us to put this kind of power in the hands of another, whether a doctor or anyone else. The idea that we can waive our right to life, and then give to another the power to take that life, requires a justification yet to be provided by anyone.

Slavery was long ago outlawed on the ground that one person should not have the right to own another, even with the other's permission. Why? Because it is a fundamental moral wrong for one person to give over his life and fate to another, whatever the good consequences, and no less a wrong for another person to have that kind of total, final power. Like slavery, dueling was long ago banned on similar grounds: even free, competent individuals should not have the power to kill each other, whatever their motives, whatever the circumstances. Consenting adult killing, like consenting adult slavery or degradation, is a strange route to human dignity.

There is another problem as well. If doctors, once sanctioned to carry out euthanasia, are to be themselves responsible moral agents—not simply hired hands with lethal injections at the ready—then they must have their own *independent* moral grounds to kill those who request such services. What do I mean? As those who favor euthanasia are quick to point out, some people want it because their life has become so burdensome it no longer seems worth living.

The doctor will have a difficulty at this point. The degree and intensity to which people suffer from their diseases and their dying, and whether they find life more of a burden than a benefit, has very little directly to do with the nature or extent of their actual physical condition. Three people can have the same condition, but only one will find the suffering unbearable. People suffer, but suffering is as much a function of the values of individuals as it is of the physical causes of that suffering. Inevitably in that circumstance, the doctor will in effect be heating the patient's values. To be responsible, the doctor would have to share those values. The doctor would have to decide, on her own, whether the patient's life was "no longer worth living."

But how could a doctor possibly know that or make such a judgment? Just because the patient said so? I raise this question because, while in Holland at the euthanasia conference reported by Maurice de Wachter elsewhere in this issue, the doctors present agreed that there is no objective way of measuring or judging the claims of patients that their suffering is unbearable. And if it is difficult to measure suffering, how much more difficult to determine the value of a patient's statement that her life is not worth living?

However one might want to answer such questions, the very need to ask them, to inquire into the physician's responsibility and grounds for medical and moral judgment, points out the social nature of the decision. Euthanasia is not a private matter of self-determination. It is an act that requires two people to make it possible, and a complicit society to make it acceptable.

Killing and Allowing to Die

Against common opinion, the argument is sometimes made that there is no moral difference between stopping life-sustaining treatment and more active forms of killing, such as lethal injection. Instead I would contend that the notion that there is no morally significant difference between omission and commission is just wrong. Consider in its broad implications what the eradication of the distinction implies: that death from disease has been banished, leaving only the actions of physicians in terminating treatment as the cause of death. Biology, which used to bring about death, has apparently been displaced by human agency. Doctors have finally, I suppose, thus genuinely become gods, now doing what nature and the deities once did.

What is the mistake here? It lies in confusing causality and culpability, and in failing to note the way in which human societies have overlaid natural causes with moral rules and interpretations. Causality (by which I mean the direct physical causes of death) and culpability (by which I mean our attribution of moral responsibility to human actions) are confused under three circumstances.

They are confused, first, when the action of a physician in stopping treatment of a patient with an underlying lethal disease is construed as *causing* death. On the contrary, the physician's omission can only bring about death on the condition that the patient's disease will kill him in the absence of treatment. We may hold the physician morally responsible for the death, if we have morally judged such actions wrongful omissions. But it confuses reality and moral judgment to see an omitted action as having the same causal status as one that directly kills. A lethal injection will kill both a healthy person and a sick person. A physician's omitted treatment will have no effect on a healthy person. Turn off the machine on me, a healthy person, and nothing will happen. It will only, in contrast, bring the life of a sick person to an end because of an underlying fatal disease.

Causality and culpability are confused, second, when we fail to note that judgments of moral responsibility and culpability are human constructs. By that I mean that we human beings, after moral reflection, have decided to call some actions right or wrong, and to devise moral rules to deal with them. When physicians could do nothing to stop death, they were not held responsible for it. When, with medical progress, they began to have some power over death—but only its timing and circumstances, not its ultimate inevitability—moral rules were devised to set forth their obligations. Natural causes of death were not thereby banished. They were, instead, overlaid with a medical ethics designed to determine moral culpability in deploying medical power.

To confuse the judgments of this ethics with the physical causes of death—which is the connotation of the word *kill*—is to confuse nature and human action. People will, one way or another, die of some disease; death will have dominion over all of us. To say that a doctor "kills" a patient by allowing this to happen should only be understood as a moral judgment about the licitness of his omission, nothing more. We can, as a fashion of speech only, talk about a doctor *killing* a patient by omitting treatment he should have provided. It is a fashion of speech precisely because it is the underlying disease that brings death when treatment is omitted; that is its cause, not the physician's omission. It is a misuse of the word *killing to* use it when a doctor stops a treatment he believes will no longer benefit the patient—when, that is, he steps aside to allow an eventually inevitable death to occur now rather than later. The only deaths that human beings invented are those that come from direct killing—when, with a lethal injection, we both cause death and are morally responsible for it. In the case of omissions, we do not cause death even if we may be judged morally responsible for it

This difference between causality and culpability also helps us see why a doctor who has omitted a treatment he should have provided has "killed" that patient while another doctor—performing precisely the same act of omission on another patient in different circumstances—does not kill her, but only allows her to die. The difference is that we have come, by moral convention and conviction, to classify unauthorized or illegitimate omissions as acts of " killing." We call them "killing" in the expanded sense of the term: a culpable action that permits the real cause of death, the underlying disease, to proceed to its lethal conclusion. By contrast, the doctor who, at the patient's request, omits or terminates unwanted treatment does not kill at all. Her underlying disease, not his action, is the physical cause of death; and we have agreed to consider actions of that kind to be morally licit He thus can truly be said to have "allowed" her to die.

If we fail to maintain the distinction between killing and allowing to die, moreover, there are some disturbing possibilities. The first would be to confirm many physicians in their already too-powerful belief that, when patients die or when physicians stop treatment because of the futility of continuing it, they are somehow both morally and physically responsible for the deaths that follow. That notion needs to be abolished, not strengthened. It needlessly and wrongly burdens the physician, to whom should not be attributed the powers of the gods. The second possibility would be that, in every case where a doctor judges medical treatment no longer effective in prolonging life, a quick and direct killing of the patient would be seen as the next, most reasonable step, on grounds of both humaneness and economics. I do not see how that logic could easily be rejected.

Calculating the Consequences

When concerns about the adverse social consequences of permitting euthanasia are raised, its advocates tend to dismiss them as unfounded and overly speculative. On the contrary, recent data about the Dutch experience suggests that such concerns are right on target. From my own discussions in Holland, and from the articles on that subject in this issue and elsewhere, I believe we can now fully see most of the *likely* consequences of legal euthanasia.

Three consequences seem almost certain, in this or any other country: the inevitability of some abuse of the law; the difficulty of precisely writing, and then enforcing, the law; and the inherent slipperiness of the moral reasons for legalizing euthanasia in the first place.

Why is abuse inevitable? One reason is that almost all laws on delicate, controversial matters are to some extent abused. This happens because not everyone will agree with the law as written and will bend it, or ignore it, if they can get away with it From explicit admissions to me by Dutch proponents of euthanasia, and from the corroborating information provided by the Remmelink Report and the outside studies of Carlos Gomez and John Keown, I am convinced that in the Netherlands there are a substantial number of cases of nonvoluntary euthanasia, that is, euthanasia undertaken without the explicit permission of the person being killed. The other reason abuse is inevitable is that the law is likely to have a low enforcement priority in the criminal justice system. Like other laws of similar status, unless there is an unrelenting and harsh willingness to pursue abuse, violations will ordinarily be tolerated. The worst thing to me about my experience in Holland was the casual, seemingly indifferent attitude toward abuse. I think that would happen everywhere.

Why would it be hard to precisely write, and then enforce, the law? The Dutch speak about the requirement of "unbearable" suffering, but admit that such a term is just about indefinable, a highly subjective matter admitting of no objective standards. A requirement for outside opinion is nice, but it is easy to find complaisant colleagues. A requirement that a medical condition be "terminal" will run aground on the notorious difficulties of knowing when an illness is actually terminal.

Apart from those technical problems there is a more profound worry. I see no way, even in principle, to write or enforce a meaningful law that can guarantee effective procedural safeguards. The reason is obvious yet almost always overlooked The euthanasia transaction will ordinarily take place within the boundaries of the private and confidential doctor-patient relationship. No one can possibly know what takes place in that context unless the doctor chooses to reveal it In Holland, less than 10 percent of the physicians report their acts of euthanasia and do so with almost complete legal impunity. There is no reason why the situation should be any better elsewhere. Doctors will have their own reasons for keeping euthanasia secret, and some patients will have no less a motive for wanting it concealed.

I would mention, finally, that the moral logic of the motives for euthanasia contain within them the ingredients of abuse. The two standard motives for euthanasia and assisted suicide are said to be our right of self-determination, and our claim upon the mercy of others, especially doctors, to relieve our suffering. These two motives are typically spliced together and presented as a single justification. Yet if they are considered independently—and there is no inherent reason why they must be linked—they reveal serious problems. It is said that a competent, adult person should have a right to euthanasia for the relief of suffering. But why must the person be suffering? Does not that stipulation already compromise the principle of self-determination? How can self-determination have any limits? Whatever the person's motives may be, why are they not sufficient?

Consider next the person who is suffering but not competent, who is perhaps demented or mentally retarded. The standard argument would deny euthanasia to that person. But why? If a person is suffering but not competent, then it would seem grossly unfair to deny relief solely on the grounds of incompetence. Are the incompetent less entitled to relief from suffering than the competent? Will it only be affluent, middle-class people, mentally fit and savvy about working the medical system, who can qualify? Do the incompetent suffer less because of their incompetence?

Considered from these angles, there are no good moral reasons to limit euthanasia once the principle of taking life for that purpose has been legitimated. If we really believe in self-determination, then any competent person should have a right to be killed by a doctor for any reason that suits him. If we believe in the relief of suffering, then it seems cruel and capricious to deny it to the incompetent. There is, in short, no reasonable or logical stopping point once the turn has been made down the road to euthanasia, which could soon turn into a convenient and commodious expressway.

Euthanasia and Medical Practice

A fourth kind of argument one often hears both in the Netherlands and in this country is that euthanasia and assisted suicide are perfectly compatible with the aims of medicine. I would note at the very outset that a physician who participates in another person's suicide already abuses medicine. Apart from depression (the main statistical cause of suicide), people commit suicide because they find life empty, oppressive, or meaningless. Their judgment is a judgment about the value of continued life, not only about health (even if they are sick). Are doctors now to be given the right to make judgments about the kinds of life worth living and to give their blessing to suicide for those they judge wanting? What conceivable competence, technical or moral, could doctors claim to play such a role? Are we to medicalize suicide, turning judgments about its worth and value into one more clinical issue? Yes, those are rhetorical questions.

Yet they bring us to the core of the problem of euthanasia and medicine. The great temptation of modem medicine, not always resisted, is to move beyond the promotion and preservation of health into the boundless realm of general human happiness and wellbeing. The root problem of illness and mortality is both medical and philosophical or religious. "Why must I die?" can be asked as a technical, biological question or as a question about the meaning of life. When medicine tries to respond to the latter, which it is always under pressure to do, it moves beyond its proper role.

It is not medicine's place to lift from us the burden of that suffering which turns on the meaning we assign to the decay of the body and its eventual death. It is not medicine's place to determine when lives are not worth living or when the burden of life is too great to be borne. Doctors have no conceivable way of evaluating such claims on the part of patients, and they should have no right to act in response to them. Medicine should try to relieve human suffering, but only that suffering which is brought on by illness and dying as biological phenomena, not that suffering which comes from anguish or despair at the human condition.

Doctors ought to relieve those forms of suffering that medically accompany serious illness and the threat of death. They should relieve pain, do what they can to allay anxiety and uncertainty, and be a comforting presence. As sensitive human beings, doctors should be prepared to respond to patients who ask why they must die, or die in pain. But here the doctor and the patient are at the same level. The doctor may have no better an answer to those old questions than anyone else; and certainly no special insight from his training as a physician. It would be terrible for physicians to forget this, and to think that in a swift, lethal injection, medicine has found its own answer to the riddle of life. It would be a false answer, given by the wrong people. It would be no less a false answer for patients. They should neither ask medicine to put its own vocation at risk to serve their private interests, nor think that the answer to suffering is to be killed by another. The problem is precisely that, too often in human history, killing has seemed the quick, efficient way to put aside that which burdens us. It rarely helps, and too often simply adds to one evil still another. That is what I believe euthanasia would accomplish. It is self-determination run amok.

Singer, *Justifying Voluntary Euthanasia*

1. Summarize the four reasons Singer gives for why it is morally worse to kill a self-conscious being. Why does he think none apply in the case of voluntary euthanasia?
2. Explain the conditions that must be met before a patient is eligible for euthanasia in the Netherlands. Which of these would not be met in nonvoluntary euthanasia?
3. Why does Singer reject the paternalistic argument against euthanasia?

Rachels, *Active and Passive Euthanasia*

1. Explain the AMA policy Rachels is challenging. How does it turn on the distinction between killing and allowing to die?
2. Why does Rachels think passive euthanasia is often morally more objectionable than active euthanasia?
3. Explain Rachels's example with Smith and Jones. Is Rachels right to suppose they are both equally to blame for their nephew's death? How does this support his argument?

Callahan, *When Self-Determination Runs Amok*

1. Explain the four categories of argument Callahan says are offered in favor of euthanasia. Where would Singer's argument fit?
2. Why does Callahan think we are right not to allow a person to sell oneself into slavery or engage in dueling? What kind of argument for euthanasia does this target?
3. Explain Callahan's distinction between causality and culpability. Why does he think we confuse these? How would this apply to the question of killing versus allowing to die?

SUGGESTIONS FOR FURTHER READING OR VIEWING

Declaration on Euthanasia. The Roman Catholic Church, 1980. www.vatican.va/roman_curia/congregations/cfaith/documents/rc_con_cfaith_doc_19800505_euthanasia_en.html.

McMahon, Jeff. *The Ethics of Killing: Problems at the Margins of Life*. Oxford: Oxford University Press. 2003.

Me Before You. 2016. A controversial though well-received film exploring the topic of euthanasia.

Singer, Peter. *Rethinking Life and Death: The Collapse of our Traditional Ethics*. New York: St. Martin's Press, 1996.

Ethics of War

INTRODUCTION TO ETHICS OF WAR

Questions about the morality of war and conduct during war span many cultures and centuries. Some questions we might want to think about include the following. Is war ever morally permissible? If so, when? Is war ever morally obligatory? If so, when? Can a lone individual be morally justified in declaring war? If so, when? Does the ability to declare war actually define the necessary and sufficient difference between a state and every other political actor (whether a corporation, a church, or an individual person)? If I personally do not know what I think about the moral justification for a particular war, should I stand with those who oppose that war, just in case they are correct? Does war set a nation on a slippery slope of not taking human life seriously enough in our moral practice? Does war morally corrupt soldiers and others who must engage in the "dirty work" of killing people and destroying their property? Can one conduct a war and treat one's enemies as if they possess human dignity or does all warfare lead to the dehumanization of one's enemies into mere targets or worse?

In the philosophical literature on the ethics of war, these and other similar questions are examined and theorized. Historically, there are three main philosophical views on the ethics of war: realism, just war theory, and pacifism. Realism is the philosophical view that war is a natural and inevitable part of human existence and as such it is simply outside the scope of morality. In other words, realists believe that moral concepts simply do not apply to questions about going to war nor conduct in war. Realism is prominent among political scientists and scholars of international relations. Thucydides's *The Talks at Melos* presents a realist account of war for our consideration.

Just war theory, on the other hand, holds that moral concepts apply both to questions about going to war (known as *jus ad bellum*) and to questions of what sort of conduct is acceptable during war (*jus en bello*). Just war theorists maintain that there are occasions when it is ethical to go to war and other occasions when war is not morally permissible. Similarly, just war theorists believe that certain conduct in war is ethically justified while other conduct is immoral despite the wartime context. Perhaps the earliest prominent proponent of just war theory was St. Augustine in the fourth century, undoubtedly a significant influence on St. Thomas Aquinas, whose view will introduce just war theory in this chapter.

Finally, pacifists agree with just war theorists that moral concepts do in fact apply to questions of war; however, pacifists maintain that war is not ever ethically justified. Bertrand Russell's essay introduces the pacifist perspective in this chapter.

READING 4.6

The Peloponnesian War

selection from *The Fifth Book*
by Thucyidides

84. The next summer went Alcibiades to Argos with twenty galleys and took thence the suspected Argives and such as seemed to savour of the Lacedaemonian faction, to the number of three hundred, and put them into the nearest of the islands subject to the Athenian state.

The Athenians made war also against the isle of Melos, with thirty galleys of their own, six of Chios, and two of Lesbos. Wherein were of their own twelve hundred men of arms, three hundred archers, and twenty archers on horseback; and of their confederates and islanders, about fifteen hundred men of arms. The Melians are a colony of the Lacedaemonians, and therefore refused to be subject, as the rest of the islands were, unto the Athenians, but rested at the first neutral; and afterwards, when the Athenians put them to it by wasting of their land, they entered into open war.

Now the Athenian commanders, Cleomedes, the son of Lycomedes, and Tisias, the son of Tisimachus, being encamped upon their land with these forces, before they would hurt the same sent ambassadors to deal with them first by way of conference. These ambassadors the Melians refused to bring before the multitude, but commanded them to deliver their message before the magistrates and the few; and they accordingly said as followeth:

85. *Athenians.* "Since we may not speak to the multitude, for fear lest when they hear our persuasive and unanswerable arguments all at once in a continued oration, they should chance to be seduced (for we know that this is the scope of your bringing us to audience before the few), make surer yet that point, you that sit here; answer you also to every particular, not in a set speech, but presently

interrupting us whensoever anything shall be said by us which shall seem unto you to be otherwise. And first answer us whether you like this motion or not?"

86. Whereunto the council of the Melians answered: "The equity of a leisurely debate is not to be found fault withal; but this preparation of war, not future but already here present, seemeth not to agree with the same. For we see that you are come to be judges of the conference, and that the issue of it, if we be superior in argument and therefore yield not, is likely to bring us war, and if we yield, servitude."

87. *Ath.* "Nay, if you be come together to reckon up suspicions of what may be, or to any other purpose than to take advice upon what is present and before your eyes, how to save your city from destruction, let us give over. But if this be the point, let us speak to it."

88. *Mel.* "It is reason, and pardonable for men in our cases, to turn both their words and thoughts upon divers things. Howsoever, this consultation being held only upon the point of our safety, we are content, if you think good, to go on with the course you have propounded."

89. *Ath.* "As we therefore will not, for our parts, with fair pretences, as, that having defeated the Medes, our reign is therefore lawful, or that we come against you for injury done, make a long discourse without being believed; so would we have you also not expect to prevail by saying either that you therefore took not our parts because you were a colony of the Lacedaemonians or that you have done us no injury. But out of those things which we both of us do really think, let us go through with that which is feasible, both you and we knowing that in human disputation justice is then only agreed on when the necessity is equal; whereas they that have odds of power exact as much as they can, and the weak yield to such conditions as they can get."

90. *Mel.* "Well then (seeing you put the point of profit in the place of justice), we hold it profitable for ourselves not to overthrow a general profit to all men, which is this: that men in danger, if they plead reason and equity, nay, though somewhat without the strict compass of justice, yet it ought ever to do them good. And the same most of all concerneth you, forasmuch as you shall else give an example unto others of the greatest revenge that can be taken if you chance to miscarry."

91. *Ath.* "As for us, though our dominion should cease, yet we fear not the sequel. For not they that command, as do the Lacedaemonians, are cruel to

those that are vanquished by them (yet we have nothing to do now with the Lacedaemonians), but such as having been in subjection have assaulted those that commanded them and gotten the victory. But let the danger of that be to ourselves. In the meantime we tell you this: that we are here now both to enlarge our own dominion and also to confer about the saving of your city. For we would have dominion over you without oppressing you, and preserve you to the profit of us both."

92. *Mel.* "But how can it be profitable for us to serve, though it be so for you to command?"

93. *Ath.* "Because you, by obeying, shall save yourselves from extremity; and we, not destroying you, shall reap profit by you."

94. *Mel.* "But will you not accept that we remain quiet and be your friends (whereas before we were your enemies), and take part with neither?"

95. *Ath.* "No. For your enmity doth not so much hurt us as your friendship will be an argument of our weakness and your hatred of our power amongst those we have rule over."

96. *Mel.* "Why? Do your subjects measure equity so, as to put those that never had to do with you, and themselves, who for the most part have been your own colonies, and some of them after revolt conquered, into one and the same consideration?"

97. *Ath.* "Why not? For they think they have reason on their side, both the one sort and the other, and that such as are subdued are subdued by force, and such as are forborne are so through our fear. So that by subduing you, besides the extending of our dominion over so many more subjects, we shall assure it the more over those we had before, especially being masters of the sea, and you islanders, and weaker (except you can get the victory) than others whom we have subdued already."

98. *Mel.* "Do you think then, that there is no assurance in that which we propounded? For here again (since driving us from the plea of equity you persuade us to submit to your profit), when we have shewed you what is good for us, we must endeavour to draw you to the same, as far forth as it shall be good for you also. As many therefore as now are neutral, what do you but make them your enemies, when, beholding these your proceedings, they look that hereafter you will also turn your arms upon them? And what is this, but to make greater the

enemies you have already, and to make others your enemies, each against their wills, that would not else have been so?"

99. *Ath.* "We do not think that they shall be ever the more our enemies, who inhabiting anywhere in the continent, will be long ere they so much as keep guard upon their liberty against us. But islanders unsubdued, as you be, or islanders offended with the necessity of subjection which they are already in, these may indeed, by unadvised courses, put both themselves and us into apparent danger."

100. *Mel.* "If you then to retain your command, and your vassals to get loose from you, will undergo the utmost of danger, would it not in us, that be already free, be great baseness and cowardice if we should not encounter anything whatsoever rather than suffer ourselves to be brought into bondage?"

101. *Ath.* "No, if you advise rightly. For you have not in hand a match of valour upon equal terms, wherein to forfeit your honour, but rather a consultation upon your safety that you resist not such as be so far your overmatches."

102. *Mel.* "But we know that, in matter of war, the event is sometimes otherwise than according to the difference of number in sides; and that if we yield presently, all our hope is lost; whereas if we hold out, we have yet a hope to keep ourselves up."

103. *Ath.* "Hope, the comfort of danger, when such use it as have to spare, though it hurt them, yet it destroys them not. But to such as set their rest upon it (for it is a thing by nature prodigal), it at once by failing maketh itself known; and known, leaveth no place for future caution.[1] Which let not be your own case, you that are but weak and have no more but this one stake. Nor be you like unto many men, who, though they may presently save themselves by human means, will yet, when upon pressure of the enemy their most apparent hopes fail them, betake themselves to blind ones, as divination, oracles, and other such things which with hopes destroy men."

104. *Mel.* "We think it, you well know, a hard matter for us to combat your power and fortune, unless we might do it on equal terms. Nevertheless we

---

1   The Greek here is exceedingly difficult, but Hobbes has at best expressed only the gist of this sentence. It means "But for those who are making a cast for their all (and hope is naturally prodigal), it (hope) is only known for what it is at the moment of failure, and even in a case where a man knows it so and guards against it, it still plagues him" (literally, "does not desert him"). The following passage explains a lot. Men in a dangerous situation might save themselves by human means. Instead, they trust to open or reasonable hope, and when these fail have recourse to the blind expectation of oracles, divination, etc.

believe that, for fortune, we shall be nothing inferior, as having the gods on our side, because we stand innocent against men unjust; and for power, what is wanting in us will be supplied by our league with the Lacedaemonians, who are of necessity obliged, if for no other cause, yet for consanguinity's sake and for their own honour, to defend us. So that we are confident, not altogether so much without reason as you think."

105. *Ath.* "As for the favour of the gods, we expect to have it as well as you; for we neither do nor require anything contrary to what mankind hath decreed, either concerning the worship of the gods or concerning themselves.[2] For of the gods we think according to the common opinion; and of men, that for certain by necessity of nature they will everywhere reign over such as they be too strong for. Neither did we make this law nor are we the first that use it made; but as we found it, and shall leave it to posterity for ever, so also we use it, knowing that you likewise, and others that should have the same power which we have, would do the same. So that forasmuch as toucheth the favour of the gods, we have in reason no fear of being inferior. And as for the opinion you have of the Lacedaemonians, in that you believe they will help you for their own honour, we bless your innocent minds, but affect not your folly. For the Lacedaemonians, though in respect of themselves and the constitutions of their own country they are wont for the most part to be generous; yet in respect of others, though much might be alleged, yet the shortest way one might say it all thus: that most apparently of all men, they hold for honourable that which pleaseth, and for just that which profiteth. And such an opinion maketh nothing for your now absurd means of safety."

106. *Mel.* "Nay, for this same opinion of theirs, we now the rather believe that they will not betray their own colony, the Melians, and thereby become perfidious to such of the Grecians as be their friends and beneficial to such as be their enemies."

107. *Ath.* "You think not, then, that what is profitable must be also safe, and that which is just and honourable must be performed with danger, which commonly the Lacedaemonians are least willing of all men to undergo [for others]."

108. *Mel.* "But we suppose that they will undertake danger for us rather than for any other; and that they think that we will be more assured unto them

---

2   A closer translation would be something like this: "Neither in what we claim nor what we do are we outside of what man thinks about the gods and what he wishes for himself."

than unto any other, because for action, we lie near to Peloponnesus, and for affection, are more faithful than others for our nearness of kin."

109. *Ath.* "The security of such as are at wars consisteth not in the good will of those that are called to their aid, but in the power of those means they excel in. And this the Lacedaemonians themselves use to consider more than any; and therefore, out of diffidence in their own forces, they take many of their confederates with them, though to an expedition but against their neighbours. Wherefore it is not likely, we being masters of the sea, that they will ever pass over into an island."

110. *Mel.* "Yea, but they may have others to send; and the Cretic sea is wide, wherein to take another is harder for him that is master of it than it is for him that will steal by to save himself. And if this course fail, they may turn their arms against your own territory or those of your confederates not invaded by Brasidas. And then you shall have to trouble yourselves no more about a territory that you have nothing to do withal, but about your own and your confederates."

111. *Ath.* "Let them take which course of these they will that you also may find by experience and not be ignorant that the Athenians never yet gave over siege for fear of any diversion upon others. But we observe that, whereas you said you would consult of your safety, you have not yet in all this discourse said anything which a man relying on could hope to be preserved by; the strongest arguments you use are but future hopes; and your present power is too short to defend you against the forces already arranged against you. You shall therefore take very absurd counsel, unless, excluding us, you make amongst yourselves some more discreet conclusion; for [when you are by yourselves], you will no more set your thoughts upon shame, which, when dishonour and danger stand before men's eyes, for the most part undoeth them. For many, when they have foreseen into what dangers they were entering, have nevertheless been so overcome by that forcible word dishonour that that which is but called dishonour hath caused them to fall willingly into immedicable calamities, and so to draw upon themselves really, by their own madness, a greater dishonour than could have befallen them by fortune. Which you, if you deliberate wisely, will take heed of, and not think shame to submit to a most potent city, and that upon so reasonable conditions as of league and of enjoying your own under tribute; and seeing choice is given you of war or safety, do not out of peevishness take the worse. For such do take the best course who, though they give no way to their equals, yet do fairly accommodate to their superiors, and towards their inferiors use moderation. Consider of it, therefore, whilst we stand off and have

often in your mind that you deliberate of your country, which is to be happy or miserable in and by this one consultation."

112. So the Athenians went aside from the conference; and the Melians, after they had decreed the very same things which before they had spoken, made answer unto them in this manner "Men of Athens, our resolution is no other than what you have heard before; nor will we, in a small portion of time, overthrow that liberty in which our city hath remained for the space seven hundred years since it was first founded. But trusting the fortune by which the gods have preserved it hitherto an unto the help of men, that is, of the Lacedaemonians, we will do our best to maintain the same. But this we offer: to be your friends, enemies to neither side, and you to depart out of our land, after agreement such as we shall both think fit."

113. Thus the Melians answered. To which the Athenians, the conference being already broken off, replied thus: "You are the only men, as it seemeth to us, by this consultation, that think future things more certain than things seen, and behold things doubtful, through desire to have them true, as if they were already come to pass. As you attribute and trust the most unto the Lacedaemonians, and to fortune and hopes, so will you be the most deceived."

114. This said, the Athenian ambassadors departed to their camp. And the commanders, seeing that the Melians stood out, fell presently to the war, and dividing the work among the several cities, encompassed the city of the Melians with a wall. The Athenians afterwards left some forces of their own and of their confederates for a guard both by sea and land, and with the greatest part of their army went home. The rest that were left besieged the place.

115. About the same time the Argives, making a road into Phliasia, lost about eighty of their men by ambush laid for them by the men of Phlius and the outlaws of their own city. And the Athenians that lay in Pylus fetched in thither a great booty from the Lacedaemonians. Notwithstanding which, the Lacedaemonians did not war upon them [as] renouncing the peace, but gave leave by edict only to any of their people that would to take booties reciprocally in the territory of the Athenians. The Corinthians also made war upon the Athenians; but it was for certain controversies of their own, and the rest of Peloponnesus stirred not.

116. The Melians also took that part of the wall of the Athenians, by an assault in the night, which looked towards the market place, and having slain the men that guarded it, brought into the town both corn and other provision,

whatsoever they could buy for money, and so returned and lay still. And the Athenians from thenceforth kept a better watch. And so this summer ended. 116. The winter following, the Lacedaemonians being about to enter with their army into the territory of the Argives, when they perceived that the sacrifices which they made on the border for their passage were not acceptable, returned. And the Argives, having some of their own city in suspicion in regard of this design of the Lacedaemonians, apprehended some of them, and some escaped.

About the same time the Melians took another part of the wall of the Athenians, they that kept the siege being then not many. But this done, there came afterwards some fresh forces from Athens, under the conduct of Philocrates, the son of Demeas. And the town being now strongly besieged, there being also within some that practised to have it given up, they yielded themselves to the discretion of the Athenians, who slew all the men of military age, made slaves of the women and children, and inhabited the place with a colony sent thither afterwards of five hundred men of their own.

On War and Murder

selection from *Summa Theologica*
by St. Thomas Aquinas

༖

FIRST ARTICLE [II–II, Q. 40, Art. 1]

Whether It Is Always Sinful to Wage War?

Objection 1: It would seem that it is always sinful to wage war. Because punishment is not inflicted except for sin. Now those who wage war are threatened by Our Lord with punishment, according to Matt. 26:52: "All that take the sword shall perish with the sword." Therefore all wars are unlawful.

Obj. 2: Further, whatever is contrary to a Divine precept is a sin. But war is contrary to a Divine precept, for it is written (Matt. 5:39): "But I say to you not to resist evil"; and (Rom. 12:19): "Not revenging yourselves, my dearly beloved, but give place unto wrath." Therefore war is always sinful.

Obj. 3: Further, nothing, except sin, is contrary to an act of virtue. But war is contrary to peace. Therefore war is always a sin.

Obj. 4: Further, the exercise of a lawful thing is itself lawful, as is evident in scientific exercises. But warlike exercises which take place in tournaments are forbidden by the Church, since those who are slain in these trials are deprived of ecclesiastical burial. Therefore it seems that war is a sin in itself.

On the contrary, Augustine says in a sermon on the son of the centurion [*Ep. ad Marcel. cxxxviii]: "If the Christian Religion forbade war altogether,

St. Thomas Aquinas, "Of War," *Summa Theologica*.

those who sought salutary advice in the Gospel would rather have been counselled to cast aside their arms, and to give up soldiering altogether. On the contrary, they were told: 'Do violence to no man . . . and be content with your pay' [*Luke 3:14]. If he commanded them to be content with their pay, he did not forbid soldiering."

I answer that, In order for a war to be just, three things are necessary. First, the authority of the sovereign by whose command the war is to be waged. For it is not the business of a private individual to declare war, because he can seek for redress of his rights from the tribunal of his superior. Moreover it is not the business of a private individual to summon together the people, which has to be done in wartime. And as the care of the common weal is committed to those who are in authority, it is their business to watch over the common weal of the city, kingdom or province subject to them. And just as it is lawful for them to have recourse to the sword in defending that common weal against internal disturbances, when they punish evil-doers, according to the words of the Apostle (Rom. 13:4): "He beareth not the sword in vain: for he is God's minister, an avenger to execute wrath upon him that doth evil"; so too, it is their business to have recourse to the sword of war in defending the common weal against external enemies. Hence it is said to those who are in authority (Ps. 81:4): "Rescue the poor: and deliver the needy out of the hand of the sinner"; and for this reason Augustine says (Contra Faust. xxii, 75): "The natural order conducive to peace among mortals demands that the power to declare and counsel war should be in the hands of those who hold the supreme authority."

Secondly, a just cause is required, namely that those who are attacked, should be attacked because they deserve it on account of some fault. Wherefore Augustine says (QQ. in Hept., qu. x, super Jos.): "A just war is wont to be described as one that avenges wrongs, when a nation or state has to be punished, for refusing to make amends for the wrongs inflicted by its subjects, or to restore what it has seized unjustly."

Thirdly, it is necessary that the belligerents should have a rightful intention, so that they intend the advancement of good, or the avoidance of evil. Hence Augustine says (De Verb. Dom. [*The words quoted are to be found not in St. Augustine's works, but Can. Apud. Caus. xxiii, qu. 1]): "True religion looks upon as peaceful those wars that are waged not for motives of aggrandizement, or cruelty, but with the object of securing peace, of punishing evil-doers, and of uplifting the good." For it may happen that the war is declared by the legitimate authority, and for a just cause, and yet be rendered unlawful through a wicked intention. Hence Augustine says (Contra Faust. xxii, 74): "The passion for inflicting harm, the cruel thirst for vengeance, an unpacific and relentless spirit, the fever of revolt, the lust of power, and such like things, all these are rightly condemned in war."

Reply Obj. 1: As Augustine says (Contra Faust. xxii, 70): "To take the sword is to arm oneself in order to take the life of anyone, without the command or permission of superior or lawful authority." On the other hand, to have recourse to the sword (as a private person) by the authority of the sovereign or judge, or (as a public person) through zeal for justice, and by the authority, so to speak, of God, is not to "take the sword," but to use it as commissioned by another, wherefore it does not deserve punishment. And yet even those who make sinful use of the sword are not always slain with the sword, yet they always perish with their own sword, because, unless they repent, they are punished eternally for their sinful use of the sword.

Reply Obj. 2: Such like precepts, as Augustine observes (De Serm. Dom. in Monte i, 19), should always be borne in readiness of mind, so that we be ready to obey them, and, if necessary, to refrain from resistance or self-defense. Nevertheless it is necessary sometimes for a man to act otherwise for the common good, or for the good of those with whom he is fighting. Hence Augustine says (Ep. ad Marcellin. cxxxviii): "Those whom we have to punish with a kindly severity, it is necessary to handle in many ways against their will. For when we are stripping a man of the lawlessness of sin, it is good for him to be vanquished, since nothing is more hopeless than the happiness of sinners, whence arises a guilty impunity, and an evil will, like an internal enemy."

Reply Obj. 3: Those who wage war justly aim at peace, and so they are not opposed to peace, except to the evil peace, which Our Lord "came not to send upon earth" (Matt. 10:34). Hence Augustine says (Ep. ad Bonif. clxxxix): "We do not seek peace in order to be at war, but we go to war that we may have peace. Be peaceful, therefore, in warring, so that you may vanquish those whom you war against, and bring them to the prosperity of peace."

Reply Obj. 4: Manly exercises in warlike feats of arms are not all forbidden, but those which are inordinate and perilous, and end in slaying or plundering. In olden times warlike exercises presented no such danger, and hence they were called "exercises of arms" or "bloodless wars," as Jerome states in an epistle [*Reference incorrect: cf. Veget., De Re Milit. i].

War and Non-resistance

Bertrand Russell

∿

The PRINCIPLE THAT it is always wrong to employ force against another human being has been held in its extreme form by Quakers and by Tolstoy, but has always been rejected by the great majority of mankind as inconsistent with the existence of civilized society. In this, no doubt, the majority of mankind are in the right. But I think that the occasions where forcible resistance is the best course are much fewer than is generally believed, and that some very great and important advances in civilization might be made if this were more widely recognized. The so-called "right of self-defence", in particular, seems to have only a very limited sphere of application, and to be often supported by arguments involving both mistakes as to political questions and a wrong conception of the best type of character.[1]

No one who holds that human conduct ought to be such as to promote certain ends—no matter what ends may be selected—will expect any absolute hard-and-fast rules of conduct to which no possible exception can be found. Not to lie, not to steal, not to murder, are very good precepts for ordinary cases: it may be, in view of the likelihood of biased judgments, that most men will act better if they always follow these precepts unquestioningly than if they consider each case on its merits. Nevertheless, it is obvious that there are cases where lying and stealing are justifiable, and the same must be said of murder by those who hold that some wars are righteous. Tolstoy does not judge conduct by its consequences: he considers actions inherently right or wrong. This makes it possible for him to say that no use of force is ever right. But if we judge conduct, as I think we ought, by its power of promoting what we consider a good life or

---

1   I touched upon this subject in a former article, in the *International Journal of Ethics* (January, 1915), but as my discussion was very brief, it was misunderstood, and seems in need of expansion. The present article is a partial reply to Professor Perry in the April number of that journal, but I have thought it better to make the reply explanatory rather than controversial.

a good society, we cannot expect such simplicity in our moral precepts, and we must expect all of them to be subject to exceptions. Whatever we may have to say must be regarded as in the nature of practical maxims, to be applied with common sense, not as logically universal rules to be tested by extreme cases.[2]

Broadly speaking, I think the use of force is justifiable when it is ordered in accordance with law by a neutral authority, in the general interest and not primarily in the interest of one of the parties to the quarrel. On this ground, the use of force by the police is justifiable, provided (as is no doubt sometimes the case) the authorities are employing the police in the general interest and not merely in the interest of the holders of power. In international affairs, if there were a Council of the Powers, strong enough to restrain any aggressive nation without great difficulty, any army or navy employed in obedience to its orders might be regarded as a police force, and justified on the same grounds on which the police are justified. I think there is more hope of ultimately achieving universal peace by this method than by the adoption of non-resistance. But this has no bearing upon the question whether non-resistance would be a good policy, if any nation could be induced to adopt it. So long as no Council of the Powers exists, there is no neutral authority to order resistance, and we have to consider the justification of repelling an attack when the nation attacked is the judge in its own cause.

The justification of non-resistance is more easily seen in the case of quarrels between individuals. If I encountered the traditional highwayman, and he demanded my money or my life, I should unhesitatingly give him my money, even if it were in my power to shoot him before he shot me. I should do this, not from cowardice or lack of spirit, but because I would rather part with money than have a man's blood on my conscience. And for the same reason, if I were compelled to engage in a duel, I would rather let my adversary shoot me than shoot him. In this I believe all humane people would agree. At the same time, if he were a worthless fellow, and I had just made an important mathematical discovery which I had not yet had time to record, it might be right to preserve my life at his expense. Arguments of this sort would justify civilized communities in defending themselves against savages. But conflicts between civilized nations are more like conflicts between rival metaphysicians, each of whom considers his own system admirable and the other man's abominable, while to outsiders it is obvious that both are equally fantastic.

In private life, most situations can be met by the double principle of neither employing force nor obeying it. It is a familiar Platonic thesis that the man who inflicts injustice is more to be pitied than the man who suffers it. But such

2 Professor Perry (page 311) confronts me with an extreme case. But I had provided for such cases by admitting that a war of self-defence is sometimes a war of principle, and justifiable on that ground.

statements are read with a smile, as charming literary paradoxes, and are not taken as practical wisdom for the guidance of life. Yet the use of force to coerce another man's will, even in those rare cases in which it is justifiable, produces a brutal and tyrannous state of mind, and is more destructive of inward peace than any misfortune that can be inflicted from without. The greatest good that can be achieved in this life is to have will and desire directed to universal ends, purged of the self-assertion which belongs to instinctive will. A man who has once known this good will not consider any private end important enough to be fought for: he may be willing to enter upon a contest of force, but if so, it will be for some end outside his own life, since what is best in his own life cannot be taken from him by another. But although he will not dictate to others for his own ends, he will also not be turned aside from universal ends by others: he will be no more willing to obey than to command. He will preserve his own liberty as scrupulously as he respects the liberty of others.

Exactly similar considerations apply to the conduct of nations, but they are obscured by traditional phrases about "honour", "patriotism", "sacred traditions", or "the protection of women and children". It is assumed that a nation which does not oppose force with force must be actuated by cowardice, and must lose whatever is valuable in its civilization. Both these are illusions. To oppose force by passive non-obedience would require more courage, and would be far more likely to preserve the best elements of the national life. It would also do far more to discourage the use of force. This would be the way of practical wisdom, if men could be brought to believe it. But I fear men are too much wedded to the belief that patriotism is a virtue, and too fond of proving their superiority to others in a contest of force. People who object to the doctrine that might is right always contend that it will be disproved by showing that might is on their own side. Yet that would only be a disproof if their side were in the wrong, and their argument shows that they really believe the doctrine they are pretending to combat. Those who genuinely disbelieve the doctrine will not attempt to disprove it by getting might on their side.

Let us imagine that England were to disband its army and navy, after a generation of instruction in the principles of passive resistance as a better defence than war. Let us suppose that England at the same time publicly announced that no armed opposition would be offered to an invader, that all might come freely, but that no obedience would be yielded to any commands that a foreign authority might issue. What would happen in this case?

Suppose, to continue the argument, that the German Government wished to take advantage of England's defenceless condition. It would be faced, at the outset, by the opposition of whatever was not utterly brutal in Germany, since no possible cloak could be found to hide the nakedness of aggression. All civilized countries, when they engage in war, find some decent excuse:

they fight, almost always, either in self-defence or in defence of the weak. No such excuse could be found in this case. It could no longer be said, as the Germans now say, that England's naval preponderance keeps other nations in bondage, and threatens the very existence of any nation which depends upon imported food. It could no longer be said that we were oppressing India, since India would be able to separate from the British Empire whenever it wished to do so. All the usual pretexts by which aggression is justified would be lacking. When America attacked Spain, it was to liberate the Cubans, against whom Spain was carrying on a war. When England attacked the Transvaal, the Poet Laureate, the *Times,* Messrs. Wehrner, Beit and Co., and the other imperialist magnates who represented the ancient traditions of the British race, solemnly assured us that our intervention was necessary for the safety of English women in Johannesburg, and for the liberation of the natives from virtual slavery to the Boers. These pleas deceived many people who, though no doubt not unwilling to be deceived, would yet have shrunk from an aggression which could not be in any way disguised. And it was said that the Boers aimed at the conquest of the whole of South Africa: we were told that, if ever England found itself entangled in a European war, Cape Colony would be overrun, and its English colonists would be subjected to a tyranny. In any civilized country, arguments of this kind are always used in justifying even the most aggressive war.

If England had no army and no navy, the Germans would be hard put to it to find a pretext for invasion. All the Liberal elements in Germany would oppose any such enterprise; so would all other nations, unless Germany offered them a share of the plunder. But let us suppose all home opposition overcome, and a force despatched to England to take possession of the country. Such a force, since it would meet with no military opposition, would not need to be large, and would not be in the state of mingled fear and ferocity which characterizes an invading army among a hostile population. There would be no difficulty in preserving military discipline, and no opportunity for the rape and rapine which have always been displayed by troops after victory in battle. There would be no glory to be won, not even enough to earn one iron cross. The Germans could not congratulate themselves upon their military prowess, or imagine that they were displaying the stern self-abnegation believed to be shown by willingness to die in the fight. To the soldierly mind, the whole expedition would be ridiculous, causing a feeling of disgust instead of pride. Perhaps a few impudent street-boys might have to have their ears boxed, but otherwise there would be nothing to lend dignity to the expedition.

However, we will suppose the invading army arrived in London, where they would evict the King from Buckingham Palace and the Members from the House of Commons. A few able bureaucrats would be brought over from Berlin to consult with the Civil Servants in Whitehall as to the new laws by which the reign of Kultur was to be inaugurated. No difficulty would be expected in managing so tame a nation, and at first almost all the existing officials would be confirmed in their offices. For the government of a large modern State is a complicated matter, and it would be thought well to facilitate the transition by the help of men familiar with the existing machinery.

But at this point, if the nation showed as much courage as it has always shown in fighting, difficulties would begin. All the existing officials would refuse to cooperate with the Germans. Some of the more prominent would be imprisoned, perhaps even shot, in order to encourage the others. But if the others held firm, if they refused to recognize or transmit any order given by Germans, if they continued to carry out the decrees previously made by the English Parliament and the English Government, the Germans would have to dismiss them all, even to the humblest postman, and call in German talent to fill the breach.

The dismissed officials could not all be imprisoned or shot: since no fighting would have occurred, such wholesale brutality would be out of the question. And it would be very difficult for the Germans suddenly, out of nothing, to create an administrative machine. Whatever edicts they might issue would be quietly ignored by the population. If they ordered that German should be the language taught in schools, the schoolmasters would go on as if no such order had been issued; if the schoolmasters were dismissed, the parents would no longer send the children to school. If they ordered that English young men should undergo military service, the young men would simply refuse; after shooting a few, the Germans would have to give up the attempt in despair. If they tried to raise revenue by customs duties at the ports, they would have to have German customs officers; this would lead to a strike of all the dock labourers, so that this way of raising revenue would become impossible. If they tried to take over the railways, there would be a strike of the railway servants. Whatever they touched would instantly become paralyzed, and it would soon be evident, even to them, that nothing was to be made out of England unless the population could be conciliated.

Such a method of dealing with invasion would, of course, require fortitude and discipline. But fortitude and discipline are required in war. For ages past, education has been largely directed to producing these qualities for the sake of war. They now exist so widely that in every civilized country almost every man is willing to die on the battlefield whenever his Government thinks the moment suitable. The same courage and idealism which are now put into war could quite easily be directed by education into the channel of passive resistance. I do not know what losses England may suffer before the present war is ended, but if they amount to a million no one will be surprised. An immensely smaller number of losses, incurred in passive resistance, would prove to any invading army that the task of subjecting England to alien domination was an impossible one. And this proof would be made once for all, without dependence upon the doubtful accidents of war.

In internal politics, in all democratic countries, the very method we have been considering is constantly practised, with continually increasing success. Even in Russia, it was the general strike which secured the Constitution of 1905. For a generation, terrorists had uselessly copied the methods of militarists by bomb-throwing and assassination; they had achieved nothing except to afford the authorities an excuse for ruthless repression—an excuse not only to the public, but also to their own consciences, since they appeared to themselves, as soldiers do, to be brave men facing death in the public service. After all the years of fruitless violence, it was the method of passive non-obedience which secured the momentary victory, afterwards lost through disunion and a return to violence. And in all the dealings of democratic Governments with labour troubles or with irreconcilable minorities, it is this same power of passive resistance that comes into play. In a civilized, highly organized, highly political State, government is impossible without the consent of the governed. Any object for which a considerable body of men are prepared to starve and die can be achieved by political means, without the need of any resort to force. And if this is true of objects only desired by a minority, it is a thousand times more true of objects desired unanimously by the whole nation.

But it may be said that, even if the Germans could not actually take over the government of England, or rob us of internal self-government, they could do two things which would injure us vitally: they could take away our Empire, and they could levy a tribute by the threat of depriving us of food supplies.

The Germans could not take away the self-governing parts of our Empire, since they would encounter there the same difficulties as would prevent them from governing England. They could take away those parts of our Empire which we hold by force, and this would be a blow to our pride: the oppression of subject races is one of the chief sources of patriotic satisfaction, and one of the chief things for which Germany envies us. But it is not a source of pride to any rational or humane man. European rule over uncivilized races is, in fact, a very sordid affair. The best of the men whom it employs are those engaged in the attempt at government, who live in exile and usually die of fever; the rest grow rich selling rum to natives or making them work in mines. Meanwhile the natives degenerate: some die of drink, some of diseases caught from white men, some of consumption in the mines; those who survive contract the vices of civilization without losing the vices of barbarism. It can only be a blessing to any nation to be deprived of this source of pride, which is a canker of corruption and immorality in the life of democratic communities.

That the Germans could levy a tribute on England by threatening our food supplies is obviously true. The ethics of such a demand would be exactly the same as that of the highwayman who demands "your money or your life". The same reasons which would lead a reasonable man to give his money rather than shoot or be shot would also lead a reasonable nation to give a tribute rather than resist by force of arms. The greatest sum that foreigners could theoretically exact would be the total economic rent of the land and natural resources of England. In fact, economic rent may be defined as what can be, and historically has been, extorted by such means. The rent now paid to landowners in England is the outcome of the exactions made by William the Conqueror and his barons. The law-courts are the outcome of those set up at that time, and the law which they administer, so far as land is concerned, represents simply the power of the sword. From inertia and lack of imagination, the English at the present day continue to pay to the landowners a vast sum to which they have no right but that of conquest. The working classes, the shopkeepers, manufacturers, and merchants, the literary men, and the men of science—all the people who make England of any account in the world—have at most an infinitesimal and accidental share in the rental of England. The men who have a share use their rents in luxury, political corruption, taking the lives of birds, and depopulating and enslaving the rural districts. This way of life is that which almost all English men and women consider the most admirable: those who are anywhere near achieving it struggle to attain it completely, and those who are more remote read serial stories about it as their ancestors would have read of the joys of Paradise.

It is this life of the idle rich which would be curtailed if the Germans exacted a tribute from England. Everything in England that is not positively harmful would be untouched: wages and other earned incomes could not be diminished without diminishing the productivity of English labour, and so lessening England's capacity for paying tribute. Our snobbish instincts, if the idle rich were abolished, might be driven, by want of other outlet, into the admiration of real merit. And if the Germans could effect this for us, they would well deserve their tribute.

It is very doubtful, indeed, whether the Germans would exact from us a larger tribute than we exact from ourselves in resisting them. There is no knowing what this war will have cost England when it ends, but we shall probably not exaggerate if we place the cost at a thousand million pounds.[3] This represents an annual payment of forty million pounds. All this, together with the annual expenditure on our Army and Navy, we might have paid to the Germans without being any poorer than we shall be when the war ends. This represents an incredibly larger tribute than we derive from India; yet the Germans assure

---

3   It is now (September, 1915) evident that this is an under-estimate.

us that we are full of commercial cunning, and that we govern India solely for our own profit. If they believe this, it is hardly to be supposed that the receipt of such a tribute would fail to satisfy them. Meanwhile we should have avoided the death of our young men, the moral degradation of almost our whole population, and the lowering of the standard of civilization slowly achieved through centuries which were peaceful in comparison with our present condition.

But, of course, all that I have been saying is fantastic, degrading, and out of touch with reality. I have been assuming that men are to some extent guided by reason, that their actions are directed to ends such as "life, liberty, and the pursuit of happiness". This is not the case. Death, slavery, and unhappiness (for others) are the chief ends pursued by States in their external relations. It is the preference of such ends to one's own happiness that constitutes patriotism, that shows a man to be free from materialism, and that raises him above the commercial, money-grubbing level of the mere shopkeeper. The Prussian feels himself noble because he is willing to be killed provided men of other nations are killed at the same time. His nobility and his freedom from commercialism consists in the fact that he desires the misery of others more than his own happiness. And there is a Prussian lurking in each of us, ready to make us reject any national advantage which is not purchased by injury to some other nation. It is this lurking Prussian in our instincts who assures us that a policy of non-resistance would be tame and cowardly, unworthy of a great and proud nation, a failure to perform our duty of chastizing an exactly similar pride in other nations.

Pride has its place among virtues, in the lives of individuals as well as in the lives of nations. Pride, in so far as it is a virtue, is a determination not to be turned aside from the ends which a man thinks good, no matter what outside pressure may be brought to bear upon him. There is pride in Condorcet, sentenced to the guillotine, spending his last days in writing a book on human progress. There is pride in those who refuse to recant their religious convictions under persecution. Such pride is the noblest form of courage: it shows that self-determination of the will which is the essence of spiritual freedom. But such pride should have as its complement a just conception of what constitutes human welfare, and as its correlative a respect for the freedom of others as absolute as the determination to preserve freedom for ourselves. Exactly the same kind of pride is good in the life of a nation. If we think ill of war, while some other nation thinks well of it, let us show our national pride by living without war, whatever temptations the other nation may put in our way to live according to their ideals rather than according to our own.

The Germans, we are given to understand, hate us with a bitter hatred, and long to believe that we feel towards them as they feel towards us; for unrequited hatred is as bitter as unrequited love. They have made it increasingly difficult not to gratify their desire; but in so far as we can keep our resistance free from bitterness we win a spiritual victory over what deserves to be combated in the enemy, which is far more important than any victory to be won by guns and bayonets.

But this kind of pride is not the kind which patriots exhort us to display. The pride that they admire is the kind which aims at thwarting others; it is the pride of power. Having suspected that the Germans desired Morocco and Mesopotamia, we were proud of the fact that we prevented them from acquiring either. Having found that the Boers desired independence, we were proud of the fact that we made them submit to our rule. This kind of pride consists merely in love of dominion. Dominion and power can only be conclusively shown by compelling others to forego what they desire. By a natural consequence, those in whom the love of power is strong are led to inflict pain and to use force against the perfectly legitimate desires of those whom they wish to subdue. In nations, this attitude is commended. Generally the heroes of a nation's history are not those who have benefited mankind, but those who have injured other nations. If we prided ourselves upon the good and not the harm that we have done, we should have put Shakespeare on the Nelson Monument, and given Apsley House to Darwin. But the citizens whom every nation honours most are those who have killed the greatest number of foreigners.

It is this pride of power which makes us unwilling to yield to others in matters of no intrinsic importance. The Germans cherish a desire to own African swamps, of which we have a superfluity. No one in England benefits by the possession of them, except a few financial magnates, mostly of foreign origin. If we were reasonable, we should regard the German desire as a curious whim, which we might gratify without any real national loss. Instead of that, we regard the German desire as a crime, and our resistance to it as a virtue. We teach school children to rejoice because so much of the map is painted red. In order that as much as possible may be painted red, we are willing to sacrifice those ideals of freedom in which we have led mankind, and, if necessary, to adopt all the worst features of the Prussian spirit. This is because we fear the external enemy, who kills the body, more than the internal enemy, who kills the soul. The soul of a nation, if it is a free soul, without slavishness and without tyranny, cannot be killed by any outward enemy. And if men would realize this, the panic fear which the nations feel one toward another would be expelled by a better pride than that of diplomatists and war-lords.

The armies and navies of the world are kept up by three causes: cowardice, love of dominion, and lust for blood.

It is cowardice that makes it difficult to meet invasion by the method of passive resistance. More courage and discipline is needed for the successful practice of this method than for facing death in the heat of battle. But I am persuaded that there is in England enough courage and enough capacity for discipline to make success in passive resistance possible, if education and moral teaching were directed to that end instead of to warlike prowess. It is cowardice also that makes men prefer the old method of trying to be stronger than your adversary (in which only one party can succeed), rather than a new method requiring imagination and a readjustment of traditional standards. Yet, if men could think outside the well-worn grooves, there are many plain facts which show the folly of conventional statesmanship. Why has Germany invaded France? Because the French have an army. Why has England attacked Germany? Because the Germans have a navy. Yet people persist in thinking that the French army and the German navy contribute to national safety. Nothing could be more obvious than the facts; nothing could be more universal than men's blindness to them.

The second reason for keeping up the armies and navies of the world is love of dominion. The Germans, in the Morocco controversy, announced that nothing of importance was to happen anywhere without their being consulted. We regarded this as monstrous arrogance; but for two centuries we had advanced the same claim as a matter of course. The matters about which diplomatists raise a pother are usually of only microscopic importance to the welfare of ordinary citizens: they are matters involving national "prestige", that is to say, the power of the State to prevent other States from doing as they wish. This power is sometimes partly based on money, but in the main it rests on armies and navies. If our navy had been smaller, we should not have been able to defeat the German desire for an Atlantic port in Morocco. It would have done us no harm if the Germans had acquired Casablanca, but we enjoyed the thought that our fiat kept them out. The procuring of such pleasures is the second purpose served by armies and navies.

The third purpose of armaments—indeed their primary and original purpose, from which all others are derivative—is to satisfy the lust for blood. Fighting is an instinctive activity of males, both animal and human. Human males, being gregarious, naturally fight in packs. It has been found that the pack tends to be more successful against other packs when fighting within the pack is as far as possible prevented. For this purpose, the law and the police have been instituted. But the shedding of human blood is still considered the most glorious thing a man can do, provided he does it in company with the rest of his pack. War, like marriage, is the legally permitted outlet for a certain instinct. But the instinct which leads to war, unlike the instinct which leads to marriage, so far from being necessary to the human race, is wholly harmful among civilized men. It is an instinct which easily becomes atrophied in a settled community: many men have hardly a trace of it. Unfortunately, as men grow older, their affections and their powers of thought decay. For this reason, and also because power stimulates the love of power, the men who have most influence in government are usually men whose passions and impulses are

less civilized than those of the average citizen. These men—the great finan-
ciers, the Ministers, and some editors of daily papers—use their position, their
knowledge, and their power of disseminating misinformation, to arouse and
stimulate the latent instinct for bloodshed. When they have succeeded, they
say that they are reluctantly forced into war by the pressure of public opinion.
Their activities are exactly analogous to those of men who distribute indecent
pictures or produce lascivious plays. They ought to be viewed in the same
light; but because of the notion that a wish to kill foreigners is patriotic and
virtuous, they are honoured as men who have deserved well of their country.
They provide an outlet for the impulse to homicide. To gratify this impulse is
the third and ultimate purpose of armies and navies.

All these three motives for armaments—cowardice, love of dominion, and
lust for blood—are no longer ineradicable in civilized human nature. All are
diminishing under the influence of modern social organization. All might
be reduced to a degree which could make them almost innocuous, if early
education and current moral standards were directed to that end. Passive
resistance, if it were adopted deliberately by the will of a whole nation, with
the same measure of courage and discipline which is now displayed in war,
might achieve a far more perfect protection for what is good in national life
than armies and navies can ever achieve, without demanding the carnage and
waste and welter of brutality involved in modern war.

Nevertheless, it is hardly to be expected that progress will come in this way,
because the imaginative effort required is too great. It is much more likely that
it will come, as the reign of law within the State has come, by the establishment
of a central government of the world, able and willing to secure obedience by
force, because the great majority of men will recognize that obedience is better
than the present international anarchy. A central government of this kind will
command assent, not as a partisan, but as the representative of the interests of
the whole. Very soon, resistance to it would be seen to be hopeless, and wars
would cease. Force directed by a neutral authority is not open to the same
abuse, or likely to cause the same long-drawn conflicts, as force exercised by
quarrelling nations each of which is the judge in its own cause. Although I firmly
believe that the adoption of passive instead of active resistance would be good
if a nation could be convinced of its goodness, yet it is rather to the ultimate
creation of a strong central authority that I should look for the ending of war.
But war will only end after a great labour has been performed in altering men's
moral ideals, directing them to the good of all mankind, and not only of the
separate nations into which men happen to have been born.

STUDY QUESTIONS FOR READINGS

Thucydides, *The Peloponnesian War*

1. How do the Athenians characterize justice? What are they trying to convince the Melians to do? Are they successful? Explain your answers.
2. What does this selection imply about the ethics of international relations and war? Is this account compelling? Explain your answers.

Aquinas, *On War*

1. What three things are required for a war to be just according to Aquinas? To what extent do you agree with Aquinas on this matter? Are there other requirements for war to be justified that Aquinas has overlooked? Explain your answers.
2. Does Aquinas' view that war can be morally justified under certain circumstances entail that any and all conduct during war is ethically acceptable? How do you think Aquinas would answer this question? How would you answer this question? Explain your answers.
3. Aquinas argues that both murder and suicide are immoral. How do you think Aquinas reconciles his views on war with such beliefs? Do you think he is able to reconcile these views consistently? Do you think his views on killing and the ethics of war seem plausible? Explain your answers.

Russell, War and Non-resistance

1. Why does Russell think that the justification of nonresistance is more easily seen in the case of individual conflict than in that of nations?
2. Why does Russell think that nonobedience requires more courage that going to war? To what extent do you agree with his account? Explain your answers.
3. Is this a practical position to take in the face of threats from other nations? Is it an ideal that we should aspire to? What does Russell think? What do you think? Explain your answers.

SUGGESTIONS FOR FURTHER READING OR VIEWING

Hacksaw Ridge. 2016. A true story film about war that raises many questions about conscientious objection (or conscientious participation) as well as religious freedom.

Nardin, Terry, ed. *The Ethics of War and Peace: Religious and Secular Perspectives.* Princeton, NJ: Princeton University Press, 1996.

The Big Red One. 1980. A film about being in the infantry during World War II written and directed by Samuel Fuller. Fuller served during World War II and earned the Silver Star, the Bronze Star, and the Purple Heart. Watch the longer 2004 edit, *The Reconstruction.* Roger Ebert's review of the film can be found at www.rogerebert.com/reviews/great-movie-the-big-red-one1980. To help the viewer gain insights into the film that they otherwise might not make, it is best to read Ebert's review after viewing the film.

Walzer, Michael. *Arguing about War.* New Haven, CT: Yale University Press, 2004.

———. *Just and Unjust Wars: A Moral Argument with Historical Illustrations.* 3rd ed. New York: Basic Books, 2000.

Treatment of Animals

INTRODUCTION TO MORAL OBLIGATION AND THE TREATMENT OF ANIMALS

The treatment of nonhuman animals raises a lot of difficult moral questions and has long been a subject of philosophical debate. Much of this debate and discussion centers on determining the basis of moral consideration. One view is that moral consideration is given in virtue of an entity's inherent value. According to proponents of this sort of view, we must give moral consideration to beings that have inherent worth so as to recognize this value no matter what. Immanuel Kant is a particularly strong advocate of this position as evidenced by the second formulation of his categorical imperative, which tells us to always act such that we treat humanity in oneself and others as an end in itself and never solely as a means. While Kant believes that only rational beings have moral worth and as such can be the only recipients of direct moral obligation, he nonetheless argues that we should treat nonhuman animals kindly as an indirect duty to humanity. Other contemporary animal rights theorists and environmental philosophers expand the Kantian framework and emphasis on inherent value beyond humanity, arguing that all "experiencing subjects of a life" or "elements of the biotic community" have inherent value that also must be recognized at all times.

A different way to think about moral consideration looks at sentience and an entity's ability to suffer as the key feature in determining moral obligation. Peter Singer argues that sentience is the basis of having an interest and that equality in the most plausible sense requires us to consider the interests of all sentient beings equally. Singer draws on the work of Jeremy Bentham, a famous utilitarian philosopher who argues that

> the day may come when the rest of the animal creation may
> acquire those rights which never could have been witholden

from them but by the hand of tyranny. The French have already discovered that the blackness of the skin is no reason why a human being should be abandoned without redress to the caprice of a tormentor. It may one day come to be recognized that the number of the legs, the villosity of the skin, or the termination of the os sacrum, are reasons equally insufficient for abandoning a sensitive being to the same fate. What else is it that should trace the insuperable line? Is it the faculty of reason, or perhaps the faculty of discourse? But a full-grown horse or dog is beyond comparison a more rational, as well as a more conversable animal, than an infant of a day, or a week, or even a month, old. But suppose they were otherwise, what would it avail? The question is not, can they reason nor can they talk but, can they suffer?[1]

Debates about the basis of moral consideration and whether we have moral obligations to nonhuman animals are ongoing with many questions about the nature and extent of such obligations, if they do in fact exist. These are the types of things to keep in mind as you read the selections in this chapter.

---

1   Jeremy Benthan. *An Introduction to the Principles of Morals and Legislation.* Edited by J. H. Burns and H. L. A. Hart. Oxford: Oxford University Press, 1970.

Duties to Animals

Immanuel Kant

∽

Of Duties to Animals and Spirits

Our author here goes on to speak of duties to beings that are above us and beneath us. But since all animals exist only as means, and not for their own sakes, in that they have no self-consciousness, whereas man is the end, such that I can no longer ask: Why does he exist?, as can be done with animals, it follows that we have no immediate duties to animals; our duties towards them are indirect duties to humanity. Since animals are an analogue of humanity, we observe duties to mankind when we observe them as analogues to this, and thus cultivate our duties to humanity. If a dog, for example, has served his master long and faithfully, that is an analogue of merit; hence I must reward it, and once the dog can serve no longer, must look after him to the end, for I thereby cultivate my duty to humanity, as I am called upon to do; so if the acts of animals arise out of the same *principium* from which human actions spring, and the animal actions are analogues of this, we have duties to animals, in that we thereby promote the cause of humanity. So if a man has his dog shot, because it can no longer earn a living for him, he is by no means in breach of any duty to the dog, since the latter is incapable of judgement, but he thereby damages the kindly and humane qualities in himself, which he ought to exercise in virtue of his duties to mankind. Lest he extinguish such qualities, he must already practise a similar kindliness towards animals; for a person who already displays such cruelty to animals is also no less hardened towards men. We can already know the human heart, even in regard to animals. Thus Hogarth, in his engravings,[1] also depicts the beginnings of cruelty, where already the children are practising it upon animals, e.g., by pulling the tail of a dog or cat; in another scene we see the progress of cruelty, where the man runs over a child; and finally the culmination of cruelty in a murder, at which point the rewards of it appear horrifying. This provides a

27:459

---

1 ['The Stages of Cruelty', 1751 – Tr.]

good lesson to children. The more we devote ourselves to observing animals and their behaviour, the more we love them, on seeing how greatly they care for their young; in such a context, we cannot even contemplate cruelty to a wolf.

Leibnitz put the grub he had been observing back on the tree with its leaf, lest he should be guilty of doing any harm to it. It upsets a man to destroy such a creature for no reason, and this tenderness is subsequently transferred to man. In England, no butcher, surgeon or doctor serves on the twelve-man jury, because they are already inured to death. So when anatomists take living 27:460 animals to experiment on, that is certainly cruelty, though there it is employed for a good purpose; because animals are regarded as man's instruments, it is acceptable, though it is never so in sport. If a master turns out his ass or his dog, because it can no longer earn its keep, this always shows a very small mind in the master. The Greeks were high-minded in such matters, as is shown by the fable of the ass, which pulled by accident at the bell of ingratitude. Thus our duties to animals are indirectly duties to humanity.

The duties to other spiritual beings are merely negative. We should never meddle in such actions as imply a *commercium,* or intercourse, with other beings. All such actions are of a kind that makes men fanatical, visionary and superstitious, and are contrary to the dignity of mankind; for that dignity includes the healthy use of reason, and if one is given to things of that sort, the sound use of reason is impossible. There may always be such beings, and all that is said of them may be true, but we are not acquainted with them, and cannot have dealings with them.

In regard to evil spirits, the situation is the same. We have just as good an idea of evil as we do of good, and refer everything evil to Hell, as we attribute everything good to Heaven. If we personify this perfect evil, we have the idea of the Devil; and have only to imagine that such a being may have influence over us, that he appears at night and stalks abroad, to be plagued with phantoms that abolish the rational use of our powers. So our duties to such beings are negative.

Our author goes on to discuss duties to inanimate objects. These also allude, indirectly, to our duties towards men. The human impulse to destroy things that can still be used is very immoral. No man ought to damage the beauty of nature; even though he cannot use it, other people may yet be able to do so, and though he has no need to observe such a duty in regard to the thing itself, he does in regard to others. Thus all duties relating to animals, other beings and things have an indirect reference to our duties towards mankind.

All Animals are Equal...

Peter Singer

ANIMAL LIBERATION may sound more like a parody of other liberation movements than a serious objective. The idea of "The Rights of Animals" actually was once used to parody the case for women's rights. When Mary Wollstonecraft, a forerunner of today's feminists, published her *Vindication of the Rights of Woman* in 1792, her views were widely regarded as absurd, and before long an anonymous publication appeared entitled *A Vindication of the Rights of Brutes.* The author of this satirical work (now known to have been Thomas Taylor, a distinguished Cambridge philosopher) tried to refute Mary Wollstonecraft's arguments by showing that they could be carried one stage further. If the argument for equality was sound when applied to women, why should it not be applied to dogs, cats, and horses? The reasoning seemed to hold for these "brutes" too; yet to hold that brutes had rights was manifestly absurd. Therefore the reasoning by which this conclusion had been reached must be unsound, and if unsound when applied to brutes, it must also be unsound when applied to women, since the very same arguments had been used in each case.

In order to explain the basis of the case for the equality of animals, it will be helpful to start with an examination of the case for the equality of women. Let us assume that we wish to defend the case for women's rights against the attack by Thomas Taylor. How should we reply?

One way in which we might reply is by saying that the case for equality between men and women cannot validly be extended to nonhuman animals. Women have a right to vote, for instance, because they are just as capable of making rational decisions about the future as men are; dogs, on the other hand, are incapable of understanding the significance of voting, so they cannot have the right to vote. There are many other obvious ways in which men and women resemble each other closely, while humans and animals differ greatly. So, it might be said, men and women are similar beings and should have similar rights, while humans and nonhumans are different and should not have equal rights.

The reasoning behind this reply to Taylor's analogy is correct up to a point, but it does not go far enough. There are obviously important differences between humans and other animals, and these differences must give rise to some differences in the rights that each have. Recognizing this evident fact, however, is no barrier to the case for extending the basic principle of equality to nonhuman animals. The differences that exist between men and women are equally undeniable, and the supporters of women's liberation are aware that these differences may give rise to different rights. Many feminists hold that women have the right to an abortion on request. It does not follow that since these same feminists are campaigning for equality between men and women, they must support the right of men to have abortions too. Since a man cannot have an abortion, it is meaningless to talk of his right to have one. Since dogs can't vote, it is meaningless to talk of their right to vote. There is no reason why either women's liberation or animal liberation should get involved in such nonsense. The extension of the basic principle of equality from one group to another does not imply that we must treat both groups in exactly the same way or grant exactly the same rights to both groups. Whether we should do so will depend on the nature of the members of the two groups. The basic principle of equality does not require equal or identical *treatment*; it requires equal consideration. Equal consideration for different beings may lead to different treatment and different rights.

So there is a different way of replying to Taylor's attempt to parody the case for women's rights, a way that does not deny the obvious differences between human beings and nonhumans but goes more deeply into the question of equality and concludes by finding nothing absurd in the idea that the basic principle of equality applies to so-called brutes. At this point such a conclusion may appear odd; but if we examine more deeply the basis on which our opposition to discrimination on grounds of race or sex ultimately rests, we will see that we would be on shaky ground if we were to demand equality for blacks, women, and other groups of oppressed humans while denying equal consideration to nonhumans. To make this clear we need to see, first, exactly why racism and sexism are wrong. When we say that all human beings, whatever their race, creed, or sex, are equal, what is it that we are asserting? Those who wish to defend hierarchical, inegalitarian societies have often pointed out that by whatever test we choose it simply is not true that all humans are equal. Like it or not we must face the fact that humans come in different shapes and sizes; they come with different moral capacities, different intellectual abilities, different amounts of benevolent feeling and sensitivity to the needs of others, different abilities to communicate effectively, and different capacities to experience pleasure and pain. In short, if the demand for equality were based on the actual equality of all human beings, we would have to stop demanding equality.

Still, one might cling to the view that the demand for equality among human beings is based on the actual equality of the different races and sexes. Although, it may be said, humans differ as individuals, there are no differences between the races and sexes as such. From the mere fact that a person is black or a woman we cannot infer anything about that person's intellectual or moral capacities. This, it may be said, is why racism and sexism are wrong. The white racist claims that whites are superior to blacks, but this is false; although there are differences among individuals, some blacks are superior to some whites in all of the capacities and abilities that could conceivably be relevant. The opponent of sexism would say the same: a person's sex is no guide to his or her abilities, and this is why it is unjustifiable to discriminate on the basis of sex.

The existence of individual variations that cut across the lines of race or sex, however, provides us with no defense at all against a more sophisticated opponent of equality, one who proposes that, say, the interests of all those with IQ scores below 100 be given less consideration than the interests of those with ratings over 100. Perhaps those scoring below the mark would, in this society, be made the slaves of those scoring higher. Would a hierarchical society of this sort really be so much better than one based on race or sex? I think not. But if we tie the moral principle of equality to the factual equality of the different races or sexes, taken as a whole, our opposition to racism and sexism does not provide us with any basis for objecting to this kind of inegalitarianism.

There is a second important reason why we ought not to base our opposition to racism and sexism on any kind of factual equality, even the limited kind that asserts that variations in capacities and abilities are spread evenly among the different races and between the sexes: we can have no absolute guarantee that these capacities and abilities really are distributed evenly, without regard to race or sex, among human beings. So far as actual abilities are concerned there do seem to be certain measurable differences both among races and between sexes. These differences do not, of course, appear in every case; they appear only when averages are taken. More important still, we do not yet know how many of these differences are really due to the different genetic endowments of the different races and sexes, and how many are due to poor schools, poor housing, and other factors that are the result of past and continuing discrimination. Perhaps all of the important differences will eventually prove to be environmental rather than genetic. Anyone opposed to racism and sexism will certainly hope that this will be so, for it will make the task of ending discrimination a lot easier; nevertheless, it would be dangerous to rest the case against racism and sexism on the belief that all significant differences are environmental in origin. The opponent of, say, racism who takes this line will be unable to avoid conceding that if differences in ability did after all prove to have some genetic connection with race, racism would in some way be defensible.

Fortunately there is no need to pin the case for equality on one particular outcome of a scientific investigation. The appropriate response to those who claim to have found evidence of genetically based differences in ability among

the races or between the sexes is not to stick to the belief that the genetic explanation must be wrong, whatever evidence to the contrary may turn up; instead
we should make it quite clear that the claim to equality does not depend on
intelligence, moral capacity, physical strength, or similar matters of fact. Equality
is a moral idea, not an assertion of fact. There is no logically compelling reason
for assuming that a factual difference in ability between two people justifies any
difference in the amount of consideration we give to their needs and interests. *The
principle of the equality of human beings is not a description of an alleged actual
equality among humans: it is a prescription of how we should treat human beings.*

Jeremy Bentham, the founder of the reforming utilitarian school of moral
philosophy, incorporated the essential basis of moral equality into his system of
ethics by means of the formula: "Each to count for one and none for more than
one." In other words, the interests of every being affected by an action are to be
taken into account and given the same weight as the like interests of any other
being. A later utilitarian, Henry Sidgwick, put the point in this way: "The good
of any one individual is of no more importance, from the point of view (if I may
say so) of the Universe, than the good of any other." More recently the leading
figures in contemporary moral philosophy have shown a great deal of agreement
in specifying as a fundamental presupposition of their moral theories some similar
requirement that works to give everyone's interests equal consideration—although
these writers generally cannot agree on how this requirement is best formulated.[1]

It is an implication of this principle of equality that our concern for others
and our readiness to consider their interests ought not to depend on what they
are like or on what abilities they may possess. Precisely what our concern or
consideration requires us to do may vary according to the characteristics of
those affected by what we do: concern for the well-being of children growing
up in America would require that we teach them to read; concern for the
well-being of pigs may require no more than that we leave them with other pigs
in a place where there is adequate food and room to run freely. But the basic
element—the taking into account of the interests of the being, whatever those
interests may be—must, according to the principle of equality, be extended to
all beings, black or white, masculine or feminine, human or nonhuman.

Thomas Jefferson, who was responsible for writing the principle of the
equality of men into the American Declaration of Independence, saw this
point. It led him to oppose slavery even though he was unable to free himself
fully from his slaveholding background. He wrote in a letter to the author of a
book that emphasized the notable intellectual achievements of Negroes in order
to refute the then common view that they had limited intellectual capacities:

> Be assured that no person living wishes more sincerely than I do,
> to see a complete refutation of the doubts I myself have entertained

and expressed on the grade of understanding allotted to them by
nature, and to find that they are on a par with ourselves ... but
whatever be their degree of talent it is no measure of their rights.
Because Sir Isaac Newton was superior to others in understanding,
he was not therefore lord of the property or persons of others.[2]

Similarly, when in the 1850s the call for women's rights was raised in the
United States, a remarkable black feminist named Sojourner Truth made the
same point in more robust terms at a feminist convention:

> They talk about this thing in the head; what do they call it?
> ["Intellect," whispered someone nearby.] That's it. What's that
> got to do with women's rights or Negroes' rights? If my cup won't
> hold but a pint and yours holds a quart, wouldn't you be mean
> not to let me have my little half-measure full?[3]

It is on this basis that the case against racism and the case against sexism must
both ultimately rest; and it is in accordance with this principle that the attitude
that we may call "speciesism," by analogy with racism, must also be condemned.
Speciesism—the word is not an attractive one, but I can think of no better term—is
a prejudice or attitude of bias in favor of the interests of members of one's own
species and against those of members of other species. It should be obvious that
the fundamental objections to racism and sexism made by Thomas Jefferson
and Sojourner Truth apply equally to speciesism. If possessing a higher degree
of intelligence does not entitle one human to use another for his or her own
ends, how can it entitle humans to exploit nonhumans for the same purpose?[4]

Many philosophers and other writers have proposed the principle of equal
consideration of interests, in some form or other, as a basic moral principle;
but not many of them have recognized that this principle applies to members
of other species as well as to our own. Jeremy Bentham was one of the few who
did realize this. In a forward-looking passage written at a time when black
slaves had been freed by the French but in the British dominions were still
being treated in the way we now treat animals, Bentham wrote:

> The day *may* come when the rest of the animal creation may
> acquire those rights which never could have been withholden
> from them but by the hand of tyranny. The French have already
> discovered that the blackness of the skin is no reason why a human
> being should be abandoned without redress to the caprice of a
> tormentor. It may one day come to be recognized that the number
> of the legs, the villosity of the skin, or the termination of the os

sacrum are reasons equally insufficient for abandoning a sensitive being to the same fate. What else is it that should trace the insuperable line? Is it the faculty of reason, or perhaps the faculty of discourse? But a full-grown horse or dog is beyond comparison a more rational, as well as a more conversable animal, than an infant of a day or a week or even a month, old. But suppose they were otherwise, what would it avail? The question is not, Can they *reason?* nor Can they *talk?* but, Can they *suffer?*[5]

In this passage Bentham points to the capacity for suffering as the vital characteristic that gives a being the right to equal consideration. The capacity for suffering—or more strictly, for suffering and/or enjoyment or happiness—is not just another characteristic like the capacity for language or higher mathematics. Bentham is not saying that those who try to mark "the insuperable line" that determines whether the interests of a being should be considered happen to have chosen the wrong characteristic. By saying that we must consider the interests of all beings with the capacity for suffering or enjoyment Bentham does not arbitrarily exclude from consideration any interests at all—as those who draw the line with reference to the possession of reason or language do. The capacity for suffering and enjoyment is *a prerequisite for having interests at all,* a condition that must be satisfied before we can speak of interests in a meaningful way. It would be nonsense to say that it was not in the interests of a stone to be kicked along the road by a schoolboy. A stone does not have interests because it cannot suffer. Nothing that we can do to it could possibly make any difference to its welfare. The capacity for suffering and enjoyment is, however, not only necessary, but also sufficient for us to say that a being has interests—at an absolute minimum, an interest in not suffering. A mouse, for example, does have an interest in not being kicked along the road, because it will suffer if it is.

Although Bentham speaks of "rights" in the passage I have quoted, the argument is really about equality rather than about rights. Indeed, in a different passage, Bentham famously described "natural rights" as "nonsense" and "natural and imprescriptable rights" as "nonsense upon stilts." He talked of moral rights as a shorthand way of referring to protections that people and animals morally ought to have; but the real weight of the moral argument does not rest on the assertion of the existence of the right, for this in turn has to be justified on the basis of the possibilities for suffering and happiness. In this way we can argue for equality for animals without getting embroiled in philosophical controversies about the ultimate nature of rights.

In misguided attempts to refute the arguments of this book, some philosophers have gone to much trouble developing arguments to show that animals do not have rights.[6] They have claimed that to have rights a being must be autonomous, or must be a member of a community, or must have the ability to respect the rights of others, or must possess a sense of justice. These claims are irrelevant to the case for animal liberation. The language of rights is a convenient political shorthand. It is even more valuable in the era of thirty-second TV news clips than it was in Bentham's day; but in the argument for a radical change in our attitude to animals, it is in no way necessary.

If a being suffers there can be no moral justification for refusing to take that suffering into consideration. No matter what the nature of the being, the principle of equality requires that its suffering be counted equally with the like suffering—insofar as rough comparisons can be made—of any other being. If a being is not capable of suffering, or of experiencing enjoyment or happiness, there is nothing to be taken into account. So the limit of sentience (using the term as a convenient if not strictly accurate shorthand for the capacity to suffer and/or experience enjoyment) is the only defensible boundary of concern for the interests of others. To mark this boundary by some other characteristic like intelligence or rationality would be to mark it in an arbitrary manner. Why not choose some other characteristic, like skin color?

Racists violate the principle of equality by giving greater weight to the interests of members of their own race when there is a clash between their interests and the interests of those of another race. Sexists violate the principle of equality by favoring the interests of their own sex. Similarly, speciesists allow the interests of their own species to override the greater interests of members of other species. The pattern is identical in each case.

Animals can feel pain. As we saw earlier, there can be no moral justification for regarding the pain (or pleasure) that animals feel as less important than the same amount of pain (or pleasure) felt by humans. But what practical consequences follow from this conclusion? To prevent misunderstanding I shall spell out what I mean a little more fully.

If I give a horse a hard slap across its rump with my open hand, the horse may start, but it presumably feels little pain. Its skin is thick enough to protect it against a mere slap. If I slap a baby in the same way, however, the baby will cry and presumably feel pain, for its skin is more sensitive. So it is worse to slap a baby than a horse, if both slaps are administered with equal force. But there must be some kind of blow—I don't know exactly what it would be, but perhaps a blow with a heavy stick—that would cause the horse as much pain as we cause a baby by slapping it with our hand. That is what I mean by "the same amount of pain," and if we consider it wrong to inflict that much pain on a baby for no good reason, then we must, unless we are speciesists, consider it equally wrong to inflict the same amount of pain on a horse for no good reason.

Other differences between humans and animals cause other complications. Normal adult human beings have mental capacities that will, in certain circumstances, lead them to suffer more than animals would in the same circumstances.

If, for instance, we decided to perform extremely painful or lethal scientific experiments on normal adult humans, kidnapped at random from public parks for this purpose, adults who enjoy strolling in parks would become fearful that they would be kidnapped. The resultant terror would be a form of suffering additional to the pain of the experiment. The same experiments performed on nonhuman animals would cause less suffering, since the animals would not have the anticipatory dread of being kidnapped and experimented upon. This does not mean, of course, that it would be *right* to perform the experiment on animals, but only that there is a reason, which is *not* speciesist, for preferring to use animals rather than normal adult human beings, if the experiment is to be done at all. It should be noted, however, that this same argument gives us a reason for preferring to use human infants—orphans perhaps—or severely retarded human beings for experiments, rather than adults, since infants and retarded humans would also have no idea of what was going to happen to them. So far as this argument is concerned nonhuman animals and infants and retarded humans are in the same category; and if we use this argument to justify experiments on nonhuman animals, we have to ask ourselves whether we are also prepared to allow experiments on human infants and retarded adults; and if we make a distinction between animals and these humans, on what basis can we do it, other than a bare-faced—and morally indefensible—preference for members of our own species?

There are many matters in which the superior mental powers of normal adult humans make a difference: anticipation, more detailed memory, greater knowledge of what is happening, and so on. Yet these differences do not all point to greater suffering on the part of the normal human being. Sometimes animals may suffer more because of their more limited understanding. If, for instance, we are taking prisoners in wartime, we can explain to them that although they must submit to capture, search, and confinement, they will not otherwise be harmed and will be set free at the conclusion of hostilities. If we capture wild animals, however, we cannot explain that we are not threatening their lives. A wild animal cannot distinguish an attempt to overpower and confine from an attempt to kill; the one causes as much terror as the other.

It may be objected that comparisons of the sufferings of different species are impossible to make and that for this reason when the interests of animals and humans clash the principle of equality gives no guidance. It is probably true that comparisons of suffering between members of different species cannot be made precisely, but precision is not essential. Even if we were to prevent the infliction of suffering on animals only when it is quite certain that the interests of humans will not be affected to anything like the extent that animals are affected, we would be forced to make radical changes in our treatment of animals that would involve our diet; the farming methods we use; experimental procedures in many fields of science; our approach to wildlife and to hunting, trapping, and the wearing of furs; and areas of entertainment like circuses, rodeos, and zoos. As a result, a vast amount of suffering would be avoided.

∽

STUDY QUESTIONS FOR READINGS

Kant, Duties to Animals

1. According to Kant, what sort of value do rational beings possess? How should we treat human beings in light of this account of value?
2. According to Kant, what sort of value do nonrational beings possess? How does he characterize such entities as opposed to his characterization of rational beings?
3. Explain Kant's characterization of animal nature mirroring human nature. What implication does this have regarding questions of moral obligation? Do we have moral obligations to animals? Do we have moral obligations regarding the treatment of animals? Explain your answers.
4. Does Kant offer a sufficient account of moral obligations regarding the treatment of animals? Why or why not?

Singer, "All Animals are Equal"

1. What is speciesism? Explain how Singer compares speciesism to racism and sexism. Are these compelling analogies? Explain your answer.
2. What sort of equality does Singer argue for? Is he advocating for equal rights and equal treatment? Explain your answers.
3. How is speciesism evidenced in human practices according to Singer? Do you agree with his account? If so, what should be done about this? Explain your answers.

SUGGESTIONS FOR FURTHER READING OR VIEWING

Regan, Tom. *The Case for Animal Rights*. Berkeley: University of California Press, 2004.

Regan, Tom, and Peter Singer, eds. *Animal Rights and Human Obligations*. Englewood Cliffs, NJ: Prentice-Hall, 1976.

Singer, Peter. *Animal Liberation*. New York: Harper Collins, 2002.

Environmental Ethics

INTRODUCTION TO ENVIRONMENTAL ETHICS

Environmental ethics is one of the newest branches of a centuries-old discipline, only gaining ground as a subset of philosophy during the last part of the twentieth century. The topic of environmental ethics raises a lot of difficult moral questions and is a rich and developing subject of philosophical debate. As is the case with questions of moral obligation and the treatment of animals, much of this debate and discussion centers on determining the basis of moral consideration. Once again the distinction between inherent value, having worth in and of itself, and instrumental value, being valuable as a tool or means to something else, is an important distinction in this discussion. Another important set of concepts to consider in this discussion is whether we ought to develop an environmental ethic that is anthropocentric (human centered), biocentric (life centered), or ecocentric (ecologically centered). Some elements of environmental ethics remain highly theoretical dealing with these sorts of problems while other areas of environmental ethics focus more on practical environmental challenges stemming from concerns about pollution, population and consumption, distribution of resources, food production, climate change, and sustainability. The two selections in this chapter focus more on the theoretical side of environmental ethics; however, it is important to consider how these views would inform and direct our actions and solutions to the practical environmental challenges facing us now and in the future.

READING 4.11

The Land Ethic

Aldo Leopold

∾

WHEN GOD-LIKE Odysseus returned from the wars in Troy, he hanged all on one rope a dozen slave-girls of his household whom he suspected of misbehavior during his absence.

This hanging involved no question of propriety. The girls were property. The disposal of property was then, as now, a matter of expediency, not of right and wrong.

Concepts of right and wrong were not lacking from Odysseus' Greece: witness the fidelity of his wife through the long years before at last his black-prowed galleys clove the winedark seas for home. The ethical structure of that day covered wives, but had not yet been extended to human chattels. During the three thousand years which have since elapsed, ethical criteria have been extended to many fields of conduct, with corresponding shrinkages in those judged by expediency only.

THE ETHICAL SEQUENCE

This extension of ethics, so far studied only by philosophers, is actually a process in ecological evolution. Its sequences may be described in ecological as well as in philosophical terms. An ethic, ecologically, is a limitation on freedom of action in the struggle for existence. An ethic, philosophically, is a differentiation of social from anti-social conduct. These are two definitions of one thing. The thing has its origin in the tendency of interdependent individuals or groups to evolve modes of co-operation. The ecologist calls these symbioses. Politics and economics are advanced symbioses in which the original free-for-all competition has been replaced, in part, by co-operative mechanisms with an ethical content.

The complexity of co-operative mechanisms has increased with population density, and with the efficiency of tools. It was simpler, for example, to define the anti-social uses of sticks and stones in the days of the mastodons than of bullets and billboards in the age of motors.

The first ethics dealt with the relation between individuals; the Mosaic Decalogue is an example. Later accretions dealt with the relation between the individual and society. The Golden Rule tries to integrate the individual to society; democracy to integrate social organization to the individual.

There is as yet no ethic dealing with man's relation to land and to the animals and plants which grow upon it. Land, like Odysseus' slave-girls, is still property. The land-relation is still strictly economic, entailing privileges but not obligations.

The extension of ethics to this third element in human environment is, if I read the evidence correctly, an evolutionary possibility and an ecological necessity. It is the third step in a sequence. The first two have already been taken. Individual thinkers since the days of Ezekiel and Isaiah have asserted that the despoliation of land is not only inexpedient but wrong. Society, however, has not yet affirmed their belief. I regard the present conservation movement as the embryo of such an affirmation.

An ethic may be regarded as a mode of guidance for meeting ecological situations so new or intricate, or involving such deferred reactions, that the path of social expediency is not discernible to the average individual. Animal instincts are modes of guidance for the individual in meeting such situations. Ethics are possibly a kind of community instinct in-the-making.

THE COMMUNITY CONCEPT

All ethics so far evolved rest upon a single premise: that the individual is a member of a community of interdependent parts. His instincts prompt him to compete for his place in that community, but his ethics prompt him also to co-operate (perhaps in order that there may be a place to compete for).

The land ethic simply enlarges the boundaries of the community to include soils, waters, plants, and animals, or collectively: the land.

This sounds simple: do we not already sing our love for and obligation to the land of the free and the home of the brave? Yes, but just what and whom do we love? Certainly not the soil, which we are sending helter-skelter downriver. Certainly not the waters, which we assume have no function except to turn turbines, float barges, and carry off sewage. Certainly not the plants, of which we exterminate whole communities without batting an eye. Certainly not the animals, of which we have already extirpated many of the largest and most beautiful species. A land ethic of course cannot prevent the alteration, management, and use of these 'resources,' but it does affirm their right to continued existence, and, at least in spots, their continued existence in a natural state.

In short, a land ethic changes the role of *Homo sapiens* from conqueror of the land-community to plain member and citizen of it. It implies respect for his fellow-members, and also respect for the community as such.

In human history, we have learned (I hope) that the conqueror role is eventually self-defeating. Why? Because it is implicit in such a role that the conqueror knows, *ex cathedra,* just what makes the community clock tick, and just what and who is valuable, and what and who is worthless, in community life. It always turns out that he knows neither, and this is why his conquests eventually defeat themselves.

In the biotic community, a parallel situation exists. Abraham knew exactly what the land was for: it was to drip milk and honey into Abraham's mouth. At the present moment, the assurance with which we regard this assumption is inverse to the degree of our education.

The ordinary citizen today assumes that science knows what makes the community clock tick; the scientist is equally sure that he does not. He knows that the biotic mechanism is so complex that its workings may never be fully understood.

That man is, in fact, only a member of a biotic team is shown by an ecological interpretation of history. Many historical events, hitherto explained solely in terms of human enterprise, were actually biotic interactions between people and land. The characteristics of the land determined the facts quite as potently as the characteristics of the men who lived on it.

Consider, for example, the settlement of the Mississippi valley. In the years following the Revolution, three groups were contending for its control: the native Indian, the French and English traders, and the American settlers. Historians wonder what would have happened if the English at Detroit had thrown a little more weight into the Indian side of those tipsy scales which decided the outcome of the colonial migration into the cane-lands of Kentucky. It is time now to ponder the fact that the cane-lands, when subjected to the particular mixture of forces represented by the cow, plow, fire, and axe of the pioneer, became bluegrass. What if the plant succession inherent in this dark and bloody ground had, under the impact of these forces, given us some worthless sedge, shrub, or weed? Would Boone and Kenton have held out? Would there have been any overflow into Ohio, Indiana, Illinois, and Missouri? Any Louisiana Purchase? Any transcontinental union of new states? Any Civil War?

Kentucky was one sentence in the drama of history. We are commonly told what the human actors in this drama tried to do, but we are seldom told that their success, or the lack of it, hung in large degree on the reaction of particular soils to the impact of the particular forces exerted by their occupancy. In the case of Kentucky, we do not even know where the bluegrass came from—whether it is a native species, or a stowaway from Europe.

Contrast the cane-lands with what hindsight tells us about the Southwest, where the pioneers were equally brave, resourceful, and persevering. The impact of occupancy here brought no bluegrass, or other plant fitted to withstand the bumps and buffetings of hard use. This region, when grazed by livestock, reverted through a series of more and more worthless grasses, shrubs, and weeds to a condition of unstable equilibrium. Each recession of plant types bred erosion; each increment to erosion bred a further recession of plants. The result today is a progressive and mutual deterioration, not only of plants and soils, but of the animal community subsisting thereon. The early settlers did not expect this: on the ciénegas of New Mexico some even cut ditches to hasten it. So subtle has been its progress that few residents of the region are aware of it. It is quite invisible to the tourist who finds this wrecked landscape colorful and charming (as indeed it is, but it bears scant resemblance to what it was in 1848).

This same landscape was 'developed' once before, but with quite different results. The Pueblo Indians settled the Southwest in pre-Columbian times, but they happened *not* to be equipped with range livestock. Their civilization expired, but not because their land expired.

In India, regions devoid of any sod-forming grass have been settled, apparently without wrecking the land, by the simple expedient of carrying the grass to the cow, rather than vice versa. (Was this the result of some deep wisdom, or was it just good luck? I do not know.)

In short, the plant succession steered the course of history; the pioneer simply demonstrated, for good or ill, what successions inhered in the land. Is history taught in this spirit? It will be, once the concept of land as a community really penetrates our intellectual life.

THE ECOLOGICAL CONSCIENCE

Conservation is a state of harmony between men and land. Despite nearly a century of propaganda, conservation still proceeds at a snail's pace; progress still consists largely of letterhead pieties and convention oratory. On the back forty we still slip two steps backward for each forward stride.

The usual answer to this dilemma is 'more conservation education.' No one will debate this, but is it certain that only the *volume* of education needs stepping up? Is something lacking in the *content* as well?

It is difficult to give a fair summary of its content in brief form, but, as I understand it, the content is substantially this: obey the law, vote right, join some organizations, and practice what conservation is profitable on your own land; the government will do the rest.

Is not this formula too easy to accomplish anything worthwhile? It defines no right or wrong, assigns no obligation, calls for no sacrifice, implies no change in the current philosophy of values. In respect of land-use, it urges only enlightened self-interest. Just how far will such education take us? An example will perhaps yield a partial answer.

By 1930 it had become clear to all except the ecologically blind that southwestern Wisconsin's topsoil was slipping seaward. In 1933 the farmers were told that if they would adopt certain remedial practices for five years, the public would donate CCC labor to install them, plus the necessary machinery and materials. The offer was widely accepted, but the practices were widely forgotten when the five-year contract period was up. The farmers continued only those practices that yielded an immediate and visible economic gain for themselves.

This led to the idea that maybe farmers would learn more quickly if they themselves wrote the rules. Accordingly the Wisconsin Legislature in 1937 passed the Soil Conservation District Law. This said to farmers, in effect: *We, the public, will furnish you free technical service and loan you specialized machinery, if you will write your own rules for land-use. Each county may write its own rules, and these will have the force of law.* Nearly all the counties promptly organized to accept the proffered help, but after a decade of operation, *no county has yet written a single rule.* There has been visible progress in such practices as strip-cropping, pasture renovation, and soil liming, but none in fencing woodlots against grazing, and none in excluding plow and cow from steep slopes. The farmers, in short, have selected those remedial practices which were profitable anyhow, and ignored those which were profitable to the community, but not clearly profitable to themselves.

When one asks why no rules have been written, one is told that the community is not yet ready to support them; education must precede rules. But the education actually in progress makes no mention of obligations to land over and above those dictated by self-interest. The net result is that we have more education but less soil, fewer healthy woods, and as many floods as in 1937.

The puzzling aspect of such situations is that the existence of obligations over and above self-interest is taken for granted in such rural community enterprises as the betterment of roads, schools, churches, and baseball teams. Their existence is not taken for granted, nor as yet seriously discussed, in bettering the behavior of the water that falls on the land, or in the preserving of the beauty or diversity of the farm landscape. Land-use ethics are still governed wholly by economic self-interest, just as social ethics were a century ago.

To sum up: we asked the farmer to do what he conveniently could to save his soil, and he has done just that, and only that. The farmer who clears the woods off a 75 per cent slope, turns his cows into the clearing, and dumps its rainfall, rocks, and soil into the community creek, is still (if otherwise decent) a respected member of society. If he puts lime on his fields and plants his crops on contour, he is still entitled to all the privileges and emoluments of his Soil Conservation District. The District is a beautiful piece of social machinery, but it is coughing along on two cylinders because we have been too timid, and too anxious for quick success, to tell the farmer the true magnitude of his obligations. Obligations have no meaning without conscience, and the problem we face is the extension of the social conscience from people to land.

No important change in ethics was ever accomplished without an internal change in our intellectual emphasis, loyalties, affections, and convictions. The proof that conservation has not yet touched these foundations of conduct lies in the fact that philosophy and religion have not yet heard of it. In our attempt to make conservation easy, we have made it trivial.

SUBSTITUTES FOR A LAND ETHIC

When the logic of history hungers for bread and we hand out a stone, we are at pains to explain how much the stone resembles bread. I now describe some of the stones which serve in lieu of a land ethic.

One basic weakness in a conservation system based wholly on economic motives is that most members of the land community have no economic value. Wildflowers and songbirds are examples. Of the 22,000 higher plants and animals native to Wisconsin, it is doubtful whether more than 5 per cent can be sold, fed, eaten, or otherwise put to economic use. Yet these creatures are members of the biotic community, and if (as I believe) its stability depends on its integrity, they are entitled to continuance.

When one of these non-economic categories is threatened, and if we happen to love it, we invent subterfuges to give it economic importance. At the beginning of the century songbirds were supposed to be disappearing. Ornithologists jumped to the rescue with some distinctly shaky evidence to the effect that insects would eat us up if birds failed to control them. The evidence had to be economic in order to be valid.

It is painful to read these circumlocutions today. We have no land ethic yet, but we have at least drawn nearer the point of admitting that birds should continue as a matter of biotic right, regardless of the presence or absence of economic advantage to us.

A parallel situation exists in respect of predatory mammals, raptorial birds, and fish-eating birds. Time was when biologists somewhat overworked the

evidence that these creatures preserve the health of game by
killing weaklings, or that they
control rodents for the farmer, or
that they prey only on 'worthless'
species. Here again, the evidence
had to be economic in order to
be valid. It is only in recent years
that we hear the more honest
argument that predators are
members of the community, and
that no special interest has the

right to exterminate them for the sake of a benefit, real or fancied, to itself. Unfortunately this enlightened view is still in the talk stage. In the field the extermination
of predators goes merrily on: witness the impending erasure of the timber wolf
by fiat of Congress, the Conservation Bureaus, and many state legislatures.

Some species of trees have been 'read out of the party' by economics-minded
foresters because they grow too slowly, or have too low a sale value to pay as
timber crops: white cedar, tamarack, cypress, beech, and hemlock are examples.
In Europe, where forestry is ecologically more advanced, the noncommercial tree
species are recognized as members of the native forest community, to be preserved
as such, within reason. Moreover some (like beech) have been found to have a
valuable function in building up soil fertility. The interdependence of the forest
and its constituent tree species, ground flora, and fauna is taken for granted .

Lack of economic value is sometimes a character not only of species or
groups, but of entire biotic communities: marshes, bogs, dunes, and 'deserts' are
examples. Our formula in such cases is to relegate their conservation to government as refuges, monuments, or parks. The difficulty is that these communities
are usually interspersed with more valuable private lands; the government
cannot possibly own or control such scattered parcels. The net effect is that
we have relegated some of them to ultimate extinction over large areas. If the
private owner were ecologically minded, he would be proud to be the custodian
of a reasonable proportion of such areas, which add diversity and beauty to his
farm and to his community.

In some instances, the assumed lack of profit in these 'waste' areas has proved
to be wrong, but only after most of them had been done away with. The present
scramble to reflood muskrat marshes is a case in point.

There is a clear tendency in American conservation to relegate to government all necessary jobs that private landowners fail to perform. Government
ownership, operation, subsidy, or regulation is now widely prevalent in forestry,
range management, soil and watershed management, park and wilderness

conservation, fisheries management, and migratory bird management, with more to come. Most of this growth in governmental conservation is proper and logical, some of it is inevitable. That I imply no disapproval of it is implicit in the fact that I have spent most of my life working for it. Nevertheless the question arises: What is the ultimate magnitude of the enterprise? Will the tax base carry its eventual ramifications? At what point will governmental conservation, like the mastodon, become handicapped by its own dimensions? The answer, if there is any, seems to be in a land ethic, or some other force which assigns more obligation to the private landowner.

Industrial landowners and users, especially lumbermen and stockmen, are inclined to wail long and loudly about the extension of government ownership and regulation to land, but (with notable exceptions) they show little disposition to develop the only visible alternative: the voluntary practice of conservation on their own lands.

When the private landowner is asked to perform some unprofitable act for the good of the community, he today assents only with outstretched palm. If the act costs him cash this is fair and proper, but when it costs only forethought, open-mindedness, or time, the issue is at least debatable. The overwhelming growth of land-use subsidies in recent years must be ascribed, in large part, to the government's own agencies for conservation education: the land bureaus, the agricultural colleges, and the extension services. As far as I can detect, no ethical obligation toward land is taught in these institutions.

To sum up: a system of conservation based solely on economic self-interest is hopelessly lopsided. It tends to ignore, and thus eventually to eliminate, many elements in the land community that lack commercial value, but that are (as far as we know) essential to its healthy functioning. It assumes, falsely, I think, that the economic parts of the biotic clock will function without the uneconomic parts. It tends to relegate to government many functions eventually too large, too complex, or too widely dispersed to be performed by government.

An ethical obligation on the part of the private owner is the only visible remedy for these situations.

THE LAND PYRAMID

An ethic to supplement and guide the economic relation to land presupposes the existence of some mental image of land as a biotic mechanism. We can be ethical only in relation to something we can see, feel, understand, love, or otherwise have faith in.

The image commonly employed in conservation education is 'the balance of nature.' For reasons too lengthy to detail here, this figure of speech fails to describe accurately what little we know about the land mechanism. A much truer image is the one employed in ecology: the biotic pyramid. I shall first sketch the pyramid as a symbol of land, and later develop some of its implications in terms of land-use.

Plants absorb energy from the sun. This energy flows through a circuit called the biota, which may be represented by a pyramid consisting of layers. The bottom layer is the soil. A plant layer rests on the soil, an insect layer on the plants, a bird and rodent layer on the insects, and so on up through various animal groups to the apex layer, which consists of the larger carnivores.

The species of a layer are alike not in where they came from, or in what they look like, but rather in what they eat. Each successive layer depends on those below it for food and often for other services, and each in turn furnishes food and services to those above. Proceeding upward, each successive layer decreases in numerical abundance. Thus, for every carnivore there are hundreds of his prey, thousands of their prey, millions of insects, uncountable plants. The pyramidal form of the system reflects this numerical progression from apex to base. Man shares an intermediate layer with the bears, raccoons, and squirrels which eat both meat and vegetables.

The lines of dependency for food and other services are called food chains. Thus soil-oak-deer-Indian is a chain that has now been largely converted to soil-corn-cow-farmer. Each species, including ourselves, is a link in many chains. The deer eats a hundred plants other than oak, and the cow a hundred plants other than corn. Both, then, are links in a hundred chains. The pyramid is a tangle of chains so complex as to seem disorderly, yet the stability of the system proves it to be a highly organized structure. Its functioning depends on the co-operation and competition of its diverse parts.

In the beginning, the pyramid of life was low and squat; the food chains short and simple. Evolution has added layer after layer, link after link. Man is one of thousands of accretions to the height and complexity of the pyramid. Science has given us many doubts, but it has given us at least one certainty: the trend of evolution is to elaborate and diversify the biota.

Land, then, is not merely soil; it is a fountain of energy flowing through a circuit of soils, plants, and animals. Food chains are the living channels which conduct energy upward; death and decay return it to the soil. The circuit is not closed; some energy is dissipated in decay, some is added by absorption from the air, some is stored in soils, peats, and long-lived forests; but it is a sustained circuit, like a slowly augmented revolving fund of life. There is always a net loss by downhill wash, but this is normally small and offset by the decay of rocks. It is deposited in the ocean and, in the course of geological time, raised to form new lands and new pyramids.

The velocity and character of the upward flow of energy depend on the complex structure of the plant and animal community, much as the upward flow of sap in a tree depends on its complex cellular organization. Without this complexity, normal circulation would presumably not occur. Structure means the characteristic numbers, as well as the characteristic kinds and functions, of the component species. This interdependence between the complex structure of the land and its smooth functioning as an energy unit is one of its basic attributes.

When a change occurs in one part of the circuit, many other parts must adjust themselves to it. Change does not necessarily obstruct or divert the flow of energy; evolution is a long series of self-induced changes, the net result of which has been to elaborate the flow mechanism and to lengthen the circuit. Evolutionary changes, however, are usually slow and local. Man's invention of tools has enabled him to make changes of unprecedented violence, rapidity, and scope.

One change is in the composition of floras and faunas. The larger predators are lopped off the apex of the pyramid; food chains, for the first time in history, become shorter rather than longer. Domesticated species from other lands are substituted for wild ones, and wild ones are moved to new habitats. In this world-wide pooling of faunas and floras, some species get out of bounds as pests and diseases, others are extinguished. Such effects are seldom intended or foreseen; they represent unpredicted and often untraceable readjustments in the structure. Agricultural science is largely a race between the emergence of new pests and the emergence of new techniques for their control.

Another change touches the flow of energy through plants and animals and its return to the soil. Fertility is the ability of soil to receive, store, and release energy. Agriculture, by overdrafts on the soil, or by too radical a substitution of domestic for native species in the superstructure, may derange the channels of flow or deplete storage. Soils depleted of their storage, or of the organic matter which anchors it, wash away faster than they form. This is erosion.

Waters, like soil, are part of the energy circuit. Industry, by polluting waters or obstructing them with dams, may exclude the plants and animals necessary to keep energy in circulation.

Transportation brings about another basic change: the plants or animals grown in one region are now consumed and returned to the soil in another. Transportation taps the energy stored in rocks, and in the air, and uses it elsewhere; thus we fertilize the garden with nitrogen gleaned by the guano birds from the fishes of seas on the other side of the Equator. Thus the formerly localized and self-contained circuits are pooled on a world-wide scale.

The process of altering the pyramid for human occupation releases stored energy, and this often gives rise, during the pioneering period, to a deceptive exuberance of plant and animal life, both wild and tame. These releases of biotic capital tend to becloud or postpone the penalties of violence.

* * *

This thumbnail sketch of land as an energy circuit conveys three basic ideas:

(1) That land is not merely soil.
(2) That the native plants and animals kept the energy circuit open; others may or may not.
(3) That man-made changes are of a different order than evolutionary changes, and have effects more comprehensive than is intended or foreseen.

These ideas, collectively, raise two basic issues: Can the land adjust itself to the new order? Can the desired alterations be accomplished with less violence?

Biotas seem to differ in their capacity to sustain violent conversion. Western Europe, for example, carries a far different pyramid than Caesar found there. Some large animals are lost; swampy forests have become meadows or plow-land; many new plants and animals are introduced, some of which escape as pests; the remaining natives are greatly changed in distribution and abundance. Yet the soil is still there and, with the help of imported nutrients, still fertile; the waters flow normally; the new structure seems to function and to persist. There is no visible stoppage or derangement of the circuit.

Western Europe, then, has a resistant biota. Its inner processes are tough, elastic, resistant to strain. No matter how violent the alterations, the pyramid, so far, has developed some new *modus vivendi* which preserves its habitability for man, and for most of the other natives.

Japan seems to present another instance of radical conversion without disorganization.

Most other civilized regions, and some as yet barely touched by civiliza-tion, display various stages of disorganization, varying from initial symptoms to advanced wastage. In Asia Minor and North Africa diagnosis is confused by climatic changes, which may have been either the cause or the effect of advanced wastage. In the United States the degree of disorganization varies locally; it is worst in the Southwest, the Ozarks, and parts of the South, and least in New England and the Northwest. Better land-uses may still arrest it in the less advanced regions. In parts of Mexico, South America, South Africa, and Australia a violent and accelerating wastage is in progress, but I cannot assess the prospects.

This almost world-wide display of disorganization in the land seems to be similar to disease in an animal, except that it never culminates in complete disorganization or death. The land recovers, but at some reduced level of complexity, and with a reduced carrying capacity for people, plants, and animals. Many biotas currently regarded as 'lands of opportunity' are in fact already subsisting on exploitative agriculture, i.e. they have already exceeded their sustained carrying capacity. Most of South America is overpopulated in this sense.

In arid regions we attempt to offset the process of wastage by reclamation, but it is only too evident that the prospective longevity of reclamation projects is often short. In our own West, the best of them may not last a century.

The combined evidence of history and ecology seems to support one general deduction: the less violent the man-made changes, the greater the probability of successful readjustment in the pyramid. Violence, in turn, varies with human population density; a dense population requires a more violent conversion. In this respect, North America has a better chance for permanence than Europe, if she can contrive to limit her density.

This deduction runs counter to our current philosophy, which assumes that because a small increase in density enriched human life, that an indefinite increase will enrich it indefinitely. Ecology knows of no density relationship that holds for indefinitely wide limits. All gains from density are subject to a law of diminishing returns.

Whatever may be the equation for men and land, it is improbable that we as yet know all its terms. Recent discoveries in mineral and vitamin nutrition reveal unsuspected dependencies in the up-circuit: incredibly minute quantities of certain substances determine the value of soils to plants, of plants to animals. What of the down-circuit? What of the vanishing species, the preservation of which we now regard as an esthetic luxury? They helped build the soil; in what unsuspected ways may they be essential to its maintenance? Professor Weaver proposes that we use prairie flowers to reflocculate the wasting soils of the dust bowl; who knows for what purpose cranes and condors, otters and grizzlies may some day be used?

LAND HEALTH AND THE A–B CLEAVAGE

A land ethic, then, reflects the existence of an ecological conscience, and this in turn reflects a conviction of individual responsibility for the health of the land. Health is the capacity of the land for self-renewal. Conservation is our effort to understand and preserve this capacity.

Conservationists are notorious for their dissensions. Superficially these seem to add up to mere confusion, but a more careful scrutiny reveals a single plane of cleavage common to many specialized fields. In each field one group (A) regards the land as soil, and its function as commodity-production; another group (B) regards the land as a biota, and its function as something broader. How much broader is admittedly in a state of doubt and confusion.

In my own field, forestry, Group A is quite content to grow trees like cabbages, with cellulose as the basic forest commodity. It feels no inhibition against violence; its ideology is agronomic. Group B, on the other hand, sees forestry as fundamentally different from agronomy because it employs natural species, and manages a natural environment rather than creating an artificial one. Group B prefers natural reproduction on principle. It worries on biotic as well as economic grounds about the loss of species like chestnut, and the threatened loss of the white pines. It worries about a whole series of secondary forest functions: wildlife, recreation, watersheds, wilderness areas. To my mind, Group B feels the stirrings of an ecological conscience.

In the wildlife field, a parallel cleavage exists. For Group A the basic commodities are sport and meat; the yardsticks of production are ciphers of take in pheasants and trout. Artificial propagation is acceptable as a permanent as well as a temporary recourse—if its unit costs permit. Group B, on the other hand, worries about a whole series of biotic side-issues. What is the cost in predators of producing a game crop? Should we have further recourse to exotics? How can management restore the shrinking species, like prairie grouse, already hopeless as shootable game? How can management restore the threatened rarities, like trumpeter swan and whooping crane? Can management principles be extended to wildflowers? Here again it is clear to me that we have the same A-B cleavage as in forestry.

In the larger field of agriculture I am less competent to speak, but there seem to be somewhat parallel cleavages. Scientific agriculture was actively developing before ecology was born, hence a slower penetration of ecological concepts might be expected. Moreover the farmer, by the very nature of his techniques, must modify the biota more radically than the forester or the wildlife manager. Nevertheless, there are many discontents in agriculture which seem to add up to a new vision of 'biotic farming.'

Perhaps the most important of these is the new evidence that poundage or tonnage is no measure of the food-value of farm crops; the products of fertile soil may be qualitatively as well as quantitatively superior. We can bolster poundage from depleted soils by pouring on imported fertility, but we are not necessarily bolstering food-value. The possible ultimate ramifications of this idea are so immense that I must leave their exposition to abler pens.

The discontent that labels itself 'organic farming,' while bearing some of the earmarks of a cult, is nevertheless biotic in its direction, particularly in its insistence on the importance of soil flora and fauna.

The ecological fundamentals of agriculture are just as poorly known to the public as in other fields of land-use. For example, few educated people realize that the marvelous advances in technique made during recent decades are improvements in the pump, rather than the well. Acre for acre, they have barely sufficed to offset the sinking level of fertility.

In all of these cleavages, we see repeated the same basic paradoxes: man the conqueror *versus* man the biotic citizen; science the sharpener of his sword *versus* science the searchlight on his universe; land the slave and servant *versus* land the collective organism. Robinson's injunction to Tristram may well be applied, at this juncture, to *Homo sapiens* as a species in geological time:

> Whether you will or not
> You are a King, Tristram, for you are one
> Of the time-tested few that leave the world,
> When they are gone, not the same place it was.
> Mark what you leave.

THE OUTLOOK

It is inconceivable to me that an ethical relation to land can exist without love, respect, and admiration for land, and a high regard for its value. By value, I of course mean something far broader than mere economic value; I mean value in the philosophical sense.

Perhaps the most serious obstacle impeding the evolution of a land ethic is the fact that our educational and economic system is headed away from, rather than toward, an intense consciousness of land. Your true modern is separated from the land by many middlemen, and by innumerable physical gadgets. He has no vital relation to it; to him it is the space between cities on which crops grow. Turn him loose for a day on the land, and if the spot does not happen to be a golf links or a 'scenic' area, he is bored stiff. If crops could be raised by hydroponics instead of farming, it would suit him very well. Synthetic substitutes for wood, leather, wool, and other natural land products suit him better than the originals. In short, land is something he has 'outgrown.'

Almost equally serious as an obstacle to a land ethic is the attitude of the farmer for whom the land is still an adversary, or a taskmaster that keeps him in slavery. Theoretically, the mechanization of farming ought to cut the farmer's chains, but whether it really does is debatable.

One of the requisites for an ecological comprehension of land is an understanding of ecology, and this is by no means co-extensive with 'education'; in fact, much higher education seems deliberately to avoid ecological concepts. An understanding of ecology does not necessarily originate in courses bearing ecological labels; it is quite as likely to be labeled geography, botany, agronomy, history, or economics. This is as it should be, but whatever the label, ecological training is scarce.

The case for a land ethic would appear hopeless but for the minority which is in obvious revolt against these 'modern' trends.

The 'key-log' which must be moved to release the evolutionary process for an ethic is simply this: quit thinking about decent land-use as solely an economic problem. Examine each question in terms of what is ethically and esthetically right, as well as what is economically expedient. A thing is right when it tends to preserve the integrity, stability, and beauty of the biotic community. It is wrong when it tends otherwise.

It of course goes without saying that economic feasibility limits the tether of what can or cannot be done for land. It always has and it always will. The fallacy the economic determinists have tied around our collective neck, and which we now need to cast off, is the belief that economics determines *all* land-use. This is simply not true. An innumerable host of actions and attitudes, comprising perhaps the bulk of all land relations, is determined by the land-user's tastes and predilections, rather than by his purse. The bulk of all land relations hinges on investments of time, forethought, skill, and faith rather than on investments of cash. As a land-user thinketh, so is he.

I have purposely presented the land ethic as a product of social evolution because nothing so important as an ethic is ever 'written.' Only the most superficial student of history supposes that Moses 'wrote' the Decalogue; it evolved in the minds of a thinking community, and Moses wrote a tentative summary of it for a 'seminar.' I say tentative because evolution never stops.

The evolution of a land ethic is an intellectual as well as emotional process. Conservation is paved with good intentions which prove to be futile, or even dangerous, because they are devoid of critical understanding either of the land, or of economic land-use. I think it is a truism that as the ethical frontier advances from the individual to the community, its intellectual content increases.

The mechanism of operation is the same for any ethic: social approbation for right actions: social disapproval for wrong actions.

By and large, our present problem is one of attitudes and implements. We are remodeling the Alhambra with a steam-shovel, and we are proud of our yardage. We shall hardly relinquish the shovel, which after all has many good points, but we are in need of gentler and more objective criteria for its successful use.

∽

READING 4.12

The Buddhist Attitude Towards Nature

Lily de Silva

Modern man in his search for pleasure and affluence has exploited nature without any moral restraint to such an extent that nature has been rendered almost incapable of sustaining healthy life. Invaluable gifts of nature, such as air and water, have been polluted with severely disastrous consequences. Man is now searching for ways and means of overcoming the pollution problem as his health too is alarmingly threatened. He also feels that it is irresponsible and morally wrong on his part to commit the future generations to a polluted planet. If man is to act with a sense of responsibility to the natural world, to his fellow human beings and to unborn future generations, he has to find an appropriate environmental ethic today to prevent further aggravation of the present pollution problem. Hence his search for wisdom and attitudes in a hitherto neglected area of knowledge, namely, religion.

Buddhism strictly limits itself to the delineation of a way of life designed to eradicate human suffering. The Buddha refused to answer questions which did not directly or indirectly bear on the central problem of human suffering and its ending. Furthermore, environmental pollution is a problem of the modern age, unheard of and unsuspected during the time of the Buddha. Therefore it is difficult to find any specific discourse which deals with the topic we are interested in here. Nevertheless, as Buddhism is a full-fledged philosophy of life reflecting all aspects of experience, it is possible to find enough material in the Pali canon to delineate the Buddhist attitude towards nature.

The word "nature" means everything in the world which is not organized and constructed by man. The Pali equivalents which come closest to "nature" are *loka* and *yathabhuta.* The former is usually translated as "world" while the latter literally means "things as they really are." The words *dhammata* and *niyama* are used in the Pali canon to mean "natural law or way."

Nature as Dynamic

According to Buddhism changeability is one of the perennial principles of nature. Everything changes in nature and nothing remains static. This concept is expressed by the Pali term *anicca*. Everything formed is in a constant process of change *(sabbe sankhara anicca)*.[1] The world is therefore defined as that which disintegrates *(lujjati ti loko)*; the world is so called because it is dynamic and kinetic, it is constantly in a process of undergoing change.[2] In nature there are no static and stable "things"; there are only ever-changing, ever-moving processes. Rain is a good example to illustrate this point. Though we use a noun called "rain" which appears to denote a "thing," rain is nothing but the process of drops of water falling from the skies. Apart from this process, the activity of raining, there is no rain as such which could be expressed by a seemingly static nominal concept. The very elements of solidity *(pathavi)*, liquidity *(apo)*, heat *(tejo)* and mobility *(vayo)*, recognized as the building material of nature, are all ever-changing phenomena. Even the most solid looking mountains and the very earth that supports everything on it are not beyond this inexorable law of change. One sutta explains how the massive king of mountains—Mount Sineru, which is rooted in the great ocean to a depth of 84,000 leagues and which rises above sea level to another great height of 84,000 leagues and which is very classical symbol of stability and steadfastness—also gets destroyed by heat, without leaving even ashes, with the appearance of multiple suns.[3] Thus change is the very essence of nature.

Morality and Nature

The world passes through alternating cycles of evolution and dissolution, each of which endures for a long period of time. Though change is inherent in nature, Buddhism believes that natural processes are affected by the morals of man.

According to the *Aggañña Sutta*,[4] which relates the Buddhist legend regarding the evolution of the world, the appearance of greed in the primordial beings—who at that time were self-luminous, subsisting on joy, and traversing in the skies—caused the gradual loss of their radiance and their ability to subsist on joy and to move about in the sky. The moral degradation had effects on the external environment too. At that time the entire earth was covered over by a very flavorsome fragrant substance similar to butter. When beings started partaking of this substance with more and more greed, on the one hand their subtle bodies became coarser and coarser. On the other hand the flavorsome substance itself started gradually diminishing. With the solidification of bodies differences of form appeared; some were beautiful while others were homely. Thereupon conceit manifested itself in those beings, and the beautiful ones started looking down upon the others. As a result of these moral blemishes the delicious edible earth-substance completely disappeared. In its place there appeared edible mushrooms and later another kind of edible creeper. In the beings who subsisted on them successively sex differentiation became manifest and the former method of spontaneous birth was replaced by sexual reproduction.

Self-growing rice appeared on earth and through laziness to collect each meal man grew accustomed to hoarding food. As a result of this hoarding habit, the growth rate of food could not keep pace with the rate of demand. Thereupon land had to be divided among families. After private ownership of land became the order of the day, those who were of a more greedy disposition started robbing from others' plots of land. When they were detected they denied that they had stolen. Thus through greed vices such as stealing and lying became manifest in society. To curb the wrong doers and punish them a king was elected by the people and thus the original simple society became much more complex and complicated. It is said that this moral degeneration of man had adverse effects on nature. The richness of the earth diminished and self-growing rice disappeared. Man had to till the land and cultivate rice for food. This rice grain was enveloped in chaff; it needed cleaning before consumption.

The point I wish to emphasize by citing this evolutionary legend is that Buddhism believes that though change is a factor inherent in nature, man's moral deterioration accelerates the process of change and brings about changes which are adverse to human well being and happiness.

The *Cakkavattisihanada Sutta* of the Digha Nikaya predicts the future course of events when human morals undergo further degeneration.[5] Gradually man's health will deteriorate so much that life expectancy will diminish until at last the average human life-span is reduced to ten years and marriageable age to five years. At that time all delicacies such as ghee, butter, honey, etc. will have disappeared from the earth; what is considered the poorest coarse food today will become a delicacy of that day. Thus Buddhism maintains that there is a close link between man's morals and the natural resources available to him.

According to a discourse in the Anguttara Nikaya, when profligate lust, wanton greed, and wrong values grip the heart of man and immorality becomes widespread in society, timely rain does not fall. When timely rain does not fall crops get adversely affected with various kinds of pests and plant diseases. Through lack of nourishing food the human mortality rate rises.[6]

Thus several suttas from the Pali canon show that early Buddhism believes there to be a close relationship between human morality and the natural environment. This idea has been systematized in the theory of the five natural laws *(pañca niyamadhamma)* in the later commentaries.[7] According to this theory, in the cosmos there are five natural laws or forces at work, namely *utuniyama* (lit. "season-law"), *bijaniyama* (lit. "seed-law"), *cittaniyama, kammaniyama,* and *dhammaniyama.* They can be translated as physical laws, biological laws, psychological laws, moral laws, and causal laws, respectively. While the first four laws operate within their respective spheres, the last-mentioned law of causality operates *within* each of them as well as among them.

This means that the physical environment of any given area conditions the growth and development of its biological component, i.e. flora and fauna. These in turn influence the thought pattern of the people interacting with them. Modes of thinking determine moral standards. The opposite process of interaction is also possible. The morals of man influence not only the psychological makeup of the people but the biological and physical environment of the area as well. Thus the five laws demonstrate that man and nature are bound together in a reciprocal causal relationship with changes in one necessarily bringing about changes in the other.

The commentary on the *Cakkavattisihanada Sutta* goes on to explain the pattern of mutual interaction further.[8] When mankind is demoralized through greed, famine is the natural outcome; when moral degeneration is due to ignorance, epidemic is the inevitable result; when hatred is the demoralizing force, widespread violence is the ultimate outcome. If and when mankind realizes that large-scale devastation has taken place as a result of his moral degeneration, a change of heart takes place among the few surviving human beings. With gradual moral regeneration conditions improve through a long period of cause and effect and mankind again starts to enjoy gradually increasing prosperity and longer life. The world, including nature and mankind, stands or falls with the type of moral force at work. If immorality grips society, man and nature deteriorate; if morality reigns, the quality of human life and nature improves. Thus greed, hatred, and delusion produce pollution within and without. Generosity, compassion, and wisdom produce purity within and without. This is one reason the Buddha has pronounced that the world is led by the mind, *cittena niyati loko.*[9] Thus man and nature, according to the ideas expressed in early Buddhism, are interdependent.

Human Use of Natural Resources

For survival mankind has to depend on nature for his food, clothing, shelter, medicine, and other requisites.

For optimum benefits man has to understand nature so that he can utilize natural resources and live harmoniously with nature. By understanding the working of nature—for example, the seasonal rainfall pattern, methods of conserving water by irrigation, the soil types, the physical conditions required for growth of various food crops, etc.—man can learn to get better returns from his agricultural pursuits. But this learning has to be accompanied by moral restraint if he is to enjoy the benefits of natural resources for a long time. Man must learn to satisfy his needs and not feed his greeds. The resources of the world are not unlimited whereas man's greed knows neither limit nor satiation. Modern man in his unbridled voracious greed for pleasure and acquisition of wealth has exploited nature to the point of near impoverishment.

Ostentatious consumerism is accepted as the order of the day. One writer says that within forty years Americans alone have consumed natural resources to the quantity of what all mankind has consumed for the last 4000 years.[10] The vast non-replenishable resources of fossil fuels which took millions of years to form have been consumed within a couple of centuries to the point of near exhaustion. This consumerism has given rise to an energy crisis on the one hand and a pollution problem on the other. Man's unrestrained exploitation of nature to gratify his insatiate greed reminds one of the traditional parable of the goose that laid the golden eggs.[11]

Buddhism tirelessly advocates the virtues of non-greed, nonhatred and non-delusion in all human pursuits. Greed breeds sorrow and unhealthy consequences. Contentment *(santutthi)* is a much praised virtue in Buddhism. [12] The man leading a simple life with few wants easily satisfied is upheld and appreciated as an exemplary character.[13] Miserliness[14] and wastefulness[15] are equally deplored in Buddhism as two degenerate extremes. Wealth has only instrumental value; it is to be utilized for the satisfaction of man's needs. Hoarding is a senseless anti-social habit comparable to the attitude of the dog in the manger. The vast hoarding of wealth in some countries and the methodical destruction of large quantities of agricultural produce to keep the market prices from falling, while half the world is dying of hunger and starvation, is really a sad paradox of the present affluent age.

Buddhism commends frugality as a virtue in its own right. Once Ananda explained to King Udena the thrifty economic use of robes by the monks in the following order. When new robes are received the old robes are used as coverlets, the old coverlets as mattress covers, the old mattress covers as rugs, the old rugs as dusters, and the old tattered dusters are kneaded with clay and used to repair cracked floors and walls.[16] Thus nothing is wasted. Those who waste are derided as "wood-apple eaters."[17] A man shakes the branch of a wood-apple tree and all the fruits, ripe as well as unripe, fall. The man would collect only what he wants and walk away leaving the rest to rot. Such a wasteful attitude is certainly deplored in Buddhism as not only anti-social but criminal. The excessive exploitation of nature as is done today would certainly be condemned by Buddhism in the strongest possible terms.

Buddhism advocates a gentle non-aggressive attitude towards nature. According to the *Sigalovada Sutta* a householder should accumulate wealth as a bee collects pollen from a flower.[18] The bee harms neither the fragrance nor the beauty of the flower, but gathers pollen to turn it into sweet honey. Similarly, man is expected to make legitimate use of nature so that he can rise above nature and realize his innate spiritual potential.

Attitude towards Animal and Plant Life

The well-known Five Precepts *(pañca sila)* form the minimum code of ethics that every lay Buddhist is expected to adhere to. Its first precept involves abstention from injury to life. It is explained as the casting aside of all forms of weapons, being conscientious about depriving a living being of life. In its positive sense it means the cultivation of compassion and sympathy for all living things.[19] The Buddhist layman is expected to abstain from trading in meat too.[20]

The Buddhist monk has to abide by an even stricter code of ethics than the layman. He has to abstain from practices which would involve even unintentional injury to living creatures. For instance, the Buddha promulgated the rule against going on a journey during the rainy season because of possible injury to worms and insects that come to the surface in wet weather.[21] The same concern for non-violence prevents a monk from digging the ground.[22] Once a monk who was a potter prior to ordination built for himself a clay hut and set it on fire to give it a fine finish. The Buddha strongly objected to this as so many living creatures would have been burnt in the process. The hut was broken down on the Buddha's instructions to prevent it from creating a bad precedent for later generations.[23] The scrupulous nonviolent attitude towards even the smallest living creatures prevents the monks from drinking unstrained water. [24] It is no doubt a sound hygienic habit, but what is noteworthy is the reason which prompts the practice, namely sympathy for living creatures.

Buddhism also prescribes the practice of *metta,* "loving-kindness" towards all creatures of all quarters without restriction. The *Karaniyametta Sutta* enjoins the cultivation of loving-kindness towards all creatures timid and steady, long and short, big and small, minute and great, visible and invisible, near and far, born and awaiting birth.[25] All quarters are to be suffused with this loving attitude. Just as one's own life is precious to oneself, so is the life of the other precious to himself. Therefore a reverential attitude must be cultivated towards all forms of life.

The *Nandivisala Jataka* illustrates how kindness should be shown to animals domesticated for human service.[26] Even a wild animal can be tamed with kind words. Parileyya was a wild elephant who attended on the Buddha when he spent time in the forest away from the monks.[27] The infuriated elephant Nalagiri was tamed by the Buddha with no other miraculous power than the power of loving-kindness.[28] Man and beast can live and let live without fear of one another if only man cultivates sympathy and regards all life with compassion.

The understanding of kamma and rebirth, too, prepares the Buddhist to adopt a sympathetic attitude towards animals. According to this belief it is possible for human beings to be reborn in subhuman states among animals. The *Kukkuravatika Sutta* can be cited as a canonical reference which substantiates this view.[29] The Jatakas provide ample testimony to this view from commentarial literature. It is possible that our own close relatives have been reborn as animals. Therefore it is only right that we should treat animals with kindness and sympathy. The Buddhist notion of merit also engenders a gentle non-violent attitude towards living creatures. It is said that if one throws dish-washing water into a pool where there are insects and living creatures, intending that they feed on the tiny particles of food thus washed away, one accumulates merit even by such trivial generosity.[30] According to the *Macchuddana Jataka* the Bodhisatta threw his leftover food into a river in order to feed the fish, and by the power of that merit he was saved from an impending disaster.[31] Thus kindness to animals, be they big or small, is a source of merit—merit needed for human beings to improve their lot in the cycle of rebirths and to approach the final goal of Nibbana.

Buddhism expresses a gentle non-violent attitude towards the vegetable kingdom as well. It is said that one should not even break the branch of a tree that has given one shelter.[32] Plants are so helpful to us in providing us with all necessities of life that we are expected not to adopt a callous attitude towards them. The more strict monastic rules prevent the monks from injuring plant life.[33]

Prior to the rise of Buddhism people regarded natural phenomena such as mountains, forests, groves, and trees with a sense of awe and reverence. [34] They considered them as the abode of powerful non-human beings who could assist human beings at times of need. Though Buddhism gave man a far superior Triple Refuge *(tisarana)* in the Buddha, Dhamma, and Sangha, these places continued to enjoy public patronage at a popular level, as the acceptance of terrestrial non-human beings such as *devatas*[35] and *yakkhas*[36] did not violate the belief system of Buddhism. Therefore among the Buddhists there is a reverential attitude towards specially long-standing gigantic trees. They are *vanaspati* in Pali, meaning "lords of the forests."[37] As huge trees such as the ironwood, the sala, and the fig are also recognized as the Bodhi trees of former Buddhas, the deferential attitude towards trees is further strengthened.[38] It is well known that the *ficus religiosa* is held as an object of great veneration in the Buddhist world today as the tree under which the Buddha attained Enlightenment.

The construction of parks and pleasure groves for public use is considered a great meritorious deed.[39] Sakka the lord of gods is said to have reached his status as a result of social services such as the construction of parks, pleasure groves, ponds, wells, and roads.[40]

The open air, natural habitats and forest trees have a special fascination for the Eastern mind as symbols of spiritual freedom. The home life is regarded as a fetter *(sambadha)* that keeps man in bondage and misery. Renunciation is like the open air *(abbhokasa)*, nature unhampered by man's activity.[41] The chief events in the life of the Buddha too took place in the open air. He was born in a park at the foot of a tree in Kapilavatthu; he attained Enlightenment in the open air at the foot of the Bodhi tree in Bodhgaya; he inaugurated his missionary activity in the open air in the sala grove of the Malas in Pava. The Buddha's constant advice to his disciples also was to resort to natural habitats such as forest groves and glades. There, undisturbed by human activity, they could zealously engage themselves in meditation.[42]

Attitude towards Pollution

Environmental pollution has assumed such vast proportions today that man has been forced to recognize the presence of an ecological crisis. He can no longer turn a blind eye to the situation as he is already threatened with new pollution-related diseases. Pollution to this extent was unheard of during the time of the Buddha. But there is sufficient evidence in the Pali canon to give us insight into the Buddhist attitude towards the pollution problem. Several Vinaya rules prohibit monks from polluting green grass and water with saliva, urine, and feces.[43] These were the common agents of pollution known during the Buddha's day and rules were promulgated against causing such pollution. Cleanliness was highly commended by the Buddhists both in the person and in the environment. They were much concerned about keeping water clean, be it in the river, pond, or well. These sources of water were for public use and each individual had to use them with proper public-spirited caution so that others after him could use them with the same degree of cleanliness. Rules regarding the cleanliness of green grass were prompted by ethical and aesthetic considerations. Moreover, grass is food for most animals and it is man's duty to refrain from polluting it by his activities.

Noise is today recognized as a serious personal and environmental pollutant troubling everyone to some extent. It causes deafness, stress, and irritation, breeds resentment, saps energy, and inevitably lowers efficiency.[44] The Buddha's attitude to noise is very clear from the Pali canon. He was critical of noise and did not hesitate to voice his stern disapproval whenever occasion arose.[45] Once he ordered a group of monks to leave the monastery for noisy behavior.[46] He enjoyed solitude and silence immensely and spoke in praise of silence as it is most appropriate for mental culture. Noise is described as a thorn to one engaged in the first step of meditation,[47] but thereafter noise ceases to be a disturbance as the meditator passes beyond the possibility of being disturbed by sound.

The Buddha and his disciples reveled in the silent solitary natural habitats unencumbered by human activity. Even in the choice of monasteries the presence of undisturbed silence was an important quality they looked for.[48] Silence invigorates those who are pure at heart and raises their efficiency for meditation. But silence overawes those who are impure with ignoble impulses of greed, hatred, and delusion. The *Bhayabherava Sutta* beautifully illustrates how even the rustle of leaves by a falling twig in the forest sends tremors through an impure heart.[49] This may perhaps account for the present craze for constant auditory stimulation with transistors and cassettes. The moral impurity caused by greed, avarice, acquisitive instincts, and aggression has rendered man so timid that he cannot bear silence which lays bare the reality of self-awareness. He therefore prefers to drown himself in loud music. Unlike classical music, which tends to soothe nerves and induce relaxation, rock music excites the senses. Constant exposure to it actually renders man incapable of relaxation and sound sleep without tranquilizers.

As to the question of the Buddhist attitude to music, it is recorded that the Buddha has spoken quite appreciatively of music on one occasion.[50] When Pañcasikha the divine musician sang a song while playing the lute in front of the Buddha, the Buddha praised his musical ability saying that the instrumental music blended well with his song. Again, the remark of an Arahant that the joy of seeing the real nature of things is far more exquisite than orchestral music[51] shows the recognition that music affords a certain amount of pleasure even if it is inferior to higher kinds of pleasure. But it is stressed that the ear is a powerful sensory channel through which man gets addicted to sense pleasures. Therefore, to dissuade monks from getting addicted to melodious sounds, the monastic discipline describes music as a lament.[52]

The psychological training of the monks is so advanced that they are expected to cultivate a taste not only for external silence, but for inner silence of speech, desire, and thought as well. The sub-vocal speech, the inner chatter that goes on constantly within us in our waking life is expected to be silenced through meditation.[53] The sage who succeeded in quelling this inner speech completely is described as a *muni,* a silent one. [54] His inner silence is maintained even when he speaks!

It is not inappropriate to pay passing notice to the Buddhist attitude to speech as well. Moderation in speech is considered a virtue, as one can avoid four unwholesome vocal activities thereby, namely, falsehood, slander, harsh speech, and frivolous talk. In its positive aspect moderation in speech paves the path to self-awareness. Buddhism commends speaking at the appropriate time, speaking the truth, speaking gently, speaking what is useful, and speaking out of loving-kindness; the opposite modes of speech are condemned.[55] The Buddha's general advice to the monks regarding speech is to be engaged in discussing the Dhamma or maintain noble silence.[56] The silence that reigned in vast congregations of monks during the Buddha's day was indeed a surprise even to the kings of the time.[57] Silence is serene and noble as it is conducive to the spiritual progress of those who are pure at heart.

Even Buddhist laymen were reputed to have appreciated quietude and silence. Pañcangika Thapati can be cited as a conspicuous example.[58] Once Mahanama the Sakyan complained to the Buddha that he is disturbed by the hustle of the busy city of Kapilavatthu. He explained that he experiences calm serenity when he visits the Buddha in the quiet salubrious surroundings of the monastery and his peace of mind gets disturbed when he goes to the city.[59] Though noise to the extent of being a pollutant causing health hazards was not known during the Buddha's day, we have adduced enough material from the Pali canon to illustrate the Buddha's attitude to the problem. Quietude is much appreciated as spiritually rewarding, while noise condemned as a personal and social nuisance.

Nature as Beautiful

The Buddha and his disciples regarded natural beauty as a source of great joy and aesthetic satisfaction. The saints who purged themselves of sensuous worldly pleasures responded to natural beauty with a detached sense of appreciation. The average poet looks at nature and derives inspiration mostly by the sentiments it evokes in his own heart; he becomes emotionally involved with nature. For instance, he may compare the sun's rays passing over the mountain tops to the blush on a sensitive face, he may see a tear in a dew drop, the lips of his beloved in a rose petal, etc. But the appreciation of the saint is quite different. He appreciates nature's beauty for its own sake and derives joy unsullied by sensuous associations and self-projected ideas. The simple spontaneous appreciation of nature's exquisite beauty is expressed by the Elder Mahakassapa in the following words:[60]

> Those upland glades delightful to the soul,
> Where the Kaveri spreads its wildering wreaths,
> Where sound the trumpet-calls of elephants:
> Those are the hills where my soul delights.
>
> Those rocky heights with hue of dark blue clouds
> Where lies embossed many a shining lake
> Of crystal-clear, cool waters, and whose slopes
> The 'herds of Indra' cover and bedeck:
> Those are the hills wherein my soul delights.
>
> Fair uplands rain-refreshed, and resonant
> With crested creatures' cries antiphonal,
> Lone heights where silent Rishis oft resort:
> Those are the hills wherein my soul delights.

Again the poem of Kaludayi, inviting the Buddha to visit Kapilavatthu, contains a beautiful description of spring:[61]

> Now crimson glow the trees, dear Lord, and cast
> Their ancient foliage in quest of fruit,
> Like crests of flame they shine irradiant
> And rich in hope, great Hero, is the hour.
>
> Verdure and blossom-time in every tree
> Wherever we look delightful to the eye,
> And every quarter breathing fragrant airs,
> While petals falling, yearning comes fruit:
> It is time, O Hero, that we set out hence.

The long poem of Talaputa is a fascinating soliloquy.[62] His religious aspirations are beautifully blended with a profound knowledge of the teachings of the Buddha against the background of a sylvan resort. Many more poems could be cited for saintly appreciation of nature, but it is not necessary to burden the essay with any more quotations. Suffice it to know that the saints, too, were sensitive to the beauties and harmony of nature and that their appreciation is colored by spontaneity, simplicity, and a non-sensuous spirituality.

Conclusion

In the modern age man has become alienated from himself and nature. When science started opening new vistas of knowledge revealing the secrets of nature one by one, man gradually lost faith in theistic religions. Consequently, he developed scanty respect for moral and spiritual values as well. With the advent of the Industrial Revolution and the acquisition of wealth by mechanical exploitation of natural resources, man has become more and more materialistic in his attitudes and values. The pursuit of sense pleasures and the acquisition of possessions have become ends in themselves. Man's sense faculties dominate him to an unrelenting degree and man has become a slave to his insatiable passions. (Incidentally the sense faculties are in Pali *indriyas* or lords, because they control man unless he is sufficiently vigilant to become their master.) Thus man has become alienated from himself as he abandoned himself to the influence of sense pleasures and acquisitive instincts.

In his greed for more and more possessions he has adopted a violent and aggressive attitude towards nature. Forgetting that he is a part and parcel of nature, he exploits it with unrestrained greed, thus alienating himself from nature as well. The net result is the deterioration of man's physical and mental health on the one hand, and the rapid depletion of non-replenishable natural resources and environmental pollution on the other. These results remind us of the Buddhist teachings in the suttas discussed above, which maintain that the moral degeneration of man leads to the decrease of his life-span and the depletion of natural resources.

Moral degeneration is a double-edged weapon, it exercises adverse effects on man's psycho-physical well being as well as on nature. Already killer diseases such as heart ailments, cancer, diabetes, AIDS, etc., are claiming victims on an unprecedented scale. In the final analysis these can all be traced to man's moral deterioration. Depletion of vast resources of fossil fuels and forests has given rise to a very severe energy crisis. It cannot be emphasized too strongly that such rapid depletion of non-renewable natural resources within less than two centuries, an infinitesimal fraction of the millions of years taken for them to form, is due to modern man's inordinate greed and acquisitiveness. A number of simple ancient societies had advanced technological skills, as is evident by their vast sophisticated irrigation schemes designed to feed the fundamental needs of several millions. Yet they survived in some countries over 2000 years without such problems as environmental pollution and depletion of natural resources. This was no doubt due to to validity of the philosophy which inspired and formed the basis of these civilizations.

In the present ecocrisis man has to look for radical solutions. "Pollution cannot be dealt with in the long term on a remedial or cosmetic basis or by tackling symptoms: all measures should deal with basic causes. These are determined largely by our values, priorities, and choices."[63] Man must reappraise his value system. The materialism that has guided his lifestyle has landed him in very severe problems. Buddhism teaches that mind is the forerunner of all things, mind is supreme. If one acts with an impure mind, i.e. a mind sullied with greed, hatred and delusion, suffering is the inevitable result. If one acts with a pure mind, i.e. with the opposite qualities of contentment, compassion, and wisdom, happiness will follow like a shadow.[64] Man has to understand that pollution in the environment has been caused because there has been psychological pollution within himself. If he wants a clean environment he has to adopt a lifestyle that springs from a moral and spiritual dimension.

Buddhism offers man a simple moderate lifestyle eschewing both extremes of self-deprivation and self-indulgence. Satisfaction of basic human necessities, reduction of wants to the minimum, frugality, and contentment are its important characteristics. Each man has to order his life on normal principles, exercise self-control in the enjoyment of the senses, discharge his duties in his various social roles, and conduct himself with wisdom and self-awareness in all activities. It is only when each man adopts a simple moderate lifestyle that mankind as a whole will stop polluting the environment. This seems to be the only way of overcoming the present ecocrisis and the problem of alienation. With such a lifestyle, man will adopt a non-exploitative, non-aggressive, gentle attitude towards nature. He can then live in harmony with nature, utilizing its resources for the satisfaction of his basic needs. The Buddhist admonition is to utilize nature in the same way as a bee collects pollen from the flower, neither polluting its beauty nor depleting its fragrance. Just as the bee manufactures honey out of pollen, so man should be able to find happiness and fulfillment in life without harming the natural world in which he lives.

Notes

All Pali texts referred to are editions of the Pali Text Society, London. Abbreviations used are as follows:

A   Anguttara Nikaya
D   Digha Nikaya
Dh   Dhammapada
Dh.A   Dhammapada Atthakatha

J   Jataka
M   Majjhima Nikaya
S   Samyutta Nikaya
Sn   Sutta-nipata
Thag   Theragatha
Vin   Vinaya Pitaka

1. A. IV, 100.

2. S. IV, 52.

3. A. IV, 100.

4. D. III, 80.

5. D. III, 71.

6. A. I, 160.

7. Atthasalini, 854.

8. Dh.A III, 854.

9. S. I, 39.

10. Quoted in Vance Packard, *The Waste Makers* (London 1961), p. 195.

11. Cp. J. I, 475 f.

12. Dh. v. 204.

13. A. IV, 2, 220, 229.

14. Dh.A. I, 20 ff.

15. Dh.A. III, 129 ff.

16. Vin. II, 291.

17. A. IV, 283.

18. D. III, 188.

19. D. I, 4.

20. A. III, 208.

21. Vin. I, 137.

22. Vin. IV, 125.

23. Vin. III, 42.

24. Vin. IV, 125.

25. Sn. vv. 143-152.

26. J. I, 191.

27. Dh.A. I, 58 ff.

28. Vin. II, 194 f.

29. M. I, 387 f.

30. A. I, 161.

31. J. II, 423.

32. Petavatthu II, 9, 3.

33. Vin. IV, 34.

34. Dh. v. 188.

35. S. I, 1-45.

36. S. I, 206-215.

37. S. IV, 302; Dh.A. I, 3

38. D. II, 4

39. S. I, 33.

40. J. I, 199 f.

41. D. I, 63.

42. M. I, 118; S. IV, 373

43. Vin. IV, 205-206.

44. Robert Arvill, *Man and Environment* (Penguin Books, 1978), p. 118.

45. A. III, 31.

46. M. I, 457.

47. A. V, 135.

48. A. V, 15.

49. M. I, 16-24.

50. D. II, 267.

51. Thag. v. 398.

52. A. I, 261.

53. S. IV, 217, 293.

54. Sn. vv. 207-221; A. I, 273.

55. M. I, 126.

56. M. I, 161.

57. M. II, 122; D. I, 50.

58. M. II, 23.

59. S. V, 369.

60. Thag. vv. 1062-1071.

61. Thag. vv. 527-529.

62. Thag. vv. 1091-1145.

63. Arvill, *Man and Environment,* p. 170.

64. Dh. vv. 1, 2

Leopold, The Land Ethic

1. What criticism does Leopold offer against traditional approaches to ethics? How does he envision the extension of ethics and the reimagined role of human beings?
2. What criticism does Leopold offer against common approaches to conservation? What substitutes are offered in place of a land ethic? What alternative does Leopold offer?
3. Explain Leopold's characterization of the land pyramid and the biotic community. What sort of value does he ascribe to all parts of the biotic community? What standard of morality does he propose as the basis for his land ethic? What do you think of Leopold's account? How would his theory change the way we live? Does it give us enough direction in resolving environmental issues such as pollution, consumption, climate change, etcetera.? Explain your answers.

De Silva, "The Buddhist Attitude Towards Nature"

1. Explain De Silva's claim that nature is dynamic and how this ties into her account of the relation between morality and nature.
2. What recommendation would Buddhism offer regarding human use of natural resources? What attitudes does Buddhism project toward animal and plant life, pollution and nature? According to Buddhist thought, how do, or ought, our attitudes influence our actions?
3. How do the values and recommendations of a Buddhist attitude toward nature fit with other accounts of ethics we have examined? Which do you find most compelling? Explain your answers.

SUGGESTIONS FOR FURTHER READING OR VIEWING

Brennan, Andrew, and Yeuk-Sze Lo. "Environmental Ethics." In *The Stanford Encyclopedia of Philosophy Stanford, edited by Edward N. Zalta. Stanford University,* Winter 2016 edition. https://plato.stanford.edu/archives/win2016/entries/ethics-environmental/.

Callicott, J. Baird. "The Conceptual Foundations of the Land Ethic." In *Companion to a Sand County Almanac,* edited by J. Baird Callicott. Madison: University of Wisconsin Press, 1987.

Naess, Arne. "The Shallow and the Deep, Long-Range Ecological Movement." *Inquiry 16* (Spring 1973).

Taylor, Paul. "Biocentric Egalitarianism." *Environmental Ethics* 3 (Fall 1981).

Moral Obligations to Others in Need

CHAPTER OUTLINE

1. Introduction to Moral Obligations to Others in Need
2. Peter Singer, "The Singer Solution to World Poverty"
3. Garrett Hardin, Lifeboat Ethics
4. Onora O'Neill, Kantianism and World Hunger
5. Study Guide Questions for Readings
6. Suggestions for Further Reading or Viewing

INTRODUCTION TO MORAL OBLIGATIONS TO OTHERS IN NEED

Questions about how we ought to act toward other people struggling to meet basic needs have been addressed by different religious traditions and philosophers over many centuries. While most people in contemporary society believe that charitable action is a good thing and worthy of praise, it is often considered supererogatory, nice but not required. In other words, charity or helping others in need is frequently considered to be different than duty. However, if we consider some of the most influential religious traditions in Western society, we see such actions are thought to be required. In fact, charity is one of the five pillars of Islam and *tzedakah,* which translates as justice, is an important requirement of Judaism. Similarly, Aristotle's virtue of generosity seems to deem charitable action a moral necessity and both Immanuel Kant and John Stuart Mill write about benevolence being an imperfect moral duty albeit for different reasons. In this chapter, we look at whether we have moral duties of benevolence in the context of global hunger and food insecurity. Peter Singer argues that there is a disconnect between what most people believe to be the right thing to do and the way they live, advocating for people to live up to the standards they articulate through action. Garrett Hardin offers a lifeboat analogy to raise questions about a duty of benevolence, and Onora O'Neill develops an account of our duty of benevolence based in the Kantian tradition.

READING 4.13

The Singer Solution to World Poverty

Peter Singer

IN THE BRAZILIAN FILM "Central Station," Dora is a retired schoolteacher who makes ends meet by sitting at the station writing letters for illiterate people. Suddenly she has an opportunity to pocket $1,000. All she has to do is persuade a homeless 9-year-old boy to follow her to an address she has been given. (She is told he will be adopted by wealthy foreigners.) She delivers the boy, gets the money, spends some of it on a television set, and settles down to enjoy her new acquisition. Her neighbor spoils the fun, however, by telling her that the boy was too old to be adopted—he will be killed and his organs sold for transplantation. Perhaps Dora knew this all along, but after her neighbor's plain speaking, she spends a troubled night. In the morning Dora resolves to take the boy back.

Suppose Dora had told her neighbor that it is a tough world, other people have nice new TVs too, and if selling the kid is the only way she can get one, well, he was only a street kid. She would then have become, in the eyes of the audience, a monster. She redeems herself only by being prepared to bear considerable risks to save the boy.

At the end of the movie, in cinemas in the affluent nations of the world, people who would have been quick to condemn Dora if she had not rescued the boy go home to places far more comfortable than her apartment. In fact, the average family in the United States spends almost one-third of its income on things that are no more necessary to them than Dora's new TV was to her. Going out to nice restaurants, buying new clothes because the old ones are no longer stylish, vacationing at beach resorts—so much of our income is spent on things not essential to the preservation of our lives and health. Donated to one of a number of charitable agencies, that money could mean the difference between life and death for children in need.

All of which raises a question: In the end, what is the ethical distinction between a Brazilian who sells a homeless child to organ peddlers and an American who already has a TV and upgrades to a better one—knowing that the money could be donated to an organization that would use it to save the lives of kids in need?

Of course, there are several differences between the two situations that could support different moral judgments about them. For one thing, to be able to consign a child to death when he is standing right in front of you takes a chilling kind of heartlessness; it is much easier to ignore an appeal for money to help children you will never meet. Yet for a utilitarian philosopher like myself—that is, one who judges whether acts are right or wrong by their consequences—if the upshot of the American's failure to donate the money is that one more kid dies on the streets of a Brazilian city, then it is, in some sense, just as bad as selling the kid to the organ peddlers. But one doesn't need to embrace my utilitarian ethic to see that, at the very least, there is a troubling incongruity in being so quick to condemn Dora for taking the child to the organ peddlers while, at the same time, not regarding the American consumer's behavior as raising a serious moral issue.

IN HIS 1996 BOOK, *Living High and Letting Die,* the New York University philosopher Peter Unger presented an ingenious series of imaginary examples designed to probe our intuitions about whether it is wrong to live well without giving substantial amounts of money to help people who are hungry, malnourished, or dying from easily treatable illnesses like diarrhea. Here's my paraphrase of one of these examples:

Bob is close to retirement. He has invested most of his savings in a very rare and valuable old car, a Bugatti, which he has not been able to insure. The Bugatti is his pride and joy. In addition to the pleasure he gets from driving and caring for his car, Bob knows that its rising market value means that he will always be able to sell it and live comfortably after retirement. One day when Bob is out for a drive, he parks the Bugatti near the end of a railway siding and goes for a walk up the track. As he does so, he sees that a runaway train, with no one aboard, is running down the railway track. Looking farther down the track, he sees the small figure of a child very likely to be killed by the runaway train. He can't stop the train and the child is too far away to warn of the danger, but he can throw a switch that will divert the train down the siding where his Bugatti is parked. Then nobody will be killed—but the train will destroy his Bugatti. Thinking of his joy in owning the car and the financial security it represents, Bob decides not to throw the switch. The child is killed. For many years to come, Bob enjoys owning his Bugatti and the financial security it represents.

Bob's conduct, most of us will immediately respond, was gravely wrong. Unger agrees. But then he reminds us that we, too, have opportunities to save the lives of children. We can give to organizations like Unicef or Oxfam America. How much would we have to give one of these organizations to have a high probability of saving the life of a child threatened by easily preventable diseases? (I do not believe that children are more worth saving than adults, but since no one can argue that children have brought their poverty on themselves, focusing on them simplifies the issues.) Unger called up some experts and used the information they provided to offer some plausible estimates that include the cost of raising money, administrative expenses, and the cost of delivering aid where it is most needed. By his calculation, $200 in donations would help transform a sickly 2-year-old into a healthy 6-year-old—offering safe passage through childhood's most dangerous years. To show how practical philosophical argument can be, Unger even tells his readers that they can easily donate funds by using their credit card and calling one of these toll-free numbers: (800) 367-5437 for Unicef; (800) 693-2687 for Oxfam America.

Now you, too, have the information you need to save a child's life. How should you judge yourself if you don't do it? Think again about Bob and his Bugatti. Unlike Dora, Bob did not have to look into the eyes of the child he was sacrificing for his own material comfort. The child was a complete stranger to him and too far away to relate to in an intimate, personal way. Unlike Dora, too, he did not mislead the child or initiate the chain of events imperiling him. In all these respects, Bob's situation resembles that of people able but unwilling to donate to overseas aid and differs from Dora's situation.

If you still think that it was very wrong of Bob not to throw the switch that would have diverted the train and saved the child's life, then it is hard to see how you could deny that it is also very wrong not to send money to one of the organizations listed above. Unless, that is, there is some morally important difference between the two situations that I have overlooked.

Is it the practical uncertainties about whether aid will really reach the people who need it? Nobody who knows the world of overseas aid can doubt that such uncertainties exist. But Unger's figure of $200 to save a child's life was reached after he had made conservative assumptions about the proportion of the money donated that will actually reach its target.

One genuine difference between Bob and those who can afford to donate to overseas aid organizations but don't is that only Bob can save the child on the tracks, whereas there are hundreds of millions of people who can give $200 to overseas aid organizations. The problem is that most of them aren't doing it. Does this mean that it is all right for you not to do it?

Suppose that there were more owners of priceless vintage cars—Carol, Dave, Emma, Fred, and so on, down to Ziggy—all in exactly the same situation as Bob, with their own siding and their own switch, all sacrificing the child in order to preserve their own cherished car. Would that make it all right for Bob to do the same? To answer this question affirmatively is to endorse follow-the-crowd ethics—the kind of ethics that led many Germans to look away when the Nazi atrocities were being committed. We do not excuse them because others were behaving no better.

We seem to lack a sound basis for drawing a clear moral line between Bob's situation and that of any reader of this article with $200 to spare who does not donate it to an overseas aid agency. These readers seem to be acting at least as badly as Bob was acting when he chose to let the runaway train hurtle toward the unsuspecting child. In the light of this conclusion, I trust that many readers will reach for the phone and donate that $200. Perhaps you should do it before reading further.

Now THAT YOU have distinguished yourself morally from people who put their vintage cars ahead of a child's life, how about treating yourself and your partner to dinner at your favorite restaurant? But wait. The money you will spend at the restaurant could also help save the lives of children overseas! True, you weren't planning to blow $200 tonight, but if you were to give up dining out just for one month, you would easily save that amount. And what is one month's dining out, compared with a child's life? There's the rub. Since there are a lot of desperately needy children in the world, there will always be another child whose life you could save for another $200. Are you therefore obliged to keep giving until you have nothing left? At what point can you stop?

Hypothetical examples can easily become farcical. Consider Bob. How far past losing the Bugatti should he go? Imagine that Bob had got his foot stuck in the track of the siding, and if he diverted the train, then before it rammed the car it would also amputate his big toe. Should he still throw the switch? What if it would amputate his foot? His entire leg?

As absurd as the Bugatti scenario gets when pushed to extremes, the point it raises is a serious one: only when the sacrifices become very significant indeed would most people be prepared to say that Bob does nothing wrong when he decides not to throw the switch. Of course, most people could be wrong; we can't decide moral issues by taking opinion polls. But consider for yourself the level of sacrifice that you would demand of Bob, and then think about how much money you would have to give away in order to make a sacrifice that is roughly equal to that. It's almost certainly much, much more than $200. For most middle-class Americans, it could easily be more like $200,000.

ISN'T IT COUNTERPRODUCTIVE to ask people to do so much? Don't we run the risk that many will shrug their shoulders and say that morality, so conceived, is fine for saints but not for them? I accept that we are unlikely to see, in the near or even medium-term future, a world in which it is normal for wealthy Americans to give the bulk of their wealth to strangers. When it comes to praising or blaming people for what they do, we tend to use a standard that is relative to some conception of normal behavior. Comfortably off Americans who give, say, 10 percent of their income to overseas aid organizations are so far ahead of most of their equally comfortable fellow citizens that I wouldn't go out of my way to chastise them for not doing more. Nevertheless, they should be doing much more, and they are in no position to criticize Bob for failing to make the much greater sacrifice of his Bugatti.

At this point various objections may crop up. Someone may say: "If every citizen living in the affluent nations contributed his or her share, I wouldn't have to make such a drastic sacrifice, because long before such levels were reached, the resources would have been there to save the lives of all those children dying from lack of food or medical care. So why should I give more than my fair share?" Another, related, objection is that the government ought to increase its overseas aid allocations, since that would spread the burden more equitably across all taxpayers.

Yet the question of how much we ought to give is a matter to be decided in the real world—and that, sadly, is a world in which we know that most people do not, and in the immediate future will not, give substantial amounts to overseas aid agencies. We know, too, that at least in the next year, the United States government is not going to meet even the very modest target, recommended by the United Nations, of 0.7 percent of gross national product; at the moment it lags far below that, at 0.09 percent, not even half of Japan's 0.22 percent or a tenth of Denmark's 0.97 percent. Thus, we know that the money we can give beyond that theoretical "fair share" is still going to save lives that would otherwise be lost. While the idea that no one need do more than his or her fair share is a powerful one, should it prevail if we know that others are not doing their fair share and that children will die preventable deaths unless we do more than our fair share? That would be taking fairness too far.

Thus, this ground for limiting how much we ought to give also fails. In the world as it is now, I can see no escape from the conclusion that each one of us with wealth surplus to his or her essential needs should be giving most of it to help people suffering from poverty so dire as to be life-threatening. That's right: I'm saying that you shouldn't buy that new car, take that cruise, redecorate the house, or get that pricey new suit. After all, a $1,000 suit could save five children's lives.

So how does my philosophy break down in dollars and cents? An American household with an income of $50,000 spends around $30,000 annually on necessities, according to the Conference Board, a nonprofit economic research organization. Therefore, for a household bringing in $50,000 a year, donations to help the world's poor should be as close as possible to $20,000. The $30,000 required for necessities holds for higher incomes as well. So a household making $100,000 could write a yearly check for $70,000. Again, the formula is simple: whatever money you're spending on luxuries, not necessities, should be given away.

Now, evolutionary psychologists tell us that human nature just isn't sufficiently altruistic to make it plausible that many people will sacrifice so much for strangers. On the facts of human nature, they might be right, but they would be wrong to draw a moral conclusion from those facts. If it is the case that we ought to do things that, predictably, most of us won't do, then let's face that fact head-on. Then, if we value the life of a child more than going to fancy restaurants, the next time we dine out we will know that we could have done something better with our money. If that makes living a morally decent life extremely arduous, well, then that is the way things are. If we don't do it, then we should at least know that we are failing to live a morally decent life—not because it is good to wallow in guilt but because knowing where we should be going is the first step toward heading in that direction.

When Bob first grasped the dilemma that faced him as he stood by that railway switch, he must have thought how extraordinarily unlucky he was to be placed in a situation in which he must choose between the life of an innocent child and the sacrifice of most of his savings. But he was not unlucky at all. We are all in that situation.

∽

Lifeboat Ethics

Garrett Hardin

∽

The Case Against Helping the Poor

ENVIRONMENTALISTS USE THE METAPHOR of the earth as a "spaceship" in trying to persuade countries, industries and people to stop wasting and polluting our natural resources. Since we all share life on this planet, they argue, no single person or institution has the right to destroy, waste, or use more than a fair share of its resources.

But does everyone on earth have an equal right to an equal share of its resources? The spaceship metaphor can be dangerous when used by misguided idealists to justify suicidal policies for sharing our resources through uncontrolled immigration and foreign aid. In their enthusiastic but unrealistic generosity, they confuse the ethics of a spaceship with those of a lifeboat.

A true spaceship would have to be under the control of a captain, since no ship could possibly survive if its course were determined by committee. Spaceship Earth certainly has no captain; the United Nations is merely a toothless tiger, with little power to enforce any policy upon its bickering members.

If we divide the world crudely into rich nations and poor nations, two thirds of them are desperately poor, and only one third comparatively rich, with the United States the wealthiest of all. Metaphorically each rich nation can be seen as a lifeboat full of comparatively rich people. In the ocean outside each lifeboat swim the poor of the world, who would like to get in, or at least to share some of the wealth. What should the lifeboat passengers do?

First, we must recognize the limited capacity of any lifeboat. For example, a nation's land has a limited capacity to support a population and as the current energy crisis has shown us, in some ways we have already exceeded the carrying capacity of our land.

Adrift in a Moral Sea. So here we sit, say 50 people in our lifeboat. To be generous, let us assume it has room for 10 more, making a total capacity of 60. Suppose the 50 of us in the lifeboat see 100 others swimming in the water outside, begging for admission to our boat or for handouts. We have several options: we may be tempted to try to live by the Christian ideal of being "our brother's keeper," or by the Marxist ideal of "to each according to his needs." Since the needs of all in the water are the same, and since they can all be seen as "our brothers," we could take them all into our boat, making a total of 150 in a boat designed for 60. The boat swamps, everyone drowns. Complete justice, complete catastrophe.

Since the boat has an unused excess capacity of 10 more passengers, we could admit just 10 more to it. But which 10 do we let in? How do we choose? Do we pick the best 10, the neediest 10, "first come, first served"? And what do we say to the 90 we exclude? If we do let an extra 10 into our lifeboat, we will have lost our "safety factor," an engineering principle of critical importance. For example, if we don't leave room for excess capacity as a safety factor in our country's agriculture, a new plant disease or a bad change in the weather could have disastrous consequences.

Suppose we decide to preserve our small safety factor and admit no more to the lifeboat. Our survival is then possible, although we shall have to be constantly on guard against boarding parties.

While this last solution clearly offers the only means of our survival, it is morally abhorrent to many people. Some say they feel guilty about their good luck. My reply is simple; "Get out and yield your place to others." This may solve the problem of the guilt-ridden person's conscience, but it does not change the ethics of the lifeboat. The needy person to whom the guilt-ridden person yields his place will not himself feel guilty about his good luck. If he did, he would not climb aboard. The net result of conscience-stricken people giving up their unjustly held seats is the elimination of that sort of conscience from the lifeboat.

This is the basic metaphor within which we must work out our solutions. Let us now enrich the image, step by step, with substantive additions from the real world, a world that must solve real and pressing problems of overpopulation and hunger.

The harsh ethics of the lifeboat become even harsher when we consider the reproductive differences between the rich nations and the poor nations. The people inside the lifeboats are doubling in numbers every 87 years; those swimming around outside are doubling, on the average, every 35 years, more than twice as fast as the rich. And since the world's resources are dwindling, the difference in prosperity between the rich and the poor can only increase.

As of 1973. the U.S. had a population of 210 million people, who were increasing by 0.8 percent per year. Outside our lifeboat, let us imagine another 210 million people, (say the combined populations of Colombia, Ecuador, Venezuela, Morocco, Pakistan, Thailand and the Philippines) who are increasing at a rate of 3.3 percent per year. Put differently, the doubling time for this aggregate population is 21 years, compared to 87 years for the U.S.

Multiplying the Rich and the Poor. Now suppose the U.S. agreed to pool its resources with those seven countries, with everyone receiving an equal share. Initially the ratio of Americans to non-Americans in this model would be one-to-one. But consider what the ratio would be after 87 years, by which time the Americans would have doubled to a population of 420 million By then, doubling every 21 years, the other group would have swollen to 354 billion. Each American would have to share the available resources with more than eight people.

But, one could argue, this discussion assumes that current population trends will continue, and they may not. Quite so. Most likely the rate of population increase will decline much faster in the U.S. than it will in the other countries, and there does not seem to be much we can do about it. In sharing with "each according to his needs," we must recognize that needs are determined by population size, which is determined by the rate of reproduction, which at present is regarded as a sovereign right of every nation, poor or not. This being so, the philanthropic load created by the sharing ethic of the spaceship can only increase.

The Tragedy of the Commons. The fundamental error of spaceship ethics, and the sharing it requires, is that it leads to what I call "the tragedy of the commons." Under a system of private property, the men who own property recognize their responsibility to care for it, for if they don't they will eventually suffer. A farmer, for instance, will allow no more cattle in a pasture than its carrying capacity justifies. If he overloads it, erosion sets in, weeds take over, and he loses the use of the pasture.

If a pasture becomes a commons open to all, the right of each to use it may not be matched by a corresponding responsibility to protect it. Asking everyone to use it with discretion will hardly do, for the considerate herdsman who refrains from overloading the commons suffers more than a selfish one who says his needs are greater. If everyone would restrain himself, all would be well; but it takes only one less than everyone to ruin a system of voluntary restraint. In a crowded world of less than perfect human beings, mutual ruin is inevitable if there are no controls. This is the tragedy of the commons.

One of the major tasks of education today should be the creation of such an acute awareness of the dangers of the commons that people will recognize its many varieties. For example, the air and water have become polluted because they are treated as commons. Further growth in the population or per-capita conversion of natural resources into pollutants will only make the problem worse. The same holds true for the fish of the oceans. Fishing fleets have nearly disappeared in many parts of the world, technological improvements in the art of fishing are hastening the day of complete ruin. Only the replacement of the system of the commons with a responsible system of control will save the land, air, water and oceanic fisheries.

The World Food Bank. In recent years there has been a push to create a new commons called a World Food Bank, an international depository of food reserves to which nations would contribute according to their abilities and from which they would draw according to their needs. This humanitarian proposal has received support from many liberal international groups, and from such prominent citizens as Margaret Mead, U.N. Secretary General Kurt Waldheim, and Senators Edward Kennedy and George McGovern.

A world food bank appeals powerfully to our humanitarian impulses. But before we rush ahead with such a plan, let us recognize where the greatest political push comes from, lest we be disillusioned later. Our experience with the "Food for Peace program," or Public Law 480, gives us the answer. This program moved billions of dollars worth of U.S. surplus grain to food-short, population-long countries during the past two decades. But when P.L. 480 first became law, a headline in the business magazine *Forbes* revealed the real power behind it "Feeding the World's Hungry Millions: How It Will Mean Billions for U.S. Business."

And indeed it did. In the years 1960 to 1970, U.S. taxpayers spent a total of $7.9 billion on the Food for Peace program. Between 1948 and 1970, they also paid an additional $50 billion for other economic-aid programs, some of which went for food and food-producing machinery and technology. Though all U.S. taxpayers were forced to contribute to the cost of P.L. 480, certain special interest groups gained handsomely under the program. Farmers did not have to contribute the grain; the Government, or rather the taxpayers, bought it from them at full market prices. The increased demand raised prices of farm products generally. The manufacturers of farm machinery, fertilizers and pesticides benefited by the farmers' extra efforts to grow more food. Grain elevators profited from storing the surplus until it could be shipped. Railroads made money hauling it to ports, and shipping lines profited from carrying it overseas. The implementation of P.L. 480 required the creation of a vast Government bureaucracy, which then acquired its own vested interest in continuing the program regardless of its merits.

Extracting Dollars. Those who proposed and defended the Food for Peace program in public rarely mentioned its importance to any of these special interests. The public emphasis was always on its humanitarian effects. The combination of silent selfish interests and highly vocal humanitarian apologists made a powerful and successful lobby for extracting money from taxpayers. We can expect the same lobby to push now for the creation of a World Food Bank.

However great the potential benefit to selfish interests, it should not be a decisive argument against a truly humanitarian program. We must ask if such a program would actually do more good than harm, not only momentarily but also in the long run. Those who propose the food bank usually refer to a current "emergency" or "crisis" in terms of world food supply. But what is an emergency? Although they may be infrequent and sudden, everyone knows that emergencies will occur from time to time. A well-run family, company, organization or country prepares for the likelihood of accidents and emergencies. It expects them, it budgets for them, it saves for them.

Learning the Hard Way. What happens if some organizations or countries budget for accidents and others do not? If each country is solely responsible for its own well-being, poorly managed ones will suffer. But they can learn from experience. They may mend their ways, and learn to budget for infrequent but certain emergencies. For example, the weather varies from year to year, and periodic crop failures are certain. A wise and competent government saves out of the production of the good years in anticipation of bad years to come. Joseph taught this policy to Pharaoh in Egypt more than 2,000 years ago. Yet the great majority of the governments in the world today do not follow such a policy. They lack either the wisdom or the competence, or both. Should those nations that do manage to put something aside be forced to come to the rescue each time an emergency occurs among the poor nations?

"But it isn't their fault!" Some kind-hearted liberals argue. "How can we blame the poor people who are caught in an emergency? Why must they suffer for the sins of their governments?" The concept of blame is simply not relevant here. The real question is, what are the operational consequences of establishing a world food bank? If it is open to every country every time a need develops, slovenly rulers will not be motivated to take Joseph's advice. Someone will always come to their aid. Some countries will deposit food in the world food bank, and others will withdraw it. There will be almost no overlap, As a result of such solutions to food shortage emergencies, the poor countries will not learn to mend their ways, and will suffer progressively greater emergencies as their populations grow.

Population Control the Crude Way. On the average, poor countries undergo a 2.5 percent increase in population each year; rich countries, about 0.8 percent. Only rich countries have anything in the way of food reserves set aside, and even they do not have as much as they should. Poor countries have none. If poor countries received no food from the outside, the rate of their population growth would be periodically checked by crop failures and famines. But If they can always draw on a world food bank in time of need, their population can continue to grow unchecked, and so will their "need" for aid. In the short run, a world food bank may diminish that need, but in the long run it actually increases the need without limit.

Without some system of worldwide food sharing, the proportion of people in the rich and poor nations might eventually stabilize. The overpopulated poor countries would decrease in numbers, while the rich countries that had room for more people would increase. But with a well-meaning system of sharing, such as a world food bank, the growth differential between the rich and the poor countries will not only persist, it will increase. Because of the higher rate of population growth in the poor countries of the world, 88 percent of today's children are born poor, and only 12 percent rich. Year by year the ratio becomes worse, as the fast-reproducing poor outnumber the slow-reproducing rich.

A world food bank is thus a commons in disguise. People will have more motivation to draw from it than to add to any common store. The less provident and less able will multiply at the expense of the abler and more provident, bringing eventual ruin upon all who share in the commons. Besides, any system of "sharing" that amounts to foreign aid from the rich nations to the poor nations will carry the taint of charity, which will contribute little to the world peace so devoutly desired by those who support the idea of a world food bank.

As past U.S. foreign-aid programs have amply and depressingly demonstrated, international charity frequently inspires mistrust and antagonism rather than gratitude on the part of the recipient nation [see "What Other Nations Hear When the Eagle Screams," by Kenneth J. and Mary M. Gergen, PT, June].

Chinese Fish and Miracle Rice. The modern approach to foreign aid stresses the export of technology and advice, rather than money and food. As an ancient Chinese proverb goes: "Give a man a fish and he will eat for a day; teach him how to fish and he will eat for the rest of his days." Acting on this advice, the Rockefeller and Ford Foundations have financed a number of programs for improving agriculture in the hungry nations. Known as the "Green Revolution," these programs have led to the development of "miracle rice" and "miracle wheat," new strains that offer bigger harvests and greater resistance to crop damage. Norman Borlaug, the Nobel Prize winning agronomist who, supported by the Rockefeller Foundation, developed "miracle wheat," is one of the most prominent advocates of a world food bank.

Whether or not the Green Revolution can increase food production as much as its champions claim is a debatable but possibly irrelevant point. Those who support this well-intended humanitarian effort should first consider some of the fundamentals of human ecology. Ironically, one man who did was the late Alan Gregg, a vice president of the Rockefeller Foundation. Two decades ago he expressed strong doubts about the wisdom of such attempts to increase food production. He likened the growth and spread of humanity over the surface of the earth to the spread of cancer in the human body, remarking that "cancerous growths demand food; but, as far as I know, they have never been cured by getting it."

Overloading the Environment. Every human born constitutes a draft on all aspects of the environment: food, air, water, forests, beaches, wildlife, scenery and solitude. Food can, perhaps, be significantly increased to meet a growing demand. But what about clean beaches, unspoiled forests, and solitude? If we satisfy a growing population's need for food, we necessarily decrease its per capita supply of the other resources needed by men.

India, for example, now has a population of 600 million, which increases by 15 million each year. This population already puts a huge load on a relatively impoverished environment. The country's forests are now only a small fraction of what they were three centuries ago, and floods and erosion continually destroy the insufficient farmland that remains. Every one of the 15 million new lives added to India's population puts an additional burden on the environment, and increases the economic and social costs of crowding. However humanitarian our intent, every Indian life saved through medical or nutritional assistance from abroad diminishes the quality of life for those who remain, and for subsequent generations. If rich countries make it possible, through foreign aid, for 600 million Indians to swell to 1.2 billion in a mere 28 years, as their current growth rate threatens, will future generations of Indians thank us for hastening the destruction of their environment? Will our good intentions be sufficient excuse for the consequences of our actions?

My final example of a commons in action is one for which the public has the least desire for rational discussion—immigration. Anyone who publicly questions the wisdom of current U.S. immigration policy is promptly charged with bigotry, prejudice, ethnocentrism, chauvinism, isolationism or selfishness. Rather than encounter such accusations, one would rather talk about other matters, leaving immigration policy to wallow in the crosscurrents of special interests that take no account of the good of the whole, or the interests of posterity.

Perhaps we still feel guilty about things we said in the past. Two generations ago the popular press frequently referred to Dagos, Wops, Polacks, Chinks and Krauts, in articles about how America was being "overrun" by foreigners of supposedly inferior genetic stock [see "The Politics of Genetic Engineering: Who Decides Who's [Defective]?" PT, June]. But because the implied inferiority of foreigners was used then as justification for keeping them out, people now assume that restrictive policies could only be based on such misguided notions. There are other grounds.

A Nation of Immigrants. Just consider the numbers involved. Our Government acknowledges a net inflow of 400,000 immigrants a year. While we have no hard data on the extent of illegal entries, educated guesses put the figure at about 600,000 a year. Since the natural increase (excess of births over deaths) of the resident population now runs about 1.7 million per year, the yearly gain from immigration amounts to at least 19 percent of the total annual increase, and may be as much as 37 percent if we include the estimate for illegal immigrants. Considering the growing use of birth-control devices, the potential effect of educational campaigns by such organizations as Planned Parenthood Federation of America and Zero Population Growth, and the influence of inflation and the housing shortage, the fertility rate of American women may decline so much that immigration could account for all the yearly increase in population. Should we not at least ask if that is what we want?

For the sake of those who worry about whether the "quality" of the average immigrant compares favorably with the quality of the average resident, let us assume that immigrants and nativeborn citizens are of exactly equal quality, however one defines that term. We will focus here only on quantity; and since our conclusions will depend on nothing else, all charges of bigotry and chauvinism become irrelevant.

Immigration Vs. Food Supply. World food banks *move food to the people*, hastening the exhaustion of the environment of the poor countries. Unrestricted immigration, on the other hand, *moves people to the food,* thus speeding up the destruction of the environment of the rich countries. We can easily understand why poor people should want to make this latter transfer, but why should rich hosts encourage it?

As in the case of foreign-aid programs, immigration receives support from selfish interests and humanitarian impulses. The primary selfish interest in unimpeded immigration is the desire of employers for cheap labor, particularly in industries and trades that offer degrading work. In the past, one wave of foreigners after another was brought into the U.S. to work at wretched jobs for wretched wages. In recent years the Cubans, Puerto Ricans and Mexicans have had this dubious honor. The interests of the employers of cheap labor mesh well with the guilty silence of the country's liberal intelligentsia White Anglo-Saxon Protestants are particularly reluctant to call for a closing of the doors to immigration for fear of being called bigots.

But not all countries have such reluctant leadership. Most educated Hawaiians, for example, are keenly aware of the limits of their environment, particularly in terms of population growth. There is only so much room on the islands, and the islanders know it. To Hawaiians, immigrants from the other 49 states present as great a threat as those from other nations. At a recent meeting of Hawaiian government officials in Honolulu, I had the ironic delight of hearing a speaker, who like most of his audience was of Japanese ancestry, ask how the country might practically and constitutionally close its doors to further immigration. One member of the audience countered: "How can we shut the doors now? We have many friends and relatives in Japan that we'd like to bring here some day so that they can enjoy Hawaii too." The Japanese-American speaker smiled sympathetically and answered: "Yes, but we have children now, and someday we'll have grandchildren too. We can bring more people here from Japan only by giving away some of the land that we hope to pass on to our grandchildren some day. What right do we have to do that?"

At this point, I can hear U.S. liberals asking: "How can you justify slamming the door once you're inside? You say that immigrants should be kept out. But aren't we all immigrants, or the descendants of immigrants? If we insist on staying, must we not admit all others?" Our craving for intellectual order leads us to seek and prefer symmetrical rules and morals: a single rule for me and everybody else; the same rule yesterday, today and tomorrow. Justice, we feel, should not change with time and place.

We Americans of non-Indian ancestry can look upon ourselves as the descendants of thieves who are guilty morally, if not legally, of stealing this land from its Indian owners. Should we then give back the land to the now living American descendants of those Indians? However morally or logically sound this proposal may be, I, for one, am unwilling to live by it and I know no one else who is. Besides, the logical consequence would be absurd. Suppose that, intoxicated with a sense of pure justice, we should decide to turn our land over to the Indians. Since all our other wealth has also been derived from the land, wouldn't we be morally obliged to give that back to the Indians too?

Pure Justice Vs. Reality. Clearly, the concept of pure justice produces an infinite regression to absurdity. Centuries ago, wise men invented statutes of limitations to justify the rejection of such pure justice, in the interest of preventing continual disorder. The law zealously defends property rights, but only relatively recent property rights. Drawing a line after an arbitrary time has elapsed may be unjust, but the alternatives are worse.

We are all the descendants of thieves, and the world's resources are inequitably distributed. But we must begin the journey to tomorrow from the point where we are today. We cannot remake the past. We cannot safely divide the wealth equitably among all peoples so long as people reproduce at different rates. To do so would guarantee that our grandchildren, and everyone else's grandchildren, would have only a ruined world to inhabit.

To be generous with one's own possessions is quite different from being generous with those of posterity. We should call this point to the attention of those who, from a commendable love of justice and equality, would institute a system of the commons, either in the form of a world food bank, or of unrestricted immigration. We must convince them if we wish to save at least some parts of the world from environmental ruin.

Without a true world government to control reproduction and the use of available resources, the sharing ethic of the spaceship is impossible. For the foreseeable future, our survival demands that we govern our actions by the ethics of a lifeboat, harsh though they may be. Posterity will be satisfied with nothing less.

Kantianism and World Hunger

Onora O'Neil

~

IV. KANTIAN APPROACHES

TO SOME FAMINE PROBLEMS

§22 A Simplified Account of Kant's Ethics

Kant's moral theory has acquired the reputation of being forbiddingly difficult to understand and, once understood, excessively demanding in its requirements. I don't believe that this reputation has been wholly earned, and I am going to try to undermine it. In §§23–26 I shall try to reduce some of the difficulties, and in §§27–30 I shall try to show the implications of a Kantian moral theory for action toward those who do or may suffer famine. Finally, I shall compare Kantian and utilitarian approaches and assess their strengths and weaknesses.

The main method by which I propose to avoid some of the difficulties of Kant's moral theory is by explaining only one part of the theory. This does not seem to me to be an irresponsible approach in this case. One of the things that makes Kant's moral theory hard to understand is that he gives a number of different versions of the principle that he calls the Supreme Principle of Morality, and these different versions don't look at all like one another. They also don't look at all like the utilitarians' Greatest Happiness Principle. But the Kantian principle is supposed to play a similar role in arguments about what to do.

Kant calls his Supreme Principle the *Categorical Imperative;* its various versions also have sonorous names. One is called the Formula of Univeral Law; another is the Formula of the Kingdom of Ends. The one on which I shall concentrate is known as the *Formula of the End in Itself.* To understand why

Kant thinks that these picturesquely named principles are equivalent to one another takes quite a lot of close and detailed analysis of Kant's philosophy. I shall avoid this and concentrate on showing the implications of this version of the Categorical Imperative.

§23 The Formula of The End in Itself
Kant states the Formula of the End in Itself as follows:

> Act in such a way that you always treat humanity, whether in your own person or in the person of any other, never simply as a means but always at the same time as an end[15]

To understand this we need to know what it is to treat a person as a means or as an end. According to Kant, each of our acts reflects one or more *maxims.* The maxim of the act is the principle on which one sees oneself as acting. A maxim expresses a person's policy, or if he or she has no settled policy, the principle underlying the particular intention or decision on which he or she acts. Thus, a person who decides "This year I'll give 10 percent of my income to famine relief" has as a maxim the principle of tithing his or her income for famine relief. In practice, the difference between intentions and maxims is of little importance, for given any intention, we can formulate the corresponding maxim by deleting references to particular times, places, and persons. In what follows I shall take the terms 'maxim' and 'intention' as equivalent.

Whenever we act intentionally, we have at least one maxim and can, if we reflect, state what it is. (There is of course room for self-deception here—"I'm only keeping the wolf from the door" we may claim as we wolf down enough to keep ourselves overweight, or, more to the point, enough to feed someone else who hasn't enough food.)

When we want to work out whether an act we propose to do is right or wrong, according to Kant, we should look at our maxims and not at how much misery or happiness the act is likely to produce, and whether it does better at increasing happiness than other available acts. We just have to check that the act we have in mind will not use anyone as a mere means, and, if possible, that it will treat other persons as ends in themselves.

§24 Using Persons as Mere Means
To use someone as a *mere means* is to involve them in a scheme of action *to which they could not in principle consent.* Kant does not say that there is anything wrong about using someone as a means. Evidently we have to do so in any cooperative scheme of action. If I cash a check I use the teller as a means, without whom I could not lay my hands on the cash; the teller in turn uses me as a means to earn

his or her living. But in this case, each party consents to her or his part in the transaction. Kant would say that though they use one another as means, they do not use one another as *mere* means. Each person assumes that the other has maxims of his or her own and is not just a thing or a prop to be manipulated.

But there are other situations where one person uses another in a way to which the other could not in principle consent. For example, one person may make a promise to another with every intention of breaking it. If the promise is accepted, then the person to whom it was given must be ignorant of what the promisor's intention (maxim) really is. If one knew that the promisor did not intend to do what he or she was promising, one would, after all, not accept or rely on the promise. It would be as though there had been no promise made. Successful false promising depends on deceiving the person to whom the promise is made about what one's real maxim is. And since the person who is deceived doesn't know that real maxim, he or she can't in principle consent to his or her part in the proposed scheme of action. The person who is deceived is, as it were, a prop or a tool—a mere means—in the false promisor's scheme. A person who promises falsely treats the acceptor of the promise as a prop or a thing and not as a person. In Kant's view, it is this that makes false promising wrong.

One standard way of using others as mere means is by deceiving them. By getting someone involved in a business scheme or a criminal activity on false pretenses, or by giving a misleading account of what one is about, or by making a false promise or a fraudulent contract, one involves another in something to which he or she in principle cannot consent, since the scheme requires that he or she doesn't know what is going on. Another standard way of using others as mere means is by coercing them. If a rich or powerful person threatens a debtor with bankruptcy unless he or she joins in some scheme, then the creditor's intention is to coerce; and the debtor, if coerced, cannot consent to his or her part in the creditor's scheme. To make the example more specific: If a moneylender in an Indian village threatens not to renew a vital loan unless he is given the debtor's land, then he uses the debtor as a mere means. He coerces the debtor, who cannot truly consent to this "offer he can't refuse." (Of course the outward form of such transactions may look like ordinary commercial dealings, but we know very well that some offers and demands couched in that form are coercive.)

In Kant's view, acts that are done on maxims that require deception or coercion of others, and so cannot have the consent of those others (for consent precludes both deception and coercion), are wrong. When we act on such maxims, we treat others as mere means, as things rather than as ends in themselves. If we act on such maxims, our acts are not only wrong but unjust: such acts wrong the particular others who are deceived or coerced.

§25 Treating Persons as Ends in Themselves

Duties of justice are, in Kant's view (as in many others'), the most important of our duties. When we fail in these duties, we have used some other or others as mere means. But there are also cases where, though we do not use others as mere means, still we fail to use them as ends in themselves in the fullest possible way. To treat someone as an end in him or herself requires in the first place that one not use him or her as mere means, that one respect each as a rational person with his or her own maxims. But beyond that, one may also seek to foster others' plans and maxims by sharing some of their ends. To act beneficently is to seek others' happiness, therefore to intend to achieve some of the things that those others aim at with their maxims. If I want to make others happy, I will adopt maxims that not merely do not manipulate them but that foster some of their plans and activities. Beneficent acts try to achieve what others want. However, we cannot seek everything that others want; their wants are too numerous and diverse, and, of course, sometimes incompatible. It follows that beneficence has to be selective.

There is then quite a sharp distinction between the requirements of justice and of beneficence in Kantian ethics. Justice requires that we act on *no* maxims that use others as mere means. Beneficence requires that we act on *some* maxims that foster others' ends, though it is a matter for judgment and discretion which of their ends we foster. Some maxims no doubt ought not to be fostered because it would be unjust to do so. Kantians are not committed to working interminably through a list of happiness-producing and misery-reducing acts; but there are some acts whose obligatoriness utilitarians may need to debate as they try to compare total outcomes of different choices, to which Kantians are stringently bound. Kantians will claim that they have done nothing wrong if none of their acts is unjust, and that their duty is complete if in addition their life plans have in the circumstances been reasonably beneficent.

In making sure that they meet all the demands of justice, Kantians do not try to compare all available acts and see which has the best effects. They consider only the proposals for action that occur to them and check that these proposals use no other as mere means. If they do not, the act is permissible; if omitting the act would use another as mere means, the act is obligatory. Kant's theory has less scope than utilitarianism. Kantians do not claim to discover whether acts whose maxims they don't know fully are just. They may be reluctant to judge others' acts or policies that cannot be regarded as the maxim of any person or institution. They cannot rank acts in order of merit. Yet, the theory offers more precision than utilitarianism when data are scarce. One can usually tell whether one's act would use others as mere means, even when its impact on human happiness is thoroughly obscure.

§26 Kantian Deliberations on Famine Problems

The theory I have just sketched may seem to have little to say about famine problems. For it is a theory that forbids us to use others as mere means but does not require us to direct our benevolence first to those who suffer most. A conscientious Kantian, it seems, has only to avoid being unjust to those who suffer famine and can then be beneficent to those nearer home. He or she would not be obliged to help the starving, even if no others were equally distressed.

Kant's moral theory does make less massive demands on moral agents than utilitarian moral theory. On the other hand, it is somewhat clearer just what the more stringent demands are, and they are not negligible. We have here a contrast between a theory that makes massive but often indeterminate demands and a theory that makes fewer but less unambiguous demands and leaves other questions, in particular the allocation of beneficence, unresolved. We have also a contrast between a theory whose scope is comprehensive and one that is applicable only to persons acting intentionally and to those institutions that adopt policies, and so maxims. Kantian ethics is silent about the moral status of unintentional action; utilitarians seek to assess all consequences regardless of the intentions that led to them.

§27 Kantian Duties of Justice in Times of Famine

In famine situations, Kantian moral theory requires unambiguously that we do no injustice. We should not act on any maxim that uses another as mere means, so we should neither deceive nor coerce others. Such a requirement can become quite exacting when the means of life are scarce, when persons can more easily be coerced, and when the advantage of gaining more than what is justly due to one is great. I shall give a list of acts that on Kantian principles it would be unjust to do, but that one might be strongly tempted to do in famine conditions.

I will begin with a list of acts that one might be tempted to do as a member of a famine-stricken population. First, where there is a rationing scheme, one ought not to cheat and seek to get more than one's share—any scheme of cheating will use someone as mere means. Nor may one take advantage of others' desperation to profiteer or divert goods onto the black market or to accumulate a fortune out of others' misfortunes. Transactions that are outwardly sales and purchases can be coercive when one party is desperate. All the forms of corruption that deceive or put pressure on others are also wrong: hoarding unallocated food, diverting relief supplies for private use, corruptly using one's influence to others' disadvantage. Such requirements are far from trivial and frequently violated in hard times. In severe famines, refraining from coercing and deceiving may risk one's own life and require the greatest courage.

Second, justice requires that in famine situations one still try to fulfill one's duties to particular others. For example, even in times of famine, a person has duties to try to provide for dependents. These duties may, tragically, be unfulfillable. If they are, Kantian ethical theory would not judge wrong the acts of a person who had done her or his best. There have no doubt been times in human history where there was nothing to be done except abandon the weak and old or to leave children to fend for themselves as best they might. But providing the supporter of dependents acts on maxims of attempting to meet their claims, he or she uses no others as mere means to his or her own survival and is not unjust. A conscientious attempt to meet the particular obligations one has undertaken may also require of one many further maxims of self-restraint and of endeavor—for example, it may require a conscientious attempt to avoid having (further) children; it may require contributing one's time and effort to programs of economic development. Where there is no other means to fulfill particular obligations, Kantian principles may require a generation of sacrifice. They will not, however, require one to seek to maximize the happiness of later generations but only to establish the modest security and prosperity needed for meeting present obligations.

The obligations of those who live with or near famine are undoubtedly stringent and exacting; for those who live further off it is rather harder to see what a Kantian moral theory demands. Might it not, for example, be permissible to do nothing at all about those suffering famine? Might one not ensure that one does nothing unjust to the victims of famine by adopting no maxims whatsoever that mention them? To do so would, at the least, require one to refrain from certain deceptive and coercive practices frequently employed during the European exploration and economic penetration of the now underdeveloped world and still not unknown. For example, it would be unjust to "purchase" valuable lands and resources from persons who don't understand commercial transactions or exclusive property rights or mineral rights, so do not understand that their acceptance of trinkets destroys their traditional economic pattern and way of life. The old adage "trade follows the flag" reminds us to how great an extent the economic penetration of the less-developed countries involved elements of coercion and deception, so was on Kantian principles unjust (regardless of whether or not the net effect has benefited the citizens of those countries).

Few persons in the developed world today find themselves faced with the possibility of adopting on a grand scale maxims of deceiving or coercing persons living in poverty. But at least some people find that their jobs require them to make decisions about investment and aid policies that enormously affect the lives of those nearest to famine. What does a commitment to Kantian moral theory demand of such persons?

It has become common in writings in ethics and social policy to distinguish between one's *personal responsibilities* and one's *role responsibilities.* So a person may say, "As an individual I sympathize, but in my official capacity I can do nothing"; or we may excuse persons' acts of coercion because they are acting in some particular capacity—e.g., as a soldier or a jailer. On the other hand, this distinction isn't made or accepted by everyone. At the Nuremberg trials of war criminals, the defense "I was only doing my job" was disallowed, at least for those whose command position meant that they had some discretion in what they did. Kantians generally would play down any distinction between a person's own responsibilities and his or her role responsibilities. They would not deny that in any capacity one is accountable for certain things for which as a private person one is not accountable. For example, the treasurer of an organization is accountable to the board and has to present periodic reports and to keep specified records. But if she fails to do one of these things for which she is held accountable she will be held responsible for that failure—it will be imputable to her as an individual. When we take on positions, we *add* to our responsibilities those that the job requires; but we do not lose those that are already required of us. Our social role or job gives us, on Kant's view, no license to use others as mere means; even business executives and aid officials and social revolutionaries will act unjustly, so wrongly, if they deceive or coerce—however benevolent their motives.

If persons are responsible for all their acts, it follows that it would be unjust for aid officials to coerce persons into accepting sterilization, wrong for them to use coercive power to achieve political advantages (such as military bases) or commercial advantages (such as trade agreements that will harm the other country). It would be wrong for the executives of large corporations to extort too high a price for continued operation employment and normal trading. Where a less-developed country is pushed to exempt a multinational corporation from tax laws, or to construct out of its meager tax revenues the infrastructure of roads, harbors, or airports (not to mention executive mansions) that the corporation—but perhaps not the country—needs, then one suspects that some coercion has been involved.

The problem with such judgments—and it is an immense problem—is that it is hard to identify coercion and deception in complicated institutional settings. It is not hard to understand what is coercive about one person threatening another with serious injury if he won't comply with the first person's suggestion. But it is not at all easy to tell where the outward forms of political and commercial negotiation—which often involve an element of threat—have become coercive. I can't here explore this fascinating question. But I think it is at least fairly clear that the preservation of the outward forms of negotiation, bargaining, and voluntary consent do *not* demonstrate that there is no coercion, especially when one party is vastly more powerful or the other in dire need. Just as our judiciary has a long tradition of voiding contracts and agreements on grounds of duress or incompetence of one of the parties, so one can imagine a tribunal of an analogous sort rejecting at least some treaties and agreements as coercive, despite the fact that they were negotiated between "sovereign" powers or their representatives.

In particular, where such agreements were negotiated with some of the cruder deceptions and coercion of the early days of European economic expansion or the subtler coercions and deceptions of contemporary superpowers, it seems doubtful that the justice of the agreement could be sustained.

Justice, of course, is not everything, even for Kantians. But its demands are ones that they can reasonably strive to fulfill. They may have some uncertain moments—for example, does advocating cheap raw materials mean advocating an international trade system in which the less developed will continue to suffer the pressures of the developed world—or is it a benevolent policy that will maximize world trade and benefit all parties, while doing no one an injustice? But for Kantians, the important moral choices are above all those in which one acts directly, not those in which one decides which patterns of actions to encourage in others or in those institutions that one can influence. And such moral decisions include decisions about the benevolent acts that one will or will not do.

§28 Kantian Duties of Beneficence in Times of Famine

The grounds of duties of beneficence are that such acts not merely don't use others as mere means but are acts that develop or promote others' ends and that, in particular, foster others' capacities to pursue ends, to be autonomous beings.

Clearly there are many opportunities for beneficence. But one area in which the *primary* task of developing others' capacity to pursue their own ends is particularly needed is in the parts of the world where extreme poverty and hunger leave people unable to pursue *any* of their other ends. Beneficence directed at putting people in a position to pursue whatever ends they may have has, for Kant, a stronger claim on us than beneficence directed at sharing ends with those who are already in a position to pursue varieties of ends. It would be nice if I bought a tennis racquet to play with my friend who is tennis mad and never has enough partners; but it is more important to make people able to plan their own lives to a minimal extent. It is nice to walk a second mile with someone who requests one's company; better to share a cloak with someone who may otherwise be too cold to make any journey. Though these suggestions are not a detailed set of instructions for the allocation of beneficence by Kantians, they show that relief of famine must stand very high among duties of beneficence.

§29 The Limits of Kantian Ethics: Intentions and Results

Kantian ethics differs from utilitarian ethics both in its scope and in the precision with which it guides action. Every action, whether of a person or of an agency, can be assessed by utilitarian methods, provided only that information is available about all the consequences of the act. The theory has unlimited scope, but, owing to lack of data, often lacks precision. Kantian ethics has a more restricted scope. Since it assesses actions by looking at the maxims of agents, it can only assess intentional acts. This means that it is most at home in assessing individuals' acts; but it can be extended to assess acts of agencies that (like corporations and governments and student unions) have decision-making procedures. It can do nothing to assess patterns of action that reflect no intention or policy, hence it cannot assess the acts of groups lacking decision-making procedures, such as the student movement, the women's movement, or the consumer movement.

It may seem a great limitation of Kantian ethics that it concentrates on intentions to the neglect of results. It might seem that all conscientious Kantians have to do is to make sure that they never intend to use others as mere means, and that they sometimes intend to foster others' ends. And, as we all know, good intentions sometimes lead to bad results, and correspondingly, bad intentions sometimes do no harm, or even produce good. If Hardin is right, the good intentions of those who feed the starving lead to dreadful results in the long run. If some traditional arguments in favor of capitalism are right, the greed and selfishness of the profit motive have produced unparalleled prosperity for many.

But such discrepancies between intentions and results are the exception and not the rule. For we cannot just *claim* that our intentions are good and do what we will. Our intentions reflect what we expect the immediate results of our action to be. Nobody credits the "intentions" of a couple who practice neither celibacy nor contraception but still insist "we never meant to have (more) children." Conception is likely (and known to be likely) in such cases. Where people's expressed intentions ignore the normal and predictable results of what they do, we infer that (if they are not amazingly ignorant) their words do not express their true intentions. The Formula of the End in Itself applies to the intentions on which one acts—not to some prettified version that one may avow. Provided this intention—the agent's real intention—uses no other as mere means, he or she does nothing unjust. If some of his or her intentions foster others' ends, then he or she is sometimes beneficent. It is therefore possible for people to test their proposals by Kantian arguments even when they lack the comprehensive causal knowledge that utilitarianism requires. Conscientious Kantians can work out whether they will be doing wrong by some act even though they know that their foresight is limited and that they may cause some harm or fail to cause some benefit. But they will not cause harms that they can foresee without this being reflected in their intentions.

Singer, "The Singer Solution to World Poverty"

1. Explain the parallels that Singer draws between Dora's scenario from the film *Central Station*, the example of Bob and the Bugatti, and the way most Americans live their daily lives. What is Singer advocating for in light of these examples?
2. What, if any, impact does the fact that other people are not doing their fair share have on my own moral obligation to others in need? Explain your answer.
3. Explain Singer's ultimate conclusion about a moral duty of benevolence. Where does this conclusion come from in his view? To what extent to you agree with Singer's conclusion? Explain your answers.

Hardin, Lifeboat Ethics

1. Explain Hardin's lifeboat analogy. What options does he consider? Which does he recommend? Explain your answer.
2. According to Hardin, how does reproduction compound the problems of the lifeboat?
3. What is a tragedy of the commons? Explain how Hardin thinks such a phenomenon will result from establishing a world food bank along with other forms of food aid and immigration.
4. Evaluate Hardin's lifeboat analogy. How compelling is his comparison and to what extent to you agree with his conclusion? Does the tragedy of the commons present a real concern regarding assistance to those in need? Explain your answers.

O'Neill, Kantianism and World Hunger

1. Explain O'Neill's characterization of a maxim and some of the different maxims that might arise in the face of poverty and the risk of famine. How are maxims relevant to determining moral obligation in Kantian ethics?
2. What does it mean to use someone as a mere means according to O'Neill? What kinds of actions must be avoided in light of this consideration on her interpretation of Kantian ethics? According to O'Neill, what does it mean to treat humanity as an end-in-itself? How does this component of the categorical imperative require us to act based on her interpretation of Kantian ethics? Explain your answers.

3. Explain how justice and beneficence impact our moral obligations to others in need in a Kantian framework according to O'Neill. What sort of obligations do we have in the context and how does O'Neill's account differ from a utilitarian account? To what extent do you agree with O'Neill's conclusions? Explain your answers.

SUGGESTIONS FOR FURTHER READING OR VIEWING

Murdoch, William W., and Allan Oaten. "Population and Food: Metaphors and the Reality." *Bioscience 25* (1975).

Singer, Peter. *The Life You Can Save*. New York: Random House, 2009.

Unger, Peter. *Living High and Letting Die*. New York: Oxford University Press, 1996.

Abortion

INTRODUCTION TO THE PROBLEM OF ABORTION

The moral permissibility of abortion is a divisive topic. The legal status of it is divisive as well. Well-intended and well-informed people hotly disagree with each other on these issues. Before any discussion of abortion begins, it is important to remember that morality and legality should not be conflated as they are two different questions—not every illegal act is immoral, and not every immoral act is illegal. An analogy might help. It is easy to imagine someone thinking that adultery should not be illegal because we probably do not to have to punish adulterers with prison or fines. However, the same person who thinks we should not make adultery illegal might nevertheless think that adultery is immoral because it involves the breaking of a promise to one's spouse. In the same way, we can easily imagine someone holding the position that abortion should remain a legal option for women to choose and the very same person teaching their own children that abortion is a morally impermissible choice to make.

Many arguments for and against the moral permissibility are familiar, but it can often seem as though they turn on matters that point to deeper disagreements between the pro-life and pro-choice camps, disagreements that often seem ultimately to be religious in nature. Frequently these arguments turn on the question of the inherent value of human life and whether a fetus (or embryo) is such a life in some relevant sense. Other disagreements turn on how we define "person" and whether the class of persons includes all humans. The two readings included here are prized among philosophers because they both avoid these familiar entanglements. Marquis makes no essential appeal to the humanity of the unborn, arguing instead from the claim that if they are killed, the unborn will be robbed of a future. Thompson defends the permissibility of abortion despite conceding, for the sake of argument, that the unborn enjoy a robust right to life.

Here are some questions to think about, or discuss with a friend, regarding the morality of abortion.

Is abortion a morally permissible choice, but not a morally praiseworthy choice, to make? Is abortion morally permissible some of the time but not morally permissible all of the time? If so, when is abortion permissible and when is it not? Is abortion morally permissible if it is not analogous to murder? Or, are there still serious reasons to think abortion is immoral even if it is not analogous to murder? Does legalized abortion set us on a slippery slope of not taking human life seriously enough in our moral practice? If I personally do not know what I think about the morality of abortion, should I stand with those who oppose abortion just in case they are correct when they compare it to murder? Shouldn't I err on the side of caution here? Does performing abortions morally corrupt doctors and nurses who must engage in the "dirty work" of performing the abortion procedure? Assuming a woman has a legal right to abortion, does it follow that other people (doctors, taxpayers, etc.) must help her get the abortion? Or, even if women have the legal right to abortion, should a (Catholic, etc.) doctor legally be able to say, "No, I will not perform an abortion"? Should taxpayers (Catholic, etc.) be able to vote against using taxes to fund clinics that perform abortions?

Why Abortion is Immoral

Don Marquis

༄

II.

In order to develop such an account, we can start from the following unproblematic assumption concerning our own case: it is wrong to kill *us*. Why is it wrong? Some answers can be easily eliminated. It might be said that what makes killing us wrong is that a killing brutalizes the one who kills. But the brutalization consists of being inured to the performance of an act that is hideously immoral; hence, the brutalization does not explain the immorality. It might be said that what makes killing us wrong is the great loss others would experience due to our absence. Although such hubris is understandable, such an explanation does not account for the wrongness of killing hermits, or those whose lives are relatively independent and whose friends find it easy to make new friends.

A more obvious answer is better. What primarily makes killing wrong is neither its effect on the murderer nor its effect on the victim's friends and relatives, but its effect on the victim. The loss of one's life is one of the greatest losses one can suffer. The loss of one's life deprives one of all the experiences, activities, projects, and enjoyments that would otherwise have constituted one's future. Therefore, killing someone is wrong, primarily because the killing inflicts (one of) the greatest possible losses on the victim. To describe this as the loss of life can be misleading, however. The change in my biological state does not by itself make killing me wrong. The effect of the loss of my biological life is the loss to me of all those activities, projects, experiences, and enjoyments which would otherwise have constituted my future personal life. These activities, projects, experiences, and enjoyments are either valuable for their own sakes or are means to something else that is valuable for its own sake. Some parts of my future are not valued by me now, but will come to be valued by me as I grow older and as my values and capacities change. When I am killed, I am deprived both of what I now value which would have been part of my future personal life, but also what I would come to value. Therefore, when I die, I am deprived of all of the value of my future. Inflicting this loss on me is ultimately what makes killing me wrong. This being the case, it would seem that what makes killing *any* adult human being prima facie seriously wrong is the loss of his or her future.[1]

How should this rudimentary theory of the wrongness of killing be evaluated? It cannot be faulted for deriving an 'ought' from an 'is', for it does not. The analysis assumes that killing me (or you, reader) is prima facie seriously wrong. The point of the analysis is to establish which natural property ultimately explains the wrongness of the killing, given that it is wrong. A natural property will ultimately explain the wrongness of killing, only if (1) the explanation fits with our intuitions about the matter and (2) there is no other natural property that provides the basis for a better explanation of the wrongness of killing. This analysis rests on the intuition that what makes killing a particular human or animal wrong is what it does to that particular human or animal. What makes killing wrong is some natural effect or other of the killing. Some would deny this. For instance, a divine-command theorist in ethics would deny it. Surely this denial is, however, one of those features of divine-command theory which renders it so implausible.

The claim that what makes killing wrong is the loss of the victim's future is directly supported by two considerations. In the first place, this theory explains why we regard killing as one of the worst of crimes. Killing is especially wrong, because it deprives the victim of more than perhaps any other crime. In the second place, people with AIDS or cancer who know they are dying believe, of course, that dying is a very bad thing for them. They believe that the loss of a future to them that they would otherwise have experienced is what makes their premature death a very bad thing for them. A better theory of the wrongness of killing would require a different natural property associated with killing which better fits with the attitudes of the dying. What could it be?

The view that what makes killing wrong is the loss to the victim of the value of the victim's future gains additional support when some of its implications are examined. In the first place, it is incompatible with the view that it is wrong to kill only beings who are biologically human. It is possible that there exists a different species from another planet whose members have a future like ours. Since having a future like that is what makes killing someone wrong, this theory

---

1   I have been most influenced on this matter by Jonathan Glover, *Causing Death and Saving Lives* (New York: Penguin, 1977), ch. 3; and Robert Young, "What Is So Wrong with Killing People?" *Philosophy*, LIV, 210 (1979):515–528.

entails that it would be wrong to kill members of such a species. Hence, this theory is opposed to the claim that only life that is biologically human has great moral worth, a claim which many antiabortionists have seemed to adopt. This opposition, which this theory has in common with personhood theories, seems to be a merit of the theory.

In the second place, the claim that the loss of one's future is the wrong-making feature of one's being killed entails the possibility that the futures of some actual nonhuman mammals on our own planet are sufficiently like ours that it is seriously wrong to kill them also. Whether some animals do have the same right to life as human beings depends on adding to the account of the wrongness of killing some additional account of just what it is about my future or the futures of other adult human beings which makes it wrong to kill us. No such additional account will be offered in this essay. Undoubtedly, the provision of such an account would be a very difficult matter. Undoubtedly, any such account would be quite controversial. Hence, it surely should not reflect badly on this sketch of an elementary theory of the wrongness of killing that it is indeterminate with respect to some very difficult issues regarding animal rights.

In the third place, the claim that the loss of one's future is the wrong-making feature of one's being killed does not entail, as sanctity of human life theories do, that active euthanasia is wrong. Persons who are severely and incurably ill, who face a future of pain and despair, and who wish to die will not have suffered a loss if they are killed. It is, strictly speaking, the value of a human's future which makes killing wrong in this theory. This being so, killing does not necessarily wrong some persons who are sick and dying. Of course, there may be other reasons for a prohibition of active euthanasia, but that is another matter. Sanctity-of-human-life theories seem to hold that active euthanasia is seriously wrong even in an individual case where there seems to be good reason for it independently of public policy considerations. This consequence is most implausible, and it is a plus for the claim that the loss of a future of value is what makes killing wrong that it does not share this consequence.

In the fourth place, the account of the wrongness of killing defended in this essay does straightforwardly entail that it is prima facie seriously wrong to kill children and infants, for we do presume that they have futures of value. Since we do believe that it is wrong to kill defenseless little babies, it is important that a theory of the wrongness of killing easily account for this. Personhood theories of the wrongness of killing, on the other hand, cannot straightforwardly account for the wrongness of killing infants and young children.[2] Hence, such theories

---

2 Feinberg, Tooley, Warren, and Engelhardt have all dealt with this problem.

must add special ad hoc accounts of the wrongness of killing the young. The plausibility of such ad hoc theories seems to be a function of how desperately one wants such theories to work. The claim that the primary wrong-making feature of a killing is the loss to the victim of the value of its future accounts for the wrongness of killing young children and infants directly; it makes the wrongness of such acts as obvious as we actually think it is. This is a further merit of this theory. Accordingly, it seems that this value of a future-like-ours theory of the wrongness of killing shares strengths of both sanctity-of-life and personhood accounts while avoiding weaknesses of both. In addition, it meshes with a central intuition concerning what makes killing wrong.

The claim that the primary wrong-making feature of a killing is the loss to the victim of the value of its future has obvious consequences for the ethics of abortion. The future of a standard fetus includes a set of experiences, projects, activities, and such which are identical with the futures of adult human beings and are identical with the futures of young children. Since the reason that is sufficient to explain why it is wrong to kill human beings after the time of birth is a reason that also applies to fetuses, it follows that abortion is prima facie seriously morally wrong.

This argument does not rely on the invalid inference that, since it is wrong to kill persons, it is wrong to kill potential persons also. The category that is morally central to this analysis is the category of having a valuable future like ours; it is not the category of personhood. The argument to the conclusion that abortion is prima facie seriously morally wrong proceeded independently of the notion of person or potential person or any equivalent. Someone may wish to start with this analysis in terms of the value of a human future, conclude that abortion is, except perhaps in rare circumstances, seriously morally wrong, infer that fetuses have the right to life, and then call fetuses "persons" as a result of their having the right to life. Clearly, in this case, the category of person is being used to state the *conclusion* of the analysis rather than to generate the *argument* of the analysis.

The structure of this anti-abortion argument can be both illuminated and defended by comparing it to what appears to be the best argument for the wrongness of the wanton infliction of pain on animals. This latter argument is based on the assumption that it is prima facie wrong to inflict pain on me (or you, reader). What is the natural property associated with the infliction of pain which makes such infliction wrong? The obvious answer seems to be that the infliction of pain causes suffering and that suffering is a misfortune. The suffering caused by the infliction of pain is what makes the wanton infliction of pain on me wrong. The wanton infliction of pain on other adult humans causes suffering. The wanton infliction of pain on animals causes suffering. Since causing suffering is what makes the wanton infliction of pain wrong and since the wanton infliction of pain on animals causes suffering, it follows that the wanton infliction of pain on animals is wrong.

This argument for the wrongness of the wanton infliction of pain on animals shares a number of structural features with the argument for the serious prima facie wrongness of abortion. Both arguments start with an obvious assumption concerning what it is wrong to do to me (or you, reader). Both then look for the characteristic or the consequence of the wrong action which makes the action wrong. Both recognize that the wrong-making feature of these immoral actions is a property of actions sometimes directed at individuals other than postnatal human beings. If the structure of the argument for the wrongness of the wanton infliction of pain on animals is sound, then the structure of the argument for the prima facie serious wrongness of abortion is also sound, for the structure of the two arguments is the same. The structure common to both is the key to the explanation of how the wrongness of abortion can be demonstrated without recourse to the category of person. In neither argument is that category crucial.

This defense of an argument for the wrongness of abortion in terms of a structurally similar argument for the wrongness of the wanton infliction of pain on animals succeeds only if the account regarding animals is the correct account. Is it? In the first place, it seems plausible. In the second place, its major competition is Kant's account. Kant believed that we do not have direct duties to animals at all, because they are not persons. Hence, Kant had to explain and justify the wrongness of inflicting pain on animals on the grounds that "he who is hard in his dealings with animals becomes hard also in his dealing with men."[3] The problem with Kant's account is that there seems to be no reason for accepting this latter claim unless Kant's account is rejected. If the alternative to Kant's account is accepted, then it is easy to understand why someone who is indifferent to inflicting pain on animals is also indifferent to inflicting pain on humans, for one is indifferent to what makes inflicting pain wrong in both cases. But, if Kant's account is accepted, there is no intelligible reason why one who is hard in his dealings with animals (or crabgrass or stones) should also be hard in his dealings with men. After all, men are persons: animals are no more persons than crabgrass or stones. Persons are Kant's crucial moral category. Why, in short, should a Kantian accept the basic claim in Kant's argument?

Hence, Kant's argument for the wrongness of inflicting pain on animals rests on a claim that, in a world of Kantian moral agents, is demonstrably false. Therefore, the alternative analysis, being more plausible anyway, should be accepted. Since this alternative analysis has the same structure as the anti-

---

3 "Duties to Animals and Spirits," in *Lectures on Ethics,* Louis Infeld, trans. (New York: Harper, 1963), p. 239.

abortion argument being defended here, we have further support for the argument for the immorality of abortion being defended in this essay.

Of course, this value of a future-like-ours argument, if sound, shows only that abortion is prima facie wrong, not that it is wrong in any and all circumstances. Since the loss of the future to a standard fetus, if killed, is, however, at least as great a loss as the loss of the future to a standard adult human being who is killed, abortion, like ordinary killing, could be justified only by the most compelling reasons. The loss of one's life is almost the greatest misfortune that can happen to one. Presumably abortion could be justified in some circumstances, only if the loss consequent on failing to abort would be at least as great. Accordingly, morally permissible abortions will be rare indeed unless, perhaps, they occur so early in pregnancy that a fetus is not yet definitely an individual. Hence, this argument should be taken as showing that abortion is presumptively very seriously wrong, where the presumption is very strong—as strong as the presumption that killing another adult human being is wrong. ...

IV.

The analysis of the previous section suggests that alternative general accounts of the wrongness of killing are either inadequate or unsuccessful in getting around the anti-abortion consequences of the value of a future-like-ours argument. A different strategy for avoiding these anti-abortion consequences involves limiting the scope of the value of a future argument. More precisely, the strategy involves arguing that fetuses lack a property that is essential for the value-of-a-future argument (or for any anti-abortion argument) to apply to them.

One move of this sort is based upon the claim that a necessary condition of one's future being valuable is that one values it. Value implies a valuer. Given this one might argue that, since fetuses cannot value their futures, their futures are not valuable to them. Hence, it does not seriously wrong them deliberately to end their lives.

This move fails, however, because of some ambiguities. Let us assume that something cannot be of value unless it is valued by someone. This does not entail that my life is of no value unless it is valued by me. I may think, in a period of despair, that my future is of no worth whatsoever, but I may be wrong because others rightly see value—even great value—in it. Furthermore, my future can be valuable to me even if I do not value it. This is the case when a young person attempts suicide, but is rescued and goes on to significant human achievements. Such young people's futures are ultimately valuable to them, even though such futures do not seem to be valuable to them at the moment of attempted suicide.

A fetus's future can be valuable to it in the same way. Accordingly, this attempt to limit the anti-abortion argument fails.

Another similar attempt to reject the anti-abortion position is based on Tooley's claim that an entity cannot possess the right to life unless it has the capacity to desire its continued existence. It follows that, since fetuses lack the conceptual capacity to desire to continue to live, they lack the right to life. Accordingly, Tooley concludes that abortion cannot be seriously prima facie wrong (*op. cit.*, pp. 46/7).

What could be the evidence for Tooley's basic claim? Tooley once argued that individuals have a prima facie right to what they desire and that the lack of the capacity to desire something undercuts the basis of one's right to it (*op. cit.*, pp. 44/5). This argument plainly will not succeed in the context of the analysis of this essay, however, since the point here is to establish the fetus's right to life on other grounds. Tooley's argument assumes that the right to life cannot be established in general on some basis other than the desire for life. This position was considered and rejected in the preceding section of this paper.

One might attempt to defend Tooley's basic claim on the grounds that, because a fetus cannot apprehend continued life as a benefit, its continued life cannot be a benefit or cannot be something it has a right to or cannot be something that is in its interest. This might be defended in terms of the general proposition that, if an individual is literally incapable of caring about or taking an interest in some X, then one does not have a right to X or X is not a benefit or X is not something that is in one's interest.[4]

Each member of this family of claims seems to be open to objections. As John C. Stevens[5] has pointed out, one may have a right to be treated with a certain medical procedure (because of a health insurance policy one has purchased), even though one cannot conceive of the nature of the procedure. And, as Tooley himself has pointed out, persons who have been indoctrinated, or drugged, or rendered temporarily unconscious may be literally incapable of caring about or taking an interest in something that is in their interest or is something to which they have a right, or is something that benefits them. Hence, the Tooley claim that would restrict the scope of the value of a future-like-ours argument is undermined by counterexamples.[6]

Finally, Paul Bassen[7] has argued that, even though the prospects of an embryo might seem to be a basis for the wrongness of abortion, an embryo cannot be

---

4   Donald VanDeVeer seems to think this is self-evident. See his "Whither Baby Doe?" in *Matters of Life and Death*, p. 233.

5   "Must the Bearer of a Right Have the Concept of That to Which He Has a Right?" *Ethics*, XCV, 1 (1984):68–74.

6   See Tooley again in "Abortion and Infanticide," pp. 47–49.

7   "Present Sakes and Future Prospects: The Status of Early Abortion," *Philosophy and Public Affairs*, XI, 4 (1982):322–326.

a victim and therefore cannot be wronged. An embryo cannot be a victim, he says, because it lacks sentience. His central argument for this seems to be that, even though plants and the permanently unconscious are alive, they clearly cannot be victims. What is the explanation of this? Bassen claims that the explanation is that their lives consist of mere metabolism and mere metabolism is not enough to ground victimizability. Mentation is required.

The problem with this attempt to establish the absence of victimizability is that both plants and the permanently unconscious clearly lack what Bassen calls "prospects" or what I have called "a future life like ours." Hence, it is surely open to one to argue that the real reason we believe plants and the permanently unconscious cannot be victims is that killing them cannot deprive them of a future life like ours; the real reason is not their absence of present mediation.

Bassen recognizes that his view is subject to this difficulty, and he recognizes that the case of children seems to support this difficulty, for "much of what we do for children is based on prospects." He argues, however, that, in the case of children and in other such cases, "potentiality comes into play only where victimizability has been secured on other grounds" (*ibid.*, p. 333).

Bassen's defense of his view is patently question-begging, since what is adequate to secure victimizability is exactly what is at issue. His examples do not support his own view against the thesis of this essay. Of course, embryos can be victims: when their lives are deliberately terminated, they are deprived of their futures of value, their prospects. This makes them victims, for it directly wrongs them.

The seeming plausibility of Bassen's view stems from the fact that paradigmatic cases of imagining someone as a victim involve empathy, and empathy requires mentation of the victim. The victims of flood, famine, rape, or child abuse are all persons with whom we can empathize. That empathy seems to be part of seeing them as victims.[8]

In spite of the strength of these examples, the attractive intuition that a situation in which there is victimization requires the possibility of empathy is subject to counterexamples. Consider a case that Bassen himself offers: "Posthumous obliteration of an author's work constitutes a misfortune for him only if he had wished his work to endure" (*op cit.*, p. 318). The conditions Bassen wishes to impose upon the possibility of being victimized here seem far too strong. Perhaps this author, due to his unrealistic standards of excellence and his low self-esteem, regarded his work as unworthy of survival, even though it possessed genuine literary merit. Destruction of such work would surely victimize its author. In such a case, empathy with the victim concerning the loss is clearly impossible.

---

8   Note carefully the reasons he gives on the bottom of p. 316.

Of course, Bassen does not make the possibility of empathy a necessary condition of victimizability; he requires only mentation. Hence, on Bassen's actual view, this author, as I have described him, can be a victim. The problem is that the basic intuition that renders Bassen's view plausible is missing in the author's case. In order to attempt to avoid counterexamples, Bassen has made his thesis too weak to be supported by the intuitions that suggested it.

Even so, the mentation requirement on victimizability is still subject to counterexamples. Suppose a severe accident renders me totally unconscious for a month, after which I recover. Surely killing me while I am unconscious victimizes me, even though I am incapable of mentation during that time. It follows that Bassen's thesis fails. Apparently, attempts to restrict the value of a future-like-ours argument so that fetuses do not fall within its scope do not succeed.

V.

In this essay, it has been argued that the correct ethic of the wrongness of killing can be extended to fetal life and used to show that there is a strong presumption that any abortion is morally impermissible. If the ethic of killing adopted here entails, however, that contraception is also seriously immoral, then there would appear to be a difficulty with the analysis of this essay.

But this analysis does not entail that contraception is wrong. Of course, contraception prevents the actualization of a possible future of value. Hence, it follows from the claim that futures of value should be maximized that contraception is prima facie immoral. This obligation to maximize does not exist, however; furthermore, nothing in the ethics of killing in this paper entails that it does. The ethics of killing in this essay would entail that contraception is wrong only if something were denied a human future of value by contraception. Nothing at all is denied such a future by contraception, however.

Candidates for a subject of harm by contraception fall into four categories: (1) some sperm or other, (2) some ovum or other, (3) a sperm and an ovum separately, and (4) a sperm and an ovum together. Assigning the harm to some sperm is utterly arbitrary, for no reason can be given for making a sperm the subject of harm rather than an ovum. Assigning the harm to some ovum is utterly arbitrary, for no reason can be given for making an ovum the subject of harm rather than a sperm. One might attempt to avoid these problems by insisting that contraception deprives both the sperm and the ovum separately of a valuable future like ours. On this alternative, too many futures are lost. Contraception was supposed to be wrong, because it deprived us of one future of value, not two. One might attempt to avoid this problem by holding that contraception deprives the combination of sperm and ovum of a valuable future like ours. But here the definite article misleads. At the time of contraception, there are hundreds of millions of sperm, one (released) ovum and millions of possible combinations of all of these. There is no actual combination at all. Is the subject of the loss to be a merely possible combination? Which one? This alternative does not yield an actual subject of harm either. Accordingly, the immorality of contraception is not entailed by the loss of a future-like-ours argument simply because there is no nonarbitrarily identifiable subject of the loss in the case of contraception.

VI.

The purpose of this essay has been to set out an argument for the serious presumptive wrongness of abortion subject to the assumption that the moral permissibility of abortion stands or falls on the moral status of the fetus. Since a fetus possesses a property, the possession of which in adult human beings is sufficient to make killing an adult human being wrong, abortion is wrong. This way of dealing with the problem of abortion seems superior to other approaches to the ethics of abortion, because it rests on an ethics of killing which is close to self-evident, because the crucial morally relevant property clearly applies to fetuses, and because the argument avoids the usual equivocations on 'human life', 'human being', or 'person'. The argument rests neither on religious claims nor on Papal dogma. It is not subject to the objection of "speciesism." Its soundness is compatible with the moral permissibility of euthanasia and contraception. It deals with our intuitions concerning young children.

Finally, this analysis can be viewed as resolving a standard problem—indeed, *the* standard problem—concerning the ethics of abortion. Clearly, it is wrong to kill adult human beings. Clearly, it is not wrong to end the life of some arbitrarily chosen single human cell. Fetuses seem to be like arbitrarily chosen human cells in some respects and like adult humans in other respects. The problem of the ethics of abortion is the problem of determining the fetal property that settles this moral controversy. The thesis of this essay is that the problem of the ethics of abortion, so understood, is solvable.

DON MARQUIS
University of Kansas

A Defense of Abortion[1]

Judith Jarvis Thompson

Most opposition to abortion relies on the premise that the fetus is a human being, a person, from the moment of conception. The premise is argued for, but, as I think, not well. Take, for example, the most common argument. We are asked to notice that the development of a human being from conception through birth into childhood is continuous; then it is said that to draw a line, to choose a point in this development and say "before this point the thing is not a person, after this point it is a person" is to make an arbitrary choice, a choice for which in the nature of things no good reason can be given. It is concluded that the fetus is, or anyway that we had better say it is, a person from the moment of conception. But this conclusion does not follow. Similar things might be said about the development of an acorn into an oak tree, and it does not follow that acorns are oak trees, or that we had better say they are. Arguments of this form are sometimes called "slippery slope arguments"—the phrase is perhaps self-explanatory—and it is dismaying that opponents of abortion rely on them so heavily and uncritically.

I am inclined to agree, however, that the prospects for "drawing a line" in the development of the fetus look dim. I am inclined to think also that we shall probably have to agree that the fetus has already become a human person well before birth. Indeed, it comes as a surprise when one first learns how early in its life it begins to acquire human characteristics. By the tenth week, for example, it already has a face, arms and legs, fingers and toes; it has internal organs, and brain activity is detectable.[2] On the other hand, I think that the premise is false, that the fetus is not a person from the moment of conception. A newly

---

1   I am very much indebted to James Thomson for discussion, criticism, and many helpful suggestions.

2   Daniel Callahan, *Abortion: Law, Choice and Morality* (New York, 1970), P 373. This book gives a fascinating survey of the available information on abortion. The Jewish tradition is surveyed in David M. Feldman, *Birth Control in Jewish Law* (New York, 1968), Part 5, the Catholic tradition in John T. Noonan, Jr., "An Almost Absolute Value in History," in *The Morality of Abortion*, ed. John T. Noonan, Jr. (Cambridge, Mass., 1970).

fertilized ovum, a newly implanted clump of cells, is no more a person than an acorn is an oak tree. But I shall not discuss any of this. For it seems to me to be of great interest to ask what happens if, for the sake of argument, we allow the premise. How, precisely, are we supposed to get from there to the conclusion that abortion is morally impermissible? Opponents of abortion commonly spend most of their time establishing that the fetus is a person, and hardly any time explaining the step from there to the impermissibility of abortion. Perhaps they think the step too simple and obvious to require much comment. Or perhaps instead they are simply being economical in argument. Many of those who defend abortion rely on the premise that the fetus is not a person, but only a bit of tissue that will become a person at birth; and why pay out more arguments than you have to? Whatever the explanation, I suggest that the step they take is neither easy nor obvious, that it calls for closer examination than it is commonly given, and that when we do give it this closer examination we shall feel inclined to reject it.

I propose, then, that we grant that the fetus is a person from the moment of conception. How does the argument go from here? Something like this, I take it. Every person has a right to life. So the fetus has a right to life. No doubt the mother has a right to decide what shall happen in and to her body; everyone would grant that. But surely a person's right to life is stronger and more stringent than the mother's right to decide what happens in and to her body, and so outweighs it. So the fetus may not be killed; an abortion may not be performed.

It sounds plausible. But now let me ask you to imagine this. You wake up in the morning and find yourself back to back in bed with an unconscious violinist. A famous unconscious violinist. He has been found to have a fatal kidney ailment, and the Society of Music Lovers has canvassed all the available medical records and found that you alone have the right blood type to help. They have therefore kidnapped you, and last night the violinist's circulatory system was plugged into yours, so that your kidneys can be used to extract poisons from his blood as well as your own. The director of the hospital now tells you, "Look, we're sorry the Society of Music Lovers did this to you—we would never have permitted it if we had known. But still, they did it, and the violinist now is plugged into you. To unplug you would be to kill him. But never mind, it's only for nine months. By then he will have recovered from his ailment, and can safely be unplugged from you." Is it morally incumbent on you to accede to this situation? No doubt it would be very nice of you if you did, a great kindness. But do you *have* to accede to it? What if it were not nine months, but nine years? Or longer still? What if the director of the hospital says, "Tough luck, I agree, but you've now got to stay in bed, with the violinist plugged into you, for the rest of your life. Because remember this. All persons have a right to life, and violinists are persons. Granted you have a right to decide what happens in and to your body, but a person's right to life outweighs your right to decide what happens in and to your body. So you cannot ever be unplugged from him." I imagine you would regard this as outrageous, which suggests that something really is wrong with that plausible-sounding argument I mentioned a moment ago.

In this case, of course, you were kidnapped; you didn't volunteer for the operation that plugged the violinist into your kidneys. Can those who oppose abortion on the ground I mentioned make an exception for a pregnancy due to rape? Certainly. They can say that persons have a right to life only if they didn't come into existence because of rape; or they can say that all persons have a right to life, but that some have less of a right to life than others, in particular, that those who came into existence because of rape have less. But these statements have a rather unpleasant sound. Surely the question of whether you have a right to life at all, or how much of it you have, shouldn't turn on the question of whether or not you are the product of a rape. And in fact the people who oppose abortion on the ground I mentioned do not make this distinction, and hence do not make an exception in case of rape.

Nor do they make an exception for a case in which the mother has to spend the nine months of her pregnancy in bed. They would agree that would be a great pity, and hard on the mother; but all the same, all persons have a right to life, the fetus is a person, and so on. I suspect, in fact, that they would not make an exception for a case in which, miraculously enough, the pregnancy went on for nine years, or even the rest of the mother's life.

Some won't even make an exception for a case in which continuation of the pregnancy is likely to shorten the mother's life; they regard abortion as impermissible even to save the mother's life. Such cases are nowadays very rare, and many opponents of abortion do not accept this extreme view. All the same, it is a good place to begin: a number of points of interest come out in respect to it.

1. Let us call the view that abortion is impermissible even to save the mother's life "the extreme view." I want to suggest first that it does not issue from the argument I mentioned earlier without the addition of some fairly powerful premises. Suppose a woman has become pregnant, and now learns that she has a cardiac condition such that she will die if she carries the baby to term. What may be done for her? The fetus, being a person, has a right to life, but as the mother is a person too, so has she a right to life. Presumably they have an equal right to life. How is it supposed to come out that an abortion may not be performed? If mother and child have an equal right to life, shouldn't we perhaps flip a coin? Or should we add to the mother's right to life her right to decide what happens in and to her body, which everybody seems to be ready to grant—the sum of her rights now outweighing the fetus' right to life?

The most familiar argument here is the following. We are told that performing the abortion would be directly killing[3] the child, whereas doing nothing would not be killing the mother, but only letting her die. Moreover, in killing the child, one would be killing an innocent person, for the child has committed no crime, and is not aiming at his mother's death. And then there are a variety of ways in which this might be continued. (1) But as directly killing an innocent person is always and absolutely impermissible, an abortion may not be performed. Or, (2) as directly killing an innocent person is murder, and murder is always and absolutely impermissible, an abortion may not be performed.[4] Or, (3) as one's duty to refrain from directly killing an innocent person is more stringent than one's duty to keep a person from dying, an abortion may not be performed. Or, (4) if one's only options are directly killing an innocent person or letting a person die, one must prefer letting the person die, and thus an abortion may not be performed.[5]

Some people seem to have thought that these are not further premises which must be added if the conclusion is to be reached, but that they follow from the very fact that an innocent person has a right to life.[6] But this seems to me to be a mistake, and perhaps the simplest way to show this is to bring out that while we must certainly grant that innocent persons have a right to life, the theses in (1) through (4) are all false. Take (2), for example. If directly killing an innocent person is murder, and thus is impermissible, then the mother's directly killing the innocent person inside her is murder, and thus is impermissible. But it cannot seriously be thought to be murder if the mother performs an abortion on herself to save her life. It cannot seriously be said that she *must* refrain, that she *must* sit passively by and wait for her death. Let us look again at the case of you and the violinist. There you are, in bed with the violinist, and the director

---

3   The term "direct" in the arguments I refer to is a technical one. Roughly, what is meant by "direct killing" is either killing as an end in itself, or killing as a means to some end, for example, the end of saving someone else's life. See note 6, below, for an example of its use.

4   Cf. *Encyclical Letter of Pope Pius XI on Christian Marriage*, St. Paul Editions (Boston, n.d.), p. 32: "however much we may pity the mother whose health and even life is gravely imperiled in the performance of the duty allotted to her by nature, nevertheless what could ever be a sufficient reason for excusing in any way the direct murder of the innocent? This is precisely what we are dealing with here." Noonan (*The Morality of Abortion*, p. 43) reads this as follows: "What cause can ever avail to excuse in any way the direct killing of the innocent? For it is a question of that."

5   The thesis in (4) is in an interesting way weaker than those in (1), (2), and (3): they rule out abortion even in cases in which both mother *and* child will die if the abortion is not performed. By contrast, one who held the view expressed in (4) could consistently say that one needn't prefer letting two persons die to killing one.

6   Cf. the following passage from Pius XII, *Address to the Italian Catholic Society of Midwives*: "The baby in the maternal breast has the right to life immediately from God.—Hence there is no man, no human authority, no science, no medical, eugenic, social, economic or moral 'indication' which can establish or grant a valid juridical ground for a direct deliberate disposition of an innocent human life, that is a disposition which looks to its destruction either as an end or as a means to another end perhaps in itself not illicit.—The baby, still not born, is a man in the same degree and for the same reason as the mother" (quoted in Noonan, *The Morality of Abortion*, p. 45).

of the hospital says to you, "It's all most distressing, and I deeply sympathize, but you see this is putting an additional strain on your kidneys, and you'll be dead within the month. But you *have* to stay where you are all the same. Because unplugging you would be directly killing an innocent violinist, and that's murder, and that's impermissible." If anything in the world is true, it is that you do not commit murder, you do not do what is impermissible, if you reach around to your back and unplug yourself from that violinist to save your life.

The main focus of attention in writings on abortion has been on what a third party may or may not do in answer to a request from a woman for an abortion. This is in a way understandable. Things being as they are, there isn't much a woman can safely do to abort herself. So the question asked is what a third party may do, and what the mother may do, if it is mentioned at all, is deduced, almost as an afterthought, from what it is concluded that third parties may do. But it seems to me that to treat the matter in this way is to refuse to grant to the mother that very status of person which is so firmly insisted on for the fetus. For we cannot simply read off what a person may do from what a third party may do. Suppose you find yourself trapped in a tiny house with a growing child. I mean a very tiny house, and a rapidly growing child—you are already up against the wall of the house and in a few minutes you'll be crushed to death. The child on the other hand won't be crushed to death; if nothing is done to stop him from growing he'll be hurt, but in the end he'll simply burst open the house and walk out a free man. Now I could well understand it if a bystander were to say, "There's nothing we can do for you. We cannot choose between your life and his, we cannot be the ones to decide who is to live, we cannot intervene." But it cannot be concluded that you too can do nothing, that you cannot attack it to save your life. However innocent the child may be, you do not have to wait passively while it crushes you to death. Perhaps a pregnant woman is vaguely felt to have the status of house, to which we don't allow the right of self-defense. But if the woman houses the child, it should be remembered that she is a person who houses it.

I should perhaps stop to say explicitly that I am not claiming that people have a right to do anything whatever to save their lives. I think, rather, that there are drastic limits to the right of self-defense. If someone threatens you with death unless you torture someone else to death, I think you have not the right, even to save your life, to do so. But the case under consideration here is very different. In our case there are only two people involved, one whose life is threatened, and one who threatens it. Both are innocent: the one who is threatened is not threatened because of any fault, the one who threatens does not threaten because of any fault. For this reason we may feel that we bystanders cannot intervene. But the person threatened can.

In sum, a woman surely can defend her life against the threat to it posed by the unborn child, even if doing so involves its death. And this shows not merely that the theses in (1) through (4) are false; it shows also that the extreme view of abortion is false, and so we need not canvass any other possible ways of arriving at it from the argument I mentioned at the outset.

2.   The extreme view could of course be weakened to say that while abortion is permissible to save the mother's life, it may not be performed by a third party, but only by the mother herself. But this cannot be right either. For what we have to keep in mind is that the mother and the unborn child are not like two tenants in a small house which has, by an unfortunate mistake, been rented to both: the mother *owns* the house. The fact that she does adds to the offensiveness of deducing that the mother can do nothing from the supposition that third parties can do nothing. But it does more than this: it casts a bright light on the supposition that third parties can do nothing. Certainly it lets us see that a third party who says "I cannot choose between you" is fooling himself if he thinks this is impartiality. If Jones has found and fastened on a certain coat, which he needs to keep him from freezing, but which Smith also needs to keep him from freezing, then it is not impartiality that says "I cannot choose between you" when Smith owns the coat. Women have said again and again "This body is *my* body!" and they have reason to feel angry, reason to feel that it has been like shouting into the wind. Smith, after all, is hardly likely to bless us if we say to him, "Of course it's your coat, anybody would grant that it is. But no one may choose between you and Jones who is to have it."

We should really ask what it is that says "no one may choose" in the face of the fact that the body that houses the child is the mother's body. It may be simply a failure to appreciate this fact. But it may be something more interesting, namely the sense that one has a right to refuse to lay hands on people, even where it would be just and fair to do so, even where justice seems to require that somebody do so. Thus justice might call for somebody to get Smith's coat back from Jones, and yet you have a right to refuse to be the one to lay hands on Jones, a right to refuse to do physical violence to him. This, I think, must be granted. But then what should be said is not "no one may choose," but only "I cannot choose," and indeed not even this, but "*I* will not *act*," leaving it open that somebody else can or should, and in particular that anyone in a position of authority, with the job of securing people's rights, both can and should. So this is no difficulty. I have not been arguing that any given third party must accede to the mother's request that he perform an abortion to save her life, but only that he may.

I suppose that in some views of human life the mother's body is only on loan to her, the loan not being one which gives her any prior claim to it. One who held this view might well think it impartiality to say "I cannot choose." But I shall simply ignore this possibility. My own view is that if a human being has any just, prior claim to anything at all, he has a just, prior claim to his own body. And perhaps this needn't be argued for here anyway, since, as I mentioned, the arguments against abortion we are looking at do grant that the woman has a right to decide what happens in and to her body.

But although they do grant it, I have tried to show that they do not take seriously what is done in granting it. I suggest the same thing will reappear even more clearly when we turn away from cases in which the mother's life is at stake, and attend, as I propose we now do, to the vastly more common cases in which a woman wants an abortion for some less weighty reason than preserving her own life.

3.   Where the mother's life is not at stake, the argument I mentioned at the outset seems to have a much stronger pull. "Everyone has a right to life, so the unborn person has a right to life." And isn't the child's right to life weightier than anything other than the mother's own right to life, which she might put forward as ground for an abortion?

This argument treats the right to life as if it were unproblematic. It is not, and this seems to me to be precisely the source of the mistake.

For we should now, at long last, ask what it comes to, to have a right to life. In some views having a right to life includes having a right to be given at least the bare minimum one needs for continued life. But suppose that what in fact *is* the bare minimum a man needs for continued life is something he has no right at all to be given? If I am sick unto death, and the only thing that will save my life is the touch of Henry Fonda's cool hand on my fevered brow, then all the same, I have no right to be given the touch of Henry Fonda's cool hand on my fevered brow. It would be frightfully nice of him to fly in from the West Coast to provide it. It would be less nice, though no doubt well meant, if my friends flew out to the West Coast and carried Henry Fonda back with them. But I have no right at all against anybody that he should do this for me. Or again, to return to the story I told earlier, the fact that for continued life that violinist needs the continued use of your kidneys does not establish that he has a right to be given the continued use of your kidneys. He certainly has no right against you that you should give him continued use of your kidneys. For nobody has any right to use your kidneys unless you give him such a right; and nobody has the right against you that you shall give him this right—if you do allow him to go on using your kidneys, this is a kindness on your part, and not something he can claim from you as his due. Nor has he any right against anybody else that *they* should give him continued use of your kidneys. Certainly he had no right against the Society of Music Lovers that they should plug him into you in the first place. And if you now start to unplug yourself, having learned that you will otherwise have to spend nine years in bed with him, there is nobody in the world who must try to prevent you, in order to see to it that he is given something he has a right to be given.

Some people are rather stricter about the right to life. In their view, it does not include the right to be given anything, but amounts to, and only to, the right not to be killed by anybody. But here a related difficulty arises. If everybody is to refrain from killing that violinist, then everybody must refrain from doing a great many different sorts of things. Everybody must refrain from slitting his throat, everybody must refrain from shooting him—and everybody must refrain from unplugging you from him. But does he have a right against everybody that they shall refrain from unplugging you from him? To refrain from doing this is to allow him to continue to use your kidneys. It could be argued that he has a right against us that *we* should allow him to continue to use your kidneys. That is, while he had no right against us that we should give him the use of your kidneys, it might be argued that he anyway has a right against us that we shall not now intervene and deprive him of the use of your kidneys. I shall come back to third-party interventions later. But certainly the violinist has no right against you that *you* shall allow him to continue to use your kidneys. As I said, if you do allow him to use them, it is a kindness on your part, and not something you owe him.

The difficulty I point to here is not peculiar to the right to life. It reappears in connection with all the other natural rights; and it is something which an adequate account of rights must deal with. For present purposes it is enough just to draw attention to it. But I would stress that I am not arguing that people do not have a right to life—quite to the contrary, it seems to me that the primary control we must place on the acceptability of an account of rights is that it should turn out in that account to be a truth that all persons have a right to life. I am arguing only that having a right to life does not guarantee having either a right to be given the use of or a right to be allowed continued use of another person's body—even if one needs it for life itself. So the right to life will not serve the opponents of abortion in the very simple and clear way in which they seem to have thought it would.

4.   There is another way to bring out the difficulty. In the most ordinary sort of case, to deprive someone of what he has a right to is to treat him unjustly. Suppose a boy and his small brother are jointly given a box of chocolates for Christmas. If the older boy takes the box and refuses to give his brother any of the chocolates, he is unjust to him, for the brother has been given a right to half of them. But suppose that, having learned that otherwise it means nine years in bed with that violinist, you unplug yourself from him. You surely are not being unjust to him, for you gave him no right to use your kidneys, and no one else can have given him any such right. But we have to notice that in unplugging yourself, you are killing him; and violinists, like everybody else, have a right to life, and thus in the view we were considering just now, the right not to be killed. So here you do what he supposedly has a right you shall not do, but you do not act unjustly to him in doing it.

The emendation which may be made at this point is this: the right to life consists not in the right not to be killed, but rather in the right not to be killed unjustly. This runs a risk of circularity, but never mind: it would enable us to square the fact that the violinist has a right to life with the fact that you do not act unjustly toward him in unplugging yourself, thereby killing him. For if you do not kill him unjustly, you do not violate his right to life, and so it is no wonder you do him no injustice.

But if this emendation is accepted, the gap in the argument against abortion stares us plainly in the face: it is by no means enough to show that the fetus is a person, and to remind us that all persons have a right to life—we need to be shown also that killing the fetus violates its right to life, i.e., that abortion is unjust killing. And is it?

I suppose we may take it as a datum that in a case of pregnancy due to rape the mother has not given the unborn person a right to the use of her body for food and shelter. Indeed, in what pregnancy could it be supposed that the mother has given the unborn person such a right? It is not as if there were unborn persons drifting about the world, to whom a woman who wants a child says "I invite you in."

But it might be argued that there are other ways one can have acquired a right to the use of another person's body than by having been invited to use it by that person. Suppose a woman voluntarily indulges in intercourse, knowing of the chance it will issue in pregnancy, and then she does become pregnant; is she not in part responsible for the presence, in fact the very existence, of the unborn person inside her? No doubt she did not invite it in. But doesn't her partial responsibility for its being there itself give it a right to the use of her body?[7] If so, then her aborting it would be more like the boy's taking away the chocolates, and less like your unplugging yourself from the violinist—doing so would be depriving it of what it does have a right to, and thus would be doing it an injustice.

And then, too, it might be asked whether or not she can kill it even to save her own life: If she voluntarily called it into existence, how can she now kill it, even in self-defense?

The first thing to be said about this is that it is something new. Opponents of abortion have been so concerned to make out the independence of the fetus, in order to establish that it has a right to life, just as its mother does, that they have tended to overlook the possible support they might gain from making out that the fetus is *dependent* on the mother, in order to establish that she has a special kind of responsibility for it, a responsibility that gives it rights against her which are not possessed by any independent person—such as an ailing violinist who is a stranger to her.

---

7 The need for a discussion of this argument was brought home to me by members of the Society for Ethical and Legal Philosophy, to whom this paper was originally presented.

On the other hand, this argument would give the unborn person a right to its mother's body only if her pregnancy resulted from a voluntary act, undertaken in full knowledge of the chance a pregnancy might result from it. It would leave out entirely the unborn person whose existence is due to rape. Pending the availability of some further argument, then, we would be left with the conclusion that unborn persons whose existence is due to rape have no right to the use of their mothers' bodies, and thus that aborting them is not depriving them of anything they have a right to and hence is not unjust killing. ...

And we should also notice that it is not at all plain that this argument really does go even as far as it purports to. For there are cases and cases, and the details make a difference. If the room is stuffy, and I therefore open a window to air it, and a burglar climbs in, it would be absurd to say, "Ah, now he can stay, she's given him a right to the use of her house—for she is partially responsible for his presence there, having voluntarily done what enabled him to get in, in full knowledge that there are such things as burglars, and that burglars burgle." It would be still more absurd to say this if I had had bars installed outside my windows, precisely to prevent burglars from getting in, and a burglar got in only because of a defect in the bars. It remains equally absurd if we imagine it is not a burglar who climbs in, but an innocent person who blunders or falls in. Again, suppose it were like this: people-seeds drift about in the air like pollen, and if you open your windows, one may drift in and take root in your carpets or upholstery. You don't want children, so you fix up your windows with fine mesh screens, the very best you can buy. As can happen, however, and on very, very rare occasions does happen, one of the screens is defective; and a seed drifts in and takes root. Does the person-plant who now develops have a right to the use of your house? Surely not—despite the fact that you voluntarily opened your windows, you knowingly kept carpets and upholstered furniture, and you knew that screens were sometimes defective. Someone may argue that you are responsible for its rooting, that it does have a right to your house, because after all you *could* have lived out your life with bare floors and furniture, or with sealed windows and doors. But this won't do—for by the same token anyone can avoid a pregnancy due to rape by having a hysterectomy, or anyway by never leaving home without a (reliable!) army.

It seems to me that the argument we are looking at can establish at most that there are *some* cases in which the unborn person has a right to the use of its mother's body, and therefore *some* cases in which abortion is unjust killing. There is room for much discussion and argument as to precisely which, if any. But I think we should sidestep this issue and leave it open, for at any rate the argument certainly does not establish that all abortion is unjust killing.

8. My argument will be found unsatisfactory on two counts by many of those who want to regard abortion as morally permissible. First, while I do

argue that abortion is not impermissible, I do not argue that it is always permissible. There may well be cases in which carrying the child to term requires only Minimally Decent Samaritanism of the mother, and this is a standard we must not fall below. I am inclined to think it a merit of my account precisely that it does *not* give a general yes or a general no. It allows for and supports our sense that, for example, a sick and desperately frightened fourteen-year-old schoolgirl, pregnant due to rape, may *of course* choose abortion, and that any law which rules this out is an insane law. And it also allows for and supports our sense that in other cases resort to abortion is even positively indecent. It would be indecent in the woman to request an abortion, and indecent in a doctor to perform it, if she is in her seventh month, and wants the abortion just to avoid the nuisance of postponing a trip abroad. The very fact that the arguments I have been drawing attention to treat all cases of abortion, or even all cases of abortion in which the mother's life is not at stake, as morally on a par ought to have made them suspect at the outset.

Secondly, while I am arguing for the permissibility of abortion in some cases, I am not arguing for the right to secure the death of the unborn child. It is easy to confuse these two things in that up to a certain point in the life of the fetus it is not able to survive outside the mother's body; hence removing it from her body guarantees its death. But they are importantly different. I have argued that you are not morally required to spend nine months in bed, sustaining the life of that violinist; but to say this is by no means to say that if, when you unplug yourself, there is a miracle and he survives, you then have a right to turn round and slit his throat. You may detach yourself even if this costs him his life; you have no right to be guaranteed his death, by some other means, if unplugging yourself does not kill him. There are some people who will feel dissatisfied by this feature of my argument. A woman may be utterly devastated by the thought of a child, a bit of herself, put out for adoption and never seen or heard of again. She may therefore want not merely that the child be detached from her, but more, that it die. Some opponents of abortion are inclined to regard this as beneath contempt—thereby showing insensitivity to what is surely a powerful source of despair. All the same, I agree that the desire for the child's death is not one which anybody may gratify, should it turn out to be possible to detach the child alive.

At this place, however, it should be remembered that we have only been pretending throughout that the fetus is a human being from the moment of conception. A very early abortion is surely not the killing of a person, and so is not dealt with by anything I have said here.

∽

Marquis, "Why Abortion is Immoral"

1. Why does Marquis think killing is wrong? Expand on what Marquis thinks we lose when we are murdered. How does Marquis's theory on why murder is wrong help to explain why we regard murder as quite possibly the worst crime?
2. What does Marquis's theory suggest about the morality of abortion?
3. Why does Marquis argue the value of the future does not need to be understood by the being with a future for it to have value?
4. Does Marquis's analysis not imply that all contraception is wrong? Why or why not?

Thompson, "A Defense of Abortion"

1. What line does Thomson admit is difficult to draw? What does Thomson think we have to admit about the unborn and human personhood?
2. Explain Thomson's "violinist" example and what it is meant to show about the morality of abortion.
3. Explain Thomson's "coat" example and what it is meant to show about the morality of abortion.
4. Explain Thomson's "barred window" example and what it is meant to show about the morality of abortion.
5. What two objections will many on the pro-choice side of the abortion debate find with Thomson's conclusions?

SUGGESTIONS FOR FURTHER READING OR VIEWING

Children of Men. 2006. An excellent science fiction film based on the premise that, in the near future, all women on earth lose the ability to have children. So, one by one we die of old age with no future generation to replace us. The film is quite thought provoking.

Hursthouse, Rosalind. "Virtue Ethics and the Problem of Abortion." *Philosophy & Public Affairs* 20, no. 3 (1991).

Noonan, John T. "An Almost Absolute Value in History." In *The Morality of Abortion: Legal and Historical Perspectives*, edited by John T. Noonan Jr. Cambridge, MA: Harvard University Press, 1970.

Tooley, Michael. "Abortion and Infanticide." *Philosophy & Public Affairs* 2, no. 1 (1972).

CPSIA information can be obtained
at www.ICGtesting.com
Printed in the USA
FSHW012305170820
73047FS

9 781516 510337